THE GREAT
FRONTIER WAR

THE GREAT FRONTIER WAR

Britain, France, and the Imperial Struggle for North America, 1607–1755

William R. Nester

PRAEGER

Westport, Connecticut
London

Library of Congress Cataloging-in-Publication Data

Nester, William R., 1956–
    The great frontier war : Britain, France, and the imperial
struggle for North America, 1607–1755 / William R. Nester.
      p. cm.
    Includes bibliographical references and index.
    ISBN 0–275–96772–7 (alk paper)
    1. United States—History—French and Indian War, 1755–1763.
    2. United States—History—French and Indian War, 1755–1763—Causes.
    3. Great Britain—Relations—France. 4. France—Relations—Great
Britain. 5. Indians of North America—Government relations—To
1789. I. Title
    E199.N48   2000
    973.2'6—dc21   99–32050

British Library Cataloguing in Publication Data is available.

Library of Congress Catalog Card Number: 99–32050
ISBN: 0–275–96772–7

First published in 2000

Praeger Publishers, 88 Post Road West, Westport, CT 06881
An imprint of Greenwood Publishing Group, Inc.
www.praeger.com

Printed in the United States of America

The paper used in this book complies with the
Permanent Paper Standard issued by the National
Information Standards Organization (Z39.48–1984).

10 9 8 7 6 5 4 3 2

To Joe Bertolini, a true friend and a great scholar

Contents

Introduction

I heard the bullets whistle, and, believe me, there is something charming
in the sound.

—George Washington

If asked when George Washington penned those valiant words, many might
well attribute them to some battle of the American Revolution. Actually,
Washington uttered them as a hotheaded, reckless, gangly youth of 23 in
the French and Indian War (1754–1763), a struggle in which he fought for
rather than against Britain. Indeed, no one was more responsible for sparking that war than Washington, first by trudging through the wilderness in
the dead of winter with a message from Virginia Governor Dinwiddie to
the French to abandon their forts in the upper Ohio River valley; then a
half year later by ordering the war's first shots when his troops ambushed
Captain Jumonville; and finally, when he ignominiously surrendered his
force at Fort Necessity and unwittingly signed a surrender document in
French naming him Jumonville's assassin! Washington was no hero on either
side of the Atlantic in that war.

What is popularly known as the "French and Indian War" was the last
and overwhelmingly the largest of five wars fought between the French and
British for mastery over the eastern half of North America. The fighting
raged not just in eastern North America but across swaths of Europe (where
it was known as the Seven Years' War), the Caribbean Islands, West Africa,
India, the East Indies, Argentina, the Philippines, and on the seas linking
those far-flung lands. The war was the first fought around the world.

Overshadowing the war's scale was its results. The last French and Indian

War was a watershed event that forever shifted the course of American history, ranking with the Revolution, Civil War, World War II, and Cold War in its powerful impact. At least one historian believes it was the nation's most decisive war. Henry Lawrence Gipson unhesitantly asserts that the "war was destined to have the most momentous consequences to the American people of any war in which they have been engaged down to our own day—consequences even more momentous than those that flowed from the victorious Revolutionary War or from the Civil War. For it was to determine for centuries to come, if not for all time, what civilization—what governmental institutions, what social and economic patterns—would be paramount in North America. It was to determine likewise whether Americans were to be securely confined, as are the people of Chile today, to a long but narrow ribbon of territory lying between the coastline and a not too distant mountain chain and whether their rivals, the French—then considered to be the greatest military power of the world and in control of the Appalachians—were to remain a permanent and effective barrier to any enjoyment of the vast western interior of the continent."[1]

Despite all of this, how much of the French and Indian War's significance seeps into America's consciousness? American historians have turned their nation's wars into publishing industries. Any large bookstore will have shelves devoted to World War II, Vietnam, and the Civil War, with smaller sections displaying books on World War I, the Korean War, and Indian wars beyond the Mississippi River. A browser can even find books on 1812 and Mexican wars. But usually one looks in vain for anything on the French and Indian War of 1754–1760, let alone those wars which preceded that final struggle between the British and French for mastery over North America. With luck one might find a recent edition of Francis Parkman's vividly written but dated *Montcalm and Wolfe.*[2] Other books on the French and Indian War do exist but are limited in analysis, scope, and/or availability.[3]

The absence is puzzling. Its wrenching global impact aside, the war certainly makes for very colorful reading with its array of inept and daring commanders, epic heroism among the troops, fierce battles and sieges, dazzlingly uniformed Europeans and Americans, warpainted Indians, creaking fleets of warships, and flags snapping in the wind.

The Great Frontier War: Britain, France, and the Imperial Struggle for North America, 1607–1755 will concentrate on exploring the events and forces leading up to the war and its first two years of combat. Chapter 1 discusses the struggle for North America over the preceding century and a half, not just between France and Britain, but the relevant Indian tribes and other European powers as well. Chapters 2 and 3 investigate the economic, political, social, and military similarities and differences among the participants. Chapters 4 and 5 explore, respectively, the fighting of 1754, in which Washington figured prominently, and that of 1755, which dwarfed the previous year's as Britain mounted four campaigns designed to defeat France's

North American empire. By the end of 1755, the fighting was stalemated like the four earlier wars. But rather than sputter to a close, in 1756 the North American war became a global war whose carnage mounted until the 1763 Treaty of Paris ended it. That broader struggle is explored in a companion volume, *The First Global War: Britain, France, and the Fate of North America, 1756–1775. The Great Frontier War* is the first book which explores in depth the roots of that first global war which decisively shifted the course of world history and prompted America's war for independence a dozen years later.

NOTES

1. Lawrence Henry Gipson, *The Great War for Empire: The Years of Defeat, 1754–1757* (New York: Alfred A. Knopf, 1959), 8:11.

2. Francis Parkman, *Montcalm and Wolfe: The French and Indian War* (1886) (New York: Capo Press, 1995).
As the final volume of a seven-book series on the British and French struggle for North America, Parkman's *Montcalm and Wolfe* is a stylistic and scholarly classic. It does not incorporate, of course, the wealth of new documents and perspectives that have emerged in the century since it was first published in 1884. Parkman has been attacked for moralizing his tale, for maintaining that "French absolutism, feudalism, and Roman institutions, magnificent and colorful as they are, are destined to go down before the Anglo-American forces of progress. . . . Parkman could ignore evidence that was not in accord with his views, permit his bias to control his judgment, or sketch characterizations that are little better than hostile caricatures" (C. Van Woodward, "Foreword," in Parkman, *Montcalm and Wolfe*, xxviii, xxx).
Perhaps Parkman is guilty as charged. But along with the accusations of promoting "great man" and "romantic" views of history, the criticism is overblown. Parkman is one the most brilliant of 19th-century historians and writers, and should be celebrated as such. Were Parkman writing today rather than then, his books would undoubtedly be quite different, benefiting from a century of scholarship and debate that has ensued since he laid his quill aside. For a book written more than a century ago, *Montcalm and Wolfe* remains a classic work of history rooted deeply in primary sources, brilliant analysis, and haunting style.

3. Two histories of the war appeared shortly after it ended. The first history of the Seven Years' War, John Entick's massive *General History of the Late War: Containing its Rise, Progress, and Events in Europe, Asia, Africa, and America,* 5 vols. (London: Edward Dilly and John Millan, 1763–1764), appeared the same year as the Treaty of Paris. It was followed a decade later by Thomas Mante's less comprehensive but better researched *History of the Late War in North America* (London: W. Strahan and T. Codell, 1792). The last two volumes of Tobias Smollet's *History of England from the Revolution to the Death of George II,* 5 vols. (London: Cooke Publisher, 1790) provides an interesting account of Britain's side of the war.
The first American histories of the war appeared in the early 19th century, the first of which was the second volume of James Grahame's *History of the United State of*

North America, From the Plantations of the British Colonies Till Their Assumption of National Independence, 4 vols. (Boston: C. C. Little & J. Brown, 1845).

In the early 1840s, the historian John Brodhead copied and in 1844 brought back to the United States 80 volumes of primary sources. Two other historians, Edmund O'Callaghan and Berthold Fernow edited these into the four-volume *Documentary History of the State of New York* (New York: Weed, Parsons, and Co., 1850–1851) and fifteen-volume *Documents Relative to the Colonial History of the State of New York* (Albany, N.Y.: Weed, Parsons, and Co., 1853–1887).

Historians have been tapping into this rich trove of material ever since. The first to do so was George Bancroft's brilliant *History of the United States*, 10 vols. (Boston: Little, Brown, 1879), followed by Samuel G. Drake, *A Particular History of the Five Years French and Indian War* (Boston: J. Munsell, 1870), an interesting if limited account.

For critical accounts of these 19th-century American historians, see Russel Baine Nye, *George Bancroft, Brahmin Rebel* (New York: Alfred A. Knopf, 1944); Mason Wade, *Francis Parkman: Heroic Historian* (New York: Viking Press, 1942); Howard Doughty, *Francis Parkman* (New York: Macmillan, 1962); Richard C. Vitzhum, *The American Compromise: Theme and Method in the Histories of Bancroft, Parkman, and Adams* (Norman: University of Oklahoma Press, 1974; W. J. Eccles, "The History of New France According to Francis Parkman," *William and Mary Quarterly* 3rd ser., 18 (1961), 163–75; R. C. Vitzhum, "The Historian as Editor: Francis Parkman's Reconstruction of Sources in Montcalm and Wolfe," *Journal of American History* 52 (1966–1967), 471–86; Francis Jennings, "A Vanishing Indian: Francis Parkman Versus His Sources," *Pennsylvania Magazine of History and Biography* (1963), 306–23; Francis Jennings, "Francis Parkman: A Brahmin Among Untouchables," *William and Mary Quarterly* 3rd ser., 42 (1985), 305–28; Wilbur R. Jacobs, *Francis Parkman: The Historian as Hero: The Formative Years* (Austin: University of Texas Press, 1991).

Three recent books by American authors explore all the wars between France and Britain in North America: Edward Hamilton, *The French and Indian Wars: The Story of Battles and Forts in the Wilderness* (Garden City, N.Y.: Doubleday & Co., 1962); Howard Peckham, *The Colonial Wars 1689–1762* (Chicago: University of Chicago Press, 1964); Douglas Edward Leach, *Arms for Empire: A Military History of the British Colonies in North America, 1607–1763* (New York: Macmillan, 1973). Leach's is by far the best of the three, providing a superb scholarly analysis of the French and Indian War, although it treats only the North American military side of that vast subject.

Francis Jennings offers his *Empire of Fortune: Crowns, Colonies, & Tribes in the Seven Years War in America* (New York: W. W. Norton, 1988) as a "reaction to, and as a replacement for, Francis Parkman's work." In some ways, Jennings' work does update Parkman's study by exploring some of the same ground with new material. Unfortunately, Jennings' ambitions remain unfulfilled. Although his book is highly informative and rooted in primary sources, it provides anything but a balanced, comprehensive overview. Like Parkman's, Jennings' account concentrates on the North American military campaigns and political issues largely without the global context in which they took place. But his book is much more narrow than Parkman's, focusing mostly on Pennsylvanian politics during the French and Indian War. The book also suffers from a confused organization and narrative in which the author at times jumps back and forth chronologically.

Lawrence Henry Gipson does try to explore the French and Indian War within the world war through his twelve-volume *The British Empire before the American Revolution* (New York: Alfred A. Knopf, 1958–1970). On the whole, Gipson's is a well-written and well-researched but meandering work, marred here and there by inaccuracies and biases.

The French and Canadians have also made important contributions to the scholarship. During the 19th and early 20th centuries, there appeared Francois-Xavier Garneau, *Histoire du Canada*, 4 vols. (Quebec: Lacour, Gayet, Robert, 1852); George Warburton, *The Conquest of Canada*, 2 vols. (London: R. Benteley, 1857); H. R. Casgrain, *Guere du Canada, 1756–1760, Montcalm et Levis*, 2 vols. (Quebec: Imprimeries de L. J. Demers & Freres, 1891); William Kingsford, *The History of Canada*, 10 vols. (London: Roswell, Hutchinson, 1887–1898); Richard Waddington, *La Guerre de Sept Ans: Histoire Diplomatique et Militaire*, 5 vols. (Paris: Firmin-Didot et Cie, 1888–1910); William Charles Henry Wood, *The Fight for Canada* (Boston: Little, Brown, 1906); Arthur Granville Bradley, *The Fight with France for North America* (Toronto: Arno Press, 1908).

For critical accounts, see Serge Gagnon, *Le Quebec et ses Historiens de 1840 a 1920* (Quebec: Pressees de l'Universite Laval, 1978); Gustave Lanctot, *Garneau, Historien National* (Montreal: Eides, 1946); James S. Pritchard, "Some Aspects of the Thought of F. X. Garneau," *Canadian Historical Review* 1 (1970), 276–91; Jean-Pierre Gaboury, *Le Nationalism de Lionel Groulx: Aspects Ideologiques* (Ottawa: Editions de l'Universite d'Ottawa, 1970).

More recent Canadian efforts have been good reads but tend to be one-sided, emphasizing to varying degrees either the British or French side of the war, and break little new ground. These include: Sigmund Samuel, *The Seven Years' War in Canada, 1756–1763* (Toronto: Ryerson Press, 1934); George F. G. Stanley, *New France: The Last Phase, 1740–1760* (Toronto: McClelland and Stewart, 1968); Guy Fregault, *Canada: The War of the Conquest, 1754–1760* (1955), trans. Margaret M. Cameron (Toronto: Oxford University Press, 1969); Gustave Lanctot, *A History of Canada*, trans. Josephine Hambleton and Margaret M. Cameron, 3 vols. (Cambridge, Mass.: Harvard University Press, 1963–1965).

THE GREAT
FRONTIER WAR

1

Trade and Conquest

He that commaundes the sea commaundes the trade, & he that is the lord of the trade of the worlde is lord of the wealth of the worlde.
—Sir Walter Raleigh, 1600

That, notwithstanding the Grants of the Kings of England, France, or Spain, the Property of these uninhabited Parts of the World must be founded upon prior Occupancy according to the Law of Nature; and it is the Seating and Cultivating of the soil & not the bare travelling through a Territory that constitutes Right.
—Lewis Burwell, 1750

I have not reply to make to your general other than from the mouths of my cannon and muskets!
—Governor Louis de Baude Frontenac's reply
to Sir William Phips' surrender demand, 1691

For over a century and a half, the French and English struggled to carve ever larger empires from the North American wilderness between the Atlantic Ocean, Rocky Mountains, Gulf of Mexico, and Hudson Bay. At first they faced not only each other but also the Spanish, Dutch and, briefly, the Swedes. Bloodshed was nearly incessant as these European powers battled among themselves and, more decisively, each fought a series of wars against various Indian tribes to establish and expand their footholds on the continent. In three mid-17th-century wars, the English defeated the Dutch (who had earlier absorbed the few Swedish settlements) and took over their North American holdings. Separately, the French and English stymied Spanish ambitions and contained them west of the Mississippi and in pockets along the Gulf Coast and northern Florida. By the late 17th century, only the French and English remained to fight over North America's eastern half. French settlements in the St. Lawrence valley were now firmly established; Quebec dispatched trading and exploring parties into the Great Lakes and Mississippi valleys that garnered an ever richer horde of furs. Along the Atlantic Coast, the English colonies developed flourishing, diversified economies and spread their hamlets as far west as the Appalachian foothills.

The character of the French and British North American "empires" differed greatly. Although the French did war against the Iroquois, Natchez, Fox, and other tribes, they did not "conquer" New France; they merely paid very high tolls to the Indians for the privilege of exploiting it. Beyond their narrow ribbon of settlement between Quebec and Montreal, or ports like New Orleans and Mobile, the New France "empire" largely consisted of several scores of ramshackle trading posts, often isolated from one another by hundreds of wilderness miles and resentful Indian tribes. None of those tribes thought themselves French subjects and would have been incensed had it been suggested that they were. Nor did they think of the annual goods dispensed by the French traders as "gifts." Of the goods received from the French, some were exchanged for "rent" and others for furs. The several hundred voyageurs, marines, and missionaries scattered across that wilderness understood clearly that their survival depended on nurturing Indian hospitality and greed, and they became quite adept at doing so by immersing themselves in Indian tongues, customs, marriage, and ambitions.

In contrast, the British had brutally conquered their empire between the Atlantic and the Appalachians with endless streams of settlers armed with muskets, diseases, and ploughs. By 1750, Britain's 1.25 million American subjects had elbowed aside or eliminated the local tribes and towered over New France's 80,000 white inhabitants. The British advantage went beyond raw numbers of settlers. British goods were better made, more abundant, and cheaper than those dispensed by the French. With such overwhelming power, the British could afford to be more assertive and less sensitive toward Indians. In doing so, they fired the hatred of most tribes against them, and even the smoldering emnity of erstwhile allies like the Iroquois and Cherokee.

Throughout the 17th century, the conflict between the French and English was waged primarily through competition for the alliances and trade of various Indian tribes. But as New France and the various English colonies expanded in territory and population, their merchants, soldiers, and privateers increasingly skirmished with each other on forest trails and the high seas. The French and English fought five wars for North America—Huguenot (1627–1629), League of Augsburg or King William's (1689–1697), Spanish Succession or Queen Anne's (1702–1713), Austrian Succession or King George's (1745–1748), and Seven Years' or French and Indian (1754–

1763). It was the final war, of course, that proved to be decisive. The last French and Indian War cannot be understood apart from the century and a half of imperialism that preceded it.

RIVAL EMPIRES

When Columbus' three ships dropped anchor in the Caribbean during his first voyage in 1492, over 500 tribes occupied regions of that sprawling continent between the Rio Grande and Arctic Ocean, with a population estimated at from 4.5 to 9 million people who spoke one of at least 200 distinct languages and countless dialects.[1] In his four voyages to the western hemisphere, Columbus never saw that land which is now the United States and Canada, let alone any of its peoples. Yet Columbus' discovery of a "New World" would unleash interrelated economic, political, military, technological, cultural, and viral forces that would forever change North America.[2]

Unlike South and Central America, whose lands and peoples were rapidly conquered by the Spanish and Portuguese, for four centuries following Columbus, European powers would fight continually over North America's spoils. Each power experienced a similar pattern of conquest: exploration and trading expeditions prepared the way for trading posts and Christian missions, which in turn often gave way to formal colonies with plantations and towns. The wars in North America and elsewhere in the western hemisphere among the European powers were frequently extensions of their wars in Europe. Yet even when periodic treaties brought a brief, tense peace to Europe, the rivalry and skirmishing continued unabated in North America.[3]

The great powers competed for New World empires through war and negotiations. In 1494, the kings of Castile and Portugal signed the Treaty of Tordesillas, which divided the New World between them. Spain rapidly exploited its treaty rights. Between 1492 and 1530, Spain conquered most of, first, the Caribbean basin and then Central and South America. The conquistadors annually hauled back to Spain vast fortunes in gold and silver.[4]

Excited by the treasures Spain had looted, other European powers hoped to find even greater gold and silver troves in as yet unconquered North America. England was the first to try. In 1497 and 1498, Henry VII dispatched John Cabot across the Atlantic to discover and claim for England whatever lands he could find. Cabot made the first recorded European visits to St. Lawrence Bay. His efforts, however, were not substantial enough for England to file a serious claim. In 1500 and 1501, Portugal's Corte-Real brothers explored that same region and established a short-lived fishing post on Cape Breton. Those Portuguese were only the most recent Europeans to drag nets off that sea's rich fishing banks; Basque fishermen may have been fishing those same waters for 50 years.[5]

Throughout the 16th century it looked as if Spain would conquer North as well as South America and thus engulf the entire western hemisphere from Newfoundland to Tierra del Fuego. Spain indeed did try. In 1513, Ponce de Leon led an expedition from San Juan, Puerto Rico up Florida's coast. The conquistadors found no gold and soon fled from showers of Indian arrows. In 1517, Hernandez de Cordoba experienced the same disappointment and resistance in Florida, as did Ponce de Leon again in 1521. Five years later, in 1526, Vasquez de Ayllon planted 200 settlers somewhere in the Cape Fear region; within a year the survivors retreated to Hispaniola. In 1528, leaving a trail of dead behind him, Panfilio de Narvaez led 400 men in five ships to land near Tampa Bay and march inland through western Florida; only four men survived to reach Mexico three years later. Between 1539 and 1543, Hernando de Soto's 600-man expedition fought and traded its way across the American southeast before its remnants sailed to safety. From 1540 to 1542, Francisco Vasquez de Coronado led a similarly fruitless attempt to find gold and other riches across the American southwest. In 1559, Tristan de Luna y Arellano sailed with thirteen ships and 500 men to Pensacola Bay. The settlement lasted until 1561 when disease and a hurricane that destroyed most of the supply fleet prompted the survivors to flee.[6]

While these various expeditions were all financial disasters, they did succeed in filling in some of the blank places on maps. News of these failures did not deter ambitious conquistadors blinded by visions of gold and slaves from mounting their own expeditions. Throughout these decades, Spanish slaving expeditions periodically sailed up the East Coast as far as Chesapeake Bay to storm villages and kidnap bewildered Indians for Caribbean plantations. While slaving raids could be successful, disease, crop failures, and Indian attacks defeated the first attempts by the Spanish to establish colonial enclaves along the coast.

The other great powers lacked the means to challenge Spain directly for control of the western hemisphere. However, enterprising ship captains could leech off Spain's successes. French, English, and Dutch privateers plucked treasure ships from the fleet sailing between Caribbean ports and Spain. In 1555, a small fleet of French privateers actually stormed and sacked Havana. But Spain was too well rooted in the Caribbean and South America for its enemies to do little more than occasionally rob it.

North America remained open for conquest. France sent Giovanni da Verrazano to explore the coast between Nova Scotia and the Carolinas in 1524. Getting wind of the voyage, Spain reacted by dispatching Esteban Gomez to chart the coast from Florida to Cape Cod in 1525. England's Henry VIII entered the rivalry when he sponsored John Rut's expedition along the East Coast in 1527. Jacques Cartier claimed the St. Lawrence watershed for France in 1534 and expanded his explorations in the region during 1535 and 1536. However, an attempt to solidify this claim, with a trading post at Cape Rouge near what later became Quebec, failed after several months. In 1541, Cartier established another settlement near the ruins of his first, but the survivors fled back to France two years later.[7]

North America's Indians had so far defeated European attempts to conquer them. European horses, armor, matchlock guns, and Bibles proved impotent in the face of Indian arrows and guerrilla tactics. It was Europe's diseases rather than its technologies or beliefs that eventually crippled native power. Smallpox and measles epidemics devastated native tribes and drastically altered the power balance. European conquest was only a matter of time, rivalry, finance, and enterprise.

After a hiatus of two decades, Versailles tried once again to establish a permanent settlement in North America, this time in the Spanish empire's backyard. In 1562, Jean Ribault led two ships and 150 men to northern Florida where he erected a cross, built a fort, and claimed that land for France. Within a year, those who had survived starvation and mutiny sailed back to France. Despite this failure, in 1564, Rene de Laudoniere landed over 200 French on the St. John's River to establish Fort Caroline. Ribault reinforced it the following year.[8]

These audacious French intrusions on the fringe of Spain's empire provoked King Philip II into mounting a sustained attempt to root a colony in North America. In 1565, he sent Pedro Menendez de Aviles with 500 soldiers, 200 civilians, and 100 colonists to take Fort Caroline. When his attack on Fort Caroline failed, Menendez sailed south 40 miles and established Fort Augustine. Leading his troops north, he launched a sneak attack that slaughtered 132 French and scattered the rest. He then marched on to capture the remnants of Ribault's relief fleet, which had been shipwrecked nearby, and executed the captain and 111 "heretics."[9] He renamed Caroline Fort San Mateo. Menendez' 1565 campaign was the first direct fighting between European powers in North America itself.

Menendez quickly expanded Spain's foothold in the region. In 1566, he sailed up the coast to establish Fort San Felipe on Parris Island. Over the next few years, he founded seven other forts along the coast from which the Spanish attempted to win from the Indians peace, Christian converts, and trade. By the early 17th century, the Spanish had over a score of missions scattered along the Gulf Coast, across northern Florida, and up the Atlantic Coast as far as South Carolina. Missionaries and explorers ranged ever deeper along the trails and villages crisscrossing the interior.

Spain's resistance coupled with religious civil war at home prevented France from mounting another expedition to North America for another 40 years. All along, however, French fishermen continued to join those from other European kingdoms in annually exploiting the Newfoundland Banks. Some enterprising French merchants sailed up the St. Lawrence as far as the Indian village of Tadoussac at the Sanquenay River mouth to buy furs there.

The English were the next power to challenge Spain's expanding foothold in North America. There, as elsewhere, the tools of English conquest were private joint stock companies chartered by the Crown with monopoly economic, political, and social rights to exploit a region in return for a percentage of the profits and obedience. When Sir Walter Raleigh received a charter from Queen Elizabeth I for his Virginia Company in 1584, the Crown had earlier granted similar monopolies to the Muscovy Company (1553) and the Levant Company (1581). The Virginia Company's charter allowed Raleigh and the other investors to take land "not actually possessed of any Christian Prince, nor inhabited by Christian People." In 1585, Raleigh established a colony on Roanoke Island; it lasted three years before it mysteriously disappeared, the remnants most likely absorbed by nearby Indians.[10]

Elsewhere in North America the English were more successful. England's first possession in the New World was Newfoundland, seized by Humphrey Gilbert in 1583 so that fishermen could more easily exploit nearby teeming fisheries. In 1586, Francis Drake succeeded in burning St. Augustine on his fleet's way to take supplies to Roanoke; the Spanish soon reestablished a new fort and town at that site. The repeated raids of Drake and other privateers on Spanish ships and settlements in the western hemisphere, along with the Roanoke colony, were attempts by England to chip away at Spanish power in the long war between those kingdoms that lasted from 1585 to 1603.[11]

The 1604 Treaty of London between England and Spain ending a generation of war brought new opportunities for English expansion in North America. In that treaty, James I accepted existing Spanish conquests in the New World but retained the opportunity for England to take any unoccupied territory. In 1605, two groups of investors, the Virginia Company and the Plymouth Company, petitioned James I for land in North America. In 1606, James I divided the claims between them, granting the Virginia Company lands between the 34th and 41st parallels and the Plymouth Company lands between the 38th and 45th parallels, leaving them both free to settle the overlapping region.

Both companies sent out colonists in 1607. The Plymouth Company's settlement on the Kennebec River failed after a year. The Virginia Company's almost failed repeatedly over the next decade. In May 1607, the Virginia Company landed 104 Englishmen to found Jamestown and attempt to discover gold in the region. Obsessed with their treasure hunt, the settlers neglected planting crops, fishing, and hunting, causing starvation and disease to kill many. Finally, Captain John Smith halted the anarchy and organized the men into farming units. Although the colony survived, Virginia financially drained its investors. The settlement would probably still have foundered had not John Rolfe established tobacco as a cash crop in 1612; Virginian tobacco exports would soon reap the fortunes that London investors had been seeking. In 1616, the Virginia Company shifted land ownership from communal to private hands, thus greatly boosting the incentive to grow crops.[12]

As if these problems of creating a viable colony were not formidable enough, Virginia was founded in the front yard of the region's most powerful Indian tribe. The Pamunkey were a confederation of 14,000 people led by Chief Powhatan, who placed his relatives as werowances (consuls) in each allied or subject town. The werowance administered his town with the local headmen, collecting taxes of corn, copper, and furs. Shortly after the English arrived, fighting broke out between them and the Pamunkey and continued off and on for decades.

The English clung to their toehold despite continual deaths from Indians, malaria, and malnutrition. Relief expeditions with more settlers and supplies arrived just when the colony neared collapse. The English survived in part by playing off the Algonquian-speaking Pamunkey against the Siouan-speaking Manahoac and Monacan in the Piedmont. Peace reigned for several years after John Rolfe married Powhatan's daughter, Pocahontas. As elsewhere, the Indians soon became dependent on European iron kettles, traps, arrowheads, hatchets, and other trade goods. Diseases swept across the region, depleting Indian populations and their fighting spirit. Despite or perhaps because of this, fighting broke out again. English expeditions then marched through the land, burning villages, slaughtering the inhabitants, and carrying away the corn. English towns were established on many of those sites.[13]

These gains were almost swept away in March 1622 when the Pamunkey led a surprise attack that wiped out one-third of Virginia's 1,200 inhabitants scattered in villages along the James Peninsula. Although the English managed eventually to defeat the Pamunkey, the expense bankrupted the Virginia Company. King James I revoked the Virginia Company's charter and asserted direct royal administration of the colony. Although Indian wars would break out periodically throughout the rest of the 17th century, Virginia's English settlements never again faced extinction and instead expanded steadily in population and territory. In April 1644, another well-planned Indian attack slaughtered over 500 settlers. Governor Berkeley promptly mustered the militia and systematically destroyed one village after another until the tribal remnants pleaded for peace.[14]

During those same decades, the French struggled to establish colonies in Nova Scotia and the St. Lawrence valley. In 1598, Mesgouez de La Roche landed 250 settlers on Sable Island off Nova Scotia; the survivors returned to France in 1603. That same year, Henry IV awarded a ten-year trade monopoly to the Sieur de Pontgrave and other investors to settle French claims to the region. De Pontgrave sailed with three ships to the New World, traded at Tadoussac, and returned with a small fortune to France. The following year, in 1604, Sieur de Monts, another investor, founded a settlement on Ile de Saint Croix in Passamaquoddy Bay. That winter scurvy killed half the inhabitants. In spring 1605, de Monts' cartographer, Samuel de Champlain, explored the coast as far down as Cape Cod before returning to Saint Croix. De Monts then decided to move his survivors to a new settlement, named Port Royal (Nova Scotia), located to trade furs from the Micmac Indians. The Micmac Chief Membertou welcomed French trade goods and arms to help him in his tribe's rivalry with the Abenaki. Membertou later became France's first Christian convert in North America.[15]

In 1608, Samuel de Champlain sailed up the St. Lawrence with three ships and established a trading post at Quebec. Only eight of his 28 men survived that first winter. Reinforcements the following spring saved Quebec from extinction. As important to the French outpost's survival was the mysterious vanishing of the Iroquois who had inhabited the St. Lawrence valley from Stadacona (Quebec) to Hochelaga (Montreal), and had so stymied Cartier. Their fate remains unknown. Most likely disease devastated them, and the remnants fled Algonquian and Huron attacks to take refuge among the Iroquois of New York. Despite their retreat, the Iroquois continued to contest the region, sending war parties against the confederation among the Montagnais at Tadoussac and the Huron and Algonquian tribes north of the upper St. Lawrence and Lake Ontario.

To promote his tiny colony's trade and safety, Champlain joined the anti-Iroquois alliance. Confident of Quebec's security, in the summer of 1609 Champlain traveled by canoe with three French and 60 Huron and Montagnais warriors up the St. Lawrence and Richelieu rivers and into Lake Champlain. On July 30, they met a war party of 200 Mohawk from the Iroquois tribe near the later site of Fort Frederic. The French remained behind a line of their allies. With arrows notched in their bows, the Mohawk advanced. Neither side fired its arrows. When the Mohawk got within 30 yards, the Huron and Montagnais parted to reveal Champlain and the other French pointing their arquebus. The Mohawk must have stood astonished and fearful—they had never before seen a firearm or a European. The French fired, killing three Mohawk chiefs and scattering the rest. Champlain's small victory solidified French friendship with the St. Lawrence valley tribes. But those and subsequent killings fired an animosity that would rage through a series of bloody wars between the French and the Iroquois for the rest of that century.[16]

The English would soon challenge the French attempts to extend their settlements south down the Atlantic Coast. In 1612, a French Jesuit mission was founded on Mount Desert Island in Penobscot Bay. That same year, the Virginia Company's Captain Samuel Argall sailed up the coast with 60 men, destroyed the mission, and then returned to Jamestown. In 1613, Argall sailed all the way to Port Royal and burned it. Argall's two attacks were the first recorded clashes between the English and French in North America. The attacks involved rival trading companies rather than kingdoms.

That year, only 43 French and about 300 English lived in all of North America. Yet, symbolically, the raids unleashed a struggle between the French and English for North America which would not be settled for nearly another century and a half.

The French gradually increased their numbers and pushed outward from tiny Quebec. In return for a fifteen-year monopoly and promise to transplant 15,000 settlers to New France, the Company of One Hundred Associates annually invested enough provisions and trade goods to keep Quebec and its slowly expanding trade alive. Although French settlers remained few, visitors were considerable; over 1,000 vessels from France and other realms annually fished and fur traded along the Grand Banks and the mouth of the Gulf of St. Lawrence.[17]

In 1615, the Huron invited Champlain to journey to their homeland in western Ontario. There Champlain, Recollect Father Joseph Le Caron, and several other French visited palisaded villages of the Huron confederation's four tribes, as well as nearby Ottawa and Neutral tribes, and learned of distant tribes scattered around the Great Lakes basin. The Huron convinced Champlain to join another war party against the Iroquois. This one was a disaster. The Iroquois repelled a Huron assault on one of their palisades and wounded Champlain, thus shattering the spell of French superiority set seven years earlier.

Meanwhile, the English continued to expand their settlements along the Atlantic Coast. By the time the *Mayflower* arrived in 1620 off what would become Massachusetts, the Wampanoag and other local tribes were used to English, French, and Dutch ships dropping anchor in their bays to trade for furs, fish, and sassafras roots, and to capture Indians for slavery. The English established short-lived trading posts at Cape Cod in 1602 and the Kennebec River mouth in 1607. An unidentified disease burned through New England between 1616 and 1618, killing as many as 90 percent of the 21,000 Wampanoag and 135,000 other Indians in the region.[18]

In 1620, Thomas Weston received Plymouth Company permission to settle families in the New World. The 100 people he recruited for his venture were divided between the dissenting "saints" (Separatists) and conformist "strangers" (Church of England). After a rough six-week crossing, the *Mayflower* first dropped anchor off Cape Cod in November and Plymouth was founded in December. That first winter, scurvy and disease killed one of every two settlers. Those who survived did so by inhabiting abandoned Wampanoag villages and looting food caches. Despite some minor skirmishes, the Plymouth settlers were spared the Indian wars that nearly destroyed the Jamestown colony. Seeking allies against the Dutch-supplied Narragansett, Massasoit, the local Wampanoag chief, chose to help rather than destroy the Plymouth colony. Former English slaves Squanto and Samoset taught the English how to grow crops and hunt in the wilderness. Thirty-five new settlers arrived in 1621 and a further 93 in 1623. Like

Virginia, Plymouth eventually prospered after its governing council agreed to privatize land and discovered wealth in wampum and furs.[19]

The desire for wealth and religious freedom led to the founding of other English colonies along North America's Atlantic Coast. "Nonseparating" Puritans founded the Massachusetts Bay Colony in 1630 and in the following decade sent settlers up the Connecticut River valley. English Catholics established Maryland in 1634. Roger Williams split with the Puritans to found Rhode Island in 1635. Two years later, the Puritans that settled the Connecticut valley broke with Massachusetts to found the colony of New Haven. By 1640, over 20,000 English had carved farms and towns throughout eastern Massachusetts, Rhode Island, Connecticut, and Long Island. Although the southern and northern English colonies edged closer to each other, for now they would remain apart.

Dutch imperialism split the English colonies. Perhaps no nation has risen from obscurity into a great power more rapidly or struggled for independence longer than the Netherlands, which achieved both simultaneously. From 1569 to 1648, seven provinces of the Spanish Netherlands fought a bloody, seemingly endless war for independence. During those same decades, Dutch merchant and war ships grew ever more powerful along the world's ocean trade routes. The Dutch established colonies on East and West Indian islands, and on enclaves dotting Africa's coast. Perhaps the greatest coup occurred in 1628 when a Dutch fleet captured that year's Spanish treasure fleet and 200,000 pounds of silver. Amsterdam emerged to rival London as Europe's most vigorous commercial center, and Paris and Rome as a cultural capital.[20]

Like the other great powers, the Dutch increasingly eyed North America as a potential source of wealth and power. In 1609, Henry Hudson sailed up the river that now bears his name, in search of the Northwest Passage to Asia. What he found instead was direct access to the rich fur country of central New York States. Dutch ships annually visited the Hudson River country between then and 1614 when the New Netherlands Company received a three-year monopoly to exploit the region. The Company promptly established Fort Nassau at present-day Albany. When the monopoly expired, the free-for-all among ambitious merchants resumed until the Dutch West Indian Company received a monopoly to the region in 1624. The Company established Fort Orange near Fort Nassau's ruins. Two years later, in 1626, it founded New Amsterdam on Manhattan Island at the mouth of the Hudson River. Over the next four decades, Dutch settlements spread not only up the Hudson River valley but were also planted in the lower Delaware and Connecticut river valleys where they competed with Swedish and Puritan settlements, respectively. Although the Puritans succeeded in squeezing the Dutch from their Connecticut settlements, their 1643 attempt to found a settlement in the Delaware valley failed. The Dutch finally absorbed New Sweden in 1655.

Fort Orange's establishment in the heart of New York would shift the regional tribal power balance. Until then neither the Five Nation Iroquois nor Four Nation Huron confederacies could prevail in their perennial struggle to defeat the other. The Iroquois recognized that if they could get Dutch guns the balance would tip in their favor. But before the Iroquois could defeat the Huron, they had to dominate the Dutch trade. In 1624, the Iroquois agreed to a truce with the French and Huron in order to defeat the Mahican, who controlled the lands surrounding the upper Hudson valley and Fort Orange. In 1628, the Mahican fled into the Lake Champlain region, abandoning their land to the eastern-most Iroquois tribe, the Mohawk. To Fort Orange, the Iroquois carried an ever greater amount of furs; between 1628 and 1633 alone, the number of skins brought to Fort Orange rose from 10,000 to 30,000.[21]

Facing these English and Dutch threats, the French redoubled their efforts to expand their North American holdings. In 1626, the Jesuits sent eight priests to New France to rival the work of the half dozen Recollet priests already proselytizing in villages up the St. Lawrence valley. In 1627, Louis XIII rechartered the Company of One Hundred Associates with a monopoly over all land from Newfoundland to Lake Huron in return for settling 4,000 people there by 1643.

Those ambitious plans were scuttled when war between England and France broke out in 1628. That year the English privateer Gervase Kirke sailed up the St. Lawrence and demanded Quebec's surrender. Champlain rejected the demand. Sailing back down the St. Lawrence, Kirke's force captured that year's supply fleet of 400 settlers and provisions crammed aboard five ships, along with nineteen nearby fishing boats; he carried away his loot and vessels to England. Kirke returned the next year with 300 men and three ships. With his ammunition and food supplies exhausted, Champlain could only surrender Quebec and its 100 inhabitants. The English also captured Port Royal in 1629, thus completing New France's conquest. These victories occurred after France and England had signed the Treaty of St. Germain-en-Laye in April 1629, which required, among other things, that New France be returned to France. If the English had held New France, they could have avoided another 130 years of warfare and rivalry with France in North America.

War also broke out in Connecticut. In 1637, the spreading settlements, land thefts, and broken promises provoked a war with the Pequot. At first, the Pequot succeeded in killing settlers, burning farms, and even besieging Fort Saybrook for over nine months. On May 25, Connecticut and Mohegan forces marched on the Pequot's Mystic River stronghold, besieged, and eventually sacked it, killing over 500 men, women, and children. Another 200 fled to the Narragansett. The prompt response and brutal massacre would cow other regional tribes from acting on their burning resentment against the English for another generation.[22]

The war prompted the leaders of Massachusetts, Plymouth, Connecticut, and New Haven colonies to form the United Colonies of New England in 1643. Laws required every community to form a militia company composed of all able-bodied men between 16 and 60 years old. In 1645, the United Colonies declared war against the Narragansett and nearly destroyed that tribe. The autonomy of the English colonies deepened in 1649 with the beheading of Charles I and subsequent civil war. Although there was no actual fighting in the American colonies, the English settlers split into royalist and parliamentarian factions. Dictator Oliver Cromwell dispatched a fleet that deposed royal governors in Virginia, Maryland, Bermuda, the Bahamas, Barbados, and Antigua. War refugees caused New England's population to double between 1640 and 1660 to 33,000. In 1660, Loyalist forces toppled Cromwell and placed Charles II on the throne.[23]

Complicating the English Civil War was the first of a series of wars between the Dutch and English (1652–1654, 1665–1667, and 1672–1674). In 1654, an English fleet commanded by Robert Sedgwick arrived at Boston to recruit for an attack on New Netherlands; the war ended before Sedgwick could launch his assault. Despite peace between England and France, New England brigands used the excuse of war to sack French posts at Port Royal, and the Penobscot and St. John rivers.

Charles II understood the potential threat colonial union posed to London's authority, and used the Dutch wars to undermine the colonists and strengthen his own power. He issued royal charters for Connecticut in 1662 and Rhode Island in 1663. In 1664, four royal investigators and 300 soldiers disembarked from three navy ships in Boston. Although the expedition's stated purpose was to conquer New Netherlands, it also declared the United Colonies illegal. The fleet sailed on to capture New Amsterdam and all of New Netherlands. The Dutch conceded these conquests to England in the 1667 Treaty of Breda. Charles II granted the land to his brother, the Duke of York, who in turn renamed both the province and New Amsterdam New York; Fort Orange became Albany.

England also expanded its empire at the expense of Spain. Under the 1670 Treaty of Madrid, Spain agreed to recognize England's colony of South Carolina and its other American colonies. This was a stunning reversal of Spanish policy, which had denied the right to North American colonies to any country other than itself and Portugal, as sanctified by Rome under the 1493 Treaty of Tordesillas. England's North American empire now stretched unbroken and unchallenged from South Carolina to Maine. The tranquility of those colonies lasted until 1675 when Indian wars again tore apart both New England and Virginia.[24]

In 1675, the Narragansett had recovered enough from their defeat three decades earlier to rechallenge English rule. That year they withdrew to an island in the Great Swamp, began raiding English settlements, and called on other tribes to join them. Unable to penetrate that flooded, jungle-like maze, the English had to delay retaliation until those waters froze over. In December, Governor Josias Winslow led a 1,150-man expedition against the Narragansett, including 517 militia from Massachusetts, 315 from Connecticut, 158 from Plymouth, and 150 Pequot and Mohegan. Those men finally overran the camp, slaughtering 97 warriors and between 300 and 1,000 women and children, while suffering 70 dead and 150 wounded. The survivors fled to join King Philip (Metacom) and the Mahican. Philip retaliated with raids that devastated the English colonies, killing hundreds of settlers. Later that year, New York Governor Edmund Andros forged an alliance with the Mohawk and got them to attack Metacom's village that winter and raid the Algonquians throughout the following year. The war sputtered to a close as Philip's Indians ran out of gunpowder and Philip himself was hunted down and killed in August 1676. No Indian war in American history was more destructive than King Philip's war—over 3,000 Indians and 1,000 colonists died in the fighting.[25]

Meanwhile, in Virginia a dispute over a hog between a farmer and the Doeg tribe led to former's murder. Fearing retaliation, the Doeg fled. The Virginia militia pursued them into Maryland where they attacked a friendly Susquehannock village in July 1675. The unprovoked attack sparked a war in which over 300 colonists and hundreds of Indians would eventually die. A civil war then broke out within the Susquehannock war. Virginia's leaders split over whether to seek peace or continue war with the Indians, with Governor Berkeley heading the peace faction and Francis Bacon the war faction. When Berkeley had Bacon removed from the council for warring against the Indians, Bacon led a rebellion against the governor. Berkeley's troops crushed Bacon's Rebellion by January 1676 and the Indians later that year. Under the Treaty of Middle Plantation, the Indian survivors ceded most of Virginia to the English and agreed to settle on reservations.[26]

These two wars dramatically shifted the power balance among Indian tribes, particularly in New England. The Algonqians' defeat allowed the Mohawk's resurgence, thus posing yet another threat to the English colonies. In 1680, Governor Andros tried to create a counterweight to the Mohawk by inviting the remnants of the defeated Algonquians of New England along with the Mahican and western Abenaki to settle at Schaghticoke 20 miles northeast of Albany. Andros also encouraged the Susquehannock survivors to journey north to settle in the Susquehanna River where they became known as Conestogas; others outright joined the Iroquois.[27]

Once again the king used the excuse of war to tighten his control over the American colonies. Charles II responded to Bacon's rebellion and the two Indian wars by establishing within the Privy Council the Lords of Trade, which would oversee the colonial governors, assemblies, and trade. Royal taxes were raised on tobacco and sugar. A series of navigation laws increasingly restricted colonial trade. In a break from his consolidation of power, Charles II did grant a proprietorship to the Quaker William Penn over both of what would become the colonies of Pennsylvania and Delaware. Charles II's successor, James II, continued to expand royal powers to control and exploit the colonies. In 1686, James II created the Dominion of New England by joining the administrations of Massachusetts, New Hampshire, Plymouth, Connecticut, and Rhode Island, and named Sir Edmund Andros to govern it. Within two years, the Dominion was expanded to include Delaware, New Jersey, and Pennsylvania. The Dominion's potential to unify the American colonies a century ahead of time died in 1688 when William of Orange deposed James II and was declared King William III. In 1689, learning of the coup, sympathizers in Boston captured Andros and his allies. In New York, Jacob Leisler led militia forces that disarmed the regular troops. In 1691, William III broke up the Dominion into its former autonomous colonies. Royal governors were appointed to all the colonies except self-governing Connecticut and Rhode Island. Massachusetts absorbed Plymouth.[28]

While various civil and international wars engulfed England and its colonies, New France struggled to survive decades of war with the Iroquois. After regaining New France in 1632, Versailles redoubled its efforts to strengthen it. Trois-Rivieres was founded in 1634 and Montreal in 1642. In 1632, Cardinal Richelieu expelled the Recollets from New France, thus allowing the Jesuits to dominate. New religious orders arrived, including the Ursulines and Soeurs Hospitalieres in 1639 and Company of the Holy Sacrament in 1642. More seigneuries were granted to encourage more settlers. The fur trade was opened to all in 1645.

The European demand for furs rapidly depleted the supply and provoked wars among the tribes. Having wiped out their own fur-bearing animals, the Iroquois stole pelts from others. In 1635, the Iroquois once again began raiding the French and their Indian allies along the St. Lawrence valley. At first, the Iroquois merely attacked convoys of fur-laden Huron canoes paddling down the Great Lakes toward New France. In the 1640s, these raids gave way to a series of "Beaver Wars" against first surrounding and then ever more distant tribes. The Iroquois objective in these wars was to destroy their rivals and capture their fur-rich lands. Hundreds of Dutch muskets gave them the means to do so. Year by year, village by village, Iroquois war parties burned enemy fields and homes, killed hundreds, and herded the survivors back to their own longhouses. The Iroquois virtually exterminated the Huron by 1649, the Petun by 1650, the Neutrals by 1651, the Erie by 1657, and the Susquehannock by 1660. The remnants of those tribes fled either to French missions along the St. Lawrence or to tribes further west; the Susquehannock headed south to Maryland and Virginia. Many of the Iroquian-speaking Huron and other tribes eventually formed a new tribe called the Wyandot, whose villages dotted Lake Erie's southwestern shore. Not every war ended in an Iroquois victory; a war against the Abenaki in the 1660s ended in stalemate. During these decades, the Iroquois also raided French settlements and killed French missionaries such as fathers Joques in 1642, Bressani in 1644, and Brebeuf and Lalemant in 1649. In all, 153 French died and 144 were captured between 1608 and 1666. Smallpox meanwhile accomplished what their enemies had failed to do—plagues in 1634 and 1661 ravaged the Five Nations. The furs looted from these wars swelled Fort Orange's warehouses, to New France's loss; in 1656 the number of furs reaching Fort Orange peaked at 46,000.[29]

The war drastically changed both the Iroquois and New France. The adoption of hundreds of captives transformed Iroquois society. Mission Indians brought with them Christianity and pro-French sentiments. However well they were treated by the Iroquois, adoptees were not inclined to raid their former nations. Captives brought with them their tribal stories, beliefs, crafts, languages, and rituals that at once enriched and diluted traditional Iroquois culture. New France would soon exploit these Iroquois weaknesses.

In Paris, Minister Jean-Baptiste Colbert determined to transform New France into a self-sufficient, diversified colony that filled rather than drained Versailles' treasury. In 1663, Colbert revoked the private company's charter and imposed direct royal rule over New France. The first objective was to stabilize the colony's security by sending it French troops. In 1664, a company from each of four regiments, the Poitou, Orleans, Lalliter, and Chambelle regiments, arrived in Quebec. Those troops were reinforced the following year with 20 companies from the Carignan-Salieres regiment, creating a combined force of 1,200 regulars commanded by Lieutenant General Alexandre de Prouville. Curiously, those troops were the first French units ever to wear uniforms—brown coats lined with grey or white.[30] In 1665, Colbert sent two energetic leaders to New France, Governor Daniel de Remy de Courcelle and Intendant Jean Talon. In 1668, Colbert ordered Talon to have each parish organize its able-bodied men into militia companies. The intendant would appoint each company's captain, who was often a retired regular officer or soldier. New France's population now totaled 3,035, of which one-third were regular soldiers while nearly all other men were in the militia. The much more reliable flintlock musket replaced the slow-firing arquebus. In addition, the French built three forts to guard the north end of Lake Champlain and the Richelieu River valley to wall off the St. Lawrence valley from Iroquois raiders. Colbert also invested royal funds into lumberyards, shipyards, and tarworks, and offered more seigneuries to encourage settlement. New France's population rose to 10,977 by 1685. Wheat production not only kept pace with the new mouths to feed, but most years actually rose to a surplus that could be exported to France.

With these measures, the military power balance shifted from the Iroquois to the French. The mere threat of a French invasion was enough to induce peace from most of the Iroquois. Exhausted from their own endless wars and a series of smallpox epidemics, by 1665 four of the Iroquois tribes accepted peace—only the Mohawk kept to the warpath. Courcelle was determined to crush the recalcitrant Mohawk. In January 1666, he led 600 French troops down the Lake Champlain and Hudson rivers in a hellish struggle to reach and attack Mohawk villages. En route, 300 died of exposure and the survivors sought shelter in Schenectady. Another 100 died as they trudged home. In October 1666, eager to overcome the previous winter's disaster, Courcelle mustered 1,300 men, including 600 regulars, 600 civilian volunteers, and 100 Huron and Algonquians, and led them toward the Mohawk villages. Although the Mohawk slipped away before Courcelle's men, the French burned four villages and destroyed their food stores. Those Mohawk who survived the winter sued for peace the following year. In 1667, the French and Five Nations signed a treaty ending war between them and opening the latter to missionaries and traders.

New France sealed the peace by dispatching priests to the Five Nations. There they found a ready audience among the hundreds of former mission Indians who had been dragged as captives to Iroquoia, as well as scores of converts among the native born. Each tribe split among neutral, pro-English, and pro-French factions whose differences over time grew ever wider and more bitter. Increasing numbers of converts migrated to one of three missions near Montreal—La Prairie, La Montagne, or Caughnawaga (Kahnawake), Cataraqui up the St. Lawrence near Lake Ontario, or the predominantly Huron mission of La Lorette near Quebec. Among the Mohawk migrants to Caughnawaga was Kateri Tekawitha, whom Rome later beatified for miracles attributed to her. Iroquois also occupied the lands north of Lake Ontario from which they had earlier driven the Huron and others during the Beaver Wars.

The French also used this peace with the Iroquois to push far up the Great Lakes and buy furs directly from those distant tribes. In 1670, Jacque Marquette founded Fort Michilimackinac at the strait between Lake Huron and Lake Michigan. In 1672, Intendant Talon dispatched Louis Jolliet to find and explore the Mississippi River. Jolliet joined with Marquette and together they paddled down the Mississippi as far as the Arkansas River before heading back. By 1674, Jolliet was in Quebec urging the government to establish trading posts down the Mississippi valley. While intrigued, Talon replied that the St. Lawrence valley's population had to grow in numbers and prosperity before they could consider colonizing more distant lands.

The French also began asserting power over nearby Lake Ontario, a region previously dominated by the Iroquois. In 1671, Courcelle led 50 men up the St. Lawrence to broker a peace between the Iroquois and western tribes. Two years later, in 1673, Governor Frontenac built upon Courcelle's limited success by leading 400 troops up the St. Lawrence and into Lake Ontario to found Fort Cataraqui (Fort Frontenac) on the northeastern shore. In 1676, the French established a trading post at the Niagara River on Lake Ontario's southwestern shore. With these two posts, the French captured much of the furs leading down from Lake Erie. Weakened by decades of war, the Iroquois could merely howl in protest.

Colbert approved these acts and implemented others that strengthened New France. British trade at Hudson Bay indirectly strengthed New France. In 1680, Colbert licensed the North Bay Company which dispatched Canadian traders to the region. He also ordered Quebec to replace all civilian trading post leaders with military officers. When Colbert died in 1683, his legacy lived on in an invigorated New France.

Among Colbert's most important acts was to grant a five-year fur trade monopoly to Rene-Robert Cavelier de La Salle in 1675. La Salle built a war ship on Lake Erie in 1679, founded St. Joseph in 1679, Fort Crevecouer in 1680, Fort Prudhomme in 1682, and Fort St. Louis in 1683. These forts linked up two strands of French power, one through the upper and western and the other through the southern Great Lakes. In 1682, La Salle led 33 French and 31 Indians in canoes down the Mississippi River all the way to the Gulf of Mexico and back. He returned to France to recruit an expedition to colonize the mouth of the Mississippi River. In 1684, he set sail with 400 men aboard four ships but could not find the Mississippi River and instead disembarked at Matagorda Bay in Texas. The survivors murdered La Salle and sailed away. It would be another three decades before the French would venture again into the Gulf of Mexico.[31]

The French trading posts became magnets for tribes throughout their surrounding regions. The Illinois confederation of a dozen affiliated bands numbered roughly 10,500 people. Increasing numbers of Illinois migrated eastward to the trading posts or to rivers that flowed down to them. This migration into lands recently claimed by the Iroquois prompted war. During the late 1670s and throughout the 1680s, Iroquois war parties ranged as far west as the Mississippi River, yet they failed to exterminate the Illinois confederacy as they had so many other tribes. A 1684 Seneca attack on Fort St. Louis was repulsed by Chevalier Henri de Baugy, 24 French, and 22 Indians. The defeat of the once seemingly invincible Iroquois proved to be the war's psychological and military turning point. In all, distance, unfamiliarity with the terrain, and enemy numbers ultimately defeated the Iroquois. The wars drove the Illinois into greater dependence on the French, not just for guns but also for advisors and troops.

The initiative passed to the French and their Indian allies. After abortive attempts by Governor Joseph Antoine le Febrve de La Barre to invade the Iroquois lands in 1684 and 1685, in 1687 his successor Jacque-Rene de Brisay de Denonville marched into the Seneca country at the head of 832 troops, 1,030 militia, and 300 Indians. Although his troops never succeeded in catching the Seneca, they did destroy several villages. The Iroquois retaliated with attacks on Fort Niagara, Fort Frontenac, and down the St. Lawrence. Weakened by both the Iroquois raids and a smallpox epidemic that killed 10 percent of New France's 11,000 settlers, Denonville negotiated a peace treaty with the Five Nations.

Whether war or peace prevailed, the Europeans continually upset existing power balances and traditions among the Indians. During the late 1670s and throughout the 1680s, the influx of French and English traders to new regions was especially disruptive as they competed for furs by cutting prices and selling muskets. Those tribes nearer the English and French traders used their muskets to settle ancient scores with more distant enemies. The Objibwa (Chippewa), for example, launched attacks against the Sioux and Fox below Lake Superior that drove those tribes west and south.

During the 1680s, the nonaggression pact of the Iroquois "League" became the alliance of the Iroquois "Confederation." The French and English alike had long treated the Five Nations as if they were one. Annual meetings at the Onondaga Council fire shifted from maintaining peace among the Five Nations to waging war and diplomacy against others. Nonetheless, there would never be a time in the confederation's history when more than three of the Five and later Six Nations simultaneously took the warpath. In fact, the council did all it could to keep peace within an increasingly divided confederation.

By 1685, over 800 French and several hundred English traders had spread across the Great Lakes, the Ohio and Mississippi valleys, and Hudson Bay. Blood was increasingly shed on lonely trails as rival French and English traders met. In 1685, the Marquis de Denonville sent Chevalier de Troyes and 90 troops to capture the three English trading posts on lower Hudson Bay, and thereby divert 50,000 furs from English to French markets. In 1686, a trading expedition dispatched by New York governor Thomas Dongan reached the Michilimackinac region to entice those tribes away from the French. Thus did French and English skirmish in the New World four years before they formally went to war in the Old.[32]

In 1689, King William's War (War of the Augsburg Succession) broke out between England and France, and soon engulfed much of Europe. William III declared war on France when Louis XIV tried to conquer the English king's native Holland and supported a Catholic Stuart claimant to the English throne. In North America, the warfare quickly assumed the characteristics that would continue through four successive wars.[33] With their armies bogged down in Europe, neither France nor England could commit significant forces to North America. London dispatched a mere four infantry companies to New York and another to Newfoundland. Versailles sent only warships to convoy its annual supply fleet to Quebec. With each war, France and England would boost the number of troops they committed to the New World. But the colonists were mostly forced to decide North America's fate on their own.

Colonial troops and their Indian allies waged war through raids and occasional major campaigns. Over the next few years, the French led war parties of Abenaki against New Hampshire and attacks composed of various tribes to the Hudson and Mohawk valleys. These raids burned Fort Casco, Fort Loyal, Salmon Falls, Schenectady, and York. In response, the English helped finance Iroquois raids along the St. Lawrence valley. An Iroquois raid in July 1689 burned the town of Lachine, a mere seven miles from Montreal. In 1690, an English raiding party voyaged up the Lake Champlain corridor to destroy La Prairie before escaping a French and Indian pursuit. That same year, William Phips led 736 men to capture Port Royal in Nova Scotia.

It was increasingly clear to colonial leaders that raiding could not win the war. In April 1691, representatives of the New England and mid-Atlantic colonies met in New York to plan and launch their first all-out attempt to conquer New France. Pieter Schuyler's raid up Lake Champlain to Montreal's outskirts caused little damage to the French. Phips, meanwhile, organized a fleet of 32 ships and 2,300 troops to sail against Quebec. His fleet anchored before Quebec on October 16 but failed to take the city by storm or destroy it with bombardment. Gales battered the fleet during its ignominious retreat, wrecking several ships and drowning 1,000 men. The expedition had been a disaster.

While life and death struggles would flare along the New England and New France frontiers, the war would be decided elsewhere. At the 1692 Battle of La Hoque, a combined English and Dutch fleet defeated the French navy. Although the war would continue to burn across Europe and the American frontier, the French were hard-pressed to supply New France in the face of British naval supremacy. Raids bloodied the frontier for another half dozen years. The governors of New France and some New England colonies offered bounties for scalps. The Iroquois suffered a humiliating defeat in 1696 when Governor Frontenac led 2,000 French and Indians to the Onondaga heartland, whose villages and crops he destroyed.

The Treaty of Ryswick abruptly ended King William's War in 1697. The French agreed to recognize William III as England's legitimate king, along with English claims to Newfoundland and Hudson Bay. Peace in Europe, however, did not extend to North America. The Abenaki continued to war against New England while the Iroquois ravaged the St. Lawrence valley. Several French expeditions along with separate Ottawa and Objibwa war parties attacked the Five Nations. Half of the Iroquois' warriors died in these wars. In 1701, the Iroquois could do nothing to prevent the French from building Fort Detroit to solidify their control over the upper Great Lakes' fur trade. Instead, that same year they meekly accepted a summons by Governor Frontenac to join representatives of 30 tribes at a Montreal council which agreed to a "Great Peace" among them all. That same year, the Iroquois signed a peace treaty with the English at Albany. In both treaties, the Iroquois promised to remain neutral in any war between France and England.

Ironically, while peace finally settled along the northern frontier, war again engulfed Europe, sparked by the death of the childless Spanish king Carlos II. Louis XIV tried to impose his grandson on the Spanish throne and thus extend French control over Spain's Italian and Flemish territory. Other great powers supported other claimants. In 1702, England officially entered what became known as Queen Anne's War or the War of the Spanish Succession. Queen Anne and her government hoped not just to contain Louis XIV's latest aggression but to use the war to seize Spain's Caribbean sugar islands and annual treasure fleet.

During the war, the periodic raids that had all along terrorized the northeast frontier increased in number and ferocity. Abenaki attacked the cities of Casco, Wells, Winter Harbor, York, and Deerfield, slaughtering hundreds of settlers and dragging hundreds of others into captivity. Caughnawaga Iroquois raided Schenectady. Iroquois raids burned and looted along the St. Lawrence valley. Western Indians attacked the Iroquois. Bounties were once again offered for enemy scalps and prisoners. Privateers captured hundreds of enemy merchant ships.

All the raiding aside, no significant campaigns occurred until 1708 when Colonel Benjamin Church launched an unsuccessful attack on Port Royal. Another attack failed the following year. Then, in 1710, an English fleet finally captured not only Port Royal but all the small French settlements dotting the Bay of Fundy. These campaigns were overshadowed in 1711 when Sir Hovenden Walker sailed toward Quebec with a fleet of 14 warships, 31 transports, and 11,000 troops, of which 4,300 were composed of seven regular regiments and 6,500 provincial troops. Walker's campaign was the first time that England had sent substantial numbers of troops to aid its American colonies. Given the expedition's fate, the regulars would have been better off not leaving England. Shortly after entering the St. Lawrence, much of the fleet ran aground in a thick fog. In all, nine ships broke up and over 900 men drowned. Walker ignominiously ordered the remnants of his command back to Boston. As Ian Steel points out, "New France's survival in 1711, as in 1690, was due to incompetence and misfortune."[34]

While King William's War had flared along Britain's northern American frontier, Queen Anne's War spread to the south. As in the northeast, victory in the southeast depended on forging Indian alliances against one's enemies. The southeast's most powerful Indian group was the Creek confederation which included seven tribes of 15,000 people in 60 villages. Enemies surrounded the Creek, including the Choctaw and Chickasaw to the west, the Guale and Apalachee allied with Spain to the southeast, and the Cherokee to the north. Hoping to get iron and guns, the Creek had invited Spanish missionaries and merchants to their realm in 1681. The Spanish faith and goods, however, spawned greeds and jealousies that threatened the fragile confederacy. By 1685, the Creek had expelled the Spaniards and invited South Carolina merchants, who left their religion at home. English-armed

Creeks began raiding Spanish missions in northern Florida along with their enemies to the west. As elsewhere, the influx of European diseases offset any material advantages. Smallpox ravaged the Creek during the 1690s. The French complicated the southeast's complex power distribution when they founded the colony of Louisiana with posts at Biloxi in 1699 and Mobile in 1701.

When news of the War of the Spanish Succession reached South Carolina, Governor James Moore organized and dispatched an expedition to take St. Augustine. While the defenders withstood the siege, a Spanish fleet arrived, forcing the English to abandon their own ships and artillery and retreat overland to South Carolina. Unable to take Florida with provincial troops, Moore then tried to exterminate it by supplying Creek war parties. The frontier war sputtered on for years, with all tribes suffering hundreds of deaths and dozens of burned villages. The French entered the fray, allying with the Choctaw against the Creek and sending privateers to seize English merchant ships. Carolinian volunteers accompanied a large Creek army that devastated the Choctaw lands in 1711. The following year, the Creek and the French signed a neutrality treaty that held until 1763.

Meanwhile, war had broken out between the three southern colonies and the Tuscarora in 1711. Over the next two years, the English launched several ever larger campaigns of Creek, Catawba, Cherokee, and provincial troops against Tuscarora villages. In 1713, Tuscarora remnants fled north all the way to New York to seek shelter among the Iroquois, who adopted them as a sixth member of their confederacy. With the Franco-Creek neutrality and Tuscarora's disappearance, the southeast escaped the large-scale fighting that engulfed the northeast during the next two Anglo-French wars.[35]

Under the 1713 Treaty of Utrecht ending Queen Anne's War, Versailles ceded English claims to Newfoundland, Hudson Bay, Acadia except for Isle Royale (Cape Breton), and Isle Saint-Jean (Prince Edward Island); recognized English sovereignty over the Iroquois; and permitted the English to trade in French territory. France's ally, Spain, lost nothing in North America, but did have to grant England the strongholds of Gibraltar and Minorca in the Mediterranean. England reaped huge benefits from the war, along with greater defense commitments.

The Utrecht Treaty is a classic example of a peace accord that sowed the seeds of future conflicts. The failure to delineate these territorial trades and fulfill other tenets unleashed a half century of conflicting claims that only war could resolve. Most controversial of all was Article 15, which seemed to allow for free trade among all the tribes and asserted British sovereignty over the Iroquois. Did free trade permit Englishmen to peddle their goods at the gates of French trading posts? If not, just where were the territories of the Iroquois and other tribes drawn? The English and French proclaimed the Iroquois as British subjects; the Iroquois rejected that distinction.

These ambiguities aside, by European standards, Utrecht inaugurated a relatively strong peace between England and France that lasted until 1744. Both sides used those 27 years to expand their respective North American empires. The French founded settlements in the Great Lakes, Mississippi valley, and Louisiana territories. In Louisiana, the French established Fort Rosalie in 1716, Fort Toulouse in 1717, and New Orleans in 1719. In the upper Mississippi valley, they established Fort de Chartres in 1720 and Fort St. Philippe in 1726. On Isle Royale in 1717, the French began building fortress Louisbourg. In 1720, the French rebuilt a trading post at the Niagara River mouth and fortified it in 1726. In 1731, Fort Frederic arose at Lake Champlain's southern narrows. In addition to these forts, the French traded at several score smaller posts scattered at cross-trails throughout the eastern woodlands, western prairies, and even high plains as far as the Assiniboine and Missouri rivers. Thus did the French construct a chain of forts and settlements in a vast crescent from the Gulf Coast, up the Mississippi valley, over to the Great Lakes, and down the St. Lawrence valley. Although the links in this chain were far apart, they served effectively as magnets for regional trade and barriers to contain the English east of the Appalachian mountains.

These French advances only spurred the English to consider ways to sever that chain. A 1735 Board of Trade report maintained that although the Appalachian Mountains "may serve at present for a very good frontier, we should not propose them for the boundary of your Majesty's Empire in America . . . British Settlements might be extended beyond them, and some small forts erected on the great Lakes . . . whereby the French communications from Quebec to the River Mississippi might be interrupted."[36]

The perennial efforts of the English to divert furs from the Great Lakes to Albany began to bear considerable fruit in the 1720s. Trade missions to the village of Irondequoit on Lake Ontario garnered furs bound for Montreal. The amount of furs reaching Albany increased tenfold between 1716 and 1724. Then, in 1725, the English established a trading post at Oswego on Lake Ontario, and fortified it in 1727. Supplies were conveyed along the 217-mile route from Albany to Oswego almost entirely by water, up the Mohawk River, over the half-dozen-mile portage of the Great Carrying Place, down Wood Creek to Lake Oneida, and then down the Onondaga River to Oswego. From there, the English canoed to the upper Great Lakes to solicit trade.

The English post on Lake Ontario was a painful thorn in the side of French Canada. The "remote Indians . . . formerly used to go down to the French at Montreal, and there buy our English goods at second Hand, at above twice the Price they now pay for them at Oswego."[37] Father Piquet worried that Fort Oswego "not only spoils our trade, but puts the English into communication with a vast number of our Indians, far and near. It is true that they like our brandy better than English rum; but they prefer

English goods to ours, and can buy for two beaver-skins at Oswego a better silver bracelet than we sell at Niagara for ten."[38]

The French responded by threatening to erect a rival post at Oswego, but they lacked the low-priced, high-quality goods that would have enabled them to compete. The rival trading posts at Oswego and Niagara made "the Six Nations' economic dependence on European trade . . . complete, and the profits flowed almost entirely in one direction."[39] This was, of course, the same pattern of dependence and exploitation that had been and would be repeated across North America. That dependence caused the Iroquois to insist that those two forts remain free from attack should another war break out between France and England.

Indian wars continued to flare up here and there along the English frontier. For years, tensions worsened between the Yamasee and the traders who buried them ever deeper in debts for goods they could no longer live without. In 1715, these animosities exploded into a revolt by the Yamasee confederation against South Carolina. With generous presents and promises, the English managed to entice the Cherokee not only to break away from the Yamasee but fight their former allies, and the Creek to withdraw into neutrality. A South Carolina campaign defeated the Catawaba and forced them into a sullen peace. Yet, despite these blows, the Yamasee fought on, killing over 400 colonists and devastating South Carolina's economy. It got so bad that, in 1719, South Carolina's proprietors handed their bankrupt colony over to the king. The war dragged on until 1728 when an English expedition destroyed a Yamasee village near St. Augustine. The Spanish refusal to help the Yamasee caused them to sue for peace.

In the northeast, fighting between New England and the Abenaki also continued for years. In 1724, an English expedition finally succeeded in destroying the center of eastern Abenaki power at Norridgewock and killing Father Sebastien Rale, who had long instigated raids on New England. Yet Dummer's War burned on until a formal peace was signed in 1727.[40]

During these decades the French fought their own frontier wars. In 1711, the French had invited the Fox to settle near Detroit. However, tensions arose between the newcomers and the existing Ottawa, Potawatomi, and Huron. Forced to choose between them, France joined its established allies in a surprise attack in 1715 that killed over 1,000 Fox and drove the survivors to Green Bay. The war dragged on for years, with the Fox eventually fighting not only the French and the three Detroit tribes, but also the Miami and Illinois as well. By 1738, the Fox population had dropped to several hundred from the 10,000 they had numbered in the 17th century. These fragments joined the Sauk in what is now eastern Iowa.

In 1729, a French land fraud provoked a Natchez attack that killed over 300 French settlers and destroyed Fort Rosalie. The French and Choctaw retaliated with an expedition that ravaged the Natchez. The Cherokee and

Chickasaw absorbed the few survivors. France's successful wars against the Fox and Natchez anchored its power at either end of the Mississippi valley. Then, a war with the Chickasaw threatened to sever that Mississippi route. In 1736, the French decided to resolve years of worsening tensions with the Chickasaw by destroying them. However, unlike the Fox and Natchez, the Chickasaw prevailed despite overwhelming odds against them. The war ended in 1739 after the Chickasaw defeated a massive army of 1,000 regulars, 88 militia, 300 blacks, and 350 Choctaw. The Chickasaw thorn would remain embedded in the French imperial side for another generation.

During this time, England and France not only remained at peace, but actually allied against Spain in an inconclusive war between 1718 and 1721. The French captured Pensacola but restored it with a peace treaty. Spain and England fought during 1728 and 1729 without a decisive victory for either side. Surprisingly, Georgia's establishment in 1733 did not immediately provoke another war. Having bolstered its northern frontiers, the Crown tried to cement its empire's southern end by issuing a charter to James Oglethorpe to found Georgia. Oglethorpe led a party of settlers to lay out Savannah in 1733 and in subsequent years established a series of forts and settlements along the coast down to the St. John's River. Despite Spanish protests against what it claimed were infringements on its territory, fighting did not break out between the two kingdoms until 1739, when Madrid's violations of its peace treaty with England led to the undeclared War of Jenkins' Ear. In 1739, an English fleet sacked Portobello, Panama. That early success, however, was eclipsed in 1740 when an expedition against St. Augustine once again failed to capture that Spanish stronghold. The English suffered an even worse disaster in 1741 when disease killed half their troops besieging Cartegena. Although Georgian troops did repel a Spanish invasion in 1742, a 1743 attack on St. Augustine once again failed miserably. Colonials provided the bulk of English troops in these campaigns. The heavy losses soured the Americans' enthusiasm for fighting far from their own homes.[41]

In 1740, the Emperor Charles VI died without a male heir. Over the next few years, most of Europe's powers joined this War for the Austrian Succession. In October 1743, the Bourbon kings of Spain and France signed the Treaty of Fontainbleau, reviving their old Family Compact. The British and French fought on the continent and oceans for at least a year before Versailles formally issued a war declaration in March 1744.[42]

In North America the struggle was known as King George's War. Once again Indian raids burned and killed along the northern frontier. Much of the fighting took place in Nova Scotia and Cape Breton. The French got in the first blow by an attack on Canso in May 1744, but failed to capture Annapolis Royal two months later. In 1745, Governor William Shirley organized an expedition of 3,000 New England troops, led by William Pepperell aboard 52 ships commanded by Admiral Peter Warren, which successfully besieged and took Louisbourg. All of the 4,460 French soldiers and civilians were transported back to France. It was a crippling blow to French power in the region. To this, the French could only respond with more raids against New England. In 1746, Rigaud de Vaudreuil led 400 Canadians and 300 Indians down the Connecticut River to capture and burn Fort Massachusetts. In June 1747, Chevalier de Niverville led a raid on New Hampshire and destroyed five forts and 100 houses. On the night of February 11–12, 1747, Captain Nicolas-Antoine Coulon de Villiers led 250 Canadians and Micmac against Grand Pre's 500 defenders commanded by Lieutenant Colonel Arthur Noble. Achieving a complete surprise, Villiers' men killed Noble and 70 of his men and captured the rest. Elsewhere, the Choctaw fought against the French from 1746 to 1749, while many Ohio valley tribes conspired but did not openly war against the French during that same period. From the Great Lakes to the Gulf, Indians looked to the English to supply their trade-goods needs.[43]

In New York, the rivalry between the French and British for an Iroquois alliance bitterly split the Longhouse. Officially, only the Mohawk fought with the British; the other tribes remained neutral. But the pressure tore each tribe into near warring factions. Many Mohawk drifted north to Caughnawaga near Montreal. Other disgruntled Iroquois migrated to the upper Ohio River valley where they became known as Mingo. Onondaga and Cayuga along with Iroquois from the other tribes flocked to the Oswegatchie mission until, by 1751, over 3,000 Iroquois had settled there. During the final French and Indian War, Oswegatchie and Caughnawaga became bases for war parties against New York, New England, and even their former kinsmen.

The war cost France much of its naval and merchant fleet. British warships and privateers reigned supreme, capturing 2,457 prizes from 1745 through 1748 alone. What ships the British did not destroy, the French often lost through mismanagement and bad luck. In spring 1746, for example, a 76-ship French fleet set sail to retake the British conquests in North America. Storms and disease killed 3,000 as the fleet reached Nova Scotia and then returned to France. The English fleet blockaded St. Lawrence Bay, provoking near starvation among the Canadians and the dwindling of Indian allies as the supply ships bringing their gifts were seized.[44]

As in previous wars, the events in North America were but sideshows to the bloodbath drenching Europe. While the British succeeded on the high seas and at Louisbourg, they barely held on in Europe. The worst threat to England occurred in 1745 when the Jacobite Stuart Prince Charles landed in Scotland and tried to spark a Scottish revolt. The threat died when the Duke of Cumberland annihilated Charles' army at Culloden in 1746 and then torched the homes of suspected Jacobite supporters.

By 1748, the European powers had exhausted their treasuries and manpower with no decisive winner. Diplomats negotiated a cease-fire in April and in October 1748 signed the Treaty of Aix-la-Chapelle. The treaty secured most of Britain's objectives including breaking up the Bourbon alliance, preserving the European power balance, and forcing France to both repudiate the Jacobite pretender to England's throne and withdraw from the Netherlands. The treaty, however, brought no change to North America; all captured territory was returned to the previous owner. Nor did the treaty clarify the imperial boundaries blurred by the 1713 Utrecht Treaty.

The decade of war against Spain and then France burned two lasting images into many Americans' memories. One was the debacle before Cartegena, where English incompetence and arrogance contributed to the deaths of thousands of colonists. The other was Louisbourg, where American initiative and courage conquered France's most powerful fortress in the western hemisphere. The Crown then shattered this colonial triumph when it restored Louisbourg with the Treaty of Aix-la-Chapelle. The war deepened a budding sense of American nationalism.[45]

The Treaty of Aix-la-Chapelle officially ended King George's War. In North America, however, King George's War was followed by six years of cold war, especially in Acadia and the upper Ohio River Valley, which finally exploded once again into open war in 1754.

ACADIA

In the postwar era, both the English and French tried to consolidate their holdings in Acadia, compete for the loyalty of the Acadians, and harass the other. The Acadian region embracing today's Cape Breton, Prince Edward Island, Nova Scotia, and New Brunswick was of enormous strategic and economic importance. The surrounding seas annually produced a wealth of fish. The region also commanded the British and French routes to their North American colonies.[46]

Historian Henry Gipson describes Acadia as "the first French and last British colony to be established in North America."[47] For a century, until 1713, the French owned Acadia, then ceded much of it to England under that year's Treaty of Utrecht. How much was ceded remained a source of bitter contention between France, who claimed the dividing line at the Chignecto Isthmus, and Britain, who asserted that Acadia included today's New Brunswick as well as Nova Scotia.

After formally taking Nova Scotia, the British administrators saw no other way to control the Acadians than to demand loyalty oaths from them. In 1717, Nova Scotia governor Richard Philips decreed that all the province's inhabitants had to swear allegiance to the British Crown. Most Acadians were willing to do so as long as they could remain neutral in any war between Britain and France. Lacking the military means to enforce his order, Philipps quietly allowed it to become a dead letter. In 1729, Governor Lawrence Armstrong also tried to enforce a loyalty oath. When the Acadians again insisted that they would sign only if they were allowed to remain neutral, Armstrong nodded his acceptance but got them to sign a document written in English, in which the Acadians unknowingly confessed their unconditional loyalty to Britain. In 1729, during his second term as governor, Philipps pulled the same trick on the Acadians. Believing that they had exacted three official acceptances of their neutrality, the Acadians would remain ignorant for two decades that London still saw them as traitors to the Crown.

Vicious fighting tore apart Nova Scotia during King George's War as the Abbe Jean Louis Le Loutre, a Spiritian missionary, rallied the Acadians to raid the British. Le Loutre was one of the more Machiavellian agents spawned before and during the French and Indian War. He explained his strategy in a letter to the Minister of Marine: "As we cannot openly oppose the English ventures, I think that we cannot do better than to incite the Indians to send word to the English that they will not permit new settlements to be made in Acadia. . . . I shall do my best to make it look to the English as if this plan comes from the Indians and that I have no part in it."[48] To win, Le Loutre would even kill the Acadian peasants he was supposedly trying to liberate. To force the Acadians to follow him, he "threatened to abandon the Acadians, withdraw their priests, have their wives and children taken from them, and if necessary have their property laid waste by the Indians."[49] These were not idle threats. When the people of Beaubassin did not aid him, Le Loutre incited Micmac to burn the village, thus driving its inhabitants to the French side of the river and denying that village to the British.

Officials in both Versailles and Quebec encouraged Le Loutre's campaign of subversion and terror against both the Acadians and the British. Du Fesne du Motel reported that "Our savages have taken a number of English scalps, the terror of these natives is unequalled, they are so frightened that they dare not leave the towns or forts without detachments, with the protection of these they go out for what is absolutely necessary."[50]

Yet, despite these efforts, Le Loutre failed to spark a general Acadian uprising. In 1748, New France Governor La Galissoniere admitted that: "Most of the poor people are of Acadian stock, they have been almost entirely abandoned by Canada and France since the Peace of Utrecht, and the English have made them believe that, having been subject formerly to the French Governor of Port Royal, they owed the same obedience to the English Governor."[51]

The Treaty of Aix-la-Chapelle converted an overt war into a covert war. On August 29, 1749, Versailles explained its policy toward Nova Scotia to the governors of New France and Isle Royale: The English "are within their rights in making in Acadia such settlements as they see fit, as long as they do not pass its boundaries, there remains for us only to bring against them as many indirect obstacles as can be done without compromising ourselves, and to take steps to protect ourselves against plans which the English can consider through the success of these settlements. The only method we can employ to bring into existence these obstacles is to make the savages of Acadia and its borders feel how much it is to their advantage to prevent the English fortifying themselves, to bind them to oppose it openly, and to excite the Acadians to support the Indians in their opposition in so far as they can do without discovery. The missionaries of both have instructions and are agreeable to act in accordance with these views."[52]

That year New France intendant Francois Bigot authorized Le Loutre to return to Nova Scotia and instigate Acadian loyalty to France and revolt against the British should another war break out. To win his mission, Le Loutre once again played on Acadian fears as well as sentiments; he threatened to loosen the Micmac on any Acadians who remained with Britain.

Meanwhile, shaken by Le Loutre's raids during the war and fearful of those yet to come, British officials debated the Acadians' fate. Massachusetts governor Shirley suggested diluting the Acadians with protestants from England and other lands. In March 1749, Lord Halifax commissioned Edward Cornwallis as governor of Nova Scotia and ordered him to gather immigrants and establish a town on Nova Scotia's eastern shore. By midsummer, 14 ships disgorged 2,500 settlers to establish Halifax. The town would not only counter the province's French population but as a naval base and fortress would counter France's Louisbourg, on Cape Breton up the coast. While strategically justified, this military buildup and settlement was expensive—costing 336,700 pounds between 1753 and 1756 alone.[53]

The Chignecto Isthmus divided British and French Acadia. There, in spring 1749, Captain Jean Luc de la Corne massed 2,500 Canadians and Indians on the western side of the Missaquash River, which flows into the Bay of Fundy. To assert British claims to the region, in 1750 Cornwallis ordered Major Charles Lawrence to advance there with two companies of troops and tell la Corne to withdraw. In April, Lawrence landed his force nearby, marched up to the Missaquash, and demanded la Corne's withdrawal. La Corne refused. The crisis defused when the opposing commanders had their men build forts on their respective sides of the Missaquash; the French built Fort Beausejour and Fort Gaspereau and the English Fort Lawrence. The French also established Fort St. Jean on the Bay of Fundy's west coast.

The confrontation proved to be a limited British victory. With a British garrison and patrols on the Chignecto Isthmus, French influence over the Acadians declined steadily. Disillusionment spread, even among those Acadians who had fled to the French lines. The farms the refugees had to carve from wilderness failed to be as bountiful as those they had abandoned. The French gave the Acadians little aid. Increasing numbers of exiles longed to return home.

The test came in 1751, when Quebec's governor ordered the Acadians to make an oath of allegiance to the French Crown and enroll in the militia. Many then fled back to British Nova Scotia. A delegation of Acadians visited Cornwallis to assure him of their loyalty as long as he protected their religious rights. Cornwallis agreed and ordered all inhabitants to take the loyalty oath to King George II before October 26, and also strictly enforced a law forbidding any trade with New France. All along the British were well aware of the dissent among the Acadian ranks west of the Missaquash. Fort Beausejour's commissary, Thomas Pichon, was a British spy and sent regular reports over to Fort Lawrence.

Upon replacing Cornwallis as governor in 1753, Lawrence wrote to the Trade Board requesting instructions for the loyalty oath. The Trade Board authorized Lawrence to impose the oath but cautioned him "to avoid giving any alarm and creating such a diffidence in their minds as might induce them to quit the province, and by their numbers add strength to the French."[54] On July 3 and 4, 1753, Acadian representatives submitted petitions to Lawrence declaring their unwillingness to swear unconditional loyalty to Britain, and pleaded for the right to remain neutral in any war with France. The Acadian refusal to unconditionally declare themselves British subjects overturned the oaths many of them had unwittingly made in 1726 and 1730. But as long as French troops sat in forts across the Missaquash, the British did not dare to imprison or banish the dissident Acadians for fear of sparking a war against both them and the neighboring French regulars, militia, and Indians.

Thus were Acadians continually torn between the British and French empires, between their legal bond to George II and their cultural bond to Louis XV. Most Acadians were willing to swear allegiance to the British Crown only if they were allowed to remain neutral in any war against France. As British subjects, the Acadians profited more easily from trade with both the Micmac and nearby Abenaki, and from smuggling with New England.

The frontier between Nova Scotia and Acadia smoldered for six years before again exploding into open war. By 1754, the English had garrisons at Halifax, Fort Edward, Annapolis Royal, and Fort Lawrence. West of the Missaquash River, the French had garrisons at Beausejour, Gaspereau, and St. Jean. Despite this tense standoff, the spark that set off the most devastating war of all between France and Britain for North America would occur elsewhere, in the Ohio valley.

THE OHIO VALLEY

Amidst King George's War, a rivalry between the English and French flared over a region that had hitherto been neglected by both. Historian Ian Steel describes the upper Ohio region as having "long been a relatively uninhabited hunting area, claimed by the Six Nations by conquest, the British colonies by charter, the French crown by discovery, and various Amerindian tribes by occupancy."[55] It was the inability of those concerned to resolve their conflicting claims that provoked the French and Indian War.

Before 1749, the French had rarely visited let alone exploited the region. The only recorded French passage was in 1739, when Governor Pierre Jean, Le Moyne de Longueuil, led an expedition of 123 French troops and voyageurs and 319 Indians through the upper Ohio region from Quebec against the Chickasaw on the lower Mississippi River. Aside from that passing French ripple, no trading posts stood in the region because there was no need for them. Indians from the Ohio valley traveled far north to French posts at Fort Sandusky on Lake Erie, Fort Miami on the Maumee River, Fort Ouiantenon on the Wabash River, or Fort Niagara on Lake Ontario's southwestern shore to sell their pelts. Why go to the Indians when the Indians went to them, reasoned the French? Anyway, the French were hard-pressed enough to garner trade from their posts scattered across the Great Lakes and upper Mississippi valley regions. There was no reason even to travel through the upper Ohio. Communications between Quebec and New Orleans were paddled via the Maumee-Wabash River route.

The French only appreciated the region when they nearly lost it. Starting in the 1730s, intrepid and ambitious English traders penetrated the rugged and thick forested maze of mountains called the Appalachians and scattered among the tribes of the Ohio valley. The Indians embraced the English merchants' higher quality, cheaper priced goods, particularly since French goods had been in short or nonexistent supply after the British navy plugged the St. Lawrence Seaway in 1745. The traders stayed even after word filtered to them through the wilderness that yet another war had broken out between England and France; the enormous profits that could be reaped among the Indians caused those traders to set aside the risk of torture, death, or captivity.

None of these traders was more skilled, daring, and lucky than George Croghan. He had arrived in Pennsylvania from Ireland as recently as 1741 and then immediately got involved deeply in the Indian trade. Croghan first traded through the Ohio country in 1742 and brought back a handsome profit. His most audacious challenge to the French occurred in 1744 when he established a trade house at the Mingo town of Cuyahoga at the river mouth of the same name. The town was a stopping point on France's Great Lakes communications and trade route. The French put a price on Croghan's head. Numerous scalphunters tracked him. But Croghan managed to evade them all in the forests or among his Indian friends. Starting in 1746, Croghan operated a trading post for several years on the triangle of land where the Allegheny and Monongahela Rivers form the Ohio River. Those few acres would soon be reckoned among the most strategic in North America. Croghan's post guarded the most prominent door between the mid-Atlantic colonies and the Ohio valley. The French and English would fight over that doorway for the next dozen years.

By 1747, Indian animosities against the French had risen to a fever pitch. The Miami, Wyandot, Iroquois, Shawnee, Choctaw, and Creek exchanged wampum belts and delegations that tried to forge a grand confederation to sweep the French from the country. Although a concerted uprising did not occur, war parties launched isolated attacks on French supply convoys and Indian trade parties en route to French posts. Miami (Twightwee) Chief Memeskia (La Demoiselle, Old Briton) not only hoisted a British flag over Pickawillany, but led his warriors to assault Fort Maumee. In 1747, Wyandot Chief Nicolas destroyed Fort Sandusky and then fled with his band to the Ohio valley. Croghan had helped instigate those and other attacks. As he traded from village to village he "persuaded the Indians to destroy the French and had so far prevailed on them, by the presents he had made them, that five French had been killed by . . . Indians . . . his views were to engross the whole trade, and to scare the French from dealing with the Indians."[56] Fearing French retaliation, Croghan abandoned his post at Cuyahoga and opened one at Pickawillany, which was far less vulnerable.

The Indian attacks threatened France's entire upper Great Lakes trade empire. The French commander at Fort Miami, Captain Raymond, lamented that "my people are leaving for Detroit. Nobody wants to stay here and have his throat cut. All the tribes who go to the English at Pickawillany come back loaded with gifts. I am too weak to meet the danger. Instead of twenty men, I need five hundred . . . if the English stay in this country we are lost. We must attack and drive them out."[57] The French did retaliate. Along the trails, French and Indian war parties waylaid English traders, confiscated their goods, and drove them back to Detroit as criminals.

Tensions rose not just with the French but among the three English colonies—Pennsylvania, Virginia, and Maryland—vying for the region's trade. In 1748, Pennsylvania's government tried to mollify those tensions by calling an April council among the three colonies and the Indian tribes from the disputed region at the Delaware town of Logstown on the Ohio River. Maryland declined the invitation. Virginia agreed to participate by proxy, sending its 200-pound contribution of presents to the Indians via Pennsylvania's Indian agent Conrad Weiser who added it to the 500 pounds worth of presents allocated by Philadelphia. With the diplomatic field cleared of its rivals, Pennsylvania's agents negotiated a treaty with the tribes that granted it rights to the region. The other provinces protested.

To resolve the dispute another council was called for July 1748 at Lancaster. Presiding over the melange of Iroquois, Delaware, Shawnee, Miami, and others living in the region was the Oneida Chief Scarouady (Monacatootha) and Seneca Chief Tanaghrisson (Half King). Under the Lancaster Treaty these chiefs signed, the Indians ceded all the lands from the Allegheny to the Ohio River to Virginia, Maryland, and Pennsylvania. It remained for those three colonies to divide that land among themselves.

In late summer, Weiser, Croghan, and Andrew Montour, a half-Seneca trader and interpreter, followed up the Lancaster Treaty by traveling through the region to attend tribal councils and distribute gifts. Stick counts by the chiefs in each upper Ohio valley village revealed a formidable number of warriors—789, of which 165 were Delaware, 163 Seneca, 162 Shawnee, 100 Wyandot, 74 Mohawk, 40 Mississauga (Chippewa subtribe), 35 Onondaga, 20 Cayuga, 15 Oneida, and 15 Mahican.[58] With only a hard couple of weeks' trek on the warpath from those villages to the settlements, it was imperative to keep those tribes happy.

Virginia only seemed to have conceded the region to Pennsylvania. In 1747, Thomas Lee and eleven other investors petitioned Williamsburg to grant them 200,000 acres in the Ohio River valley. On November 6, Governor Gooch forwarded their request to the Board of Trade. After receiving the query on December 15, the Board studied it for a month and then, on January 19, 1748, wrote Gooch requesting his advice on any difficulties he foresaw that could arise from the purchase. Gooch got the Board's letter on June 5; in his June 16 reply, he admitted the sale "might possibly give umbrage to the French." Shortly after getting Gooch's letter on August 15, the Board endorsed and forwarded it to the Privy Council. On November 24, the Privy Council approved and returned the petition to the Board which in turn, on December 13, submitted to the Privy Council its final report on the matter and instructions to Gooch to carry out the petition. It had taken little more than a year for London to approve a vast land grant in disputed territory that could "give umbrage to the French."[59]

Meanwhile, the partners formed the Ohio Company of Virginia which, on October 18, 1748, directly petitioned London for a 500,000-acre land grant, more than twice the size of its original request. Along with expanding the ranks of investors to include most of Virginia's council and many prominent men, they further greased their plea by offering a cut to John Hanbury, a hugely rich Quaker tobacco and fur trader in London with considerable influence at court and throughout the colonies. Hanbury agreed. On January 11, 1749, Hanbury presented the Ohio Company petition to the government.[60]

Led by its anti-French president, George Montagu Dunk, Earl of Halifax, the Board of Trade quickly passed the measure and forwarded it to the king. Acting on Halifax's advice, on March 16, 1749, George II sent an order to Virginia Lieutenant-Governor Gooch to issue an initial grant of 200,000 acres of land west of the Allegheny Mountains from the Ohio forks down to the Kanawha River, and an additional 300,000 acres if the Ohio Company settled 100 families on their land within seven years and erected a fort. The goal was classically mercantilist: "to greatly promote the consumption of our shipping and navigation, and extend your Imperial Majesty's empire in America."[61] That rider to the grant stipulating a fort and settlers would eventually lead to war with France. As Francis Jennings put it, the "heedless greed of these few headstrong men lit a fire in the wilderness that spread to become a conflagration throughout the world."[62]

However, the first government to bitterly protest the concession was not that of France but of Pennsylvania. Citing Pennsylvania's 1748 treaty with the Ohio valley tribes, both Proprietor Thomas Penn and Governor James Hamilton vainly denounced the grant as infringing on their colony's territory. The western land claims of Virginia, Maryland, and Pennsylvania overlapped. The Indians rejected any surveying team that might help resolve the dispute. Regardless, Pennsylvanians, Virginians, and other Americans continued to compete fiercely and sometimes violently with each other as they plied their trades throughout the region.

While the colonies squabbled over the territory, the French acted. The influx of British traders in the Ohio valley deeply worried Governor Roland Michel, Baron de La Galissoniere. In 1749, he ordered Captain Joseph Pierre Celoron de Blainville to lead an expedition into the region to chase away the British and intimidate the tribes into an unquestioned allegiance to France. On June 14, Celoron set out from Lachine with his interpreter, the half-Seneca Lieutenant Daniel Marie Chabert de Joncaire de Clausonne, 14 officers, 20 soldiers, 180 Canadians, and a score of Indians in 23 canoes. They paddled up the St. Lawrence, across Lake Ontario, portaged around Niagara Falls, and then skimmed along Lake Erie. At Presque Isle, they portaged over to Riviere des Boeuf (French Creek) and paddled down it to the Allegheny River, and then down it to the Ohio River.

At river confluences Celoron nailed to trees lead plates that stated: "Year 1749, in the reign of Louis Fifteenth, King of France, We, Celoron, commanding the detachment sent by the Marquis de La Galissoniere, commander-general of New France, to restore tranquility in certain villages of these cantons, have buried this plate at [place, date] . . . as a token of renewal of possession heretofore taken of the aforesaid streams, as the preceding Kings of France, have enjoyed or ought to have enjoyed it, and which they have upheld by force of arms and treaties, notably by those of Ryswick, Utrecht, and Aix-la-Chapelle."

Although the inhabitants of most villages fled at word of his approach, Celoron did manage to conduct councils at Logstown, Old Shawnee Town, and Pickawillany. At these councils, he informed the startled and resentful chiefs that they and their people were French subjects and should expel the English. Each council threatened to explode into violence, none more than at Old Shawnee Town where the Indians and French pointed muskets at each other before Celoron's gifts and Joncaire's eloquence soothed the crisis. At Pickawillany, Memeskia took the gifts and vaguely promised to return his people to Fort Miami as Celoron requested, only later to refuse to do so.

En route, Celoron ordered those British traders he encountered to leave immediately and not return. With one party of traders he sent a letter to Pennsylvania governor James Hamilton in which he warned that "I have been much surprised to find traders belonging to your government in a country to which England never had any pretension. . . . Those whom I have just encountered . . . I have treated with all possible courtesy, though I had a right to regard them as interlopers . . . their undertaking being contrary to . . . the peace treaty signed over fifteen months ago. I hope, Sir, that you will be so good as to prohibit that trade in the future. . . . I know our Governor . . . would be very sorry to be forced to have recourse to any violence, but his orders are very strict not to suffer any foreign traders within his government."[63] New York governor Clinton became aware of the Celoron expedition in December 1750, when a Cayuga chief presented one of the lead plates to Indian trader William Johnson at a council at his home. Governor Clinton sent it on to the Board of Trade.

Celoron returned to Montreal on November 9, 1749 to offer the governor a gloomy prospect for French ambitions in the region. He reported that British goods not only sold for one-fourth the cost of French goods but were of superior quality. As if these disadvantages were not debilitating enough, the French also lacked the number of merchants or easy access to the region that the British enjoyed. He concluded that "the nations of these localities are very badly disposed towards the French, and are entirely devoted to the English. I do not know in what way they could be brought back."[64] In reporting to Versailles the results of Celoron's expedition, Governor de la Jonquiere urged that "we must establish one or more trading posts on the Belle Riviere or its vicinity, and especially toward its headwaters. Those posts might have the inconvenience of making contraband trade easier . . . this ought to be risked, because without it the English would undoubtedly locate there, and through this would be in a position to penetrate to all our trading posts and cut the communication with Louisiana."[65]

Celoron's just completed expedition and the Ohio Company's proposed expedition to the region upped the pressure on Pennsylvania to boost its effort or lose its claims to its rivals. On his own initiative, in early 1750, Croghan convinced the Delaware and Mingo to allow him to expand his trade cabin at the forks of the Ohio into a full-scale trading post. Delighted with the concession, Croghan hurried back to Philadelphia to gain backing for the expedition.

Strapped for cash and eager to avoid any commitment that might drag the province into war, the Quaker-dominated assembly rejected any scheme that entangled Pennsylvania in conflict with its neighbors and France. While it shelved his treaty the assembly sent Croghan back to the Miami with a gift to oil that flowering friendship. The assembly also rejected Penn's offer of 400 pounds to build and 100 pounds annually thereafter to maintain such a post. Finally, it spurned an offer by Governor Clinton to help sway Ohio valley Indian loyalties by convening their representatives at a council in Albany. However, in September, the assembly did grant another gift for the Indians when it learned that the French had erected a trading post at Venango on the Allegheny River.

The assembly's refusal to participate in a united colonial front toward the Indians angered not only Pennsylvania's Indian traders but all those sympathetic to British expansion beyond the Allegheny Mountains. Yet, other governors had similar problems getting their assemblies to finance trade and peace with the Indians. Clinton condemned his assembly for having "not given one farthing for Indian affairs, nor for a year past have they provided for the subsistence of the garrison at Oswego, which is the key for the commerce between the colonies and the inland nations of Indians."[66]

Virginia too stumbled, even after the Ohio Company received its grant. Most of Virginia's leaders seemed largely indifferent or outright hostile to the Ohio Company's fate. Although some prominent Virginians had invested in the Ohio Company, most Burgess members had not. Many had invested in one or more of about 20 land companies that hoped to reap their own huge grants beyond the Appalachian Mountains. Thus they opposed devoting public funds to bail out the private enterprise of their rivals.[67]

Throughout these crucial years, Virginia's actual governor was William Anne Keppel, Earl of Albemarle, who remained at his estate in England largely indifferent to his faraway dominion. As in most other colonies, Virginia's real ruler was its lieutenant-governor who actually resided in Williamsburg. In August 1749, William Gooch finally resigned as lieutenant-governor, having served in the post since 1727. Three council members—John Robinson, Thomas Lee, and Lewis Burwell—briefly filled the lieutenant-governor's chair while London chose a successor. Although Lee served simultaneously as lieutenant-governor and Ohio Company president, ill health prevented him from energetically performing either role, let alone using one post's power to advance his interests in the other.

Upon Burwell's death, George II appointed Robert Dinwiddie to the post. It seemed a proper choice. Dinwiddie had served the king in the New World since 1727 when he became Bermuda's customs official and from 1738 to 1749 as surveyor-general for the southern district of colonies. Ironically, Dinwiddie's appointment to lieutenant-governor was dated July 4. Dinwiddie's policies and personality would greatly contribute to American independence. His insistence on collecting a pistole fee on land patents and surveys would provoke the deep-seated American aversion to taxes, while the deadlock over the issue between governor and burgess would impede Virginia's war effort. His arrogance and tactlessness seemed to personify the worst excesses of English rule. All that was in the future.[68]

Meanwhile, the relationship started out well enough. At Dinwiddie's November 20, 1750 inauguration, the assembly speakers mixed lavish greetings to their new governor with references to the assembly's rights and privileges and former lieutenant-governor Gooch as "our great protector and bene-factor." Dinwiddie's inaugural address allayed any fears or misgivings the Virginians may have had. On the heels of a succession of sickly governors, Dinwiddie brought vigor to his office. From the time he entered the governor's palace, Dinwiddie sought to enlist closer ties with the Indians and to that end commissioned intelligence reports on their numbers, customs, and attitudes, and conducted diplomacy by letter with the chiefs. He also corresponded with his other governors over a range of subjects, particularly those of Pennsylvania and Maryland with whom Virginia's interests clashed in the Ohio valley. His reports to the Board of Trade throughout 1751, 1752, and 1753 included ever more alarming assessments of the French threat to the Ohio River country.[69] However, the project of closest interest to Dinwiddie was to help the Ohio Company, in which he had bought an ample share, exploit its Ohio valley grant.

On September 11, 1750, two months before Dinwiddie took office, Christopher Gist and eleven other men had set off for the region to invite the tribes to a council at Fredericksburg the following spring. Gist wore two hats on his expedition. The House of Burgess paid him 20 pounds to act as messenger to the Indians while the Ohio Company gave him 150 pounds to explore the territory for possible settlement sites to fulfill the obligations of their land grant. Then age 44, Gist was a good choice to head the expedition, as he had spent decades on the frontier as a farmer, surveyor, trader, and hunter.

Gist appeared before the Logstown Council on November 25. At first, he was received no more courteously than Celoron. Gist feared that "they began to suspect me, and said, I was come to settle the Indians' Land, and they knew I should never go home again safe." He dampened their threats by claiming he conveyed a message "from the King, by order of the President of Virginia."[70] The Indians understood the difference between murdering a representative from some company and the king's messenger.

To complicate matters, Pennsylvania's agent, Croghan, was at Logstown when Gist arrived. Although from rival provinces and paymasters, the two frontiersmen hit it off. Croghan actually presented Gist to the chiefs before inviting them to a council at Logstown in spring of 1751. Gist then traveled throughout the region to survey it secretly for the Ohio Company before returning to Williamsburg to make his report.

While Indian, French, and Pennsylvanian intrigues stymied Gist's diplomatic efforts, the Virginia Company suffered succession crises. Ohio Company president Thomas Lee died in November 1750, depriving both Virginia and the Ohio Company of their leaders. Lawrence Washington assumed the Ohio Company's presidency before dying in 1751. Despite these setbacks, the Ohio Company did make some progress. In 1750, the Ohio Company erected a trading post where Wills Creek flows into the Potomac

River. Two years later, it built another post where Red Stone Creek joins the Monongahela River.

Meanwhile, the French made another diplomatic push in the region. After Governor La Galissoniere returned to France in 1750, he drew up with Etienne de Silouette a report on the English threat to the Ohio valley and submitted it to Versailles. War Minister Rouille sent orders to the new French governor, Jacque Pierre de Taffanel de La Jonquiere, to expel the English traders from the region and establish a French post at the Ohio forks. Jonquiere sent Lieutenant Joncaire, a half dozen soldiers, and five canoes laden with gifts back to the Ohio valley to solidify whatever gains Celoron had made the previous year. Joncaire's party wintered high on the Allegheny River and proceeded to the Ohio in spring 1752.

On May 20, Joncaire and his party arrived at Logstown just two days after that year's council had convened. The council involved a three-way tug-of-war among France, Virginia, and Pennsylvania for permission to build forts in the upper Ohio valley. The day after his arrival, Joncaire appeared before the council, called on the Indians to remain loyal to France, and distributed his gifts. The Indians rejected Joncaire's appeal. Deeply discouraged, Joncaire resumed his diplomatic mission down the Ohio River.

A few days later, Croghan rose to pass out gifts and request a fort at the Ohio forks for Pennsylvania. In doing so, he exceeded his instructions which confined his diplomacy to signing a friendship treaty. The Indians did sign a treaty with Croghan that appeared to grant his request for a fort. Another Pennsylvania agent, Andrew Montour, denied that the Indians had actually agreed to the fort. Pennsylvania's assembly would reject Croghan's treaty.

Finally, it was Gist's turn to speak on behalf of Virginia. He asked the chiefs for a treaty that not only permitted the Ohio Company to build a fort at the forks but also ceded 200,000 acres of surrounding land. He capped his argument with the claim that the treaty he presented to them merely reaffirmed concessions they had made under the 1744 Lancaster Treaty. On May 31, as the chiefs heatedly debated Gist's request, there ground ashore at Logstown three canoes laden with 700 pounds worth of Virginia gifts. Yet, even after Gist distributed them, it would take another two weeks of negotiations and feasts before all the chiefs agreed to sign. On June 13, 1752, the Treaty of Logstown granted Virginia a trading post at the Ohio forks and 200,000 acres of land. Gist hurried back to Williamsburg with the treaty.

Croghan, meanwhile, journied on to Pickawillany where he negotiated a treaty with Memeskia's Miami, and representatives of the Wabash and Piankashaw that allied Pennsylvania with those tribes. The treaty was an impressive feat of diplomacy. Croghan's efforts were complicated when, amidst negotiations, four Ottawa arrived to urge Memeskia to rejoin the French alliance. Memeskia rejected their request and sent them away. Croghan's elation would eventually fade—he had no authority to make such a treaty and the assembly later denounced it along with his Logstown agreement.

As if the attempts by Virginia and Pennsylvania to negotiate with the Ohio valley tribes were not complicated enough by their own rivalry, divisions among and within those tribes, the various assemblies' refusal to grant enough gifts, and French enticements to those Indians to spurn the English, the Iroquois refused to accept any results from such councils. The Iroquois hoped to close the Ohio valley to both the English and the French. Claiming sovereignty over the Ohio tribes, the Iroquois refused to allow those Indians to negotiate for themselves. Only the Onondaga council could decide the fate of the Ohio tribes. Pennsylvania's chief agents to the Indians, Croghan and Weiser, sharply disagreed over the issue, with Croghan encouraging the Ohio tribes to assert their independence and Weiser maintaining that they should remain bowed to the Iroquois.

Meanwhile, Versailles was dissatisfied with Jonquiere's failure to follow orders, and made its feelings known in a letter to him: "Last year you wrote that you would soon drive the English from the Ohio; but private letters say that you have done nothing. This is deplorable. If not expelled, they will seem to acquire a right against us. Send force enough to drive them off, and cure them of all wish to return."[71] Whether Jonquiere intended to make such an effort will remain unknown. He died on March 17, 1752.

The French accomplished through war what they could not accomplish through trade and diplomacy. Acting independently, on June 21, 1752, Charles Langlade led 250 Ottawa, Chippewa, and Potawatomi against Pickawillany, destroying it and killing, among others, Memeskia, whom they boiled and ate along with an English trader's heart. Three other English traders were carried away to Detroit as captives. Most of Pickawillany's warriors were attending the Logstown Council when the attack occurred. They returned to find their village in ashes and many of their relatives and neighbors dead.

Langlade's attack shoved the power balance throughout the region from Britain back to France. It cowed the surviving Miami into renouncing their alliance with the British and returning to the French. Other tribes soon followed. Terror-stricken British traders throughout the region hastily packed up and fled east across the Appalachian Mountains to the settlements beyond. Croghan later estimated that he alone lost 16,000 pounds and that there were 52 men killed or captured by the French before 1754.[72]

On July 1, 1752, Ange Duquesne de Menneville, Marquis Duquesne, arrived at Quebec to serve as the new governor-general with clear instructions from Versailles that the British have "no right to the River Ohio. We had discovered it long before they . . . had known it, and we have resorted to it when no other Indians were there but the Chaouanons, with whom they were at war, and who have always been our friends."[73]

Duquesne acted decisively. Attempting to build upon Langlade's successful raid, he ordered his frontier commanders to imprison all British traders found in the Ohio River valley. Throughout the rest of 1752 and into 1753, Duquesne assembled a 2,200-man expedition at Fort Niagara commanded by Captain Paul Marin de La Malgue. In early spring, Marin led his troops westward along Lake Erie's southern shore until he reached Presque Isle on May 15. While some of his troops built Fort Presque Isle, others cut a road over to the headwaters of Riviere aux Boeufs (French Creek) where they built Fort Le Boeuf and 150 piroques with which to descend the Ohio River valley.

At Fort Le Boeuf Marin called a council of the region's tribes, to whom he dispensed presents and whom he warned not to trade with the British. While most other chiefs snatched away the gifts, Tanaghrisson openly condemned the French presence: "With this belt we detain you and ask you to have them cease setting up the establishments you want to make. All the tribes have always called upon us not to allow it. . . . I shall strike at whoever does not listen to us. . . . We ask you only to send us what we need, but not to build any forts there." Marin sternly replied that he would "continue on my way, and if there are any persons bold enough to set up barriers to hinder my march, I shall knock them over so vigorously that they may crush those who made them."[74] Upon this tense standoff, a Shawnee delegation arrived to reject Tanaghrisson's assertion and welcome the French. Undeterred, later that year Tanaghrisson would deliver two more demands that the French depart before his final warning that December.

Shortly after Tanaghrisson and his followers stalked away, Marin began preparations to build a fort where French Creek joins the Allegheny River. Low water in the rivers and illness among the troops kept Marin from pushing on to the Ohio forks. Disease, overwork, and malnutrition killed over 400 of the expedition's 2,300 men, including Marin who succumbed on October 29, 1753. Before dying, Marin sent all but 300 of his surviving troops back to Montreal. Captain Jacques Legardier de Saint Pierre took over briefly before resigning in December. Captain Pierre Pecaudy de Contrecoeur then assumed command.

Reviewing the emaciated survivors, Duquesne questioned the expedition's wisdom. Appalled, the governor "could not help being touched by the pitiable state to which fatigues and exposures had reduced them. Past all doubt, if these emaciated figures had gone down the Ohio as intended, the river would have been strewn with corpses, and the evil-disposed savages would not have failed to attack the survivors, seeing they were but spectres."[75]

The Indians, however, sought to expell the French by diplomacy rather than war. Scarouady led 98 Mingo, Shawnee, Wyandot, Miami, and Delaware to Virginia and Pennsylvania to elicit their help in ejecting the French. In September at Winchester, the delegation met with Virginian commissioner William Fairfax who promised to give the Indians arms and a Virginian fort at the Ohio forks. On September 12, Scarouady replied that the

Indians welcomed the arms but "We now request you may not build that Strong-House at the Forks for we intend to keep our Country clear of Settlements during these troublesome Times. As to the French, we have sent to warn him off our Lands; & if they will not hear us, We are ready to make them feel our Hatchets, for we intend to turn Our Hatchets against them."[76]

Scarouady's rejection of Fairfax's promise to build a fort embarrassed the Virginians. The Ohio Company had already planned to erect a fort there. Fairfax also announced that Virginia had elicited a promise from the Cherokee, Chickasaw, and Catawaba to attack the French. This time it was Scarouady's turn to be embarrassed. He heatedly made his feelings known—those tribes were Iroquois enemies. For them to attack the French in the Ohio River valley would mean invading lands claimed by the Iroquois. Scarouady warned Fairfax that he would have to negotiate a formal peace between the Iroquois and those tribes before they would be allowed to enter the Ohio valley. Fairfax agreed. Scarouady was further troubled when the Delaware and Shawnee delegates met privately with Fairfax to request recognition and special treatment. The council must have seemed a rude setback for Scarouady—he came asking for arms and instead he got promises of an English fort on the Ohio River, invasion by Iroquois enemies, and the assertion of independence by hitherto Iroquois subjects like the Delaware and Shawnee.

Scarouady had little better luck at the October council in Carlisle, Pennsylvania. The council became mired in a Shawnee request that colonial officials help free some of their people held in South Carolina. Once again, the Shawnee assertion challenged Iroquois supremacy and sidetracked discussion of the French threat to the Ohio River valley. Eventually, the council returned to the main issue. Pennsylvania's representatives, Andrew Montour and George Croghan, negotiated a treaty in which the colony promised to supply 800 pounds worth of goods to the tribes in return for an alliance against the French. Eventually, Pennsylvania made good on both promises. Officials secured the release of the Shawnee prisoners and Croghan delivered goods to the Indians in January 1754.

Yet all these efforts to push back the French came to nothing. Tanaghrisson, who first confronted the French "like a Lyon roaring out Destruction, came back like a Sheep with Tears in his Eyes, and desired the English to go away, for that the French who were coming down the River Ohio in two hundred Canoes would hurt them and make Spoil of their Goods."[77] Scarouady and the other Ohio River valley representatives came back from Winchester and Carlisle disillusioned that the British were capable of doing anything more for their defense than make promises and offer a few presents. The alliance was stillborn.

The English failure to forge a solid alliance with the Ohio tribes followed a similar reverse earlier that summer at a council with the Iroquois. On June

16, 1753, Mohawk Chief Hendrick stood, locked eyes with Governor Clinton, and proclaimed: "Brother when we came here to relate our Grievances about our Lands, we expected to have something done for us. . . . Nothing shall be done for us. . . . [A]s soon as we come home we will send up a belt of Wampum to our Brothers the 5 Nations to acquaint them the Covenant is broken between you and us. So brother you are not to expect to hear of me any more, and Brother we desire to hear no more of you."[78]

New York's defense all but collapsed with the words of King Hendrick. The Mohawk had been the only Iroquois tribe that had consistently supported the British. Their villages were only several score miles from Albany and had consistently acted as a buffer against war parties of French and Indians from other tribes, including those of the Six Nations. Their entreaties on behalf of the British at Onondaga had frequently blunted the calls of others for war against the colonies. Now, if war broke out, the Mohawk would not only allow French and Indian war parties through their land, they might well join them. Hendrick's statement also destroyed the British claim to the Ohio River valley by dint of their suzerainty over the Iroquois. The Iroquois rejection of neutrality on top of the French expedition to the upper Ohio would lead to the Albany Conference of 1754.

The 1753 Marin expedition to establish forts at Presque Isle and Le Boeuf provided a crisis severe enough to spur the Cabinet Council into action. The word of Marin's expedition first arrived in a May 15 letter from Oswego's commander to William Johnson, who then spread the news to the colonial governors. In a June 16 letter, Dinwiddie reported the Marin expedition to the Board of Trade, adding his hope that "you will think it necessary to prevent the French taking Possession of the Lands on the Ohio, so Contiguous to Our Settlements, or indeed in my private Opinion they ought to be prevented making any Settlements to the Westward of Our present Possession."[79] Dinwiddie then asked for instructions to deal with the French threat.

The Board of Trade received Dinwiddie's letter on August 11. Initially, the Board and the Cabinet split over how to respond to Marin's expedition. Although officially backing British claims to the region, most felt that the French claims were stronger and Duquesne's incursion probably justified. Lord Holderness, the Secretary of State for the Southern Department, swung the government behind a tougher policy. In a document penned on August 28, Holderness sent Dinwiddie detailed instructions on how to manage the growing crisis on the frontier. While cautioning Dinwiddie to remain strictly on the defensive, Holderness authorized him to build forts on the upper Ohio River to prevent the French from taking it, and to call out the militia to defend those forts and the frontier. Aware of Virginia's military weakness, he had arranged for 30 4-pounder cannon to be sent to the colony. In addition, he asked Dinwiddie to act as the Crown's intermediary with the other governors as the crisis unfolded. Dinwiddie now held explicit power to repel a French incursion: "If You shall find, that any Number of Persons . . . shall presume to erect any Fort or Forts within the Limits of Our Province of Virginia . . . You are to require of Them peaceably to depart . . . & if, notwithstanding Your Admonitions, They do still endeavor to carry out any such unlawful and unjustifiable Designs, We do hereby strictly charge, & command You to drive them off by Force of Arms."[80]

The crisis also prompted London to force the colonials to cooperate rather than compete with one another. Confusion, mistrust, and cheating reigned when each province was allowed to negotiate its own treaties with the Indians. The Indians played off the colonies against each other, provoking them into bidding wars and carting away the riches each paid for peace. It had long been obvious to leaders in London and the colonies alike that they could buy a far cheaper and more resilient peace if they could simply forge a united negotiating front against the Indians.

On September 18, 1753, the Board sent orders to the governors of New York, Pennsylvania, Maryland, Massachusetts, Virginia, New Jersey, Maryland, and New Hampshire to send delegates to a grand council with the Iroquois. Its orders to the governors declared: "His Majesty having been pleased to order a Sum of Money to be issued for Presents to the Six Nations of Indians, and to direct his Governor of New York to hold an Interview with them for delivering these Presents, for burying the Hatchet, and for renewing the Covenant Chain with them, We think it our duty to acquaint you therewith."[81] After the necessary exchanges of letters, a date for the Albany assembly was set for June 14, 1754. Governor Clinton was given the duty of inviting and hosting the delegates.

GEORGE WASHINGTON'S MISSION

The pressure on Dinwiddie to act decisively hit him from all directions, from his superiors in London, Ohio Company investors, and the French themselves. The French had already built a chain of three forts from Lake Erie to the Allegheny River. In spring 1754, they would likely erect a fort at the Ohio forks itself, thus squeezing off that vast region from the Crown and Ohio Company. An August 1753 letter from William Trent, an Ohio Company agent at Wills Creek, made the stakes Dinwiddie faced extremely clear: "The Eyes of all the Indians are fixed upon you. You have it now in your Power with a small Expense to save this whole Country for his Majesty, but if the Opportunity is missed it will never be in the Power of the English to recover it but by a great Expence and the United Force of all the Colonies. . . . The French tell the Indians in all their Speeches that they will drive the English over the Allegeny Mountains."[82]

Lacking the military means to drive out the French, Governor Dinwiddie opted for simply telling them to leave. The man Dinwiddie chose as his message-bearer was George Washington.[83] In all, it was an excellent choice, both for the mission and subsequent American history. Although then only 21 years old, Washington carried with him some limited frontier experience. At age 16, he had helped survey the future site of Alexandria and then parts of the Shenandoah Valley for Virginia's largest landowner, William Fairfax, whose ancestors had received from King Charles II a five-million-acre land grant between the Rappahanock and Potomac Rivers. During those several months, Washington camped in the wilderness and observed, though hardly got to know, some settlers and Indians. Washington got the job because his half-brother Lawrence and Fairfax were both Ohio Company investors. The following year in 1749 Washington was named surveyor of Culpepper County, the first public office of his illustrious career. Washington and Dinwiddie first met in 1751 when the young man called on the lieutenant-governor to report on then-invalid Lawrence's efforts as Ohio Company president. Impressed with Washington, in February 1753 Dinwiddie appointed him as one of four adjutant majors of Virginia's militia, Washington's first military command.

Washington certainly looked the part of a military officer. At six foot, four inches tall, he towered over most other men of his time. As an expert rider and dancer, he proved to be as physically tough as he was graceful. With a personality as aloof as his height, Washington tended to awe those around him. Beneath that imposing facade, however, was a quick-tempered, rash young man who tended to follow his heart even when more experienced advisors urged him to take more reasoned paths.

On October 30, Dinwiddie ordered Washington to journey to the Ohio valley, council with the Indians, and hand the French a letter from Dinwiddie demanding that they immediately leave the region. Washington departed that same day to carry out his mission.

On November 1, two days after Dinwiddie bade adieu to Washington, he convened the House of Burgess and asked them to provide money to raise 200 armed men to counter the worsening French threat. Instead of discussing that request, the assembly raised the issue of the pistole fee (a surcharge on land sales) Dinwiddie pocketed before he would register a land sale. When Dinwiddie justified his fee, the assembly bluntly declared it unlawful because "subjects cannot be deprived of the least part of their property without their consent."[84] The assembly declared it would appropriate no money until Dinwiddie promised to revoke the fee. Dinwiddie refused, thus foregoing any means of backing with military power his threat to the French.

Washington, of course, would remain blissfully unaware of all this until he returned to Williamsburg three months later. At Fredericksburg, he engaged Jacob Van Braaum to be his French interpreter. From there the two hurried to Alexandria where they purchased supplies and horses. At Wills Creek, Washington hired Christopher Gist to be his guide, along with four other men to help haul supplies. From there they took the well-trod path to John Fraser's trading house where Turtle Creek joined the rain-swollen Monongahela River. Washington and Gist took Fraser's canoe, leaving their four packers and Van Braam to travel over land. They camped for two days where the Monongahela and Allegheny Rivers join to form the Ohio River. Washington surveyed the ground as a possible location for the Ohio Company's future fort. After the other men joined them, Gist led the party to Logstown seventeen miles down the Ohio River.

At Logstown on November 26, Washington met with Tanaghrisson, Scarouady, Shingas, and other chiefs. He requested they remain loyal to the English and provide him an escort to the French forts. At first, Tanaghrisson reasserted that the Indians wanted neither British nor French forts in the Ohio region. However, after three days of negotiations, he agreed to an English fort at the forks and to be one of four Indians who would accompany Washington to Fort Le Boeuf. Tanaghrisson carried with him a wampum belt that he promised to throw before the French as he ordered them to leave.

On December 4, they reached Fort Machault commanded by Captain Philip Thomas Joncaire, Sieur de Chabert, who invited Washington and his entourage to dinner. Washington reported that the French "treated [us] with the greatest Complaisance. The Wine, as they dos'd themselves pretty plentifully with it, soon banish'd the restraint which at first appear'd in their Conversation, & gave license to their Tongues to reveal their Sentiments more freely. They told me it was their absolute Design to take Possession of the Ohio and, by G—, they wou'd do it; for tho' they were sensible, that the English cou'd raise two Men for their one, yet they knew their Motions were too slow and dilatory to prevent any Undertaking of theirs."[85]

For three days, Joncaire entertained them, all the while plying Tanaghrisson and the other chiefs with drink, gifts, and promises to swing them to his side. Befuddled by all this, Tanaghrisson at first refrained from delivering the protest that he had earlier rehearsed repeatedly before Washington. However, on the morning of December 6, Tanaghrisson "came to my Tent quite Sober, & insisted very much that I shou'd stay & hear what he had to say to the French. . . . About 10 oClock they met in Council, the King spoke . . . & off'd the French Speech belt . . . which Monsieur Joncaire refused to receive; but desired him to carry to Fort Le Boeuf."[86]

They left the next morning and, after four days of slogging through snow, freezing rain, and mud, reached Fort Le Boeuf on the evening of December 11. The next morning, Washington and his delegation were ushered before Fort Le Boeuf's commander, Captain Jacques Legardier de Saint-Pierre, a veteran frontier soldier who had served in Acadia, the Lake of the Woods region, and Fort Toulouse. They delayed their council until they were joined by Captain Louis Le Gardeur de Repentigny, Fort Presque Isle's commander. The sight of the gangly but dignified young man standing before St. Pierre must have astonished him, a feeling that surely swelled as he read the letter from Governor Dinwiddie that Washington handed him. In his letter, Dinwiddie politely but firmly expressed his surprise that the French would occupy lands "so notoriously known to be the Property of the Crown of Great Britain. . . . I must desire You to acquaint me by whose Authority and Instructions You have lately marcht from Canada with an arm'd Force, & Invaded the King of Great Britain's Territories . . . it becomes my Duty to require Your peaceable departure . . . I persuade myself You will receive & entertain Major Washington with the Candour and Politeness natural to Your Nation; & it will give me the greatest Satisfaction if you return him with an Answer suitable to my wishes for a very long and lasting Peace between Us."[87]

St. Pierre resisted an immediate reply to Dinwiddie's claim that the Ohio valley was British territory and that the French must leave immediately. Instead, he complied with Dinwiddie's request that he entertain Washington and the Indians. Washington accused St. Pierre of "plotting every Scheme that the Devil & Man cou'd invent, to set our Indians at Variance with us. . . . I can't say that ever in my Life I suffer'd so much Anxiety as I did in this affair."[88] It worked. Once again soaked with drink, Tanaghrisson refused to make the expulsion speech he had promised Washington. As he had at Fort Machault, Washington took advantage of his wait to make detailed sketches of Fort Le Boeuf defenses and garrison.

On December 14, St. Pierre handed Washington his formal reply to Dinwiddie's letter: "As to the summons you send me to retire, I do not think myself obliged to obey it. Whatever may be your instructions, I am here by virtue of the orders of my General, and I entreat you, Sir, not to doubt for a moment that I have a firm resolution to follow them with all the exactness and determination which can be expected of the best officer."[89]

A century and a half of imperial rivalry between France and Britain converged on Washington and St. Pierre as they exchanged letters from their respective governments. War still was far from inevitable. Adept diplomacy and compromise could have diffused the crisis smoldering in the upper Ohio valley. But war would indeed explode on that frontier the next year, and Washington would order his troops to fire that war's first volley.

NOTES

1. John D. Daniels, "The Indian Population of North America in 1492," *William and Mary Quarterly* 49 (1992), 298–320; Ray Allen Billington and Martin Ridge, *Westward Expansion: A History of the American Frontier*, 5th ed. (New York: Macmillan, 1982), 20–21.

2. Karen O. Kupperman, *Settling with the Indians: The Meeting of English and Indian Cultures 1580–1640* (Totowa, N.J.: Rowman & Littlefield, 1981); William W. Fitzhugh, ed., *Cultures in Contact: The Impact of European Contacts on Native American Institutions, A.D. 1000–1800* (Washington, D.C.: Smithsonian Institute

Press, 1985); Bruce G. Trigger, "Early Native American Responses to European Contact: Romantic versus Rationalistic Interpretations," *Journal of American History* 77 (1990–1991), 1195–1215.

3. J. H. Elliott, *The Old World and the New, 1492–1650* (Cambridge: Cambridge University Press, 1970); Douglas C. North and Robert Paul Thomas, *The Rise of the Western World: A New Economic History* (Cambridge: Cambridge University Press, 1976); Ralph Davies, *The Rise of the Atlantic Economies* (Ithaca, N.Y.: Cornell University Press, 1973); Peter Parry, "Colonial Development and International Rivalries Outside Europe," in R. B. Wernham, ed., *The New Cambridge Modern History,* vol 3 (Cambridge: Cambridge University Press, 1968), 540–42; John F. Ferling, *A Wilderness of Miseries: War and Warriors in Early America* (Westport, Conn.: Greenwood Press, 1980).

4. J. H. Elliott, *Imperial Spain, 1469–1716* (New York: St. Martin's Press, 1963); Lyle N. McAlister, *Spain and Portugal in the New World, 1492–1700* (Minneapolis: University of Minnesota Press, 1971); Carl Ortwin Sauer, *Sixteenth Century North America* (Berkeley: University of California Press, 1971); D. B. Quinn, ed., *New American World: A Documentary History of North America to 1612,* 5 vols. (New York: Arno and Bye, 1979); Henry Kamen, *Spain, 1469–1714: A Society in Conflict* (London: Longman, 1983); John Lynch, *Spain, 1516–1598: From Nation State to World Empire* (Oxford: Oxford University Press, 1992); Hugh Thomas, *Conquest: Montezuma, Cortes, and the Fall of Old Mexico* (New York: Simon and Schuster, 1993).

5. David B. Quinn, *England and the Discovery of America, 1481–1620* (New York: Knopf, 1974); Francis Jennings, *The Invasion of America: Indians, Colonialism, and the Cant of Conquest* (Chapel Hill: University of North Carolina Press, 1975); Ian K. Steele, *Warpaths: Invasions of North America, 1513–1765* (New York: Oxford University Press, 1994).

6. Jerald T. Milanich and Susan Mibrath, eds., *First Encounters: Spanish Explorations in the Caribbean and the United States, 1492–1570* (Gainesville: University of Florida Press, 1989).

7. Sauer, *Sixteenth Century North America*; Marcel Trudel, *The Beginnings of New France, 1524–1663* (Toronto: McClelland and Stewart, 1973); Carl Ortwin Sauer, *Seventeenth Century North America* (Berkeley: University of California Press, 1980); Lawrence C. Worth, ed., *The Voyages of Giovanni da Verrazzano, 1524–1528* (New Haven, Conn.: Yale University Press, 1970).

8. Philip Wayne Powell, *Soldiers, Indians, & Silver: The Northward Advance of New Spain, 1550–1600* (Berkeley: University of California Press, 1969).

9. Eugene Lyon, *The Enterprise of Florida: Pedro Menendez de Aviles and the Spanish Conquest of 1565–1568* (Gainesville: University of Florida Press, 1976), 47; Paul E. Hoffman, *The Spanish Crown and the Defense of the Caribbean, 1565–1568: Precedent, Patrimonialism, and Royal Parsimony* (Baton Rouge: University of Louisiana Press, 1980).

10. Theodore K. Rabb, *Enterprise and Empire: Merchant and Gentry Investment in the Expansion of England, 1575–1630* (Cambridge, Mass.: Harvard University Press, 1967).

11. Mary Frear Keeler, ed., *Sir Francis Drake's West Indian Voyage, 1585–86* (London: Hakylut Society, 1981); James Leitch Wright, Jr., *Anglo-Spanish Rivalry in North America* (Athens: University of Georgia Press, 1971).

12. Charles McLean Andrews, *The Colonial Period of American History*, 4 vols. (New Haven, Conn.: Yale University Press, 1934–1938); George F. Willison, *Behold Virginia: The Fifth Crown* (New York: Harcourt, Brace, and Company, 1952); Philip L. Barbour, ed., *The Complete Worlds of Captain John Smith, 1580–1631*, 3 vols. (Chapel Hill: University of North Carolina Press, 1986); Helen C. Roundtree, *The Powhatan Indians of Virginia: Their Traditional Culture* (Norman: University of Oklahoma Press, 1992); Helen C. Roundtree, *Powhatan's People: The Powhatan Indians of Virginia through Four Centuries* (Norman: University of Oklahoma Press, 1990).

13. V. Earle Carville, "Environment, Disease, and Mortality in Early Virginia," in Thad Tate and David Ammerman, eds., *The Chesapeake in the Seventeenth Century* (Chapel Hill: University of North Carolina Press, 1979); Darrett B. Rutman, "The Virginia Company and Its Military Regime," in Darrett B. Rutman, ed., *The Old Dominion: Essays for Thomas Perkins Abernethy* (Charlottesville: University of Virginia Press, 1964); J. Frederick Fausz, "An 'Abundance of Blood Shed on Both Sides': England's First Indian War, 1609–1614," *Virginia Magazine of History and Biography* 98 (1990), 9–16.

14. Alden T. Vaughan, " 'Expulsion of the Savages' ": English Policy and the Virginia Massacre of 1622," *William and Mary Quarterly* 35 (1978), 57–84; J. Frederick Fausz, "The 'Barbarous Massacre' Reconsidered: The Powhatan Uprising of 1622 and the Historians," *Explorations in Ethnic Studies* 1 (1978), 16–36; J. Frederick Fausz, "Fighting Fire with Firearms: The Anglo-Powhatan Arms Race in Early Virginia," *American Indian Culture and Research Journal* 3 (1979), 39–47; William L. Shea, *The Virginia Militia in the Seventeenth Century* (Baton Rouge: Louisiana State University Press, 1983).

15. H. P. Biggar, ed., *The Works of Samuel de Champlain*, 6 vols. (Toronto: Champlain Society, 1922–1936); Bruce G. Trigger, *Natives and Newcomers: Canada's "Heroic Age" Reconsidered* (Montreal: McGill–Queens University Press, 1985); G. S. Graham, *Empire of the North Atlantic: The Maritime Struggle for North America* (Toronto: University of Toronto Press, 1950); Gustave Lanctot, *A History of Canada: From the Treaty of Utrecht to the Treaty of Paris, 1713–1763*, trans. Josephine Hambleton and Margaret M. Cameron, 3 vols. (Cambridge, Mass.: Harvard University Press, 1963–1965); W. J. Eccles, *The Canadian Frontier, 1535–1760* (New York: Holt, Rinehart and Winston, 1969); W. J. Eccles, *France in America* (New York: Harper and Row, 1972).

16. Robert Goldstein, *French-Iroquois Diplomatic and Military Relations 1609–1701* (The Hague: PMA Publishing Corp., 1969); John A. Dickinson, "La Guerre Iroquoise et la mortalite en Nouvelle-France, 1608–1666," *Revue d'Histoire de l'Amerique Francaise* 36 (1982–1983), 31–54.

17. Eccles, *Canadian Frontier*, 24.

18. Catherine Marten, "The Wampanoags, in the Seventeenth Century: An Ethnological Study," *Occasional Papers in Old Colony Studies* 2 (1970), 3–40; Neal Salisbury, *Manitou and Providence: Indians, Europeans, and the Making of New England, 1500–1643* (New York: Oxford University Press, 1982); William Cronon, *Changes in the Land: Indians, Colonists, and the Ecology of New England* (New York: Hill and Wang, 1983); Dean R. Snow and Kim M. Lanphear, "European Contact and Indian Depopulation in the Northeast: The Timing of the First Epidemics," *Ethnohistory* 35 (1988), 15–33.

19. William Bradford, *Of Plymouth Plantation, 1620–1647*, ed. Samuel E. Morison (New York: Knopf, 1952); George F. Willison, *Saints and Strangers* (New York: Reynal and Hitchcock, 1945); George D. Langdon, *Pilgrim Colony: A History of New Plymouth, 1620–1691* (New Haven, Conn.: Yale University Press, 1966).

20. Maurice Aymard, ed., *Dutch Capitalism, World Capitalism* (Cambridge: Cambridge University Press, 1981); Jonathan I. Israel, *Dutch Primacy in World Trade, 1585–1740* (Oxford: Clarendon Press, 1989).

21. Steele, *Warpaths*, 114.

22. Alfred Goldsworthy Bailey, *The Conflict of European and Eastern Algonkian Cultures, 1504–1700* (Toronto: University of Toronto Press, 1969).

23. Harry M. Ward, *The United Colonies of New England, 1643–1690* (New York: Vantage Press, 1961); Sir Charles Harding Firth, *Cromwell's Army: A History of the English Soldier during the Civil Wars, the Commonwealth, and the Protectorate* (London: Methuen, 1962); David S. Lovejoy, *The Glorious Revolution in America* (1972) (reprint, Middletown, Conn.: Wesleyan University Press, 1987).

24. Donna Merwick, "Becoming English: Anglo-Dutch Conflict in the 1670s in Albany, New York," *New York History* 62 (1981), 389–414; Charles H. Lincoln, ed., *Narratives of the Indian Wars, 1675–1699* (1913) (reprint, New York: Barnes and Noble, 1958).

25. Neal Salisbury, "Indians and Colonists in Southern New England after the Pequot War: An Uneasy Balance," in Laurence M. Hauptman and James D. Wherry, eds., *The Pequots in Southern New England: The Fall and Rise of an American Indian Nation* (Norman: University of Oklahoma Press, 1990), 81–95; H. L. Peterson, "The Military Equipment of the Plymouth and Bay Colonies, 1620–1690," *New England Quarterly* 20 (1947), 197–208; Douglas E. Leach, "The Military System of Plymouth Colony," *New England Quarterly* 24(1951), 342–64; Douglas Edward Leach, *Flintlock and Tomahawk: New England and King Philip's War* (New York: Macmillan, 1958); Patrick M. Malone, "Changing Military Technology Among the Indians of Southern New England, 1600–1677," *American Quarterly* 25 (1973), 49–71; Arthur J. Worrall, "Persecution, Politics, and War: Roger Williams, Quakers, and King Philip's War," *Quaker History* 66 (1977), 73–86; Philip Ranlet, "Another Look at the Causes of King Philip's War," *New England Quarterly* 61 (1988), 79–100; Steven T. Katz, "The Pequot War Reconsidered," *New England Quarterly* 64 (1991), 26–34; Alfred A. Cave, "Who Killed John Stone? A Note on the Origins of the Pequot War," *William and Mary Quarterly* 49 (1992), 509–21.

26. Francis Jennings, "Glory, Death, and Transfiguration: The Susquehannock Indians in the Seventeenth Century," *Proceedings of the American Philosophical Society* 112 (1968), 15–53; Wilcomb E. Washburn, *The Governor and the Rebel: A History of Bacon's Rebellion in Virginia* (Chapel Hill: University of North Carolina Press, 1957).

27. Elisabeth Tooker, "The Demise of the Susquehannock: A 17th Century Mystery," *Pennsylvania Archeologist* 54 (1984), 1–10.

28. Stephen Saunders Webb, *1676: The End of the American Independence* (New York: Knopf, 1984); Lovejoy, *The Glorious Revolution in America*; Richard R. Johnson, *Adjustment to Empire: The New England Colonies, 1675–1715* (New Brunswick, N.J.: Rutgers University Press, 1981); William Pencak, *War, Politics, & Revolution in Provincial Massachusetts* (Boston: Northeastern University Press, 1981).

29. Daniel K. Richter, *The Ordeal of the Longhouse: The Peoples of the Iroquois*

League in the Era of European Colonization (Chapel Hill: University of North Carolina Press, 1992), 64, 71; Steele, *Warpaths*, 117; See also ibid., chapters 3–7; Daniel K. Richter and James H. Merrell, eds., *Beyond the Covenant Chain: The Iroquois and Their Neighbors in North America, 1600–1800* (Syracuse, N.Y.: Syracuse University Press, 1987; Richard Aquila, "Down the Warrior's Path: The Causes of the Southern Wars of the Iroquois," *American Indian Quarterly* 4 (1978), 211–21; Raoul Naroll, "The Causes of the Fourth Iroquois War," *Ethnohistory* 16 (1969), 51–81; Elisabeth Tooker, "The Iroquois Defeat of the Huron: A Review of the Causes," *Pennsylvania Archeologist* 33, no. 1–2 (1963), 115–23; Keith F. Otterbein, "Huron vs. Iroquois: A Case Study in Inter-Tribal Warfare," *Ethnohistory* 26 (1979), 141–52; Thomas Elliot Norton, *The Fur Trade in Colonial New York, 1686–1776* (Madison: University of Wisconsin Press, 1974).

30. Rene Chartrand, *The French Soldier in North America* (Bloomfield, Ont.: Museum Restoration Service, 1984), 8; Jack Verney, *The Good Regiment: The Carignan-Salieres Regiment in Canada, 1665–1668* (Montreal: McGill-Queens, 1991).

31. Ian K. Steele, *Guerrillas and Grenadiers: The Struggle for Canada, 1689–1760* (Toronto: McClelland and Stewart, 1969); Patricia Galloway, ed., *La Salle and His Legacy: Frenchmen and Indians in the Lower Mississippi Valley* (Jackson: University of Mississippi Press, 1982); Anka Muhlstein, *La Salle: Explorer of the North American Frontier* (New York: Arcade Publishing, 1992).

32. Eccles, *Canadian Frontier*, 110; W. J. Eccles, *Canada Under Louis XIV 1663–1701* (Toronto: McClelland and Stewart, 1964), 1:653; 2:98–105; Steel, *Betrayals*, 137.

33. For overviews, see Peckham, *Colonial Wars*; Leach, *Arms for Empire*; Steele, *Warpaths*.

34. Steele, *Warpaths*, 158; Gerald S. Graham, ed., *The Walker Expedition to Quebec, 1711* (Toronto: Champlain Society Publications 32, 1953).

35. Douglas Brown, *The Catawba Indians: The People of the River* (Columbia: University of South Carolina Press, 1966); Verner W. Crane, *The Southern Frontier: 1670–1732* (Ann Arbor: University of Michigan Press, 1929); David H. Corkran, *The Creek Frontier, 1540–1783* (Norman: University of Oklahoma Press, 1967); Patricia D. Woods, "The French and the Natchez Indians in Louisiana, 1700–1731," *Louisiana History* 19 (1978), 421–38; W. Slitt Robinson, *The Southern Colonial Frontier, 1607–1763* (Albuquerque: University of New Mexico Press, 1979); Patricia D. Woods, *French-Indian Relations on the Southern Frontier, 1699–1762* (Ann Arbor: University of Michigan Press, 1980).

36. Edmund O'Callaghan and Berthold Fernow, eds., *Documents Relative to the Colonial History of the State of New York* (hereafter cited as NYCD), 15 vols. (Albany, N.Y.: Weed, Parsons, and Co., 1853–1887), 5:624–45.

37. Cadwallader Colden, *The History of the Five Nations of Canada (1747)* (New York: AMS Press, 1973), pt. 3, pp. 42–43; Richter, *Ordeal of the Longhouse*, 249.

38. Richter, *Ordeal of the Longhouse*, 268.

39. Colin G. Calloway, *The Western Abenaki of Vermont, 1600–1800: War, Migration, and the Survival of an Indian People* (Norman: University of Oklahoma Press, 1991).

40. Steele, *Warpaths*, 163,164–65.

41. John Tate Lanning, *The Diplomatic History of Georgia: A Study of the Epoch of Jenkins' Ear* (Chapel Hill: University of North Carolina Press, 1936); A. M. Wil-

son, *French Foreign Policy during the Administration of Cardinal Fleury, 1726–1743* (Cambridge: Cambridge University Press, 1936); Robert L. Meriwether, *The Expansion of South Carolina, 1729–1765* (Kingsport: University of Tennessee Press, 1940); Larry E. Ivers, *British Drums on the Southern Frontier: The Military Colonization of Georgia, 1733–1749* (Chapel Hill: University of North Carolina Press, 1974).

42. Walter Louis Dorn, *Competition for Empire, 1740–1763* (New York: Harper and Row, 1940).

43. Steele, *Warpaths*, 170–73.

44. Lawrence Henry Gipson, *Zones of International Friction: The Great Lakes Frontier, Canada, the West Indies, India, 1748–1754* (New York: Alfred A. Knopf, 1952), 298.

45. Albert Harkness, "Americanism and Jenkins' Ear," *Mississippi Valley Historical Review* 37 (June 1950), 57–91; Richard L. Merritt, *Symbols of American Community, 1735–1775* (New Haven, Conn.: Yale University Press, 1966).

46. W. S. MacNutt, *The Atlantic Provinces: The Emergence of Colonial Society 1712–1857* (Toronto: McClelland and Stewart, 1965); Andrew Hill Clark, *Acadia: The Geography of Early Nova Scotia to 1760* (Madison: University of Wisconsin Press, 1968); L. F. S. Upton, *Micmacs and Colonists: Indian–White Relations in the Maritimes, 1713–1867* (Vancouver: University of British Columbia Press, 1979).

47. Gipson, *Zones*, 3.

48. Quoted in Gerard Finn, "Le Loutre, Jean-Louis," in *Dictionary of Canadian Biography* (Toronto: University of Toronto Press, 1966–), 4:453–58; John Clarence Webster, *The Career of the Abbe Le Loutre in Nova Scotia with a Translation of His Autobiography* (Shedia, N.B.: Privately Printed, 1933).

49. Stanley, *New France*, 73.

50. Quoted in J. S. McLennan, *Louisbourg from Its Foundation to Its Fall: 1713–1758* (1918) (Halifax, N.S.: The Book Room Limited, 1994), 190.

51. Quoted in McLennan, *Louisbourg*, 184.

52. Can. Arch. vol. ii, 292, quoted in McLennan, *Louisbourg*, 190.

53. Francis Jennings, *Empire of Fortune: Crowns, Colonies, & Tribes in the Seven Years War in America* (New York: W. W. Norton and Company, 1988), 118.

54. Board of Trade to Lawrence, March 4, 1754, selections from Thomas B. Atkins, ed., *Public Documents of the Province of Nova Scotia* (hereafter known as PDPNS (Halifax, N. S.: Charles Annand, 1869), 207.

55. Steel, *Warpaths*, 179. See also Paul A. W. Wallace, *Indians in Pennsylvania* (Harrisburg, Pa.: Historical and Museum Commission, 1961); Charles A. Hanna, *The Wilderness Trail, or the Ventures and Adventures of Pennsylvania Traders on the Allegheny Path*, 2 vols. (New York: Putnam and Sons, 1911); Thomas Perkins Abernethy, *Western Lands and the American Revolution* (1937) (New York: Russell and Russell, 1959).

56. Quoted in Nicholas B. Wainwright, *George Croghan: Wilderness Diplomat* (Chapel Hill: University of North Carolina Press, 1959), 15.

57. Abstract of Dispatches from Canada, 1749, NYCD 10:201.

58. C. A. Weslager, *The Delaware Indians: A History* (New Brunswick, N.J.: Rutgers University Press, 1991), 206.

59. Gooch to Board of Trade, November 6, 1747, in Kenneth P. Bailey, ed., *The Ohio Company Papers, 1747–1817, Being Primarily Papers of the "Suffering Traders" of Pennsylvania* (hereafter cited as Bailey, *Ohio Company Papers*) (Arcata, Calif.: Ar-

thur H. Clark, 1947), 23–24; Gooch to Board of Trade, June 16, 1748, ibid.; Privy Council to Gooch, November 24, 1748, ibid.; Board of Trade to Privy Council, December 13, 1748, ibid.; see also Kenneth P. Bailey, *The Ohio Company of Virginia and the Westward Movement, 1748–1792* (Glendale, Calif.: Arthur H. Clark Company, 1939); Alfred P. James, *The Ohio Company: Its Inner History* (Pittsburgh: University of Pittsburgh Press, 1959).

60. Thomas Lee to Board of Trade, October 18, 1749, in Bailey, *Ohio Company Papers*; Petition of John Hanbury, [1748], ibid.

61. Privy Council order to Board of Trade, March 16, 1749, in Bailey, *Ohio Company Papers*; Privy Council order to Board of Trade concerning Hanbury's petition, February 9, 1749, ibid.

62. Jennings, *Empire of Fortune*, 13.

63. Celoron to Hamilton, August 6, 1749, NYCD 6:532–23.

64. Quoted in Donald Kent, *The French Invasion of Western Pennsylvania* (Harrisburg: Pennsylvania Historical and Museum Commission, 1954), 9–10.

65. De la Jonquiere to Minister of Marine, September 20, 1749, *Wilderness Chronicles of Northwestern Pennsylvania*, ed. Sylvester K. Stevens and Donald H. Kent (hereafter cited as Stevens, *Wilderness Chronicles*) (Harrisburg: Pennsylvania Historical Commission, 1941), 27.

66. Clinton to Bedford, July 30, 1750, NYCD, 6:578–79.

67. For details of other land companies, see Gipson, *Zones*, 257–58.

68. Louis Knott Koontz, *Robert Dinwiddie, His Career in American Colonial Government and Westward Expansion* (Glendale, Calif.: Arthur H. Clark, 1941).

69. Dinwiddie to Board of Trade, August 1751, in R. A. Brock, ed., *The Official Records of Robert Dinwiddie, Lieutenant Governor of the Colony of Virginia, 1751–1758* (1883) (hereafter cited as Brock, *Dinwiddie Papers*) (reprint, New York: AMS Press, 1971); *Dinwiddie Papers*, January 20, 1752, ibid.; December 10, 1752, ibid.; June 16, 1753, ibid.

70. November 25, 1750, in William M. Darlington, ed., *Christopher Gist's Journals* (Cleveland: Arthur H. Clark, 1893).

71. Quoted in Francis Parkman, *Montcalm and Wolfe: The French and Indian War* (New York: Da Capo Press, 1995), 47–48.

72. George Croghan to Jeffrey Amherst, September 26, 1763, in James Sullivan and A. C. Flick, eds., *The Papers of William Johnson*, 14 vols. (hereafter cited as *Johnson Papers*) (Albany: State University of New York, 1921–1965), 10:823–25.

73. Instructions to Duquesne, April 1752, NYCD, 10:242–454.

74. Both quotes in Kent, *French Invasion*, 46–51.

75. Duquesne to Rouille, November 29, 1753, NYCD, 10:255.

76. Fairfax to Dinwiddie, November 22, 1753, C.O., 5:1328, 47–72, in Brock, *Dinwiddie Papers*.

77. Richard Peters to T. Penn, July 5, 1753, ms., Penn Mss., Off. Corr. 6:73, Historical Society of Pennsylvania.

78. Conference Minutes, New York, June 16, 1753, NYCD, 6:788.

79. Dinwiddie to Board of Trade, June 16, 1753, in Brock, *Dinwiddie Papers*; see also Stoddart to Johnson, May 15, 1753, in Stevens, *Wilderness Chronicles*, 72–73; Pennsylvania Report on French Activities, May 25, 1753, ibid., 74–76.

80. Holderness to Dinwiddie, August 28, 1753, in Brock, *Dinwiddie Papers*; see also T. R. Clayton, "The Duke of Newcastle, the Earl of Halifax, and the American

Origins of the Seven Years' War," *The Historical Journal* (Cambridge, England) 24: 3 (September 1981), 576–78, 591; Basil Williams, *The Whig Supremacy, 1714–1760,* 2nd ed., rev. by C. H. Stuart, *Oxford History of England* (Oxford: Clarendon Press, 1962).

81. Board of Trade Circular Instructions to Colonial Governors, September 18, 1753, NYCD, 6:802.

82. Trent to Dinwiddie, August 1753, in Bailey, *Ohio Company Papers.*

83. Hugh Cleland, *George Washington in the Ohio Valley* (Pittsburgh: University of Pittsburgh Press, 1955); James Thomas Flexner, *George Washington: The Forge of Experience, 1732–1775* (Boston: Little, Brown, and Company, 1965).

84. Quoted in Koontz, *Dinwiddie*, 214.

85. Donald Jackson, ed., *The Diaries of George Washington, 1748–65,* vol. 1 (hereafter cited as Jackson, *Washington Diaries*) (Charlottesville: University of Virginia Press, 1976), 1:144.

86. Jackson, *Washington Diaries,* 1:146.

87. Dinwiddie to St. Pierre, October 31, 1753, NYCD, 10:258.

88. Jackson, *Washington Diaries,* 1:152.

89. St. Pierre to Dinwiddie, December 15, 1753, NYCD, 10:258.

2

Economies and Societies

To withstand the violence of the cold winters, one ought to have his blood composed of brandy, his body of brass, and his eyes of glass.
—Baron Lahontan, 1686

In my person alone resides the sovereign power. . . . To me alone belong the legislative power, unconditional and undivided. All public order emanates from me. My people and I are one.
—Louis XV, 1766

We shall be as a city upon a hill. The eyes of all people are upon us.
—John Winthrop, 1630

These colonies are deeply tinged with all the vices and bad qualities of the mother country; and indeed, many parts of it are peopled with those that the law or necessity has forced upon it. Notwithstanding these disadvantages . . . this will, some time hence, be a vast empire, the seat of power and learning. Nature has refused them nothing.
—James Wolfe, 1758

We shall not speak of the rights of the natural owners of the country, which these great powers entirely discount, even though the natives find it strange that others should fight for a country where the author of life has, in their view, created them, where they have always lived & of which the bones of their ancestors have had possession from the beginning of time.
—Captain Pierre Pouchot, 1754

Two great and expanding empires went to war in 1754. The tentacles of the French and British empires extended beyond North America's eastern half to enclaves in the West and East Indies, West Africa, and India's coast. Impressive as those scattered holdings looked on maps, their value varied considerably. Ironically, the English and French alike derived greater revenues from their tiny Caribbean sugar islands than all the furs, tobacco, pitch, and lumber shipped from their vast North American colonies. Nonetheless, beyond Europe, Versailles and Whitehall devoted the most treasury and blood to the struggle for North America.

Mercantilism served as the intellectual foundation for the imperial policies of both France and Britain. Under mercantilism, the government and merchants are partners in promoting a virtuous cycle of wealth and power. The government wields a mix of trade barriers, regulations, and subsidies to domestic industries in order to maximize exports from and minimize imports to the realm. The resulting annual trade surpluses translate into ever greater amounts of hard currencies like gold and silver pouring into the kingdom. Through duties and taxes, a cut of this coin drops into royal coffers, while the rest pours as profits into the targeted industries. The government diverts some of its revenues into an ever more powerful army and navy that can defend and expand the empire. The industrial leaders, meanwhile, invest in more production at home and ventures abroad. Colonies served as captive markets for excess domestic production and captive suppliers of goods that could not be made at home. The larger and more economically diverse the empire, the more virtuous the mercantilist cycle of wealth and power.

Although both kingdoms followed mercantilism, their success in implementing that strategy differed greatly, as did their relative power and vitality. In the mid-18th century, of the two mother countries, France's 20 million people were four times larger than Britain's 5.8 million. While France's empire was run by nobles lodged in the spendid baroque palace of Versailles outside Paris, the British managed theirs from the cramped warren of buildings in London known as Whitehall. Superficially, it would appear that France had the upper imperial hand.

Yet Britain's smaller population was gifted by a far more dynamic merchant fleet, entrepreneurial class, and banking world, all of which worked together to build and manage a rich empire. The imperial gap was nowhere greater than in North America. By virtually every raw indicator of power, the American colonies overshadowed New France. Comparing their respective populations in 1750, New France's 70,000 colonists, including 51,000 Canadians, were outnumbered by the 1,062,000 white and 242,100 black colonists in the American colonies by a nearly one-to-seventeen ratio. While New France was a chronic drain on Versailles' treasury, each of the American colonies enjoyed a prosperous, diversified, and, if need be, self-sufficient economy.[1]

What of the colonists themselves? Were they little more than impoverished and exploited pawns in the hands of Versailles or Whitehall? To varying degrees, the Americans and Canadians alike managed to assert considerable personal autonomy and lead lives that surpassed in wealth and liberty that of their counterparts in their respective motherlands. Determining how wealthy the average American or Canadian of that era was by today's standards, however, is an impossible task. Most families made the bulk of their own clothes, shelter, furnishings, and food, the value of which was unrecorded. Barter rather than coin underwrote most trade. Still, most people enjoyed lives of relative material abundance. Although most people died in their fifties, a high birth rate overcame the shorter longevity. Despite the war's carnage, the populations of the American colonies and New France both expanded by 1760 when there were 1,593,600 Americans, of which 1,267,800 were white and 325,800 black, and 63,100 Canadians.[2]

The North American empires of Britain and France cannot be understood apart from the Indian tribes that inhabited much of the claimed territory and were anxiously sought by both sides as allies in trade and war. Here too the English had certain advantages over the French. English goods were better made, more abundant, and cheaper than French goods, all of which made American traders generally more welcome than their Canadian counterparts at a village. What the French lacked in economic heft they compensated for with a more sophisticated understanding of and sensitivity to Indian ways, longer contact and thus more entrenched relations with most tribes west of the Appalachians, and, if need be, the ability to mobilize enough Canadians and Indians to intimidate villages with wavering loyalty.

THE FRENCH EMPIRE

During the late 17th century, while parliamentarians fought to impose a constitutional monarchy on the English king, Louis XIV, during his long reign from 1661 to 1715, expanded his monarchical powers, although they were never quite "absolute." Louis XIV bequeathed to his great grandson, Louis XV, splendor and wealth unsurpassed in European history. Louis XV lived in the grand palace and gardens of Versailles with its several hundred courtiers, 10,000 servants, 3,000 horses, 217 carriages, 150 pages, 30 physicians, and 68-million-livres budget in 1751 alone, one-quarter of all government revenues.[3]

On the surface, France in the mid-18th century "was unquestionably an absolute monarchy. The King held all the powers: executive; legislative, subject to registration, but that could be imposed on the Parlement; even judicial, since the Council acted as a court of the last resort, able to confirm or annul the Parlements' decisions. He was able to tax pretty much as he liked, and to spend the State's revenue exactly as he saw fit. He declared war, negotiated and ratified all treaties, whether of peace or commerce. He could raise troops or disband them. He could govern with the help of one minister, or several, or none. He could, and did, order censorship of all printed matter, whether books or periodicals. He appointed bishops and abbots, as well as civil servants and military officers. He gave patents of nobility, titles, honors of all kinds. No one could stop him or bring him to account."[4]

Like so many kings, Louis XV cared more for the joys of the hunt, table, and bed than for state affairs. Although quite intelligent, he was no intellectual. A minister or philosopher could briefly capture his flighty attention with arguments spiced with wit and compassion. The king might then make some momentous or trivial decision before his mind drifted back to more sensuous pursuits.

His avoidance of power is understandable. He replaced Louis XIV as king on September 1, 1715. Not only was the "Sun King" a tough act to follow, but Louis XV was plunked onto the throne at age five, hardly the prime of life for decisive rule. He was a shy boy who would become a shy man. Throughout his reign, Louis XV revelled in etiquette, perhaps as much to hide from as to control his nobility. Louis XV reigned but never truly ruled. From his ascension, he was guided by a series of powerful advisors. The Sun King's will appointed the Duc d'Orleans as Regent and Andre-Hercule de Fleury, Bishop of Frejus, as tutor. To increase his hold over the king, the Regent took Louis XV back from Versailles to Vincennes in Paris. The Regency abolished the ministries and governed through a Council of Regency that presided over councils for War, Navy, Finances, Interior, and Church. The system proved unwieldy and inefficient. The Regent increasingly bypassed the council's advice and decided on his own. When the Duc d'Orleans' decrees proved no more capable of governing France, he reluctantly bowed to other powerful court figures and factions to dismantle much of his power. In 1718, the Council of Regency was abolished, the ministries reconstructed, and the court returned to Versailles. Louis XV was crowned at Reims on October 23, 1722, and declared of age on February 16, 1723. Yet he remained firmly the puppet of his advisors as the Royal Regency became the Royal Council. The Duc d'Orleans died in 1723, and, from the inevitable power struggle, de Fleury emerged to become the power behind the throne until his own death in 1743.

When de Fleury died, the king declared to his ministers, "Gentlemen, I have just become Prime Minister." Henceforth, Louis XV regularly attended the King's Council meetings that actually made policy and decided overall strategy, and dutifully initialed the laws, budgets, and edicts drafted in his name. The King's Council included the war, marine, foreign affairs, and comptroller-general or treasury ministries. These ministers ran their fiefs out of their palaces with little more than a handful of scribes and requisition clerks. One minister followed another as his predecessor fell to royal disfavor, court intrigue, or his own blunders of venality or policy. The turnover crimped the development of an experienced, united policy-making team that could plan, run, and win the war that expanded around the world after 1754.

One notable exception defies the persistent shuffling of ministers. From 1743 until he was dismissed in disgrace in 1757, Marc Pierre de Voyer, the Marquis d'Argenson, served as France's War Minister. In the midst of war he was followed by his inexperienced and timid nephew, Marc-Rene, the Marquis de Palmy. In 1758, France received its most able War Minister for that war, Charles Fouquet, the Duc de Belle-Isle, who had been a professional soldier all his adult life. Unfortunately, Belle-Isle was then a near invalid 73 years of age. When he died in January 1761, Etienne-Francois, Duc de Choiseul, took his place. Choiseul skillfully extracted France from that disastrous war.

The Marine Ministry was founded in 1669 to manage the growing empire's civil and military policies. Five Marine Ministers served during the war: Jean-Baptiste de Machault d'Arnouville to February 1757, Peirenc de Moras to May 1758, the Marquis de Massaic to November 1758, Nicolas-Rene Berryer to October 1761, and the Duc de Choiseul to April 1766. Except for Choiseul, none of these individuals showed much enthusiasm or imagination in executing their duties.

During the war, four men served as foreign minister—Antoine-Louis Rouille to June 1757, Abbe de Bernis to December 1758, Etienne-Francois, Duc de Choiseul to October 1761, and the Duc de Praslin to April 1766. Choiseul was by far the most talented of the lot but headed the foreign ministry when the war was all but lost. At most he and his cousin Praslin could simply try to negotiate the best peace for France.

Four treasury ministers or comptroller-generals struggled with the Herculean task of funding the Seven Years' War along with a host of other budgetary commitments, vital and frivolous alike: the Peirenc de Moras to August 1757, Jean de Boullongne to March 1759, Etienne de Silhouette to November 1759, and Henri-Lionard Jean-Baptiste Bertin to December 1763. No matter how hard they tried, each failed in turn. Although from 1756 through 1762, Versailles raised more than one billion livres in revenues, that treasury fell far short of expenses. By December 1760, the War Ministry alone was 80 million livres in debt.[5] As tax receipts fell short of expenditures, Versailles had to borrow. Much of the money and supplies that fueled France's armies and navies came from two sources: the financier Jean Paris de Montmartel and his brother, the merchant Joseph Duverney Paris, who were also close friends with Madame Pompadour. Although he took their money, Louis discarded their advice to cut expenses and expand the tax base. Louis hoped to gain more money by debasing the livre; the more money his mint coined, the less it could buy. In the war's last years, Louis XV had to grovel for huge loans before Spain's King Carlos III and various European bankers, only to have his requests denied because France was no longer thought to be credit-worthy. In the end, Louis XV was forced to melt down his royal silver into coin, an action that had no discernable effect on waging the war but certainly reduced the splendor of his reign.

At Versailles, as in any royal court, a myriad of the ambitious sought to rule behind the throne. If Louis had a prime minister, it was his former mistress and best friend, Jean-Antoinette Poisson, Marquise de Pompadour. She had a sometimes decisive say on most royal policies, including appointments and campaign strategies. She approved or rejected ministers, cut deals with members of France's elite and foreign diplomats alike, and joined policy debates. Symbolizing her political and cultural powers, she helped establish both the Ecole Militaire in 1751 and Sevres porcelin factory in 1752. She herself fashioned a salon that nurtured some of France's greatest artists, philosophers, and wits. She persuaded Louis XV to ease his censorship and tolerate, if not patronize, the Encyclopedists. In doing all of this, she became the lightning rod for France's policies. Unable to attack the king, dissidents instead pilloried his mistress. She was blamed for France's humiliating defeats and its bankruptcy. Pompadour could symbolize only wrong; she received no credit for French victories.[6]

At best, the policy making was chaotic. Bernis, who served as an unofficial prime minister for much of the war, wrote in 1755 that there was "no unity in the Council, open warfare between M. de Argenson and M. de Machault, gross disrespect in the discussions, no proper subordination. M. le prince de Conti, without being a minister, was consulted on almost everything, Mme. de Pompadour was openly at odds with the prince, and the King held the balance in the midst of these divisions. Add [to this] the display of the most scandalous luxury, the misery of the people, no true talent in the Council, not a courageous citizen at Court [and] no competent general on land or sea just before the onset of a war."[7]

Little talent for administration or war could be gleaned from the vast nobility whose members squeezed into Versailles from every corner of France. The nobility was split between "la noblesse d'epee" whose ancestors had achieved knighthood under the Franks, and "la noblesse de la robe" who had over the centuries purchased high office from the Crown. Not surprisingly, those wielding France's swords cast disdainful eyes on the newly gowned nobility manning the kingdom's ministries and courts, as much for the latters' short pedigrees as for their corruption. In return, the noblesse de la robe reserved a rich laughter for the frequent ineptness of the former on the battlefield. However contemptuous they may have been of one another, those two classes did together leech their wealth off the sweat of the realm's peasants, artisans, and merchants. Louis XV had little control over his nobles; at most he could dispose of the more troublesome ones by issuing lettres de cachet, which either exiled or imprisoned them. Although many gifted and devoted officers and officials arose from ranks of both noble classes, most also shared a frivolity, selfishness, extravagance, and indifference to France's fate that sapped the government's ability to wage a continental, let alone a global, war.

Among the nobility, the greatest check to the king's power were the thirteen regional parlements charged with registering and enforcing royal laws, officially approving any nobleman who came of age or succeeded another, or judging civil and criminal trials involving the nobility. Like most other administrative positions, those of Parlement were bought or inherited. Parlements were a thorn in the royal side and complicated Versailles' task of governing. When the parlements had emerged in the 14th century, they merely registered new laws; eventually they evaluated them. If a law was poorly written or contradicted other laws, Parlement might send a "remonstrance" to the king. Legally, the king could reject the remonstrance and issue a letter of command (lettres de jussion) that forced Parlement to register the law. Parlement eventually remonstrated not just royal laws but edicts directed at them. The king could then call a "bed of justice" (lit de justice) in which he appeared before Parlement to demand their acquiescence.

Not surprisingly, the Paris Parlement, with its jurisdiction encompassing Versailles, 230 judges (conseillers), and twelve superior magistrates (presidents), was the most powerful. Throughout the war the Paris Parlement defied Louis XV on appointments to the Grand Conseil, the vingtieme tax, unigenitus bull, and the Jesuits, among other issues. How much this tug of war between king and Parlement impeded the war effort, however, is impossible to say.

Far more debilitating to the achievement of Versailles' ambitions were the wretched economic and social conditions that later provoked a revolution. While Britain was embarking on the industrial revolution, France's economy remained as feudal as its nobility. A tiny aristocracy and small merchant class exploited all others. Just as Versailles practiced mercantilism for all of France, the nobles did so for their respective provinces. France was one kingdom split among several score local economies, each severed from the others by bewildering webs of regulations and duties that stunted trade, investment, and innovation. In France, as in other societies capped by exclusive elites, mostly the little people paid taxes. Tax collectors then pocketed much of the wealth they gouged from peasants and townspeople, rather than transferring it to the states.

As inflation and expenses soared, and the economy and revenues stagnated, Louis XV briefly listened to physiocrats like Jean-Claude Vincent de Gornay, Francois Quesnay, Pierre-Samuel du Pont, and Anne-Robert-Jacques Turgot who urged the abolition of internal trade barriers. He did make a half step toward reform. On September 17, 1754, Versailles abolished all domestic duties on grain. The measure helped circulate more grain at cheaper prices, while taking wealth from the nobles and petty officials alike who had pocketed the high duties. Redistributing wealth from the rich to the poor was at once good economics and bad politics. The howls of protest from the rich ensured that it would be the last reform that Louis made.

In stark contrast to its bleak economy, France's cultural sun never shone as brightly as it did during the mid-18th century. It was the age of Voltaire's acid wit and Rousseau's romantic introspection. Many other luminaries in political philosophy, literature, music, sculpture, painting, architecture, and charm crowded Parisian salons. The age spawned a mix of baroque, rococo, and neoclassical arts such as the music of Jean Philippe Rameau, the paintings of Francois Boucher, Jean Fragonard, or Jean Baptiste Simeon Chardin, the sculpture of Verbeeckt, the tapestries and carpets from the factories of Aubusson and Gobelin, the lacquerware of the brothers Martin, the neoclassical architecture of Jacque Ange Gabriel or the porcelain of Sevres. Although the age of Moliere, Racine, and Corneille was long past, theater flourished through the Comedie Francaise and Comedie Italienne. The nobility and litterati immersed themselves in the lighthearted antics displayed in a Watteau or Fragonard painting; few were concerned about the fate of France's North American empire.

That vast wilderness empire was a little-appreciated counterpart to Versailles' brilliance. Versailles claimed for New France all those lands between the Rocky and Appalachian Mountains, and the Gulf of Mexico and Hudson Bay. As in most of Britain's American colonies, the initial monopoly charter to a private firm to New France eventually gave way to royal rule. For New France's first half century, a succession of companies with royal charters enjoyed monopoly rule and exploitation but, through a dearth of finance and competence, failed to establish a dynamic, populous, and, most importantly, profitable New France. By 1663, the entire colony's French population numbered only 2,200. The burden of supplying these people and all their other operations sank the Company of One Hundred Associates under an ever growing debt mountain, just as it had all previous enterprises.

In March 1663, the Company of One Hundred Associates surrendered its charter to Louis XIV. For the next century, Versailles would directly rule New France, nominally by the king, actually by the Ministry of Marine which administered the province by setting its policies, appointing its governors, approving any initiatives, and financing its survival.

New France had a dual government. The governor-general or governor served as the commander in chief of all provincial and regular troops, the king's spokesman for Indian relations, and the colony's ceremonial leader. He alternated residences between Quebec, the official capital, from August through December, and Montreal from January through July. Residing at Quebec, the intendant was essentially the governor's prime minister with administrative duties in finances, trade, provisions, the courts, food supplies, hospitals, famine relief, bureaucrats, the police, war munitions, and the royal storehouses. The intendant's bureaucracy was divided among a Bureau de la Marine that administered the royal storehouses, a Domaine d'Occident that collected customs duties and rents for royal lands and trading posts, and Grand Voyer who oversaw roads and town planning. The number of royal officials serving the governor or intendant was small, only 218 by 1755.[8]

Although the governor-general presided over all of New France, he ruled directly over Canada which included the St. Lawrence and Great Lakes watersheds, and indirectly over Louisiana which extended from the Gulf Coast north up the Mississippi's eastern watershed, and Isle Royale which also included Acadia west of the Chignecto Isthmus and Isle St. Jean. Every year, the Marine Ministry sent separate instructions with the annual supply fleets to the governor at Quebec, and to the lieutenant-governors of Louisiana at New Orleans and Isle Royale at Louisbourg, respectively. The governor and lieutenant-governors annually sent detailed reports on their provinces' conditions and policies to Versailles.

As in many British colonies, New France's government grew more rather than less restrictive over time. For three decades after 1647, the landowners and merchants of Quebec, Montreal, and Trois-Rivieres elected syndics or representatives to advise the governor. Then, in 1664, the king created, for the Royal Province of New France, a Sovereign Council that included the governor, intendant, bishop, attorney-general, and five councilors who would discuss and overcome problems plaguing the province. The Sovereign Council allowed the syndics to atrophy during the 1670s and finally abolished it. Instead, lieutenant-governors ruled over those three towns, and presided over their respective royal courts. In 1702, the Sovereign Council was renamed the Superior Council and its councilors were increased to twelve. Other than those changes, the council existed only to render advice when asked by the governor and serve as the highest court of appeals. In 1708, Quebec's merchants did receive permission to meet annually and elect representatives to discuss local concerns with the intendant. The merchants of Montreal and Trois-Rivieres got the same privilege in 1717. Yet a benevolent feudalism rather than democracy characterized these annual sessions between New France's merchant elite and the intendant. Paternalism was as important in guiding French administration as mercantilism. Historian William Eccles points out that "poverty was not regarded as a sin or crime, but as a fault in the fabric of society that had to be mended."[9] The government provided hospitals, orphanages, and food to the needy. In all, however, paternalism was no better implemented for New France than mercantilism.

In 1754, while over two million people crowded the American colonies, only about 70,000 people of French descent inhabited the vast realm of New France, of which 55,000 were in Canada, 5,000 in Acadia, and 10,000 in Louisiana. Most Canadians lived in the narrow strip along the St. Lawrence River valley between Quebec and Montreal. With 8,000 people

Quebec was the largest town, followed by 5,000 in Montreal, and 800 in Trois-Rivieres. A tiny political, economic, and social elite of 400 families peaked New France's society, including about "131 seigneurs, of whom some were commoners; 106 gentlemen and notables; 119 merchants, 22 lawyers and 13 doctors. There were also about 40 notaries."[10]

If Quebec was the administrative and cultural capital, Montreal was New France's real working headquarters, serving as the center for the fur trade and Indian diplomacy. Each May, Indian emissaries gathered at the Ramezay palace where the governor dispensed presents and promises. The governor, in turn, dispatched from Montreal annual canoe fleets with trade goods and instructions for post commanders scattered across New France's far reaches. Some canoe fleets paddled up the Ottawa River, portaged over the divide, and spread out into the western Great Lakes and beyond. Other canoes struggled up the St. Lawrence, into Lake Ontario and Lake Erie, and then by rivers into the Ohio country. The strand of each route knotted in the Mississippi River. At strategic points along these routes stood one of many trading posts, each with a motley collection of voyageurs, marines, artisans, and, sometimes, a missionary or two.

Garnering furs and gathering souls were deemed thoroughly compatible goals. In addition to his secular duties, Louis XV also headed the Catholic Church in France. Recollet missionaries had arrived in New France as early as 1608; Jesuits followed in 1611. In 1632, Versailles restricted the Recollets from the Indians, allowing the Jesuits to dominate for a quarter century until the Sulpicians were permitted to set up a church in Montreal in 1659. In 1639, two female religious orders were established in New France, Marie de l'Incarnation led an Ursuline mission and Mere Maire-Guet de Saint-Ignace, an Augustines Hospitalieres de l'Hotel Dieu mission. The first bishop was appointed to New France in 1658, but was commanded by Rome; the position was made the Bishopric of Quebec in 1674 and thereafter was controlled by Versailles. In 1756, of Canada's 163 priests, 84 were secular, 30 Sulpician, 25 Jesuit, and 24 Recollet; 81 were born in Canada and the remainder in France.[11] Protestantism was outlawed and its adherents barred from the colony.

New France was divided into church parishes, of which Canada had 124. Each parish struggled to meet expenses by garnering a tax of one-twenty-sixth of a peasant's wheat harvest; Versailles also made generous annual subsidies to the Bishop, which were poorly redistributed. Only 44 parishes were wealthy enough that they could support themselves with local tithes; the rest scraped by on Royal subsidies. One in every three parishes were so poor they could not afford their own priests. Members of those congregations had to travel elsewhere if they sought the comforts of mass, confession, baptism, or sanctified marriage and burial.

The parishes were the center of civil as well as religious authority. While many parishes wanted priests, all had officials appointed by the governor.

To each parish the governor assigned a captain de malice or militia captain who not only ensured that all able-bodied men between ages 16 and 60 attended drills and campaigns, but also supervised public works, welfare, and law enforcement.

As the captains ruled the parishes, the local seigneurs or landlords reigned. Starting in 1634, seigneuries were granted to those who promised to settle immigrants in New France, in all 238 seigneuries by the 1750s, which averaged about 35,000 acres or 55 square miles. The Church received about one-quarter of these grants.[12] Virtually all these grants were narrow strips of land fronting the St. Lawrence and extending inland between Quebec and Montreal. Strictly speaking, although court favorites received grants, they were not necessarily lords; among the seigneurs were commoners as well as noblemen. Seigneurs had both duties and rights, and mostly exercised neither. Although the seigneurs, theoretically, had the right to collect 10 percent of the peasants' income as rent, most were content to live off wealth reaped from their own estates. The 1711 Edict of Marly required all seigneurs to develop or else lose their land; it was not enforced until 1741. In all, about 200 families formed Canada's aristocracy. Unlike their French counterparts, Canadian aristocrats were allowed to engage in trade.

New France was never more than a vast drain on Versailles' annual budget. By 1753, Quebec had run up 3,495,675 livres in debt to Versailles.[13] How could such a potentially rich land impoverish Versailles? New France's administration was just as profligate and corrupt as that of its mother kingdom. Corruption, sloth, and incompetence characterized French rule from the highest officials to the lowliest laborers. The bureaucracy was corrupt from top to bottom, with each official along the way pocketing a bribe with each transaction. Personnel fiefdoms riddled the bureaucracy; officials were accountable not to the "people" or even the "state," but solely to the patron who had put them in office. Fort commanders pocketed salaries and supplies for false names on muster rolls. Local officials sold everything they could steal from the government. Famine relief supplies went to the highest bidder rather than to the needy. Likewise, royal presents designed to keep the Indians loyal ended up on the black market. The numbers of Indians on the warpath was inflated; officials took the goods that should have gone to those imaginary warriors. Well-to-do draft-dodgers could buy one-year exemptions from military service. Throughout his journal, Louis Bougainville cited case after case of corruption, despairing all along of the vast waste of the king's money. He estimated that two-thirds of the supplies sent by Versailles were stolen and the other third sold by commanders when they should have been given away.[14]

Most corrupt of all was Francois Bigot, New France's Intendant since 1748.[15] Bigot shamelessly abused his powers to build an enormous patronage and corruption machine that stretched to every parish, town, and fort across the province. Bigot's henchmen included his lieutenant, Joseph Cadet, a former butcher who was made New France's commissary-general; Jean Victor de la Marre Varin, the naval commissary; Jean-Baptiste Martel, the king's storekeeper at Quebec; Captain Francois le Mercier, the artillery commander; and the governor's brother Rigaud Vaudreuil. The tentacles of Bigot's machine reached across the Atlantic. La Porte, the Marine Minister's secretary, opened all correspondence from New France, judiciously diverting to Bigot any letters critical of the intendant's management. The merchant house Gradis and Son at Bordeaux conspired with Bigot to falsify records and fence stolen goods.

Bigot's machine skimmed money from virtually every enterprise in New France, including 2 percent of the fur trade. Perhaps the most common and lucrative means of theft was to overcharge the king for goods and services. From 1756 to 1758, Bigot and his gang charged Versailles 23 million francs for goods that cost only 11 million francs. The scam usually went like this: One of Bigot's lackeys would contract with the Gradis and Sons firm at Bordeaux to sell him goods which he imported duty-free by claiming they were the king's. Bigot then convinced the Colonial Minister that Versailles should buy supplies from Canada rather than ship them there, since he claimed that Canada already had three years of supplies on hand. He then sold the king, at huge markups, the supplies he had imported from Gradis and Sons. Bigot then turned around and sold the supplies reimported from France at highly inflated prices. The Canadians dubbed each of Bigot's warehouses at Quebec and Montreal "La Friponne," or "The Cheat." Bigot's most outrageous scam was to accuse peasants of hoarding grain and order soldiers to confiscate it; send it to France in royal ships and sell it to the king; and then plead for the king to give it back to New France to avert the famine he had created. With the grain back in his hands, Bigot would then sell it back to the peasants who had originally grown it, at grossly inflated prices.

To many, Bigot was as repulsive as he was rich; apparently his body was as corrupt as his politics: He "was an ugly man, small and overweight. He had unruly yellowish hair piled above an unattractive face covered with pimples. Suffering from nasal scabs that gave out an unpleasant odour, he spent vast sums of money on perfumes and fragrant waters to conceal his affliction. One of his many servants was always standing at his side with an armful of hankerchiefs scented with various eaux de toilette. The sweet sickly smell permeated the small room that served as his office."[16] What Bigot lacked in physical charm, he seems to have overcome with the ability to attract men and women to his side, although one suspects that his abundant wealth and power may have been his most important lure. While Louis XV had Madame Pompadour to enliven his bed, salon, and policies, Bigot had Madame Angelique Renaud d'Avene des Meloizes, the wife of Captain Michel Jean Hugues Pean. Bigot got rid of the husband by assigning him to distant frontier posts.

What role did the governor play in the corruption game? During the years leading up to and throughout the French and Indian War, New France had a succession of governors. Roland-Michel Barrin de La Galissoniere, Marquis de La Galissoniere was New France's acting but unofficial governor from 1747 to 1749. New France's official governor was Jacque-Pierre de Taffenel de La Jonquiere, Marquis de La Jonquiere who was appointed to the post in 1746, but did not arrive until August 14, 1749 and served until his death at Quebec in March 1752. Ange Duquesne de Menneville, Marquis Duquesne ruled from then until 1755 when he received permission to return to the navy. Pierre de Rigaud de Vaudreuil de Cavagnial, Marquis de Vaudreuil reached Quebec on June 23, 1755 and remained governor until he surrendered New France on September 8, 1760. Bigot's corruption machine preceded Galissoniere and thrived until the conquest. Although Vaudreuil was the only governor to be charged with corruption, and was acquitted, each governor undoubtedly benefited from Bigot's machine.

What explains the virulence of this corruption? As always, Parkman put it well: "Honesty could not be expected from a body of men clothed with arbitrary and ill-defined powers, ruling with absolute sway an unfortunate people who had no voice in their own destinies, and answerable only to an apathetic master three thousand miles away. Nor did the Canadian Church, though supreme, check the corruptions that sprang up and flourished under its eye."[17] Louis Bougainville grew ever more critical of New France during his five years there. In December 1758, he reported to Versailles that "Canada . . . has been ignored, delivered entirely into the hands of a small number of people who are rendered despotic by the great distance at which they find themselves from the sovereign power, who seek only to build up quick fortunes in a new land in order to enjoy it in Europe, and who have good reasons to wish that the clouds covering the country be never dispelled. This country finds itself exhausted . . . its government is bad. . . . We live from day to day. . . . In brief, it is a land of abuse, of ignorance, of prejudice, of everything monstrous in politics."[18]

Corruption damaged French power in several ways. Had Canada been administered by honest officials, it might have turned a handsome profit for the king. As it was, France was better off cutting that perennial financial drain. The more money and goods that lined official pockets, the less there was with which to finance Indian alliances and campaigns against the English. Worst of all, corruption even drove some men to treason. Bougainville maintains that Louisbourg's merchants were so greedy that they sold out their country when they stood to profit from it: "They surrender the place in order to secure under the capitulation that the citizens keep their property. . . . The Commissary reports an inventory of only what remains in the King's storehouse at the surrender, and makes no mention of the goods carried into the city, which go to his profit. M. B[igot] did the same in 1745. He got the inhabitants to request the commander to surrender, and the commander subsequently surrendered under the pretext of not being able to restrain revolting inhabitants, as well as a mutinous garrison."[19]

Despite all of this, most Canadians appear to have been fatalistic about the practice, concerned mostly with reaping what they could from the system. The spoils permeating the administration from the parishes and remote posts up to the intendant and governors undoubtedly did exploit Canadians through higher prices and shortages of goods and even food. But corruption was no worse in New France than in France itself.

As if New France's corruption were not debilitating enough, mercantilism backfired for Versailles in New France, which for a century and a half drained rather than enhanced the kingdom's wealth. Versailles stunted New France's development by smothering most entrepreneurship under royal monopolies. The fur trade was successively controlled by the Company of One Hundred Associates, the Company of East India, the Canada Company, and the Company of India. In the fishing industry, the Bayonne Company monopolized whaling, the Sieur Corva and Associates salmon, and the Sieur Pascund walruses and seals. Favored individuals enjoyed monopoly licenses over commodities like flour, vegetables, slaughterhouses, and so on. Only two small-scale industries were allowed, the Saint Maurice iron works at Trois-Rivieres and the shipbuilding works at Quebec. Despite royal subsidies, both the iron and ship works were chronic money-losers because of bad management and inadequate supplies.[20]

Furs and fish were the pillars of New France's economy. Furs accounted for one-quarter of all wealth changing hands and nearly all of New France's exports. Of 1,548,588 livres worth of furs exported in 1754, beaver accounted for 505,319 livres or one-third the value. Among some of the other skins were 293,658 livres in buckskins, 182,324 livres in marten, 176,477 livres in wildcat, and 130,145 livres in bearskins. Over 150 years, the fur trade ran a series of boom-and-bust cycles as supply, demand, and price shifted according to changing fashions, overtrapping, war disruptions, and the availability of trade goods. Fishing was the second most important source of wealth. On the war's eve, over 3,000 vessels and 15,000 fishermen of all nationalities annually hauled in over 500,000 pounds worth of wealth.[21]

New France suffered chronic trade deficits. Typical was the year 1754 when it exported only 1,719,683 livres worth of goods and received 5,202,461 livres worth of imports, for a deficit of 3,482,778 livres. All luxury goods, firearms, ammunition, gunpowder, and wine were imported. Each year Versailles dispatched ships filled with presents for the Indians and supplies for the garrisons. Despite its being a perpetual drain on Versailles' budget, in good years Canada supplied important products such as dried fish, fish oil, flour, horses, lumber, iron, ginseng, and salt to France and its Caribbean colonies.

How did New France finance this perennial deficit? France's currency consisted of three units, in which one livre equaled twenty sols, and twelve derniers a sol. Even more than Britain's American colonies, New France suffered a severe coinage shortage. What little coin entered the colony was whisked away to pay for imports. Most trade was barter. Since New France had no taxes, Quebec could only supplement its subsidies from Versailles with customs duties. Eventually, Quebec chose to finance New France's chronic budget and trade deficit with an ever-growing mountain of ever-worsening credit. In 1684, Intendant Jacques de Meulles came up with the idea of issuing credit on playing cards which could be reimbursed for specie once it arrived with the annual supply fleet. Up to the 1760 conquest, Versailles periodically stamped out and revived card money as the imperative for credit rose and fell in relation to the varying degrees to which the system stimulated inflation and corruption.

Smuggling alleviated the shortages caused by corruption and mercantilism. Both Versailles and Whitehall forbade their respective Canadian and American subjects to trade with each other. What Americans and Canadians could not do legally, they did illegally. Smuggling was rampant between Montreal and Albany, Acadia and New England, the upper Great Lakes and Oswego, and the American colonies and French West Indian islands. War did not eliminate that trade; it only trimmed its volume and raised its costs. The reason for the trade was simple. The Canadians had a surplus of furs, fish, and sugar but lacked good quality, abundant, and inexpensive manufactured goods. For these they turned to the Americans who enjoyed such goods in abundance but wanted those commodities.

Despite the India Company's monopoly and law against trading in the American colonies, many furs trapped by Indians or Canadians ended up in British hands. For several important reasons, British goods cost less and were more numerous and better made than French goods. The St. Lawrence River iced over half the year and was perilous to shipping the other half, thus disrupting the flow of goods to New France. In contrast, the American coastline was ice-free all the way up to Maine. As if climate was not a big enough disadvantage, French manufacturers simply could not produce goods on the same scale and of the same quality as their rivals across the English Channel. Finally, like monopolies anywhere, Canada logically favored selling a few goods at high prices rather than the converse.

New France prices were generally two to three times higher than American prices. From its founding in 1624, Albany became a magnet for Indian and Canadian traders who aspired to a better return on their furs. In 1698, a gun cost a trader two beavers in Albany and five in Montreal, a blanket one beaver in Albany and two in Montreal, 40 pounds of lead one beaver in Albany and three in Montreal. Mohawk and Jesuit missionaries at the Iroquois town of Caughnawaga served as middlemen in the Lake Champlain trade. The founding of Oswego in 1726 made it even more likely that Canadian furs would find their way to British rather than French markets.

At Oswego, Canadians and Indians received a standard four livres, four sous per pound weight compared to only three livres, five sous at French posts, including nearby Fort Niagara. As Cadwallader Colden pointed out in 1726, "our Indian Traders not only have a double Price for their Indians Goods but likewise buy the Goods they sell to the Indians at half the Price the French Indian traders do—the French Traders must be ruined . . . before now if they had not found means to carry their Beaver to Albany where they get double the Price they must have sold for in Canada."[22]

As Daniel Richter notes, irony underlay this trade: "French vendors at Niagara and Montreal depended in large part upon Albany suppliers for strouds, wampum, and other goods tailored to the tastes of Indian consumers, and without the illicit Albany–Montreal traffic, they could never have successfully competed with Oswego. After the repeal of all restrictions on the north–south trade in 1731, as commerce with the Six Nations and western Indians simultaneously shifted to Oswego, exchanges with Montreal became the principal business of Albany merchants and their Indian customers. Thus furs traded at French Niagara were likely to end up at Albany, where Canadian Iroquois would exchange them on behalf of Montreal merchants for English manufactures that would in turn be shipped to Niagara to be bartered for more furs. To some degree, then, the French and English western posts were parallel retail branches of the same wholesale trade."[23]

Versailles experimented with various means to regulate the fur trade, but none were powerful enough to prevent traders or trappers from selling their furs at Albany or Oswego after 1726. In 1681, hoping to gain some of the lost revenues, the government tried issuing licenses (conges) to the better-connected entrepreneurs. The smuggling continued. Versailles abolished licenses in 1686 and tried cracking down. A small revenue source died while the abuse went on. Licensing was restored in 1716. Colonial officials largely turned a blind eye to the lucrative trade. Bribes allowed officials themselves to benefit directly from smuggling.

The Enlightenment shining brightly in Paris and elsewhere failed to illuminate New France. The province lacked the intellectual or artistic vigor of even Britain's American colonies. There was no representative assembly in which dissident voices or petitions could be raised. No newspapers or even printing press could legally exist in New France. With no public and few private libraries, few books changed hands. As early as 1635, the Jesuits did found a College at Quebec, but it immersed its students in dogma rather than speculation. Duties rather than rights shaped peoples' lives.

Despite the exploitive corruption, intellectual and artistic void, long, harsh winters, and often failed harvests that brought most people to starvation's brink, Canadians overall were generally better off than their counterparts in France. There were no direct taxes in New France. Canadian peasants did not have to pay the tax on their production (taille) or the salt tax that impoverished French peasants. Traders, however, did pay a 25 percent export tax on all beaver pelts. Although there was a 10 percent duty on wine, spirits, and tobacco, and, from 1749, a 3 percent duty on all other imports, these did not raise prices to exhorbitant amounts. Governors and intendants quickly shot down periodic suggestions by Versailles that higher taxes be imposed. In addition to their militia duties, peasants were required to serve a day or two annually on improving local roads or bridges. None of these restrictions were crippling. In all, most Canadians managed to lead lives of pleasure, adequately fulfilled material needs, and a gradually expanding national self-awareness.

A Canadian identity slowly, steadily emerged, forged in those settlements and posts isolated in wilderness and given voice by such works as Samuel de Champlain's *Voyages* (1632), Pierre Boucher's *Histoire veritable et naturelle . . . du Canada* (1664), Louis-Armand de Lom d'Arce de Lahonton's *Nouveaux voyaes* and *Dialogues* (1703), or Joseph-Francois Lafitau's *Moeurs des sauvages ameriques* (1724). Students acquired literacy and theology from the Jesuit College at Quebec, the Sulpicians' Seminary at Montreal, and the Ursiline Academy at Quebec. Not long after arriving in Canada, Bougainville wrote, "What a country, my dear brother, and what patience is needed to bear the slights that people go out of their way to lay on us here. It seems as though we belonged to a different nation, even a hostile one."[24] Bougainville, of course, was correct. The 55,000 French-speaking inhabitants of Canada were no longer French—over the preceding century and a half, they had become Canadian.

Refuge in a distant land only partially explains the growth of Canadian nationalism. Like the Americans, the Canadians gradually became aware of their cultural distinctness through the neglect and exploitation of their colonial overlords. However, unlike the Americans, the Canadians never developed the democratic institutions and values at any level that could reflect and excite their nationalism. Independence for Canadians would come a century later than for Americans. Even then, Canadians spurned revolution in favor of a devolution of power that kept them nomimally subject to whatever queen or king sat in London.

Why did Versailles cling to such a financial disaster as New France? In royal eyes, New France's strategic and prestige value far outweighed its maintenance costs. The colony's territorial claims and chain of trading posts up the St. Lawrence and Great Lakes and down the Mississippi locked the British into a narrow strip between the Appalachians and the Atlantic. But throughout the war, as British armies slowly crushed Canada, Versailles dispatched only limited troops and supplies to New France. With as much relief as anything else, Versailles would write off the continental-sized burden with the 1763 Treaty of Paris.

THE BRITISH EMPIRE

The British Empire was a far-flung hodgepodge of 15 million diverse peoples subordinated to 31 different administrations ranging from autonomous colonies like Connecticut or Rhode Island to East India Company "factories."[25] London had patched together this empire from pieces of overseas territory acquired more by treaties of cession with local rulers than outright conquest; the attraction of wealth won obedience from natives more readily than the fear of British arms. Chartered private monopolies were far more important than the Royal Navy in this imperial expansion.

Presiding over Britain's vast empire at mid-century sat King George II. Ideally, the king could still call and dismiss Parliament, and veto parliamentary bills. Armed with the power of appointment through his "civil list," the king enjoyed a rich source of patronage and thus influence. He approved and dismissed all high-ranking positions of state. Likewise, he could issue new titles and other honors as he wished. His proclamations were law. Those below him had to consult the king on all important matters. He headed the Church of England, army, and navy. The king could reach deep into his wealth and extract enough to buy votes and voices for his policies.

Yet, in an age of "absolute" monarchs, George II's power was largely ceremonial. Ever since the Glorious Revolution of 1688, the king reigned while Parliament ruled. The Bill of Rights (1689) and Act of Settlement (1701) ensured a constitutional rather than absolute monarchy for Britain. Parliament had offered the throne to William in 1688 and George in 1714; what it offered, it could theoretically take away. In all, the king merely ratified decisions made elsewhere. No king had exercised his veto right since 1714. His power was confined to that of persuading those around him who held real power, and appointing and firing those targeted by his advisors.

George II was as active and brave a king as he could be under England's constitutional monarchy. He actually led his troops into battle at Dettingen in 1747. Although the government's leaders may have admired the king's bravery, they marginalized him politically. When he was especially exasperated, George II could speak wistfully of retiring to Hanover, a none too veiled threat to provoke a constitutional crisis. Few took such threats to abandon England seriously; some welcomed them. The king got along no better with the Crown Prince, Frederick, than he did with Parliament. George II despised his son and may have had decidedly mixed feelings when the man died in 1751. The king got along better with the new Crown Prince, his grandson and namesake who would become George III. Born in 1683, George II was 71 years old when the war broke out in 1754. His age increasingly showed.

While the king reigned, Parliament ruled through its "power of the purse," which meant power over policy. The Septennial Act of 1716 required elections to be held at least once every seven years, although the king could dismiss Parliament and call for new elections at any time. A bill became law only after both houses passed it and the king signed it. Although the House of Lords held 216 seats in the 1750s, rarely did more than a handful of lords show up to conduct business. The House of Lords' most important function was to fill positions in the Privy Council and Cabinet. During the mid-18th century, the House of Commons held 558 seats that included 415 boroughs; 94 English and Welsh counties; 45 Scottish counties; two each from the universities of Oxford Cambridge; and one from each of the Cinque Ports. Of a population of 5.8 million Britons, voting restrictions of varying degrees of severity restricted the franchise to 245,000 male voters, of which the boroughs contributed 85,000 and the counties 160,000. To vote in the county elections, one had to be a freeholder with an annual income of 40 shillings; electoral requirements varied among the boroughs and other districts. The nationally disenfranchised included Catholics, Jews, Quakers, agnostics, criminals, women, and other "undesirables."

Corruption was the true ruler of British politics. Some of the boroughs were notoriously "rotten" in confining the electorate to a handful. Sarum, William Pitt's first district, had only five voters. Of course, the fewer voters a district harbored, the greater the chance that an election simply went to the highest bidder. One hundred and eleven boroughs were in the "pockets" of wealthy patrons who sold them to whomever pleased them. No secret ballot existed in any district; elections were held by a show of hands and voices, a practice that allowed the stronger party to intimidate the weaker into compliance.

England's government was much more complex than the strained partnership between Crown and Parliament. Imperial policy was debated, decided upon, and implemented largely among the Cabinet Council, Privy Council, and Board of Trade with their overlapping powers and members. Ministers were at once members of Parliament and the Cabinet; some were also on the Privy Council, Board of Trade, and various committees.

A descendant of the notorious Star Chamber, the Privy Council was supposedly the power behind the throne. Its committees investigated issues and proposed remedies. Laws passed by all the colonies except Connecticut, Maryland, and Rhode Island were not legal until the Privy Council approved them. Once appointed, privy councilors served for the king's lifetime. The Privy Council's chief duty was to advise the king and convey his wishes to Parliament.

Although not mentioned in any of the documents composing Britain's "Constitution," the Cabinet Council made policy. It had emerged from the Privy Council in the early 18th century to address specific issues and duties. Over time the Cabinet Council nudged the Privy Council aside in importance, and now included ministers both with and without portfolio. Decisions were reached after debate and consensus. The most important foreign policy ministers were those of the Exchequer, Admiralty, War, and Navy; the Secretary of State for the Northern Department which dealt with northern European affairs, and the Secretary of State for the Southern Department with duties over the empire and southern Europe. Although no official prime minister existed, one man usually presided.

The king did not attend Cabinet meetings but merely ratified its decisions, sometimes with pointed questions and protests, more often with merely a royal sigh. He dared not do more. As the fates of Charles I and James II had revealed, British kings ultimately were expendable, occasionally with extreme prejudice. The king had to be highly sensitive to the tenuous coalitions in the Cabinet among the bitterly opposed factions. George II, for example, hated William Pitt, but the "Great Commoner's" parliamentary and popular power forced the king to accept him into the government.

A special body to administer the empire predated the Cabinet and its Secretary of State for the Southern Department. At first the Privy Council administered colonial policy. Then, in 1634, almost two decades after Virginia's founding, the Crown created a Commission of Plantations to formulate and implement imperial policy. The name was changed to the Committee on Trade and Plantations in 1650, and then split into a Council of Trade and Council for Foreign Plantations in 1660. These were recombined into the Lord Commissioners for Trade and Plantations in 1675, and renamed the Board of Trade in 1696. With the Secretary of State for the Southern Department, the Board's sixteen members devised policies for the governors and approved or rejected colonial laws. Mostly, the Board rubberstamped all but 5.5 percent of colonial laws, although it did overturn about 30 percent of colonial court decisions. The Board of Trade worked closely with colonial agents and merchants to formulate policies.[26]

In the mid-18th century, England was largely a one-party state ruled by Whigs. The Whig Party had emerged in 1679 in opposition to Charles II and his royalist coterie known as the Tories, whose influence had diminished ever since 1688. By the 1750s, the distinction between parliamentarian Whigs and royalist Tories had disappeared; virtually all supported a constitutional monarchy ruled by Parliament. In all, party loyalty counted for little in Parliament. The concept of being a Whig or Tory was vague at best. The Whig Party had become a multi-party system in itself, split into factions built around personalities, wealth, and power rather than sets of ideas and policies. Only 20 to 30 of 558 members were beholden to ministers for their seats; everyone else was more or less independent. Unable to coerce a majority, a ministry's power rested on its ability to persuade members to vote its way. Lacking a party let alone party discipline, chief ministers were successful to the degree that they understood and could manipulate the prejudices, interests, sentiments, and pocketbooks of most in Parliament.

From Robert Walpole's fall as chief minister in 1739, two brothers dominated the Whig Party through 1754, and thus the Cabinet and the British Empire. Henry Pelham and Thomas Pelham-Holles, the Duke of Newcastle, had used their vast wealth and political skills to create and run a machine that was largely synonymous with the government. Pelham and Newcastle had installed their cronies in most other ministries, while saving the most powerful positions for themselves. Pelham was the chief minister who served formally as First Lord of the Treasury and Chancellor of the Exchequer. Newcastle had served as Secretary of State for the Southern Department from 1724 to 1748, and then took over as Secretary of State for the Northern Department. Of the constellation of parliamentarians more or less aligned with the Pelham faction, the most important would prove to be William Pitt, although that was not evident before the war.

The Pelham faction's power was shadowed by another faction's rise. In 1745, George II appointed his son, William Augustus, the Duke of Cumberland, to the relatively minor post of captain general. From then until his resignation in 1757 after he ignominiously surrendered his Army of Observation at Kloster-Zeven, Cumberland's tenure was marked by controversy and scandal, capped by that spectacular failure. Yet during that time, his rise in power was checked only once—as George II's mental powers waned, Cumberland unsuccessfully lobbied Parliament to become his regent.

Some feared that Cumberland aspired to become another Cromwell. No evidence exists proving that Cumberland ever aspired to overthrow England's parliamentary system in favor of an absolute monarchy, let alone a military dictatorship. Yet, his bluster and grabs for ever-greater policy-making power certainly provoked the fear that he aspired to do so. That fear helped prolong the Pelham faction's power.

Theoretically, Cumberland could only recommend and not command policy. However, his ambition, assertiveness, and royal father led him to acquire, eventually, a very important seat at the policy table as he argued proposals directly with the king or any minister. Cumberland's power begat more power. He became the nucleus for a parliamentary faction that eventually included Halifax, Sandwich, Bedford, Richmond, Marlborough, Anson, and Fox, along with the parliamentary votes of most former or current army officers. While Cumberland was the faction's symbolic leader, John Russell Bedford, the Duke of Bedford, was its first actual leader, followed by Henry Fox in 1754.

Although the Pelham and Cumberland factions were fierce political foes, the former had no choice but agree to draw the latter into the inner circle of policy making. In 1751, the Cumberland faction forced Pelham to quell a push by some in Parliament to abolish the position of captain general. Then, the Pelham faction's power teetered on the brink of collapse when Henry died in 1754. As one price for becoming chief minister, Newcastle had to allow Cumberland to sit in its meetings when North American affairs were discussed. This swung the Cabinet Council's power seesaw toward the captain general and Fox, who dominated policy during the first few years of the war. Fox had served as war secretary for ten years from 1746 through November 1755 when he was named Secretary of State for the Southern Department.

It was this military faction that William Pitt would have to overcome to take power and guide Britain to victory in the Seven Years' War. Cumberland's humiliating surrender in 1757 gave Pitt the opportunity to become chief minister and pack the Cabinet with old and new Pelham faction members. From then until New France's conquest, Pitt dominated British strategy.

Presiding over the world's most dynamic economy, Whitehall had far less trouble raising revenues than Versailles. Tariff receipts from the British Isles and Empire poured into the Exchequer. Unlike France, England was one large united market. Agriculture and trade were the backbones of English wealth; manufacturing was just moving beyond the cottage to the factory. Money oiled the workings of the British Empire; in 1750, there were 20 banks in London alone while dozens of merchant houses loaned and borrowed. Bankers and the government believed in hard currency; paper money accounted for only 2 percent of all transactions.

Britain's aristocrats were not as parasitic as those of France. Many dirtied their hands with trade or manufacturing enterprises and thus expanded the wealth of both themselves and England. They were also far better educated. Universities at Oxford and Cambridge educated many of Britain's political and economic elite; London's law schools—Lincoln's Inn, Middle Temple, Inner Temple, and Gray's Inn—provided legal and oratory training. Some of this wealth, enterprise, and learning trickled down to their lessers. While two-thirds of the population were peasants, perhaps one in five could be considered middle class.

No society on earth was more urbanized than England's. For hundreds of years, the enclosure movement whereby landowners converted crop to pasture land had driven away peasants into the dank towns and cities. In 1754, London swelled with 600,000 people and a dynamic economy whose growth engines were finance, trade, and manufacturing. The empire's second, third, and fourth cities were Bristol with 75,000 people, Manchester with 50,000, and Liverpool with 22,000; trade dominated the economies of Bristol and Liverpool, textile manufacturing that of Manchester. The expanding middle class in all the cities were islands of prosperity surrounded by abject poverty and decadence. Gambling dens and brothels lined streets crowded with gin addicts, prostitutes, and pickpockets.

It was the England of William Hogarth's *The Rake's Progress*, Henry Fielding's *Tom Jones*, and George Handel's "Water Music" that fought and won the Seven Years' War. Stunning as these gifts were, in all, the mid-18th century was not the high point in England's cultural history. In glaring contrast to France's Enlightenment, only one major political philosopher bestrode the intellectual stream of that age: David Hume, with his *Treatise on Human Nature* (1739) and *Treaties of Political Discourses* (1752). Perhaps England's other great thinkers were too busy making money to bother with the underlying principles behind its creation and the political and moral quandaries it posed. The Royal Society for Improvement of Natural Knowledge continued to promote debate and studies, but no great scientist emerged during that era. Likewise, the theater lived off the brilliant play-wrights of earlier eras. England's tranquil intellectual waters were stirred by the emergence of the English novel as an art form, with the bawdy satires of Henry Fielding's *Joseph Andrews* (1742) and *Tom Jones* (1739), Tobias Smollet's "adventures" of *Roderick Random* (1748) and *Peregrin Pickle* (1751), and the sentimental moralism of Samuel Richardson's *Pamela* (1740) and *Clarisa* (1747). William Hogarth dominated painting as thoroughly as Hume did political philosophy, offering scathing social commentaries through his "Harlot's Progress," "Marriage a la Mode," and "Rake's Progress" series. The press, meanwhile, churned out thousands of books, pamphlets, newspapers, and journals to satisfy the tastes of an increasingly literate public.

As in France, few of Britain's intellectual or political elite thought much about their empire across the Atlantic. Unlike that of France, Britain's North American empire boosted rather than drained the home economy. By the 1750s, thirteen separate colonies stretched along the Atlantic Coast of Britain's North American empire. They differed markedly in population size, political system, and economic vitality. A 1755 compilation found that Nova Scotia had 4,000 inhabitants, New Hampshire 25,000, Massachusetts 200,000, Rhode Island 30,000, Connecticut 100,000, New York 55,000, New Jersey 75,000, Pennsylvania 220,000, Maryland 100,000, Virginia 125,000, North Carolina 56,000, South Carolina 25,000, and Georgia 3,000. But each of these colonies enhanced England's wealth and power.[27]

The importance of the American colonies to English prosperity was nicely captured by a 1756 letter from the prominent London merchant, John Thomlinson, to Lord Granville: "As our Foreign Trade is certainly the Source of all our Wealth, and consequently our Strength, Then our American Collonies and plantations must absolutely be of the utmost conciquence to the defense, wellfare, & happiness of These Kingdomes, As the Trade with Those collonies & plantations are of greater advantage to us than all other Foreign Trades we are in possession of, as this very Trade brings in a far greater Ballance to the increase of our National Stock, Than all our other Foreign Trades put together; And also Employs More Shipping, breedes & Employs more Seamen, More Artificers Manufactureres, &c than all the Rest . . . this Trade must still continue soley our Own; And this our most daingerous Rivalls in Trade, and most implacable Enemies the French . . . are makeing every effort . . . to wrest this inestimable Fountain of wealth & strength out of our hands, and should they ever succeed, how must we then be distresse'd to keep up our Fleets & Armys in so repectable a manner as we have hitherto done."[28]

Mercantilism dominated Britain's imperial and trade policies as it did in all other European powers. As early as 1549, the author of *A Discourse of the Commonweal of This Realm of England* captured mercantilism's essence when he wrote: "We must always take heed that we buy no more of strangers than we do sell them; for so we should impoverish ourselves and enrich them."[29] To this end, Parliament regulated colonial trade in three ways, by requiring all trade to be carried in English or American ships, by enumerating goods that could be exported only to Britain, and by listing goods that could not be exported directly from one colony to another.

The Crown's first mercantilist act occurred as early as 1621 when it ordered Virginia to export its tobacco only to English ports. Starting with the first Navigation Act in 1651, Parliament regulated American colonial trade by imposing 80 laws through 1750. Whitehall added ever more "enumerated" goods to a list that had to be conveyed by British or American ships via English ports. These "enumerated" goods included molasses, copper ore, tar, lumber, sugar, hemp, iron ore, rice, cotton, tobacco, and pitch. Any goods not on the list could be traded directly with foreign countries but still had to be shipped in American or British ships. The 1663 Staple Act was the first of a half dozen that required all goods sent to or from the colonies to be shipped in English or American ships. The law was a boon to the British Empire's shipping interests but kept prices high for consumers. Under a 1696 Navigation law, vice-admiralty courts were established in the colonies to enforce the restrictions and collect duties. The 1699 Woolens Act forbade the export of wool yarn or products from one colony to another. The law was designed to protect English woolen manufacturers from any colonial production other than at the household craft level. The 1732 Hat Act and 1750 Iron Act were similar attempts by Parliament simultaneously to boost English manufacturing of those two industries while repressing any American enterprises. The Iron Act not only forbade Americans to export any iron or steel production to other colonies, but outlawed any mills for slitting and rolling iron or forges for plating or making steel.[30]

Britain's mercantilist policies were "a patchwork of restrictive laws conceived in a spirit of arrogance and administered with an inefficiency that invited evasion."[31] Nonetheless, formidable as those laws seemed on paper, Whitehall supervised rather than ruled its empire. To administer those colonies, the king appointed governors, customs clerks, and admiralty judges. Those officials presided over what had long been mostly self-governing colonies. The navigation acts would have crippled colonial commerce had they been strictly enforced; in practice, officials turned a blind eye to them. Merchants artfully dodged the laws; smuggling was rampant. Likewise, entrepreneurs found ways around some manufacturing restrictions. The colonies were encouraged to produce pig and bar iron to be refined by English mills and forges. By 1775, the American colonies accounted for one-seventh of global pig iron production. A rough balance of payments may have actually existed between Britain and the American colonies by the mid-18th century, as America's merchandise trade deficit was offset by exports of raw and semi-finished goods, and ships, besides British payments for officials, troops, and reimbursements for colonial defense expenditures. British spending in the colonies peaked from 1756 through 1763 when the Treasury dispensed 7,984,000 pounds, of which the army accounted for 5,489,000 pounds, the navy 966,000 pounds, colonial reimbursements 1,078,000 pounds, colonial administration 261,000 pounds, the Ordnance Board 160,000, and other expenditures 30,000 pounds. This financial inflow exceeded America's 7,287,000-pound trade deficit for those years. After the war, the thirteen American colonies reverted to a severe balance-of-payments deficit.[32]

The English aversion to large standing armies extended across the Atlantic where only a few scattered, understrength regular companies were posted. Colonists were responsible for their own defense. The idea that the king needed to quarter a large army in the colonies to squash an American rebellion was unthinkable. Although some worried about swelling American identity, lack of cooperation, and grievances, they assumed that the perpetual French threat would constrain it.

Despite superficial differences among them, to varying extents each colony's government was rooted in democratic principles, practices, and institutions. The American colonies were founded and developed during the Enlightenment or Age of Reason when European political philosophers propounded concepts of political and economic liberty justified by natural law. Any exploration of natural law revealed self-evident truths, or "Common Sense" as Thomas Paine would call them. Among these truths were the inalienable rights of life, liberty, and property identified by John Locke. To be morally legitimate, governments had to reflect and protect such essential rights and truths. In the American colonies, far from the greedy powers of England's Crown and aristocracy, these values and their institutions became ever more deeply rooted.

Some English and Americans alike feared that in the colonies, liberty dissolved all too easily into anarchy. New York Council member Cadwallader Colden complained that "the Inhabitants of the Northern Colonies are all so nearly on a level . . . [of] licentiousness, under the notion of liberty . . . that they are impatient under all kind of superiority and authority. . . . The Merchants in America are so accustomed to despise all Laws of Trade . . . the People of America are fond of elective Officers. . . . I think the success in Government depends more on the choice which His Majesty's Ministers make of the Persons to govern us, than on anything else."[33]

Others complained that the reverse was true, that Parliament and local elites were eroding American liberties. Theoretically, governments are supposed to develop from depotisms into liberal democracies. Among some American colonies the opposite happened—initial political tolerance and rights gave way to increased restrictions. One by one all the colonial assemblies eventually imposed property requirements for voters and legalized slavery. In Virginia, for example, the assembly approved a property qualification in 1670; in 1699, the standard was raised so that only freeholders of 25 or more acres could vote.

An American colony was ruled by one of three types of arrangements—charter, proprietor, or royal. Six of the first nine American colonies were founded by joint stock companies chartered by the Crown. During the late 17th century, however, the Crown revoked most of the charters after decades of misrule and bankruptcy by the private companies, and asserted direct or royal rule. Other colonies like Maryland, New York, New Jersey, the Carolinas, and Pennsylvania started as proprietorships or personal fiefdoms granted by the king. Proprietors proved to be just as corrupt and inefficient as companies in administering colonies. By the 1750s, the king had ended most proprietorships and ruled directly, leaving only two extant. Thomas and Richard Penn enjoyed a joint proprietorship over Pennsylvania and the Lower Countries on the Delaware, while the Calvert family still owned Maryland. When the war broke out, the king ruled eight of the thirteen colonies.[34]

Each colony had a governor and an assembly. Although the Crown or proprietors appointed most governors, the citizens of Connecticut and Rhode Island elected their own. Many of the colonies' governors were really lieutenant-governors. The actual governors remained at their vast estates in England to enjoy the title as royal sinecures. Regardless of whether a governor or lieutenant-governor sat in the colonial mansion, like the king, he theoretically enjoyed an array of powers. A governor could command the colony's land and sea forces, pardon criminals, administer the law, convene and dismiss the assembly and veto its laws, appoint judges to civil and criminal courts, name the members of his executive council, and issue legally binding proclamations. In reality, the assembly used its "power of the purse" to inhibit a governor's ambitions as thoroughly as the Parliament did that of the king. Unlike the king, governors were beholden to a higher power—the Privy Council—which issued secret policy instructions that the governor struggled to push through the assembly, and named and dismissed governors at will.

What today's laws would condemn as a conflict of public and private interests would in those days be considered a most fortunate convergence of interests—at least for those involved. The governors and officials dispatched by the Crown to the American colonies unashamedly used their positions to enrich themselves by padding their salaries with all sorts of "fees," tempered only by vague, unspoken limits of appearance and amount. Of secondary importance was fulfilling the Crown's policies. To London's entreaties to do so, the governors would simply cite the intransigence of the colonial assemblies.

The assemblies varied considerably in structure, law-making powers, and the qualifications to vote and run for office. Only Pennsylvania had a unicameral legislature; all others had a popularly elected lower house and appointed upper house. In most colonies, laws passed by assemblies and governors had to be approved by the Parliament and king. Rhode Island, Connecticut, and Maryland alone did not have to submit their laws for parliamentary scrutiny. Maryland's charter was unique in freeing it from taxation by Parliament.

No colonial governor escaped a tug-of-war with his assembly over power, perks, policy, and prestige. All the colonial assemblies fiercely defended their accumulated rights. With their miserliness and sensitivity to an intrusion on their prerogatives, the colonial assemblies frustrated their governors. American independence, or at least aversion to taxation, was already well established by 1754. Time after time, to the outrage of the governors and London alike, the colonial assemblies voted down appropriations to supply their own forces in the field. Any governor would have echoed Nova Scotia governor Charles Lawrence's bitter complaints: "the business of calling an Assembly. The present Posture & Situation of Our Provincial Affairs, the uncertain Event of the Differences between Us and our treacherous neighbors, with a thousand other untoward Circumstances render in my Opinion all Proposals and Projects for an Assembly at this critical Conjuncture chimerical. . . . For I know nothing so likely to obstruct and disconnect all Measures for the public Good, as the foolish Squabbles that are attendant upon Elections & the Multitude by Persons Qualified in their own Imaginations only, as able Politicians."[35]

North America proved to be as much a political graveyard for governors as for generals. The strain of constantly fighting on three fronts—with the provincial assembly, Whitehall, and the French and Indians—eventually crushed most governors. Some were dismissed, like Massachusetts governor William Shirley in April 1757. Others, exhausted, resigned, like Virginia's acting governor Robert Dinwiddie in January 1758. Nearly all were embittered by the experience.

Two other institutions shaped colonial government. Executive councils enjoyed executive, legislative, and judicial duties by serving as advisory bodies to the governor who appointed its half dozen members, reviewing bills, and acting as the colony's highest court of appeals. District courts had considerable power not only to judge alleged civil or criminal cases but shared with town meetings such duties as regulating the economy; raising taxes; maintaining roads, ports, and bridges; and overseeing the militia. Courts were particularly important in local government among the southern colonies, whose populations were relatively dispersed and thus could not easily attend town meetings.

Each colony promoted its interests in London through an agent who was given powers similar to those of ambassadors. To curry favorable policies, agents ran the full gauntlet of Britain's political system—Parliament, the Council Cabinet, the Board of Trade, the Privy Council, the Treasury, and even members of the royal family. They spent most of their time with Parliament, defending laws passed by colonial assemblies, pressing Parliament for more money, buttonholing and trying to sway prominent parliamentarians with arguments and the occasional bribe.[36]

The rivalry and jealousy among the colonies themselves was as fierce as that between governor and assembly. Nearly all the colonies held extravagant claims for western land beyond the Appalachian Mountains, some from "sea to sea." Many of these claims overlapped; nearly all were uncharted. War erupted between England and France in 1754 partly because of the competition between Virginian and Pennsylvanian traders for the wealth of the Ohio valley. The Ohio Company's Virginia investors sought and received from the Crown permission to own land in the upper Ohio River valley, already claimed not only by France but by Pennsylvania. In 1750, learning of the Ohio Company's plans, Pennsylvania proprietor Thomas Penn offered 400 pounds of his own money to finance an expedition to get there and build a fort first. Although the assembly rejected his offer, it did appropriate 1,250 pounds in presents for the Indians that year and 1,260 pounds for 1751. Virginia's stake in the upper Ohio valley varied with the very different investment interests of its two succeeding lieutenant-governors as much as anything else: "Gooch was interested primarily in internal development rather than in expansion to the west, either for Virginia or for Britain. He, for instance, had taken stock in an iron mine; Dinwiddie put his faith in the Ohio Company."[37]

Although America's Constitution firmly separates church and state as an essential component of liberal democracy, in the colonial era the two were intricately linked. Religion dominated the lives of most colonial Americans. In those days, freedom of religion did not mean tolerance for all beliefs but the ability of the dominant sect's adherents to impose their beliefs on others in the community and colony. Most sects reflected the pessimism, materialism, pervasion of evil, and harsh judgment of eternal damnation by God emphasized by Calvinism. Laws demanded weekly church attendance. Those absent were fined; in some cases repeat offenders were pilloried, flogged, and, during the early colonial era, even put to death. A church anchored every community. The Bible provided social as well as spiritual guidance; the sermon was the most common form of public address. Most political leaders helped guide their churches as well; two of every three men who signed the Declaration of Independence were vestrymen.[38]

The Society of Friends, or Quakerism, was the odd religion in the American colonies. The Quakers believed in equality, human goodness, informality, and toleration—values endorsed by most Americans today but condemned as subversive and irreverent by most colonists then. Quaker William Penn's 1682 Frame of Government for the colony he received from Charles II the previous year tolerated the practice of different religions. Of the thirteen colonies, only Pennsylvania allowed Catholics to publicly celebrate mass. In 1734, the assembly rejected a demand by Governor Thomas Penn that Catholics be denied that right.[39]

In one area the Quakers were notoriously intolerant—they refused to swear allegiance to any power other than God. Their refusal to take an oath to a court, army, government, or even the king provoked their persecution in England and subsequent flight to America. Since their beliefs prevented them from swearing allegiance to the king, the Quaker-dominated assembly continually elected as their deputy-governor non-Quakers who could take such an oath. Quaker pacifism continually frustrated the efforts of other colonies to fight the French and Indians. The assembly continally voted down attempts by Pennsylvania's deputy-governor to appropriate money to wage war against the Crown's enemies.

Church and education were as thoroughly entwined as church and state. The three earliest colleges, Harvard (1636), William and Mary (1693), and Yale (1701), were all chartered as schools for the dominant religious sect in those colonies. Presbyterians founded Princeton (1746), Baptists Brown (1765), Indian missionaries Dartmouth (1769), and Anglicans and Presbyterians the College of Philadelphia (University of Pennsylvania, 1753) and King's College (Columbia, 1756). Despite their religious orgins, at each of those colleges, scholarship escaped dogma. Those schools produced many of America's revolutionary leaders. William and Mary alone would eventually educate sixteen members of the Continental Congress, four signers of the Declaration of Independence, and four presidents. Then, as now, law was the great road to take for political advancement, and thus the most popular course of study at college. Lawyers would number 25 of the 56 signers of the Declaration of Independence and 31 of the 51 delegates to the Constitutional Convention.

If genuine freedom of religion was wanting in most colonies, Americans had made greater progress toward freedom of the press. The first American printing press was set up in Cambridge as early as 1639. By the French and Indian War's end, all the major cities and every colony had a newspaper, and there were over 60 printing presses throughout the colonies. In addition to newspapers, from 1639 through 1763 those presses produced over 10,808 almanacs, pamphlets, magazines, and books. Some of these were best-sellers, including 141,257 copies of Benjamin Franklin's *Poor Richard's Almanack* between 1752 and 1765. Those press owners were largely free to print what they willed. In 1735, freedom of the press was the subject of the landmark case of John Peter Zenger, who was acquitted of a politically motivated seditious libel charge. The decision dampened subsequent urges to sue on that charge.[40]

America's world of high culture was not confined to political tracts. An increasingly vigorous intellectual and cultural life was stirring in the American colonies. Early on, writers grappled with the New World's history, starting with John Smith's *General Historie of Virginia, New England, and the Summer Isles* (1624), and extending through Increase Mather's *A Breife History of the Warr with the Indians in New England* (1676), Thomas Prince's *Chronological History of New England* (1726), Cadwallader Colden's *History of the Five Indian Nations* (1726), and William Byrd's *History of the Dividing Line* (1728). Other writers targeted more select aspects of history, such as Roger Williams' linguistic work, *A Key into the Language of America* (1643), or John Williams' captivity narrative, *The Redeemed Captive Returning Unto Zion* (1707). That American genre, the discovery and development of oneself, emerged during the colonial era, best exemplified by Jonathan Edwards' spiritual journey in his *Personal Narrative* (1745) and Benjamin Franklin's transformation into a Renaissance man in his *Autobiography*, begun in 1771. Religion colored many early histories such as William Bradford's *Of Plimouth Plantation*, (1630–51), Cotton Mather's *Magnalia Christi Americana* (1702), and George Alsop's *New England Rarities* (1672). The American colonies produced a wealth of theological works, of which the more prominent were Thomas Hooker's *The Application of Redemption* (1656), Jonathan Mayhew's *Two Sermons on the Nature, Extent, and Perfection of Divine Goodness* (1750), Jonathan Edwards' *Sinners in the Hands of an Angry God* (1741), and his masterly *History of the Work of Redemption* (1774). Among the early American contributions to physics were Cadwallader Colden's *First Causes of Action* (1746) and *Principles of Action in Matter* (1751). Lewis Evans' *Geographical, Philosophical, and Mechanical Essays* (1755–1756) were subjects explored by several learned societies, including Philadelphia's Philosophical Society, founded by Benjamin Franklin in 1743; New York's Society for the Promotion of the Arts, Agriculture, and Oeconomy (1764); and the Virginian Society for the Promotion of Usefull Knowledge (1772). American poets explored a range of subjects, including love, in Anne Bradstreet's "To My Dear and Loving Husband" (1650), spirituality in Edward Taylor's "Meditations" (1682–1725), satire in Ebenezeer Cook's "The Sot-Weed Factor" (1728), and patriotism in "The Glory of America" (1771) jointly composed and read by Philip Freneau and Hugh Henry Breckinridge at their Harvard graduation.

As for the fine arts, some early painters like Augustine Clement, Joseph Allen, Gustavus Hesselius, Charles Bridges, John Smibert, and John Wollston migrated to America and then began or enhanced their careers. Others like American-born John Singleton Copley or Benjamin West interrupted early careers in the colonies to become expatriot painters in London. Charles Wilson Peale was the most skilled of those who spent their entire lives painting in America. Early American music included such compositions as James Alexander's "Ballads" (1734), James Lyon's "Urania" (1761), and William Billings' "The New England Psalm-Singer" (1770). Other flourishing arts included silversmithing, furniture making, mezzotints, engraving, gravestone carving, clockmaking, and gunmaking. Dancing, theater, and concerts were popular in most towns but distinct American versions had not yet been developed. American high culture budded during the colonial era; it would blossom following the Revolution.[41]

Each colony allowed ever-greater freedom to own enterprises and property.[42] As in New France, land and other property in the colonies were once collectively owned by the founding companies. That communalism did not last long. For a decade following Jamestown's founding in 1607, the Virginia Company owned all property and tried to care for its employees. The results were problems familiar to communalism—low productivity, high costs, and inefficiency. In 1619, the Virginia Company finally abandoned the unworkable system and distributed its land to willing workers, thus embarking the colony on sustained economic expansion. Tenants scratching out subsistence became farmers with incentives to improve their lives with hard work, innovation, and the development of markets. To varying degrees, other colonies experienced a similar shift from collective to private land ownership patterns.

No colony was founded on higher ideals than Georgia. James Oglethorpe and 21 other trustees listed in Georgia's 1732 charter were all philanthropists determined to create an ideal society based on charity, hard work, community-owned land, and redemption of the fallen. Private ownership of land or slaves was outlawed as morally debilitating. Since the trustees paid for all Georgia's expenses, there was no taxation, and thus no need for a representative assembly. These ideals and institutions were eventually abandoned as unworkable, as human weaknesses like corruption, incompetence, jealousy, and laziness, to name a few, proved stronger than lofty ideals. By 1750, the trustees had grudgingly allowed for the private ownership of land and human beings.[43]

Each colony's wealth derived from its own unique mix of sources, but agriculture was the foundation.[44] At first, the settlers failed to produce enough crops to feed themselves, let alone harvest a surplus for export. Colonial agriculture eventually flourished only after farmers meshed Indian crops, land clearing, planting, and harvesting techniques with those they brought from Europe. Farmers usually planted half their fields with Indian corn and the other half with European crops. Farmers lived off the hardy Indian corn while supplementing their diets and incomes from other crops.

The seemingly endless amount of land prompted farmers to be careless with its use. Mid-18th-century essayist Jared Eliot succinctly captured the mentality of most farmers: "when our fore-fathers settled here, they entered a land which probably never had been Ploughed since the Creation; the Land being new they depended upon the natural Fertility of the Ground,—which served their purpose very well, and when they had worn out one piece they cleared another, without any concern to amend their Land, except a little helped by the Fold and Cart-dung. . . . Seduced by the fertility of the soil on first settling, the farmers think only of exhausting it as soon as possible, without attending to their own interest in a future day: this is a degree of blindness which in sensible people one may fairly call astonishing."[45] George Washington himself remarked that "the aim of farmers in this country, if they can be called farmers, is not to make the most they can from the land, which is, or which has been, cheap, but the most of the labour, which is dear; the consequence of which has been, much ground has been scratched over and none cultivated or improved as it ought to have been."[46] The exhaustion of eastern soils coupled with a population ever swelling from the birthrate and immigration was the greatest spur for Americans to head westward.

The fur trade was a mainstay of the early colonial economies. However, its importance steadily diminished as adjacent forests were trapped and hunted out and colonial economies diversified. Regions differed in the furs they produced, with beaver pelts dominating the north and deerskins the south.[47]

Although Parliament severely restricted the manufacture of most finished goods in the American colonies, it did encourage the manufacture of some goods destined for the British navy or shipping like hemp, masts, yards, turpentine, pitch, tar, bowsprits, and entire ships. Shipbuilding was the industrial bulwark for many ports in the northern colonies. Artisans made a vast range of products for domestic consumption including glass, guns, furniture, barrels, textiles, and so on.[48]

Forced to buy so many English goods, the colonies suffered annual trade deficits with England. The effects of trade varied considerably from one colony to the next. Southern ports like Charlestown, Wilmington, Norfolk, Fredericksburg, and Alexandria tended to be simply transshipment points while northern ports like Baltimore, Philadelphia, New York, Newport, and Boston had more diversified economies that included insurance, shipbuilding, rope walks, fishing, and other businesses. As such, northern ports had far larger populations than southern ports. Regardless of the port, perhaps as much as 75 percent of trade was carried in American rather than English ships.[49]

Americans, like Canadians, evaded mercantilist restrictions with smuggling. In addition to smuggling with Canada via the Oswego, Lake Champlain, and Nova Scotia routes, American merchants also conducted an extensive and highly profitable trade with the West Indies. To create a false paper trail, goods often were transshipped at Dutch islands like St. Eustatius and Curacao, Denmark's St. Thomas, or the port of Monte Cristi in Spain's Hispaniola. In late 1758, Madrid announced "free port" status for Monte Cristi, which was just across the bay from the French Haitian ports of Port Dauphin and Cap Francois. From then until the war's end, hundreds of American merchant ships dropped anchor in Monte Cristi. Lord Loudoun complained to Whitehall in 1757 that "the Truth is no Rule or Law has any force in this Country, and all of them . . . carry'd on a Trade with the Enemy the whole time. They take Clearances to the British Islands and give Security; they trade notwithstanding with the Dutch and Spanish at Hispaniola: they go to St. Christo, make a sham Sale of their Ships and Cargo to the Spaniards, put Spanish Crews on board who carry the Ship to St. Francis, at the Cape sells the cargo to the French, loads with Sugar and Molasses, brings her back to the Owners who come directly home with her again . . . the French will be supplied with everything they want in spite of all the Regulations."[50]

Despite all the economic diversity, barter rather than coin underwrote most American transactions. England's currency had three units: the pound sterling worth 20 shillings, and the shilling worth 12 pence. Few of these coins circulated in the colonies. The reason for the shortage was simple— Parliament refused to allow any colonial mint to open and limited the amount of coin reaching the colonies to money spent on military procurement. As a result, the most common coin in the colonies was not the English shilling but the Spanish piece of eight or *real*, earned by American merchants selling their products to Spain and its colonies. Through trade, a variety of other currencies circulated in lesser amounts, including those of France, Holland, and Portugal. Whitehall thoroughly approved of such sales, which enriched the empire with foreign coin. Parliament's laws of 1704 and 1708 tried to set the exchange rate of one Spanish *real* to six English shillings. Colonists tended to ignore the official exchange rate and use black market rates.

Private bills of exchange and promissory notes filled the official currency void. Warehouse certificates for commodities, especially tobacco, were popular. Governors and assemblies would approve a loan to an investor secured on his land and distributed by the province's "land bank." Generally, an investor could borrow up to one-half his land's value. This was not enough to supply the demand for currency. Eventually, all the colonial governments issued paper money unbacked by specie to pay for their transactions. Most colonies carefully restricted their paper money supply and eventually bought back old issues with taxes to avoid sparking inflation. During the 1720s, however, the four New England provinces and South Carolina flooded the economy with paper money. Parliament responded in 1731 by freezing all issues. Although the New England colonies briefly reined in their issues, eventually they were once again recklessly printing paper money. In 1751, Parliament passed the Currency Act forbidding any new issues until the old debts were paid off.[51]

Americans largely enjoyed longer, easier, and more prosperous lives than their counterparts in the motherland. Whether skilled or unskilled, colonial labor was scarce and thus fetched wages from 30 to 100 percent higher than in England. The population soared from 38,000 whites and 1,200 blacks in 1650 to 412,000 whites and 60,000 blacks in 1720, to 1,674,800 whites and 456,900 blacks in 1770. Overall, in today's dollars, per capita income may have grown from $677 in 1650 to $964 in 1720, or 0.3 percent annually, and to $1,264 by 1774 or 0.4 percent annually. The war boosted the economies of supply centers like Boston, New York, Philadelphia, Albany, Charleston and scores of frontier towns on campaign and supply routes. Class differences were more blurred in the American colonies than probably anywhere else in the world. The freedom to start a business and own land allowed an unprecedented amount of socioeconomic mobility. The greater prosperity allowed people to marry somewhat earlier than in England—from 20 to 23 years of age for women and 24 to 26 for men in the American colonies, compared to around 25 for women and 26 to 28 for men in the mother country. With an earlier start and healthier surroundings, American families tended to have more children than English families, six or seven compared to around five.[52]

These differences were recognized by British subjects on both sides of the Atlantic and prompted a continual migration westward across the ocean. Why did people emigrate to the colonies? The exact reasons, of course, varied from one individual to the next. But opportunities to own land, practice a trade, freely worship with one's sect, or join relatives already over there were among the most common reasons. A poll of 2,532 people and their dependents, none of whom were indentured servants, conducted by the British Register of Emigration from 1773 to 1776, found that most were "seeking to better themselves, or planning to 'plant' themselves on American soil, or hoping to establish a 'settlement' for their families there, or expecting to join relatives with whom they had been in communication, or assuming that they would be able to engage abroad in crafts and trades for which they had been trained."[53] These hopes would have differed little from those who preceded them for a century and a half.

Those were the "pull" reasons. Many were "pushed" from the British Isles and elsewhere by bankruptcy, the loss of their land, crimes they had committed, deportation, rising prices, stagnant wages, grinding poverty, religious persecution, and primogeniture. Overpopulation threatened to worsen the already dismal lives of most of His Majesty's subjects. The "enclosure movement," whereby landowners converted crop fields to sheep grazing lands to capitalize on the textile industry's expansion, displaced hundreds of thousands of peasants. The English law mandating primogeniture or the inheritance of all property by the oldest son forced younger brothers to survive through enterprise. Improved farm techniques at once raised productivity and made redundant hundreds of thousands of other peasants.[54]

The American colonies were a refuge from all of this. Sermons, pamphlets, and company recruiting offices helped sway potential colonists. Some migrants could afford their own passage and living expenses while they established themselves in America. Most arrived as indentured servants, their passage paid by masters for whom they would work for as long as the next seven years.[55]

Nonetheless, socioeconomic differences split the American colonies into north and south, piedmont and tidewater, established and frontier settlements, and among the slave, poor, middle, and upper classes. Most colonists accepted these differences. The fiery Massachusetts minister John Winthrop succinctly expressed this belief that class differences were not only natural but just, when he declared: "God Almightie in his most holy and wise providence, hath soe disposed of the Condition of Mankinde, as in all times some must be rich, some poore, some highe and eminent in power and dignitie; others meane and in subjection."[56]

Of all those class differences, no greater chasm existed than that between slaves and the rest of the population. The first slaves may have arrived in the American colonies as early as 1619 in Virginia. Throughout the 17th century slaves gradually supplanted indentured servants as a cheap labor source. Slave prices dropped steadily as the trade between Africa and the colonies expanded, thus increasing the ready supply while the wages for white labor rose. By 1660, the colonies began enacting laws regulating slavery. Although slavery existed in every colony, slaves were far more common in the south with its large tobacco, rice, and indigo plantations and unhealthy summer climate. By 1750, there were over 240,000 people of African origin in the American colonies, about 95 percent of whom were slaves.[57]

Political and economic differences aside, a range of common characteristics and interests bound the Americans, the most important of which was a rising sense of nationalism. An American identity evolved early among the colonists, nurtured by the vast ocean that separated them from their mother country, the development of their own institutions, customs, and history, and the open disdain that most English held for them. Most Americans identified strongly with the ideals of John Winthrop's "The City on the Hill" sermon, which compared the church-dominated towns and farm communities carved from America's wilderness as spiritual beacons to oppressed peoples everywhere. They continually cited their "rights as Englishmen" to protest heavy-handed treatment by Parliament or the Crown. By the 1750s, most Americans had turned their backs on the corrupt, effete old world of Europe to embrace a new world of spiritual, economic, and political freedom. They had become Americans.

THE INDIANS

To varying degrees, all of the tribes scattered across the eastern half of the continent were dragged into the century-and-a-half rivalry between the French and British for the mastery over North America. That rivalry provoked tremendous shifts in the distribution of power, culture, and population among the tribes. Disease and war wiped out numerous tribes like the Susquehannock, Powhatan, and Mohican, to name a few. The remnants of some defeated tribes that fled and over time partially transformed their identity, like the Huron into the Wyandot. Other tribal fragments were absorbed into the victorious tribes like the Iroquois. In Canada, some tribes like the Potawatomi, Huron, or Chippewa clustered around French missions and trading posts. In the English colonies, tribes like the Shawnee and Delaware fled before the advance of white settlers. Bands split from tribes to form an autonomous tribe of their own, like the Mingo from the Iroquois. Tribes whose villages had once lived as neighbors became increasingly distant, as did the Delaware who had migrated either to the upper Delaware, upper Ohio, or upper Susquehanna valleys.

Ironically, the survival of the first European settlers to arrive in North America depended on the skills and generosity of neighboring Indians. Over time that dependence was reversed. But the degree of that reversal differed greatly between English and French colonists. The Indian dependence on the English deepened as the American economies became increasingly diversified and the fur trade diminished in relative importance. New France never achieved the economic diversity and dynamism of the English colonies. Instead, New France and the tribes under its influence shifted from French dependence on the Indians to mutual dependence.

Daniel Richter identifies four traumatic phases in the relations between Indians and Europeans, each of which further weakened the surviving natives: "first came massive depopulation from imported diseases; next, a slide into economic dependence on trade with Europeans; then ensnarement in the imperial struggles of powerful French and English colonial neighbors; finally, direct incursions on . . . territory and sovereignty."[58] Ever since Columbus' ships first reached the Caribbean in 1492, diseases caused the most devastating impact. Epidemics swept across regions of the western hemisphere sometimes a generation or two before the first traders or conquerors arrived.[59]

But other effects of European imperialism could be just as traumatic. Whether the French or English outright conquered or simply "crowded" the Indians, they presented each tribe with a terrible and barely understood dilemma. To survive, the Indians had to assimilate not only European technological but also intellectual and even spiritual ways. Europeans transformed Indians from the stone age into the iron age. European goods were passed from tribe to tribe across continents long before the recipients saw their first European. The deepening dependence on European goods destroyed traditional crafts like pottery, basketry, pipes, bows and arrows, and longhouses, to be replaced by muskets, metal pots, knives, hatchets, glass beads, and log cabins. Cattle, sheep, pigs, and chickens grazed or rooted around villages. These adaptations raised living standards at a terrible cost.

Technologies and culture are tightly interwoven. The more foreign goods the tribes took, the more they lost their traditional cultures and became dependent on European values. The result was the eventual assimilation of the Indians into appendages of today's American and Canadian cultures. Thomas Pownall observed that after decades of being cheated by Europeans the Iroquois "are no longer that plain simple People they were once, but are become wily and covetous and encrease in Jealousy and suspicion as they encrease in Guile and Avarice."[60]

The British and French sought deerskins in the south and furs, especially beaver pelts, in the north. Deerskins were used as cheap and thin leather for European clothes. Beaver pelts were valued for European hats because the inner hairs used for felt had tiny barbs that matted together and shed far less easily than other fur. Beaver skin had two layers of fur, one long and the other short. Processing a pelt required removing the outer fur to get at that fine inner felt. Indian customs aided this process. When Indians wore their beaver robes their body heat and grease wore off that outer hair. Traders especially prized such robes. Beaver trapping occurred during the winter months when pelts were the thickest; trading during the summer months when trails and rivers were easily followed.[61]

If his luck, skill, and courage held, a trader could enrich himself through the beaver trade. In the trade's early days, one could hand an Indian a livre's or pound's worth of goods for pelts that might fetch 200 times that in Paris or London. Values changed over time. The growing demand for beavers destroyed them across the continent while the demand increased in Europe. Indians understood this and charged more for their steadily dwindling supply of pelts.

No trade good was more destructive of Indian life than alcohol. Indians drank to get drunk. Indians considered those drunk to be unresponsible for any mayhem that ensued. The diversion of village wealth into drunken binges tore apart each member's commitment to once sacred socioeconomic duties. Farming, hunting, fishing, elders, and children were neglected. To get drunk and while drunk, Indians might trade away all their property, including their wives and children. Deep resentments might explode in murder and destruction. The Indians "pardon murder committed by drunkards. A drunken man is a sacred person. According to them it is a state so delicious that it is permitted, even desirable, to arrive at; it is their paradise."[62]

The first sight of Indians invariably startled Europeans, and must have taken a long time for most to get used to, if ever. French Captain Pierre Pouchot remarked that "Indians gladly wear rings on all their fingers. Men make up their faces more than women. They can sometimes spend three or four hours on their makeup. It can be said that they are more concerned about it than any affected young woman in France. The care they devote to prettying themselves, or coloring their faces artistically red, black & green with symmetrical patterns that they sometimes change two or three times a day, leaves nothing natural exposed except for their eyes & teeth. . . . Their hair is no wider on their head than a priest's skullcap. It is cut to the length of a finger, swept up in a topknot with grease & powdered with vermillion in the middle. They leave two locks of hair which they enclose in two silver tubes the length of a finger or arrange in a tail with a woggle of porcupine skin. They also stick several birds' feathers in their hair, which forms a kind of crest. When a young man has made war, he cuts away the hair from around his ear & attaches a piece of lead to it in such a way that the weight stretches this cartilage, thus forming an opening in which a rolled gaiter can be placed. They wind around it a brass wire and in the middle they place tufts of feathers or colored hair. These ears come down to their shoulders and flap when they walk. When they travel through the forest, they put a strap around their foreheads to hold in their ears so they are not torn in the brush. They only keep their ears for as long as they are sober for as soon as they fight when they are drunk, they tear them off one another. As a result, there are few men of advanced age who have whole ears. They pierce the tendon of the nose & insert in the hole a small ring with a little silver triangle that dangles over the mouth."[63]

For most Europeans, the Indians looked, acted, and thought the same. Bougainville admits that he sees "no difference in the dress, ornaments, dances, and songs of these different nations. They are naked save for a breechcloth, and painted in black, red, and blue, etc. Their heads are shaved and feathers ornament them. In their lengthened ear [lobes] are rings of brass wire. They have beaver skins for covering, and carry lances, arrows, and quivers made of buffalo skin . . . these Indians are erect, well made, and almost all of great height. They pass the night there singing and dancing."[64]

In reality, the tribes differed greatly in appearance, belief, behavior, and custom. At least some Europeans were sensitive to such nuances. After several years in New France, Pouchot observed that through frequent contact with the Indians one "can, without speaking to them, judge from their features as well as from the way they dress which nation they belong to."[65]

Nonetheless, the superficial similarities outweighed the differences. Across the northeast, Indians fortified their villages with palisades and ditches. Within, the Indians dwelled communally in longhouses composed of bark over bent sapling frames, and sometimes 100 or more feet long. Families crowded around firepits in segments of the longhouse. Privacy was minimal, with sleeping platforms and animal hide partitions along with blinding smoke and perpetual dimness obscuring the inhabitants. Elsewhere, extended families crowded into wigwams of bark over half-dome wooden frames.

Each sex had its own role. Men hunted, fished, and warred; women planted and gathered. Relations between men and women were relaxed. Marriage and divorce were easy and frequent. Sexuality was largely unconstrained despite the close quarters of the longhouse and wigwam. Couples would abstain from sex during menstruation, pregnancy, for days before embarking on a raid, and for a year or more after childbirth. In most tribes, descent was through a mother's lineage. Husbands went to live with their wives; children joined their mother's clan. Thus, a mother's brother rather than her husband might be the more important male influence on children. Children were raised lovingly and permissively. Indian "men & women are deeply attached to their children . . . & keep them clean. . . . Indian women nurse their infants for two or three years & more. . . . It is very rare that they beat their children. . . . Up to the age of thirteen or fourteen, the children have nothing else to do except play."[66]

Tribal governments varied, but few had European-style autocratic leaders. Councils of elder men governed most tribes and reached decisions by consensus. Each tribe was divided into clans, each of which had its own longhouse or houses, and its own guardian elders. Headmen achieved their status through reputations for bravery when young and generosity and wisdom as elders. Sometimes an elder would allow a more eloquent younger warrior to speak on his behalf. Europeans often confused these powerful orators and war leaders with the actual tribal chiefs. Women were allowed to speak in some councils like those of the Iroquois; however, in most tribes they were excluded.

In all, Indians enjoyed far more individual freedom than even the Americans, who continually insisted on their "natural" liberty and rights in disputes with London. The Indians recognize "only voluntary subordination. Each person is free to do as he pleases. The village chiefs and the war chiefs can have influence, but they do not have authority, still their influence over the young men depends on how much they exert it, and upon their attention to keeping the kettles full, so to say."[67] Indian life could be idyllic when food was abundant, peace reigned, and the weather was mild: "All these Indians passed the time while they were held up in bathing and amusing themselves. They swim like fish, diving and remaining underwater a long time."[68]

Notions of private property were hazy. Utensils, food, blankets, pots, and other items frequently changed hands to accommodate needs. Individuals achieved status by giving away rather than accumulating wealth. Elaborate rituals of gift-giving accompanied funerals, marriages, and diplomatic or trading missions. Hospitality demanded that male guests be fed, housed, and sometimes bedded with daughters or even wives.

Fields were communally owned. By planting squash, beans, and corn together, Indians retained the soil's fertility far longer than the single-crop fields of the Europeans. The "three sisters" worked together—bean vines would grow up the cornstalk while the squash vines spread rapidly across the ground to choke off weeds. The legumes took nitrogen from the air. The women also garnered nuts and berries for food; firewood; and reeds and bark for baskets. Villages lasted a couple of decades before the fields lost their fertility and the surrounding forest its firewood. The tribe then abandoned that site for another.

Gifts were the lubricant for Indian relationships.[69] Gifts were given to celebrate a child's naming ceremony, purchase a bride, succor the aggrieved, or polish a "chain of friendship" whether between individuals, families, clans, or nations. Status, wealth, and generosity were closely linked. The wealthier man or group gave more to the poorer than they received. The notion of "Indian giving" among whites came from the Indian practice of giving some token gift and then expecting it or some equivalent to be returned, enhanced with additional goods. When the French or British dispensed gifts, they were expected to vary the amounts and types in relation to the recipients' respective ranks. Muskets, gunpowder, shot, clothing, blankets, mirrors, rings, vermillion, lace, flints, hatchets, knives, gorgets, and, above all, rum or other spirits were common gifts. The French and English alike enhanced their diplomacy by sending a tribe a gunsmith to repair weapons and other metal implements, as well as act as an unofficial hostage.

The nature of warfare changed dramatically after the Europeans arrived. Until then, warfare was ritualized as lines of warriors wearing reed-armor approached each other and exchanged barrages of insults and arrows. Few died in the exchanges. European diseases devastated tribes, thus creating unprecedented needs to fill the places of vacant loved ones with captives and scalps. Trade competition provoked devastating wars over hunting and trapping grounds and trade routes. European weapons gave the Indians unprecedented power to destroy their enemies. Warfare became ever more savage with the enemy's annihilation the goal. French and English bounties for scalps made killing enemies as desirable as taking captives. Some practices continued. Scalping was universally practiced long before and after the Europeans arrived, as were, for many tribes including the Iroquois, variations of both ritual and subsistence cannibalism. When a village decided to send warriors to the French or British the chief would give the ally a bundle of red-dyed sticks to show how many warriors had been committed to the war.[70]

To varying degrees, warfare was an integral part of each tribe's culture. Blood feuds or "mourning wars" provoked most bloodshed. Indians did not endure the deaths of loved ones and neighbors stoically, but immersed themselves in long periods of mourning that could involve self-neglect, laceration, or even mutilation, and attacks on other tribes. When someone died, his or her place and name had to be filled by bringing captives or scalps back from the warpath. Indians sublimated grief and avenged deaths through war, which usually stimulated more grief and the need for vengeance when warriors failed to return or the raid provoked deadly enemy counterattacks. Clans rather than villages initially tended to go to war, but dragged in the entire tribe as enemies retaliated. Thus were tribes trapped in a vicious, never-ending war cycle.[71]

Mourners sought captives, to be tortured to death shortly after their arrival or adopted as family members. Whatever his ultimate fate, upon reaching the village a male captive had to run a gauntlet of club-wielding men, women, and children. Some tribes feasted and honored enemy warriors before tormenting them by the vilest possible means and in some tribes eating in bouts of ritualistic cannibalism. Yet those prisoners who were spared torture often experienced a dazzling change in treatment. Many families would adopt captives, including men, to replace loved ones lost in warfare. After a period of hazing and far longer socialization, the captive gradually became assimilated into the tribe. Most Indians lacked the racism of the Europeans.[72]

In all, the economic rationale for adopting or selling captives usually outweighed the emotional satisfaction of torturing them to death. No trade good was more lucrative or prestigious than slaves. The taking and ransoming of captives prevailed throughout peace and war alike. The French markets for captives far exceeded those in the English colonies. The *New York Mercury* reported, in 1755, that one "cannot make Money half so fast any other Way, as by taking Englishmen, and selling them for Slaves; and the French are very ready to buy them; for when they buy a Man, or Woman for 3 or 400 Livres, they pay in Paper Money or Goods, and they will ask double in Silver; and they make 'em live and work like Negro's, till they pay just what they ask."[73]

Like Europeans, spirituality was as important for Indians as war or commerce. Each tribe had its own creation myths and believed in some sort of "Master of Life" or "Great Spirit" that presided over countless spirits of the earth, rocks, waters, winds, and animals. All living and nonliving things had their own spiritual power. Humans tapped into that spiritual power through reverence and rituals, either directly by addressing its holder or indirectly by fulfilling the ethical duties of caring for one's neighbors. Dreams were the most common means of communicating with the spirit world, followed by tobacco-smoking rituals with effigy head pipes.

Everyone had his own guardian spirit that, if honored, could guide and protect him through life. Through various devotions, Indians communed with both the Master of Life and their guardian spirit. Guardian spirits were usually revealed through a vision quest of prolonged fasting, prayer, and solitude. Bougainville described the native religions as "crude paganism and still in its infancy. Each makes a god of the object that strikes his [fancy], the sun, the moon, the stars, a snake, a moose, in fact all visible beings, animate or inanimate. They have, however, a way of determining the object of their worship. They fast for two or three days. After this preparation, calculated to make them dream, the first thing which in their sleep presents itself to their excited imagination becomes the god to which they devote the rest of their days. It is their "Manitou." They invoke it for their fishing, hunting, and war. It is to it that they sacrifice."[74]

Shamans not only aided the spiritual devotions of the individual or village, but also served as doctors and psychologists by curing diseases, interpreting dreams, demanding sacrifices to quell animosities from humans or spirits, and leading religious rituals. Even a condescending European like Bougainville could be awed by the spiritual power evoked by the shamans: "the old men who remained here yesterday made medicine to learn the news of their brothers. The hut shook, the medicine men sweated drops of blood, and at last the devil came and told them that their brothers would return shortly with scalps and prisoners. A medicine man in the medicine house is just like the priestess of Delphi . . . evoking the shades."[75]

Dreams were perhaps the most common path to the spirit world. While today's psychologists use dreams to understand a patient's past and present, shamans interpreted dreams to reveal the future of not just the dreamer but sometimes the whole village. A bad dream could keep a warrior at home or break up an entire war party.

Indians believed in the Master of Life and Heaven, but did not originally believe in the Devil or Hell. As Bougainville himself admits, the notion of a Devil was a European intrusion into native beliefs: "The belief in two spirits, one good, the other bad, the one inhabiting the heavens, the other the bowels of the earth, now established among them, goes back only to the time they commenced trade with the Europeans. Originally, they recognized only 'Manitou.' Besides they say that the Master of Life who created them was brown and beardless, while he who made the Frenchmen was white and bearded." They had more difficultly believing "in punishments and rewards after death, only a state like that of life, a more happy one nevertheless, for they think that the dead live in villages situated beyond the setting sun, where they have vermillion and tobacco in abundance."[76] The dead were buried with their personal effects so that they could arrive at that blissful village fully prepared.

Mission Indians meshed their traditional beliefs with Christianity. At the Lake of the Two Mountains mission, 20 miles up the St. Lawrence from Montreal, "Indians of three different nations live there, Nipissings, Algonkins, and Iroquois. They have three separate groups of houses, although all united in the same village. They have a common church, which is attractive and properly ornamented. Two Sulpician missionaries are in charge, one for the Nipissings and the Algonkins, the other for the Iroquois. The Indians go to pray in the church three times a day, each in his own tongue, and they attend with exemplary devotion. They serve as choir boys and chanters. The men sit on one side and the women on the other, and the choir formed by the latter is very melodious. The cabins are well enough built but very filthy. There is a special council house for each nation and a large one, which must be three hundred feet long, for the general councils of the three nations."[77]

By the 1750s, a century and a half of trade and war with the Europeans had eroded or destroyed many Indian traditions. The closer a tribe was to the European settlements, the greater the changes. Single-family cabins had largely replaced multi-family longhouses. Palisaded villages gave way to dispersed clusters of hamlets. Epidemics and wars had ravaged tribal populations, spirit, and unity. Increasing numbers of men worked for daily wages for the whites as scouts, porters, and hunters. Indians discarded the belief that the land was sacred and owned by all; now they eagerly sold out parcels to white governments and settlers. The rivalry between French and English merchants, and Catholic and Protestant missionaries for Indian hearts, minds, weapons, and wealth inevitably splintered every tribe into bitterly opposed factions.

Nonetheless, the tribes differed greatly in their relative power, allies, enemies, and customs. Indians east of the Mississippi spoke dialects of one of four language groups—Algonquian, Iroquoian, Siouan, and Muskogean. Algonquian was the most widely spoken language, followed by Iroquoian, Muskogean, and Siouan. As in other regions around the world, a common language did not guarantee common sentiments or interests. The Iroquois, for example, during the 17th century, warred against nearly all surrounding and even distant tribes regardless of how much or little they shared linguistically.

As with any nation anywhere on earth, a tribe's relative power depended on many things—its population compared to that of its enemies, the proximity of both Indian and European enemies and allies, the quality of its morale, cohesion, and leadership, the availability of guns, and the abundance of wealth and food. Despite their steady decline, most tribes retained some measures of power. The most important was the ability to play off the French and English against each other.

The Five and later Six Nations of the Iroquois League or Longhouse were by far the most powerful tribal group and most important in shaping the rivalry between the English and French for a century and a half.[78] Iroquois power rested as much on their location as on their unity. Stretching westward from the French to the northeast and the Dutch and later the English from the southeast, the Iroquois empire was at once close enough to the rival European powers to play them off against each other and far enough away to evade conquest for over two centuries. The Iroquois made the most of their access to and refuge from the slowly expanding French and British Empires. Iroquois war parties were but days from attacking trade routes snaking through Lake Ontario to the north, the upper Susquehanna River to the south, and the Hudson River to the east.

Iroquois power diminished steadily over time. Disease, war, and cultural assimilation eliminated the tribal buffers between the Iroquois and the Europeans. English pioneers carved farms and villages from the wilderness up the Mohawk valley, the Iroquois Longhouse's eastern end. Epidemics, military defeats, and enculturation eroded Iroquois fighting strength and spirit. Each tribe, along with the entire confederacy, split among pro-French, pro-British, and neutral factions.

By the 1750s, although the Iroquois retained considerable fighting and political strength, their power was sharply diminished from a century earlier. Although populations depleted by war and pestilence had contributed to Iroquois decline, economics played a more important role. Richter argues that "the Iroquois who remained in their traditional homelands were becoming minor players in a game of shrinking economic importance to Euro-Americans. Having never possessed prime hunting territories of their own, they had thrived in the best of times either by raiding for or trading for pelts hunted by their native neighbors. With both alternatives now closed, the Six Nations were sinking into irrelevance in a region more and more dominated by Euro-Americans."[79]

As with other confederations, language differences split the Iroquois. They even lacked a common word to describe themselves, with the League called the Haudenosaunee by the Seneca and the Kanosoni by the Mohawk. From west to east across central New York were the most numerous of the Iroquois, the Seneca, then the Cayuga, Onondaga, Oneida, and Mohawk. The Iroquoian-speaking Tuscarora joined the League in the 1710s to live near the Seneca after being driven from North Carolina. In council the Tuscarora were allowed to speak but not vote.

The Iroquois League was not an alliance against other tribes but a non-aggression pact whose members agreed not to fight among themselves. The League was formed sometime in the 16th century by Hiawatha, whose diplomatic gifts brought peace to those perpetually warring tribes. Fifty sachems met annually for a grand council at Onondaga, where they would renew their pact by reciting the epic stories of its founding.

Diplomacy with other tribes or the Europeans was conducted through similar rituals. Delegations were met before the village where a preliminary council took place to cool passions fired by war and fear. The delegation was then paraded inside the village to a feast. After a day or two of socializing, the Iroquois and foreign delegation would meet at the council house where they feasted, told stories, consoled each other for their losses, and exchanged presents. From opposite sides of the fire, the Iroquois and the foreign delegation then made speeches and debated the always interrelated issues of war, peace, status, and trade.

The Iroquois seemingly favored the British for several reasons. British goods were more abundant, less expensive, and of better quality. If the Iroquois could bring other tribes into trade with the British, they increased their own status and wealth as middlemen. And, finally, the Iroquois and British could not have found a better go-between than William Johnson. Yet, the Iroquois had survived a century and a half of French and British rivalry by playing them off against each other.

To the south of Iroquoia on the upper Susquehanna River lived mostly Delaware, with shards of other tribes.[80] At some time in the late 17th century, the Iroquois had designated the Delaware as "women" who were prohibited from conducting diplomacy or war on their own. Instead, Iroquois diplomats would negotiate on their behalf at councils with the whites or Indians. At a 1754 council an Iroquois faction signed away those Delaware lands to Connecticut's Susquehanna Company.

That same year, the Delaware Chief Teedyuscung moved his band from the Moravian mission of Gnadenhutten near Bethlehem to the Wyoming valley of the upper Susquehanna. Shortly after arriving, he learned of the land sale to the Susquehanna Company. Incensed, he rejected both that deal and his tribe's vassalage to the Iroquois. Most Delaware and other Indians living in the region, who had long chaffed under the Iroquois yoke, rallied to his side. Throughout the war, Teedyuscung succeeded in asserting his tribe's independence for three important reasons. The Iroquois had lost too much manpower and were too bitterly divided to war against him. As a Moravian convert, Teedyuscung was a favorite with that sect and the Quakers, and thus received their powerful support. Finally, however much they may have differed on other issues, Pennsylvania's assemblymen and other leaders were united in opposing any claims by Connecticut or other colonies for land they asserted as their own.

In the middle and upper Ohio River valley lived three clusters of diverse bands. Near where the Monongahela and Allegeny Rivers join to form the Ohio River lived bands of Shawnee, Delaware, and Iroquois or Mingo, along with fragments of other tribes that had split off from their brethen in the mid-18th century and sought refuge from the pressure of English settlers and the Iroquois in the remote regions. Shawnee, Delaware, and Wyandot villages broke clearings in the upper Muskingum River. Shawnee villages stood where the Kanawha and Scioto Rivers met the Ohio.[81]

From the 1730s until 1754, English traders dominated this region despite Celoron's 1749 incursion. Like all Indians, those in the Ohio valley desired European-manufactured goods but rejected English settlement. During these decades, the Iroquois League claimed sovereignty over the upper Ohio valley tribes. Presiding over these peoples were two transplanted Iroquois chiefs, the Seneca Tanaghrisson or Half King and Oneida Scarouady, who both lived at Logstown, about eighteen miles downriver from the Ohio forks. Through 1754, they maintained the loyalty of most of these Indians to the English while Delaware Chief Shingass rallied those Indians bitterly opposed to the English. But with Washington's surrender that year and Braddock's debacle in 1755, most Indians shifted to Shingas and the victorious French. For four years, war parties from the upper Ohio valley devastated the Virginia, Maryland, and Pennsylvania frontiers. These raids mostly ended only after General Forbes led an army to capture Fort Duquesne in November 1758.

Several hundred miles further west lived a cluster of tribes along the Maumee-Wabash watershed. That route between Lake Erie and the Ohio River was the most tenuous link between Quebec and New Orleans. Along that route lived the Miami (Twigthwee) and the related tribes, the Piankashaw, Wea, Kickapoo, Mascouten, and Ouiatenon, and a Wyandot or Huron band led by Chief Nicholas on Sandusky Bay. The French tried to anchor the loyalty of these tribes with Fort Vincennes on the lower and Fort Ouiantenon on the upper Wabash River, Fort Miami on the Maumee River, and Fort Sandusky near the Wyandot. The influx of English traders with their cheaper and better-made goods in the 1730s and 1740s increasingly strained the tribes' relations with the French.

Miami Chief Memeskia, known by the French as La Demoiselle and the English as Old Briton, then openly broke with the French, led his band from the shelter of Fort Miami, and formed a new town of Pickawillany on the Miami River in 1748. There he welcomed English traders and warned the French to stay away. In 1750, Memeskia went so far as to circulate war belts to tribes between the Mississippi River and Appalachian Mountains for a simultaneous attack that would wipe out the French forever. The alliance never took place. The Illinois sent word to the French of the conspiracy. The French sent their own envoys to the tribes to maintain their loyalty. The Miami killed several French traders in 1752, prompting a raid by Canadians, the Ottawa, and led by Charles Langlade that destroyed Pickawillany. The attack cowed the tribes in that region to remain loyal to France throughout the war.

Further west along the Mississippi River, between the mouths of the Ohio and Missouri Rivers and in the Illinois River watershed, lived the Illinois Confederation which included a dozen small, linguistically related bands. Further up the Mississippi River valley, along the Wisconsin and Fox Rivers and Lake Michigan, lived the Potawatomi, Mesquakie, and Sauk. Above the Wisconsin River along the Mississippi River lived the Dakota. Objibwa bands dotted the shores of Lake Superior and westward. Ottawa villages clustered near Fort Michilimackinac between Lakes Michigan and Huron. Around Fort Detroit gathered the most diverse array of tribes, including Ottawa, Huron, and Potawatomi. All of these tribes were too remote to be influenced by the English even during the 1740s. In addition to Detroit and Michilimackinac, the French retained firm influence over the region's tribes with Forts de Chartres, Vaudreuil, La Baye, St. Charles, and La Jonquiere. In some years, hundreds of warriors from those distant tribes would journey east to fight alongside the French.

Throughout the Great Lakes, the Iroquois influence over other tribes disappeared somewhere west of Niagara Falls. Most tribes were loyal to the French but some villages leaned toward the English. The founding of Oswego on Lake Ontario in 1726 diverted an increasing amount of furs coming down the Great Lakes to New York, while the arrival of mostly Virginian and Pennsylvanian traders on Lake Erie's southern shore in the 1730s took back furs to their respective colonies. From then, the French had increasing trouble retaining the loyalty of some tribes in those regions. For example, the Wyandot or Huron band living near Detroit remained grudgingly loyal to France while another Wyandot band led by Chief Nicholas lived on Sandusky Bay and flirted with the English. In 1747, warriors from Chief Nicholas' band murdered five French traders. Nicholas then conspired with tribes around Detroit to raise the scalping knife against the French. The plan was betrayed, the attack failed, and Nicholas took his band into the Ohio valley where he died the following year. The French dominated those tribes residing west and north of Lake Erie. The Ottawa, Huron, Potawatomi, and Mississauga remained loyal to the French for the war's duration and each year supplied warriors for the long journey east to raid in the Lake Champlain and Mohawk valleys.[82]

The French also dominated the regions from Niagara to the Gulf of St. Lawrence, and from there down the Atlantic Coast to Maine. Most of the Indians along the St. Lawrence had been catholicized with missions for the Iroquois at La Presentation on the upper St. Lawrence River and Caughnawaga near Montreal; Iroquois, Nipissing, and Algonquians at the Lake of the Two Mountains Mission 20 miles up the St. Lawrence from Montreal; the Abenaki at the St. Francis mission where the St. Francis River reaches the St. Lawrence east of Montreal; or the Huron at Lorette outside Quebec. In Acadia, the largely Catholic Micmac raided the British in Nova Scotia while the Abenaki of what is now Maine continually harassed the upper New England settlements.[83]

The Cherokee were to the southeastern Indians what the Iroquois were to the northeast Indians—the most powerful tribe in the region and largely neutral toward the English.[84] About 10,000 Cherokee lived in about 60 towns divided into clusters from the Lower towns along the Tugaloo River north, and the Over Hills towns along the upper Tennessee River. Like other Indians, the Cherokee complained that the English traders cheated them, forced them ever deeper into debt, wiped out the game, and addicted them to rum and manufactured goods for survival.

South Carolina, led by Governor Hugh Glen, dominated relations with the Cherokee. Glen tried to alleviate these complaints by dividing the Cherokee country into 20 districts and licensing one trader for each district. Illegal traders inevitably found ways around these restrictions and the abuses continued. More effective was Glen's strategy of playing on the traditional animosities between the Cherokee and Creek to deepen each's dependence on England. By trying to broker a peace in the war that broke out between the Creek and Cherokee in 1751, Glen managed to increase his influence over them both. Glen asserted even more influence when he succeeded in gaining the Lower Cherokee permission to build Fort Prince George in their midst in 1753.

Like other tribes, the Cherokee played their own divide-and-rule game. They sent delegations not only to South Carolina, but to Virginia, Georgia, and North Carolina to solicit gifts and better trade deals. With each colony, the Cherokee threatened to join the French should the English continue neglecting their complaints. Cherokee chiefs also visited the Shawnee and Delaware towns along the Ohio River to press for a common front against the English and French. During the war years, Little Carpenter (Attakulla-kulla) gradually became the Cherokee's leading chief.

Glen's efforts did keep the Cherokee loyal to England when the war with France first broke out. Fort Loudoun was built in the Over Hill country in 1756. In 1758, several hundred Cherokee briefly joined the Forbes expedition against Fort Duquesne. Yet, in 1759 depredations by returning Cherokee warriors along the frontier sparked a war that would burn along South Carolina's frontier for two bloody years.

After the Cherokee, the Creek were the greatest potential enemy to the southern colonies. The Creek were divided into clusters of upper villages along the Coosa and Oakfuskie Rivers and lower villages along the Chattahoochie and Flint Rivers. The Spanish, French, and English with their advanced posts at St. Augustine, Fort Toulouse, and Fort Frederica all vied for Creek trade and friendship. The Creek largely remained peaceful during the war because the English paid them off with trade goods.

Among the other southeastern tribes, the small Catawba tribe on the Catawba River in the South Carolina Piedmont formed a strategic bulwark between that colony and northern raiders. Glen wed the Catawba to South Carolina with generous gifts, regulated trade, and promises not to allow any white settlers in their territory. Glen was also successful in exploiting the hatred between the Chickasaw, located on the upper Yazoo River, and Louisiana to British advantage with traders, gifts, and diplomacy, best conducted by James Adair in the 1740s and early 1750s. Glen failed to woe the Choctaw, in villages along the upper Pearl and Tombigbee Rivers, away from the French before and during the war. If war was, to varying degrees, a possibility with all of the tribes, trade was the constant force in their relationship between the southern colonies. The deerskin trade was an essential pillar of South Carolina's economy when never less than 150,000 pounds of skins were exported annually from Charleston from 1731 to 1765, with lesser amounts from Georgia, North Carolina, and Virginia.[85]

While the importance of any particular tribe or even group of tribes to the struggle between France and England varied considerably, the Indians would never be decisive in any war fought between the two European powers. The final war was won by overwhelming British naval and land power. At best, an Indian alliance meant that fewer of one's own settlers and more of the enemy's would be butchered. Even then, frontier commanders often questioned whether that was worth all the frustrations, treasury, and diplomacy needed to rally those Indians to their banner. Nonetheless, what is important is that the French and English acted on the belief that Indians were the fulcrum of power in the New World.

NOTES

1. Population of British North America, August 1755, in E. B. O'Callaghan and Berthold Fernow, eds., *Documents Relative to the Colonial History of the State of New York* (hereafter cited as NYCD), 15 vols. (Albany, N.Y.: Weed, Parsons, and Co., 1853–1887), 6:993; Capilation List of Canada, NYCD, 10:271–75; John J. McCusker and Russell R. Menard, *The Economy of British America, 1607–1789* (Chapel Hill: University of North Carolina Press, 1991), 112, 172; James M. Cassady, *Demography in Early America* (Cambridge, Mass.: Harvard University Press, 1969); Robert V. Wells, *The Population of the British Colonies in North America before 1776: A Survey of Census Data* (Princeton, N.J.: Princeton University Press, 1975); W. J. Eccles, *France in America* (New York: Harper and Row, 1972); J. Hamelin, *Economie et Societe en Nouvelle-France* (Quebec, 1960); W. J. Eccles, *Canada Under Louis XIV, 1663–1710* (Toronto: McClelland and Stewart, 1964); George F. G. Stanley, *New France: The Last Phase, 1744–1760* (Toronto: McClelland and Stewart, 1968); Bruce A. Cox, ed., *Native People, Native Lands* (Ottawa: Carleton University Press, 1988); Gustave Lanctot, *A History of Canada: From the Treaty of Utrecht to the Treaty of Paris, 1713–1763*, trans. Josephine Hambleton and Margaret M. Cameron, 3 vols. (Cambridge, Mass.: Harvard University Press, 1963–1965).

2. McCusker and Menard, *Economy of British America*, 112, 203; Robert V. Wells, *The Population of the British Colonies in America Before 1776: A Survey of Census Data* (Princeton, N.J.: Princeton University Press, 1975). Although 70,000 people in New France is the standard figure, a more comprehensive survey found 82,000 people in 1759. However, that number undoubtedly included the French soldiers and sailors in the province. Montcalm to Belle Isle, April 12, 1759, NYCD 10:962.

3. Will Durant and Ariel Durant, *Rousseau and Revolution, A History of Civilization in France, England and Germany from 1756, and in the Remainder of Europe from 1715 to 1789* (New York: Simon and Schuster, 1967), 84; Olivier Bernier, *Louis the Beloved: The Life of Louis XV* (Garden City, N.Y.: Doubleday and Co., 1984); Michel Antoine, *Louis XV* (Paris: Librairie Artheme Fayard, 1989).

4. Bernier, *Louis the Beloved*, 102.

5. Lee Kennett, *The French Armies in the Seven Years' War: A Study in Military Organization and Administration* (Durham, N.C.: Duke University Press, 1967), 90, 94.

6. Nancy Mitford, *Madame de Pompadour* (New York: Random House, 1953).

7. Cardinal de Bernis, Memoires et Lettres (Paris, 1866), 204, quoted in Bernier, *Louis the Beloved*, 175.

8. Lanctot, *History of Canada*, 123.

9. W. J. Eccles, *The Canadian Frontier, 1534–1760* (New York: Holt, Rinehart, and Winston, 1969), 69.

10. Lanctot, *History of Canada*, 203–4; Capilation List of Canada, NYCD, 10: 271–75.

11. Lanctot, *History of Canada*, 126.

12. Lawrence Henry Gipson, *Zones of International Friction: The Great Lakes Frontier, Canada, the West Indies, India, 1748–1754* (New York: Alfred A. Knopf, 1952), 10–11.

13. Ibid., 26.

14. Edward Hamilton, ed., *Adventure in the Wilderness: The American Journals of Louis Antoine de Bougainville, 1756–1760* (hereafter cited as Hamilton, *Bougainville Journal*) (Norman: University of Oklahoma Press, 1964), 201.

15. Guy Fregault, *Francois Bigot: Administrateur Francais*, 2 vols. (Montreal: Universite de Montreal Institute d'Histoire de l'Amerique Francaise, 1948).

16. Laurier LaPierre, *1759: The Battle for Canada* (Toronto: McClelland and Stewart, 1990), 110–11.

17. Francis Parkman, *Montcalm and Wolfe: The French & Indian War* (1884) (New York: Da Capo Press, 1995), 320–21.

18. Hamilton, *Bougainville Journal*, 218.

19. Quoted in Yves F. Zoltvany, *The Government of New France: Royal, Clerical, or Class Rule* (Scarborough, Ont.: Prentice-Hall, 1971), 22.

20. Lanctot, *History of Canada*, 113–14.

21. Gipson, *Zone*, 24–25, 56; Harold Innis, *The Cod Fisheries: The History of An International Economy* (New Haven, Conn.: Yale University Press, 1940), vii.

22. Colden's Memoir on the Fur Trade, NYCD, 5:726–33; Return of Western Tribes at Oswego, NYCD, 6:538; NYCD, 9:404–9.

23. Daniel Richter, *The Ordeal of the Longhouse: The Peoples of the Iroquois League in the Era of European Colonization* (Chapel Hill: University of North Carolina Press, 1992), 269; Stanley Nider Katz, *Newcastle's New York: Anglo-American Politics, 1732–1753* (Cambridge, Mass.: Harvard University Press, 1968); George A. Ralyk, *Nova Scotia's Massachusetts: A Study of Massachusetts–Nova Scotia Relations, 1630–1784* (Montreal: McGill–Queen's University, 1973).

24. Bougainville to his brother, November 7, 1756, Public Archives of Canada, Bougainville Transcripts, MG 18, K10, I.

25. For the most comprehensive account of the British Empire, see Lawrence Henry Gipson, *The British Empire before the American Revolution*, 12 vols. (New York: Alfred A. Knopf, 1952–1958), from which much of the following information was taken.

26. Alison Gilbert Olson, "Relations with the Parent Country: Britain," in Jacob Ernest Cooke, ed., *Encyclopedia of the North American Colonies*, vol. 1 (New York: Charles Scribner's Sons, 1993), 335; Arthur Herbert Basye, *The Lords Commissioners of Trade and Plantations, Commonly Known as the Board of Trade, 1748–1782* (New Haven, Conn.: Yale University Press, 1925); Alison G. Olson, "The Board of Trade and London-American Interest Groups in the Eighteenth Century," in Peter Marshall and Glyn Williams, eds., *The British Atlantic Empire before the American Revolution* (London: Frank Cass, 1980), 33–51; Ian K. Steel, *The Politics of Colonial Policy: The Board of Trade in Colonial Administration, 1696–1720* (Oxford: Oxford University Press, 1968).

27. Population of Britain's American Colonies, 1755, NYCD, 6:993; Daniel Boorstin, *The Americans: The Colonial Experience* (London: Sphere Books, 1959); James M. Smith, ed., *Seventeenth Century America* (Chapel Hill: University of North Carolina Press, 1959); Oliver P. Chitwood, *A History of Colonial America* (New York: Harper & Bros., 1961); Max Savelle and Robert Middlekauff, *A History of*

Colonial America (New York: Holt, Rinehart and Winston, 1964); David G. Sweet and Gary B. Nash, eds., *Struggle and Survival in Colonial America* (Berkeley: University of California Press, 1981).

28. John Thomlison to Granville, December 13, 1756, in Stanley Pargellis, ed., *Military Affairs in North America, 1748–1763: Selected Documents from the Cumberland Papers in Windsor Castle (1936)* (reprint, Hamden, Conn.: Archon Books, 1969), 257.

29. Mary Dewar, ed., *A Discourse of the Commonweal of this Realm of England Attributed to Sir Thomas Smith* (Charlottesville: University of Virginia Press, 1969), 63.

30. Oliver M. Dickerson, *The Navigation Acts and the American Revolution* (New York: Octagon, 1978).

31. Page Smith, *A New Age Begins: A People's History of the American Revolution* (New York: Penguin Books, 1976), 141.

32. Curtis P. Nettels, *The Emergence of a National Economy, 1775–1815* (New York: M. E. Sharpe, 1962), 42; Julian Gwyn, "British Government Spending and the North American Colonies, 1740–1775," in Peter Marshall and Glyn Williams, eds., *The British Atlantic Empire before the American Revolution* (London: Frank Cass, 1980), 77, 74–84.

33. Colden to Halifax, August 3, 1754, in Pargellis, *Military Affairs*, 19–21.

34. Stephen Saunders Webb, *1676: The End of American Independence* (New York: Knopf, 1984).

35. Lawrence to Halifax, December 9, 1755, in Pargellis, *Military Affairs*, 157; Jack P. Greene, *The Quest for Power: The Lower Houses of Assembly in the Southern Royal Colonies, 1689–1776* (1963) (reprint, New York: W. W. Norton, 1972); Alan Rogers, *Empire and Liberty: American Resistance to British Authority, 1755–1763* (Berkeley: University of California Press, 1974).

36. Michael Kammen, *A Rope of Sand: The Colonial Agents, British Politics, and the American Revolution* (Ithaca, N.Y.: Cornell University Press, 1968); Max Savelle, *The Origins of American Diplomacy: The International History of Anglo-America, 1492–1763* (New York: Macmillan, 1967).

37. Louis Knott Koontz, *Robert Dinwiddie, His Career in American Colonial Government and Westward Expansion* (Glendale, Calif.: Arthur H. Clark, 1941), 168.

38. Carl Bridenbaugh, *Mitre and Sceptre: Transatlantic Faiths, Ideas, Personalities, and Politics, 1689–1775* (New York: Oxford University Press, 1962).

39. John Tracy Ellis, *Catholics in Colonial America* (Baltimore: Helicon Press, 1965); Jay P. Dolan, *The American Catholic Experience: A History from Colonial Times to the Present* (Garden City, N.Y.: Doubleday and Co., 1985).

40. Charles E. Clark, "The Colonial Press," in Jacob Ernest Cooke, ed., *The Encyclopedia of the North American Colonies* (New York: Charles Scribner's Sons, 1993), 3:111–22.

41. Emory Eliot, ed., *American Literature: A Prentice-Hall Anthology*, vol. 1 (Englewood Cliffs, N.J.: Prentice-Hall, 1991); James Thomas Flexner, *First Flowers of Our Wilderness: American Painting* (Boston: Houghton Mifflin, 1947); Carl Bridenbaugh, *The Colonial Craftsman* (Chicago: University of Chicago Press, 1950); Ian Quimby, ed., *The Craftsman in Early America* (New York: W. W. Norton, 1984).

42. Edwin J. Perkins, *The Economy of Colonial America* (New York: Columbia

University Press, 1980); Stuart Bruchey, *Enterprise: The Dynamic Economy of a Free People* (Cambridge, Mass.: Harvard University Press, 1990); W. Elliott Brownlee, *Dynamics of Ascent: A History of the American Economy* (New York: Alfred A. Knopf, 1974); Ross M. Robertson, *History of the American Economy* (New York: Harcourt Brace Jovanovich, 1973); Carole Shammas, "How Self-Sufficient Was Early America," *Journal of Interdisciplinary History* 13 (1982), 247–72; Theodore K. Rabb, *Enterprise and Empire: Merchant and Gentry Investment in the Expansion of England, 1575–1630* (Cambridge, Mass.: Harvard University Press, 1967).

43. Larry E. Ivers, *British Drums on the Southern Frontier: The Military Colonization of Georgia, 1733–1749* (Chapel Hill: University of North Carolina Press, 1974).

44. Lewis C. Gray, *History of Agriculture in the Southern United States to 1860* (Washington, D.C.: Carnegie Institute, 1933); Percy Wells Bidwell and John I. Falconer, *History of Agriculture in the Northern United States, 1620–1860* (Washington, D.C.: Carnegie Institute, 1925); Max G. Schumacher, *The Northern Farmer and His Markets During the Late Colonial Period* (New York: Arno Press, 1975).

45. Harry J. Carman and Rexford G. Tugwell, eds., *Jared Eliot: Essays Upon Field Husbandry in New England, and Other Papers, 1748–1762* (New York: Columbia University Press, 1934), 137.

46. Quoted in Bidwell and Falconer, *History of Agriculture*, 119.

47. Thomas Elliot Norton, *The Fur Trade in Colonial New York, 1686–1776* (Madison: University of Wisconsin Press, 1974).

48. Victor S. Clark, *History of Manufacturing in the United States, 1607–1860*, 3 vols. (Washington, D.C.: Carnegie Institute, 1929); James T. Shepherd and Gary M. Walton, *Shipping, Maritime Trade, and the Economic Development of Colonial North America* (Cambridge: Cambridge University Press, 1972); Charles F. Carroll, *The Timber Economy of Puritan New England* (Providence, R.I.: Brown University Press, 1973).

49. James A. Henretta, *The Evolution of American Society, 1700–1815: An Interdisciplinary Analysis* (Lexington, Mass.: D.C. Heath, 1973), 78–79; Carl Bridenbaugh, *Cities in the Wilderness: The First Century of Urban Life in America* (New York: Alfred A. Knopf, 1955).

50. Loudoun to Cumberland, June 22, 1757, in Paragellis, *Military Affairs*, 376; Richard Pares, *Colonial Blockade and Neutral Rights, 1739–1763* (Oxford: Oxford University Press, 1938).

51. Curtis P. Nettels, *The Money Supply of the American Colonies Before 1720* (Madison: University of Wisconsin Press, 1934); Leslie V. Brock, *The Currency of the American Colonies, 1700–64* (New York: Arno Press, 1975); Joseph Albert Ernest, *Money and Politics in America, 1755–65: A Study in the Currency Act of 1764 and the Political Economy of Revolution* (Chapel Hill: University of North Carolina Press, 1973); E. James Ferguson, *The Power of the Purse* (Chapel Hill: University of North Carolina Press, 1961).

52. Russel Menard, "Growth and Welfare," in Jacob Ernest Cooke, ed., *Encyclopedia of the North American Colonies* (New York: Charles Scribner's Sons, 1993), 467–82; Richard B. Morris, *Government and Labor in Early America* (New York: Columbia University Press, 1946); Alice Hanson Jones, *Wealth of a Nation to Be: The American Colonies on the Eve of the Revolution* (New York: Columbia University Press, 1980), 78; James M. Cassady, *Demography in Early America* (Cambridge,

Mass.: Harvard University Press, 1969); Arthur W. Calhoun, *A Social History of the American Family* (New York: Barnes & Noble, 1945).

53. Bernard Bailyn, *Voyagers to the West: A Passage in the Peopling of America on the Eve of Revolution* (New York: Alfred A. Knopf, 1986), 199–200.

54. C. G. A. Clay, *Economic Expansion and Social Change: England, 1500–1700*, 2 vols. (Cambridge: Cambridge University Press, 1984); Eric Kerridge, *The Agricultural Revolution* (London: Allen & Unwin, 1973).

55. Abbott Emerson Smith, *Colonists in Bondage: White Servitude and Convict Labor in America, 1607–1776* (Chapel Hill: University of North Carolina Press, 1947); Winthrop D. Jordan, *White Over Black* (Chapel Hill: University of North Carolina, 1968); David W. Galenson, *White Servitude in Colonial America: An Economic Analysis* (Cambridge: Cambridge University Press, 1981); David Cressy, *Coming Over: Migration and Communication Between England and New England in the Seventeenth Century* (Cambridge: Cambridge University Press, 1987).

56. Quoted in Stuart Bruchey, ed., *The Colonial Merchant: Sources and Readings* (New York: Harcourt, Brace, & World, 1966), 95; Gary B. Nash, *Class and Society in Early America* (Englewood Cliffs, N.J.: Prentice-Hall, 1970).

57. Edmund S. Morgan, *American Slavery, American Freedom: The Ordeal of Colonial Virginia* (New York: W. W. Norton, 1975).

58. Richter, *Ordeal of the Longhouse.*

59. Wagner E. Stearn and Allen E. Stearn, *The Effect of Small-pox on the Destiny of the American Indian* (Boston: B. Humphries, 1945); Daniel K. Richter, Essay Review of Henry F. Dobyns, *Their Numbers Became Thinned: Native American Population Dynamics in Eastern North America, William and Mary Quarterly* 3rd ser., 41 (1984), 649–53; Russell Thorton, *American Indian Holocaust and Survival: A Population History Since 1492* (Norman: University of Oklahoma Press, 1987); Susan Johnston, "Epidemics: The Forgotten Factor in Seventeenth Century Native Warfare in the St. Lawrence Region," in Bruce A. Cox, ed., *Native Peoples, Native Lands* (Ottawa: Carleton University Press, 1988); Sherburne F. Cook, "The Significance of Disease in the Extinction of the New England Indians," *Human Biology* 44 (1973), 485–508.

60. Thomas Pownall, "Notes on Indian Affairs," Huntington Library, LO 460, HL.

61. Harold A. Innis, *The Fur Trade in Canada: An Introduction to Canadian Economic History* (New Haven, Conn.: Yale University Press, 1930); Paul Chrisler Phillips, *The Fur Trade*, vol. 1 (Norman: University of Oklahoma Press, 1961); Arthur J. Ray, *Indians in the Fur Trade: Their Role as Trappers, Hunters, and Middlemen in the Lands Southwest of Hudson Bay, 1660–1870* (Toronto: University of Toronto Press, 1974); Murray G. Lawson, *Fur: A Study in English Mercantilism, 1700–1775* (Toronto: University of Toronto Press, 1975); Arthur J. Ray and Donald Freeman, *"Give Us Good Measure": An Economic Analysis of Relations Between the Indians and the Hudson's Bay Company Before 1763* (Toronto: University of Toronto Press, 1978); Calvin Martin, *Keepers of the Game: Indian-Animal Relationships and the Fur Trade* (Berkeley: University of California Press, 1978); Shepard Krech, ed., *Indians, Animals, and the Fur Trade: A Critique of Keepers of the Game* (Athens: University of Georgia Press, 1981); W. J. Eccles, "A Belated Review of Harold Adams Innis, The Fur Trade in Canada," *Canadian Historical Review* 60 (1983), 341–

441; W. J. Eccles, "The Fur Trade and Eighteenth Century Imperialism," *William and Mary Quarterly* 3rd ser., 40 (1983), 341–62.

62. Hamilton, *Bougainville Journal*, 225.

63. Brian Leigh Dunnigan, ed., *Memoirs on the Late War in North America Between France and England, by Pierre Pouchot* (cited hereafter as Dunnigan, *Pouchot Memoirs*) (Youngstown, N.Y.: Old Fort Niagara Association, 1994), 443–44.

64. Hamilton, *Bougainville Journal*, 118.

65. Dunnigan, *Pouchot Memoirs*, 440.

66. Ibid., 446–47.

67. Hamilton, *Bougainville Journal*, 134.

68. Ibid., 126.

69. Wilbur R. Jacobs, *Wilderness Politics and Indian Gifts: The Northern Colonial Frontier, 1748–1763* (Lincoln: University of Nebraska, 1950).

70. Daniel K. Richter, "War and Culture: The Iroquois Experience," *William and Mary Quarterly*, 3rd ser., 60 (1983), 528–59.

71. Howard H. Peckham, ed. "Thomas Gist's Indian Captivity, 1758–1759," *Pennsylvania Magazine of History and Biography* 80:3 (July 1956), 285–311; J. Norman Heard, *White Unto Red: A Study of the Assimilation of White Persons Captured by Indians* (Methuen, N.J.: Scarecrow Press, 1973); Colin G. Calloway, ed., *North Country Captives: Selected Narratives of Indian Captivity from Vermont and New Hampshire* (Hanover, N.H.: University Press of New England, 1992); John Demos, *The Unredeemed Captive: A Family Story from Early America* (New York: Vintage Books, 1995).

72. Keith F. Otterbein, "Why the Iroquois Won: An Analysis of Iroquois Military Tactics," *Ethnohistory* 11 (1964), 56–63; Sherburne F. Cook, "Interracial Warfare and Population Decline among the New England Indians," *Ethnohistory* 20 (1973), 1–24; James Axtell and William C. Sturtevant, "The Unkindest Cut; or, Who Invented Scalping?" *William and Mary Quarterly* 3rd ser., 37 (1980), 451–72; Thomas S. Abler, "Iroquois Cannibalism: Fact Not Fiction," *Ethnohistory* 27 (1980), 309–26; Thomas S. Abler and Michael H. Logan, "The Florescence and Demise of Iroquoian Cannibalism: Human Sacrifice and Malinowski's Hypothesis," *Man in the Northeast*, no. 35 (Spring 1988), 1–26.

73. *New York Mercury*, August 11, 1755, quoted in Coleman, *New England Captive*, 2:298–300; Steele, *Betrayal*, 10–18; Alden T. Vaughan and Edward W. Clark, eds., *Puritans Among the Indians: Accounts of Captivity and Redemption, 1676–1724* (Cambridge, Mass.: Harvard University Press, 1981).

74. Hamilton, *Bougainville Journal*, 133.

75. Ibid., 55–56.

76. Ibid., 133, 134.

77. Ibid., 122.

78. George T. Hunt, *Wars of the Iroquois* (Madison: University of Wisconsin Press, 1960); Georgiana C. Nammack, *Fraud, Politics, and Dispossession of the Indians: The Iroquois Land Frontier in the Colonial Period* (Norman: University of Oklahoma Press, 1969); Francis Jennings, *The Invasion of America* (Chapel Hill: University of North Carolina Press, 1975); Francis Jennings, *The Ambiguous Iroquois Empire: The Covenant Chain Confederation of Indian Tribes with English Colonies* (New York: W. W. Norton, 1984); Francis Jennings, William N. Fenton, Mary A. Druke, and

David R. Miller, eds., *Iroquois Indians: A Documentary History of the Six Nations and Their League* (Woodbridge, Conn.: Research Publications, 1985); Richard Aquila, *The Iroquois Restoration: Iroquois Diplomacy on the Colonial Frontier, 1701–1754* (Detroit: Wayne State University Press, 1983); Francis Jennings et al., *The History and Culture of Iroquois Diplomacy: An Interdisciplinary Guide to the Treaties of the Six Nations and Their League* (Syracuse, N.Y.: Syracuse University Press, 1985); Daniel K. Richter, "Iroquois vs. Iroquois: Jesuit Mission and Christianity in Village Politics, 1642–1686," *Ethnohistory* 32 (1985), 1–16; Daniel K. Richter, "Up the Cultural Stream: Three Recent Works in Iroquois Studies," *Ethnohistory* 3rd ser., 32 (1985), 363–69; Daniel Richter and James H. Merrell, eds., *Beyond the Covenant Chain: The Iroquois and Their Neighbors in Indian North America, 1600–1800* (Syracuse, N.Y.: Syracuse University Press, 1987); Daniel K. Richter, "Cultural Brokers and Intercultural Politics: New York–Iroquois Relations, 1664–1701," *Journal of American History* 75 (1988–1989), 40–67.

79. Richter, *Ordeal of the Longhouse*, 270–71.

80. C. A. Weslager, *The Delaware Indians: A History* (New Brunswick, N.J.: Rutgers University Press, 1991); Stephen Auth, *The Ten Years' War: Indian-White Relations in Pennsylvania, 1755–1765* (New York: Garland Publishers, 1989); Anthony F. C. Wallace, *King of the Delawares: Teedyuscung, 1700–1763* (1949) (reprint, Syracuse, N.Y.: Syracuse University Press, 1990).

81. James H. Howard, *Shawnee: The Ceremonialism of a Native American Tribe and Its Cultural Background* (Athens: University of Ohio Press, 1981).

82. Richard White, *The Middle Ground: Indians, Empires, and Republics in the Great Lakes Regions, 1650–1815* (Cambridge: Cambridge University Press, 1991); Helen Blair, ed., *The Indian Tribes of the Upper Mississippi Valley & Region of the Great Lakes* (1911) (reprint, Lincoln: University of Nebraska Press, 1996); W. Vernon Kinietz, *The Indians of the Western Great Lakes, 1615–1760* (1940) (reprint, Ann Arbor: University of Michigan Press, 1996); Helen Hornbeck Tanner, *Atlas of Great Lakes Indian History* (Norman: University of Oklahoma Press, 1987).

83. Alfred Goldsworthy Bailey, *The Conflict of European and Eastern Algonkian Cultures, 1504–1700*, 2nd ed. (1937) (reprint, Toronto: University of Toronto Press, 1969); Laurence M. Hauptman and James D. Wherry, eds., *The Pequots in Southern New England: The Fall and Rise of an American Indian Nation* (Norman: University of Oklahoma Press, 1990); Colin Calloway, *The Abenaki* (New York: Chelsea House, 1989).

84. Verner W. Crane, *The Southern Frontier, 1670–1732* (Ann Arbor: University of Michigan Press, 1929); Theda Perdue, *Slavery and the Evolution of Cherokee Society, 1540–1866* (Knoxville: University of Tennessee Press, 1979); J. Leitch Wright, Jr., *The Only Land They Knew: The Tragic Story of the American Indians in the Old South* (New York: The Free Press, 1981); James Howlett O'Donnell III, *Southeastern Frontiers: Europeans, Africans, and American Indians, 1513–1840, A Critical Bibliography* (Bloomington: Indiana University Press, 1982); Peter H. Wood, Gregory A. Waselkov, and M. Thomas Hatley, eds., *Powhatan's Mantle: Indians in the Colonial Southeast* (Lincoln: University of Nebraska Press, 1989); James H. Merrell, *The Indians' World: Catawbas and Their Neighbors from European Contact Through the Era of Removal* (Chapel Hill: University of North Carolina Press, 1989); Daniel H. Usner, *Indians, Settlers, & Slavers in a Frontier Exchange Economy: The Lower Mississippi Valley Before 1783* (Chapel Hill: University of North Carolina Press,

1992); Charles Hudson, *The Southeastern Indians* (Knoxville: University of Tennessee Press, 1976); John Richard Alden, *John Stuart and Southeastern Colonial Frontier* (New York: Gordian Press, 1966).

    85. Crane, *Southern Frontier*, 11.

3

Armies and Navies

Let Americans fight Americans.

—Duke of Newcastle

Col. Preble, who, I remember, was a harsh man, swore he would knock the first man down who should step out of his first ranks which greatly surprised me, to think that I must stand still to be shot at.

—Private David Perry, 1755

The Way to secure Peace is to be prepared for War.

—Benjamin Franklin

For in the end, they are a necessary evil.

—Louis Antoine de Bougainville, 1756

When French and British subjects once again marched and sailed off to war against each other in 1754, their militaries were completely asymmetrical. France's vast land forces dwarfed Britain's while the English fleet outgunned France's by more than two to one. In 1755, France fielded 150,000 infantry in 236 battalions, 53,000 militia in 107 battalions, 30,000 cavalry in 214 squadrons, and 3,800 gunners. In contrast, Britain started the war with about 30,000 troops in 48 understrength regiments. It was in seapower that Britain excelled, with its fleet numbering 130 warships with 50 or more guns, compared to a mere 57 warships of such firepower in the French fleet. War forced both kingdoms to mobilize enormous amounts of more men and weapons to feed to the slaughter. By the war's end, Britain deployed 140,000 soldiers and marines in 124 regiments to France's 330,000. The

British fleet expanded to almost 300 vessels by 1763 while France's diminished to 40 warships of all kinds.[1]

The imbalance between these two militaries at once reflected the two kingdoms' differing populations, traditions, and geography, and shaped their respective strategies. Facing formidable potential enemies just beyond its eastern and southwestern borders, France's wars were won or lost on the continent. With 20 million people, France had a huge pool of men eligible to don a uniform and musket. Given its endowments, limitations, and challenges, France naturally relied on large armies to defend and expand its realm, leaving fewer resources available to invest in its navy.

With 6 million people, Britain had less than one-third the manpower pool available to France. The sea, however, was worth several hundred thousand soldiers for Britain's defense. For Britons that vast oceanic moat had advantages that went beyond those of economy and defense against foreign enemies. Oliver Cromwell's dictatorship during the 1650s had made Britons leery of a large standing army, and that moat allowed them to do without one. Britain relied on overwhelming naval power not just to defend itself but to dominate sea lanes to the far-flung empires of its own and other kingdom's making.

Nonetheless, despite its superior seapower and distant, lucrative colonies, British security was thought to lie primarily over the channel rather than beyond the oceans. For hundreds of years, English policy sought to keep Holland and Flanders free from great power rule. Throughout the 17th and 18th centuries, England had periodically sided with Hapsburg Austria to war against Bourbon Spain and France when those kingdoms sought to conquer Holland and neighboring small principalities that could provide a launch for the invasion of the British Isles.

Britain's continental ties deepened following the ascension of a Hanoverian to the English throne in 1714. Throughout the 18th century, British foreign policy was dominated by the king's dual responsibilities as English monarch and Hanover elector. Although he resided in England, the king presided over two separate realms, administrations, revenues, budgets, armies, and peoples. Although it was a second-rate power, Hanover could muster up to 40,000 troops. That small, professional army defended a principality surrounded by greater powers like France, Austria, and Prussia. Thus was Britain's security thought inseparable from the independence of Hanover and the Netherlands.

English policy protected these commitments by deftly manipulating Europe's power balance against any ambitious potential hegemony. Acting firmly on the strategy that "the enemy of my enemy is my friend," the English used generous subsidies, leavened occasionally by contingents of British redcoats, to keep small and great powers in the field against any enemies that threatened the Netherlands or Hanover. Not every Briton accepted these "national" interests. Throughout his career in Parliament and after becoming prime minister in December 1756, William Pitt worked ceaselessly to challenge those assumptions and promote his visions of British interests in an expanding global empire. The resulting policy combined defending Britain's continental ties with a drive to plant the Union Jack on all French colonies around the world.

As overwhelming as French land and British seapower appeared, both were limited in their application. Land warfare of that era was confined to relatively small, professional armies maneuvering in relatively short campaigns punctuated by a battle or two. Likewise, fleet admirals and warship captains were constrained by strict rules of engagement that smothered tactical initiative. The opposing kings, Louis XV and George II, with their respective "absolute" and "constitutional" powers, also found their hands tied beyond the fawning and sometimes mocking courts immediately surrounding them. The ability to mobilize a realm's entire population, industry, and natural resources for war would not reach a ruler's hands until after 1789. At best, Louis XV and George II not only could muster a mere fraction of their kingdoms' potential warpower, they lacked the administrative ability even to measure accurately that potential. War remained largely a duel of professionals. Unless their homes and fields happened to be on a line of march or battle, or a family member was in uniform, most peasants and townspeople remained untouched by the fighting.

The ability to wage war in North America was even more limited. In the 150 years since France and England had first rooted colonies in North America, those two countries had fought four wars and constantly jockeyed for Indian furs and loyalties. When the English and French fought, their wars consisted mostly of large-scale raids designed to disrupt, rather than sustained campaigns to vanquish the enemy. Provincial troops and Indian allies provided the bulk of either side's forces, swelled occasionally by handfuls of regulars.

All that would change in 1755. That year, both London and Versailles first shipped large numbers of regular troops to North America. For the next five years, regular troops would provide the backbone and muscle of most campaigns. That war in North America, however, pitted a French David against a British Goliath. British naval superiority inhibited France from sending over enough troops to win, even if Versailles could have diverted significant numbers from its European campaigns. Britain, meanwhile, could send over as many troops as it could recruit. Likewise, with a mere one-twentieth the inhabitants of Britain's colonies, France's population advantage disappeared in North America. Only so many Canadian peasants could be plucked from their fields and into the ranks. Although Canada did mass a formidable militia at Quebec in 1759, like home guards everywhere its military prowess was second-rate at best.

The French could defend their North American empire only by constantly distracting the lumbering and constantly growing British giant with well-executed offensives that threatened Albany from the Mohawk valley or Lake Champlain. And that is exactly what the French did. Despite their overall inferior numbers, the French were more effective in concentrating their meager forces at key points. During the war's first three years, the French stiff-armed the British with bloody defeats at the Monongahela, Oswego, Fort William Henry, and Fort Carillon. But once the French lost the initiative, their defeat was practically inevitable.

The British eventually won by sheer weight of numbers. British navy warships and hundreds of privateers cut off New France from the annual supplies of troops, food, gunpowder, and Indian presents that enabled it to survive. Armies of British infantry regulars and provincials, bateauxmen, axmen, and teamsters crawled up against, embraced, and crushed French strongpoints on Lake Champlain and Lake Ontario, at Fort Louisbourg, the Ohio forks, and, finally, the St. Lawrence valley. By 1759, Pitt had concentrated elements of 32 regiments and 30,000 troops in North America. Outgunned and starving, the French eventually had to surrender.

Yet, it took seven years for all that to happen. The campaigns and results of the French and Indian War cannot be understood apart from the nature of warfare in North America and at sea, and the varying roles that Indians played in every campaign.

THE ART OF NORTH AMERICAN WARFARE

When George Washington ordered his troops to fire on Jumonville's encampment in 1754, he sparked the fifth war between Britain and France in North America. That war would lead to Britain's conquest of New France.

The first three previous wars fought between France and Britain for North America—Huguenot (1627–1629), King William's (1689–1697), Queen Anne's (1702–1713), and King George's (1744–1748), were indecisive for several reasons. Each of those wars was the appendage of far greater wars engulfing Europe. North America's fate thus hung on the outcome of battles and negotiations across the Atlantic Ocean. The American empires, despite their vastness and potential wealth, were but sideshows. At best, London and Paris could divert to their respective colonies only limited amounts of money, munitions, warships, and troops, along with ample encouragement.[2]

Nor could either Versailles or Whitehall mobilize enough of their colonists into the ranks for a decisive thrust against the other. The respective numbers of Americans and Canadians were important but never decisive. Although the ratio of 20 Americans to every Canadian prevailed from 1609 through 1763, the British had more than enough manpower to prevent conquest but not enough to conquer. The French offset their disadvantage by mobilizing Canadian and Indian raiders much more effectively than the English. The American population advantage was further undercut by the policy of most English colonies until 1755 of remaining removed from the wars that did not directly affect them. The front-line provinces of Massachusetts, New Hampshire, and New York usually fought alone; sometimes they received minor contributions from other provinces. Neither war nor peace had ever descended everywhere at once along the frontier. Somewhere at virtually any time, American colonists feared an Indian attack. For over 150 years, warfare in North America consisted mostly of small-scale raids and short-lived battles and sieges along the frontier. The 1711 Walker expedition against Quebec and 1745 Louisbourg campaign were exceptional.

But perhaps the most important element that prevented either side from gaining a decisive victory in their wars was topography. In 1754, a vast, largely trackless wilderness buffer separated the British and French North American empires. After exploring the Hudson-Champlain frontier in 1749, the Swedish naturalist Peter Kalm reported that "not a human being lives in these waste regions and no Indian villages are found there."[3] That wilderness buffer was broken by three narrow and easily defended corridors that led to New France—the St. Lawrence Seaway, Lake Champlain, and Lake Ontario.

In three of the four previous wars, British forces had never succeeded in breaking through any of those corridors and decisively invading the heart of New France. The fifth war, however, would prove decisive. For the first time, London committed vast numbers of regiments and warships to North America. Inevitably, the sheer numbers of British regulars, American volunteers, and Indian allies would break through the French forts guarding Canada's strategic corridors—Louisbourg, Quebec, Carillon, Niagara—and conquer the heartland.

Topography did not completely advantage the French. The British could supply their troops far more easily than the French could theirs. The British enjoyed both command of the sea and easy supply routes to most of their forces in North America. Aside from Braddock's disastrous and Forbes' victorious thrusts against Fort Duquesne, most British campaigns extended along well-trodden roads that originated in seaports like New York, Boston, or Philadelphia. In contrast, while America's ports fronted the ocean, French ships had to sail 400 miles up the St. Lawrence just to dock at Quebec, and a further 160 treacherous miles before reaching Montreal. Even after a load of supplies had successfully run the gauntlet of British warships and was deposited at Montreal, it still had to be conveyed to distant forts at places like Niagara, Carillon, Duquesne, Detroit, Michilimackinac, and beyond.

If topography imposed advantages and disadvantages on both sides, climate favored the English. Snow fell and rivers froze two weeks earlier and lasted two weeks longer in the Great Lakes and St. Lawrence regions than it did south of the Appalachian divide. Thick ice sheets in the Gulf of St. Lawrence cut off New France from the outside world for three to four months. Canadian growing seasons were short; crop failures from early freezes were frequent. That combined with the British blockade to make malnutrition nearly chronic and starvation frequent throughout New France. In contrast, American ports remained open year-round and inland rivers were navigable for roughly an extra month. Louis Bougainville explained that "the English have winter a month later and spring a month earlier than we. Moreover, their troops in going into winter quarters go from a warm country into one which is no less so, and their route is by way of the King's Highway in which two carriages can go abreast, and the rivers are navigable at all times."[4]

Yet, English commanders never capitalized on this climatic advantage. The mind-numbing boredom and limited supplies available at frontier posts prompted commanders on both sides to withdraw their colonial levies and most regulars early each winter to the settlements and then return them to the frontier once the ice and snow had melted in the spring. But the French consistently won the race back to the frontier forts. French reinforcements swelled the ranks of defenders at forts like Carillon and Niagara long before English expeditions arrived. If they started at all, English campaigns up Lake Champlain and Lake Ontario or even against Louisbourg did not move until July and sometimes even August.

Just as the French mobilized their troops on the frontier faster in the spring, they were never truly snowbound in the winter. They used sledges dragged by draft animals to communicate with their isolated wilderness posts during the winter. A shortage of draft animals, however, limited the amount of supplies that could be transported during those months. Raiding continued during the winter as Indians and Canadians struggled through snowdrifts to attack isolated posts, settlements, and supply convoys in the corridors linking Albany with Oswego and Fort Edward, the Nova Scotia settlements and forts, and the New England and middle colonies' frontier. Although most winter raiding parties numbered a score or so, a few had several hundred, and one, Rigaud's 1757 attack on Fort William Henry, consisted of 1,300 Indians and troops.

As in any war, geography limited the range of successful strategies for either side. At best, given their inferior amounts of troops, supplies, and ships, the French could merely stave off defeat; conquest of the English colonies was an impossibility. There were simply not enough French soldiers and supplies available in North America to take, let alone hold, say, Boston or New York. Although the French army in Europe far outnumbered Britain's, Versailles lacked the naval power to convey them safely to the New World.

With these limitations, a successful French strategy depended on launching limited offensives and continuous large-scale raids to bloody, wear down, and throw the British off balance. Fort Edward and then Albany were the logical focal points of any major offensive. A vigorous French attack there would crimp British offensives elsewhere as forces and supplies were diverted for Albany's defense. A major French offensive anywhere else would simply divert and ultimately drain vital military resources, thus leaving Canada weaker rather than stronger.

If an Albany offensive failed, survival depended on concentrating most French troops and supplies at Quebec and Carillon, the two most important fortresses guarding the heart of French Canada. It mattered little what happened at Fort Duquesne or even Fort Niagara and Fort Louisbourg. Those all were sideshows. If the British were strong enough to take Quebec, Montreal surely would fall, and then the game was lost.

In sum, a successful French strategy in North America depended on deft diplomacy to keep as many Indians allied or neutral as possible; constant raids to drain the frontier and colonial governments of money, men, and supplies; and well-organized, well-supplied, and well-led campaigns against Albany. Ultimately, however, a French victory in North America depended on what happened on the high seas and in Europe. To Versailles, New France was but a secondary front to the epic struggle waged in Europe. Fearing that to send more meant to lose more, throughout the war, Versailles dispatched only a trickle of troops and supplies to Canada. Given Britain's overwhelming command of the sea, the French could hardly have sent much more if they had so desired.

The optimum British strategy to win the war in North America was, of course, the opposite of France's. That strategy was eventually established by William Pitt.[5] For his vision and determination to win a global war of conquest, Pitt looms far above the political leaders on either side of the Channel. Just how important was Pitt to Britain's overwhelming victory? Had not Pitt headed the government from December 1756 to October 1761, the war in North America might well have sputtered to an indecisive close like previous struggles. It was Pitt who shifted Britain's strategy from merely defeating the French to conquering New France.

After entering the Cabinet in 1756, Pitt clearly brought a drive and focus to British policy that other ministers lacked. No one was more committed to destroying and swallowing the French Empire. To that end, Pitt devised a grand strategy for systematically demolishing the French Empire around the world. Ideally, that strategy involved committing only enough British troops and subsidies to the continent to divert French strength, while it used its naval superiority to expand Britain's empire at France's expense. For Pitt even to acknowledge British interests on the continent was quite a turnaround from the years he spent in Parliament criticizing even the slightest commitment there. Strategic as well as political rationales helped Pitt recognize that by keeping Prussia, Hanover, and other German allies in the war, Britain diverted from France financial and military forces that could be deployed in North America.

But Pitt's strategy was not flawless. From 1757 to 1761, he committed enormous amounts of troops and treasury to pinprick raids along the French coast that undermined the war efforts of Whitehall rather than Versailles. He annually called on colonial governors to mobilize far more provincial forces than were needed for most campaigns; those troops consumed enormous amounts of equipment, weapons, provisions, transportation, and time that could have been better employed elsewhere. Pitt's generals were at best an uninspiring lot, including Amherst, who was overwhelmingly mediocre, and Abercromby, who is best remembered for blindly marching his army into a slaughtering field. While Pitt is lauded for tapping Wolfe to take Quebec, that expedition nearly turned out as disastrous as Abercromby's before Fort Carillon.

Pitt understood that the key to British victory in North America lay first in corking the St. Lawrence Seaway. Time was on Britain's side. Canada was not self-sufficient—it depended on frequent and heavily laden supply ships to provide enough powder, lead, muskets, grain, and trade goods for its inhabitants to sustain themselves. The British navy outgunned and outsailed its French counterpart by three ships to one. Canada, thus, was at the mercy of the British navy. Once an effective British naval blockade severed that slender supply line, Canada would then wither on the vine.

But harvesting that fruit depended on besieging Quebec with overwhelming numbers of amply supplied British regulars, and then sailing further up the St. Lawrence and taking Montreal. Provincial forces elsewhere at Lake George, Oswego, Nova Scotia, and along the Pennsylvania, Maryland, and Virginia frontiers merely needed to hold the line.

Hindsight makes that strategy the most economical British victory. But in the real world, strategy is shaped by a myriad of competing political factions, perceptions, and traditions. Year after year, the British tried and failed to implement multi-pronged offensives against Forts Duquesne, Niagara, Carillon, and Louisbourg. Eventually, all those forts fell, but at an enormous and largely unnecessary cost in treasury and blood.

The fifth war for North America was unlike any that preceded it. In his three years in Canada, General Montcalm found that the "nature of war in this colony has totally changed. Formerly the Canadians thought they were making war when they went on raids resembling hunting-parties—now we have formal operations; formerly the Indians were the basis of things, now they are only auxiliaries. We now need other views, other principles. I say this; but the old principles remain."[6] Montcalm's aid, Louis de Bougainville, also noticed the change: "Now war is established here on the European basis. It is no longer a matter of making a raid, but of conquering or being conquered. What a revolution! What a change . . . townsmen, bankers, merchants, officers, bishops, parish priests, Jesuits, all plan this [war], speak of it, discuss it, pronounce on it."[7]

Warfare now embraced not only large-scale raids, but European-style field battles and sieges. Open field battles of the era in Europe were relatively simple. Opposing armies lined up their regiments end to end, studded that front with artillery batteries, anchored each flank with cavalry squadrons, and kept several regiments in reserve. Infantry and cavalry alike defended and advanced in three or more parallel ranks. The only element of this type of battle missing in North America was cavalry. Neither the French nor the British sent any cavalry squadrons to their colonies. Commanders deployed rangers and Indians for the traditional cavalry roles of scouting and screening, and in battle often anchored their lines with provincial troops rather than horsemen.

Few open field battles occurred during the war, of which the fights at Abraham (1759) and St. Foy (1760) before Quebec were the most significant. Much more common were British assaults on fortified lines, such as at Fort Carillon (1758), Gabarus Bay near Louisbourg (1758), and Beauport near Quebec (1759). The French too made such assaults, most notably on William Johnson's entrenchments at Lake George (1755) and Belle Famille at Niagara (1758). Of those five assaults, only the seaborne attack on the fortified French beaches at Gabarus Bay succeeded, and only then when some troops found an undefended cove and Wolfe shifted his attack to there.

Amphibious warfare played a major role in British campaigns in North America, Europe, the Caribbean, India, and the Philippines. Just what contributed to a successful amphibious assault? James Wolfe learned valuable lessons from a failed 1757 landing at Rochefort that he later practiced at Louisbourg and Quebec: "I have found that an admiral should endeavour to run into an enemy's port immediately after he appears before it; that he should anchor the transport ships and frigates as close as he can to the land; that he should reconnoitre . . . as quick as possible, and lose no time in getting the troops on shore; that previous directions should be given in respect to landing the troops, and a proper disposition made for the boats of all sorts, appointing leaders and fit persons for conducting the different divisions . . . in an affair depending on vigor and dispatch, the Generals should settle their plan of operations, so that no time should be lost in idle debate . . . when the sword should be drawn; that pushing on smartly is the road to success . . . that the honor of one's country is to have some weight; and that, in particular circumstances and times, the loss of a thousand men is rather an advantage to a nation than otherwise, seeing that gallant attempts raise its reputation and make it respectable; whereas the contrary appearances sink the credit of a country, ruin the troops, and create infinite uneasiness and discontent at home."[8]

Whether it was an attack against the enemy in open field or behind fortifications, observers detected national differences in how such battles were waged. Captain John Knox compared the temper of French and British troops: "their whole detachment ran down the precipice with a ridiculous shout and manned their works. I have often reflected upon the absurdity of this practice in the French, who entertain a high opinion of their own discipline and knowledge in the art of war; there is nothing that can be more absurd than such noise in engaging an enemy . . . it . . . must tend to defeat all regularity and good order among themselves, because their men are thereby confused and are rendered incapable of paying attention to their officers or their duty; it is a false courage. How different, how nobly awful and expressive of true valour is the custom of the British troops! They do not expend their ammunition at an immense distance; and, if they advance to engage or stand to receive the charge, they are steady, profoundly silent and attentive, reserving their fire until they have received that of their adversaries, over whom they have a tenfold advantage; there are cases where huzzaing may be necessary, but those are very rare; the practice is unmilitary in an army or body of regulars; and experience plainly shows us that the troops who, in perfect silence, engage an enemy, waiting for their first fire, will always preserve a superiority."[9]

European-style sieges were more common than assaults. A siege involves days or even weeks of digging trenches and emplacing batteries ever closer to the enemy's fortress and then bombing it into rubble. Throughout the war, once an army besieged a fortress it invariably took it, as Monckton did at Beausejour (1755), Montcalm at Oswego (1756) and Fort William Henry (1757), Amherst at Louisbourg (1758), Johnson at Niagara (1759), Murray, having taken command upon Wolfe's death, at Quebec (1759), and Amherst at Fort Levis (1760). Other commanders won by default when the defenders abandoned their fortress before a siege began such as at Forts Duquesne, Carillon, and Frederic (all in 1759), and Isle aux Noix (1760). It was customary for besiegers to allow valiant defenders to surrender with "honors of war," which meant allowing them to march out with their muskets and swords clubbed, accompanied by one cannon with a gunner holding a burning wick. However, after the slaughter of several score or more British troops by Indians at Fort William Henry, most British commanders denied that honor to the French.

Artillery was relatively unimportant in field battles but decisive in any siege. At best, cannon played an auxiliary role in standup fights, whether it was in the open pastures before Quebec and Fort Carillon or dense woods at Lake George and the Monongahela. In those battles, the side prevailed that best massed and directed its musket fire. However, at fortresses like William Henry, Louisbourg, Frontenac, and Niagara, cannon, howitzers, and mortars were essential in battering down the defenders' walls and psyches.

Likewise, thousands of massed muskets were impotent against well-constructed entrenchments, let alone fortress walls. Abercromby's name might today be associated with competence rather than stupidity if he had devoted a day to bringing up and placing his guns, and the following day to unleashing an artillery bombardment that systematically destroyed the French breastworks before Fort Carillon. His massed regiments then could have swept away the remnants of the French troops rather than being torn apart before their lines.

Full-scale wilderness battles were less frequent than those in open fields.[10] Not surprisingly, the French mostly prevailed in the forest. The largest French and Indian forest victories over the British forces occurred at the Monongahela (1755), the Bloody Morning Scout near Lake George (1755), and Fort Duquesne (1758). The only significant large-scale woods fight in which the British, largely composed of American bateauxmen, held their own was on the Oswego River (1756).

While such grand wilderness battles were rare, there were dozens of forest skirmishes with a score or so of combatants on either side. Although the French and Indians tended to prevail in such fights, it was a myth that the British were unfamiliar with guerrilla warfare: "For more than a decade, European armies had utilized and fought Balkan pandours, Austrian and Dutch partisans, the French Regiment de Grassin, and Scottish Highlanders in the '45. All these opponents used irregular warfare, including raids, ambushes, and skirmishes from cover. Military manuals of the 1740s and 1750s, including those of Franz von Der Trenck, La Croix, Turpin, de Crisse, and Maurice, Comte de Saxe, all discussed partisan combat, or la petite guerre. Although Braddock's library is not known, fellow officers Henry Bouquet, John Forbes, George Townsend, and James Wolfe were familiar with these works."[11]

However, it took three years before the English generals applied to North America the principles of irregular warfare they had supposedly learned a decade earlier in Europe.[12] In 1758, Lord Loudoun required each regiment to train for irregular fighting as well as form a company of light infantry and a company of riflemen. It was Jeffrey Amherst who created the "thin red line" by forming his regiments into two rather than three ranks because "the enemy have very few regular troops to oppose us, and no yelling of Indians, or fire of Canadians, can possibly withstand two ranks, if the men are silent, attentive, and obedient to their officers."[13]

No British commander was a greater wilderness fighter than New Hampshire frontiersman Robert Rogers. In the fall of 1757, Rogers wrote a manual on wilderness warfare to help new recruits, especially officers, learn their trade. Described as the "first written manual of warfare in the New World," Rogers' tactics combined a dynamic mix of audacity and prudence, and can be ranked with those of other great guerrilla leaders.[14] The bottom line of any operation is to surprise the enemy while avoiding ambush. Every patrol should march in single file and be protected by point men, flankers, and rear guards. Larger forces should be split into three columns, each with their own point men, flankers, and rear guard. In wet ground, troops should move abreast to minimize tracks. Undiscovered troops communicate through bird and hand signals. Upon spotting the enemy, all take cover in front and rear lines by twos, with each man in the front rank alternatively firing and reloading. Some of the reserve rank should be sent to reinforce the flankers to block encirclement and in turn encircle the enemy. Others of the rear fill gaps in the front line. When hard-pressed, the front line retreats behind the rear which then becomes the front. Fire on the enemy is continuous. If surrounded, a two-lined square is formed. If the enemy is superior, escape into the night in small groups that scatter through the forest. If the enemy gives way, the pursuit presses upon them with the flankers advancing the fastest to cut them off. Half a party keeps watch half the night, and the others the rest of the night. The entire party should awaken and take arms before dawn as that is when the Indians most often attack. Before moving out, scouts are dispatched in a wide circle around camp to ensure the enemy has not prepared an ambush. Avoid popular springs, fords, and shorelines. If followed, circle back and ambush the pursuers. Even at a fort, rangers should be ready to move out within a minute. Rogers ends his narrative by emphasizing that every situation is different and officers and men alike must be ready immediately to adapt it to their advantage.

While war of any kind is horrible, wilderness warfare was fought with an especially vicious savagery. Combatants not only often tortured and murdered any enemies they captured, but women and children as well. Both the French and British colonial leaders offered bounties for the scalps of their enemies, with no regard for age or gender. General Shirley commanded Rogers to "distress the French and their allies, by sacking, burning, and destroying their houses, barns, barracks, canoes, battoes, &c. and by killing their cattle of every kind; and at all times to endeavour to way-lay, attack, and destroy their convoys of provisions by land and water, in any part of the country."[15] And at times both sides even resorted to biological warfare. The Iroquois dumped animal remains and other filth in streams from which the British drew water. During the 1763 siege of Fort Pitt, the British commander ordered blankets of smallpox victims to be given to the Indians.[16]

Not only did the strategy shift from limited to total war, but by the war's latter years any lingering remnants of chivalry between opposing officers dissolved into a savagery that matched that of the Indians. By 1759, shortly after his fleet anchored beyond cannon shot of Quebec and his men were rowed ashore, General Wolfe issued orders for them "to burn and lay waste the country."[17] Wolfe later ordered his gunners to bombard Quebec into rubble, slaughtering civilians and soldiers alike. When Montcalm responded by floating down his second flotilla of fire rafts against the British fleet, Wolfe sent him word that "if the enemy presume to send down any more fire rafts, they are to be made fast to two particular transports, in which are all the Canadian and other prisoners, in order that they may perish by their own base interventions."[18] Desperate times called for desperate measures. Montcalm threatened to set the "savages" loose on Quebec's citizens when they begged him to surrender the town to avert any more destruction.

No matter what kind of campaign or battle was being fought, commanders wrestled with the same problems of intelligence, negotiations, prisoners, and supply. Commanders usually made important decisions only after consulting their officers. These councils of war not only tapped into collective wisdom but also allowed "a commander to give up an operation without himself carrying the full burden of blame."[19] Officers could not begin to make a rational decision without obtaining and analyzing information about the enemy's strengths, weaknesses, deployments, and intentions. Here, while Indian and colonial scouts were important, even more so were deserters and prisoners who had an intimate understanding of their side's numbers, morale, supplies, and, sometimes, even the commander's intentions.

Most prisoners were taken following a siege whose conclusion was negotiated between opposing commanders. In those days, the white flag was not the universal sign of truce or surrender. Contrary to popular belief, the French battle flag was all white; golden fleur de lis emblazoned only the royal standard. When either side wished to speak with the enemy, they waved the predominant color of the enemy's flag. Thus did the French display a red flag and the British a white flag. A commander then sent a trusted officer into the enemy's line to convey his surrender terms. One major decision that the besieging commander had to make was whether to retain or parole prisoners. It made more sense, especially for the hard-pressed French, to parole rather than keep prisoners who ate up enormous amounts of food and diverted troops to serve as their guards. Paroled troops consumed their own nation's provisions while waiting on the sidelines for their promise to expire. Of course, there was always the chance that paroled troops might well be sent back into battle, as Lord Loudoun did with the troops paroled at Fort William Henry.

Whether they were on campaign or in camp, solders had to be fed, armed, and clothed, something that took armies of butchers and bakers, along with teamsters, stevedores, farmers, rowers, drovers, and weavers, and makers of muskets, gunpowder, cannons, boats, ships, barrels, ropes, tools, and wagons to accomplish. Even where paths broke through the wilderness it was often easier to transport a large military force by boat. Transportation on rivers and lakes was usually by flat-bottomed bateaux or round-hulled whaleboats, both of which had pointed prows and sterns. Birchbark canoes were, of course, most common where the tree was ubiquitous, as in the St. Lawrence valley and upper New England. Elsewhere, Indians traveled by dugout canoes (piroque) while the Iroquois often used elmbark canoes.

No permanent French or British armies existed. For each campaign they devised, Versailles or Whitehall had to create a new army from available regiments and commanders. As the largest permanent units, regiments formed the army's backbone, although they varied considerably in size from one to four battalions. Ideally, each British battalion numbered about 850 men in twelve 60-man companies which included ten of regular infantry, one light infantry company for scouting and skirmishing, and one grenadier company of the physically toughest and largest men for shock troops. French battalions numbered 525 troops and 31 officers in twelve line (fusilier) companies and one grenadier company. Most British regiments had only one battalion; with four battalions, the 60th Royal Americans was a notable exception. During the Seven Years' War, however, some regiments were authorized to recruit a second battalion. Most French regiments had two to four battalions.

The practice of concentrating the biggest and toughest soldiers in the regiment's grenadier company tended to rob the line companies of their best men. Grenadier companies were split into two platoons with each to anchor an end of the regiment's line. In some battles or even campaigns a general might group the grenadier companies into one elite regiment. Amherst did so at Louisbourg and Wolfe at Quebec; both used their grenadier regiments to lead assaults. Here the advantage in combat prowess was offset by the inexperience of grenadier companies from rival regiments with maneuvering and fighting as one cohesive unit.

In both armies, most regiments were owned, not by the king or state, but by the lords whose feudal ancestors first raised the unit, or by extremely wealthy men who chose to raise and lead a new regiment. Likewise, officer commissions were for sale at prices that escalated with rank. Only the extremely wealthy could buy the highest ranks. Purchased commissions helped bolster aristocratic power at the expense of battlefield prowess. Few officers knew anything of the art or science of war. In all European armies, the "officer corps subordinated the military values of expertise, discipline, and responsibility to the aristocratic values of luxury, courage, and individualism. The aristocrat was an amateur at officership; it was not for him a vocation with ends and standards of its own, but an incidental attribute of his station in society."[20] Many criticized the system and the unprofessional officers it bred. Pitt pilloried the commanders' "Want of Application to Geography, the different Arts of War and Military Discipline; their Insolence to the inferior Officers, and Tyranny over the common Men. . . . [Their] Extravagance, Idleness, and Luxury . . . few seem to be affected with any other Zeal than that of aspiring to the highest Posts, and grasping the largest Salaries."[21]

Officers looked as well as acted like aristocrats. In both armies, they wore white wigs or powdered their long hair white, a practice extended to the ranks for dress parades. The use of flour for that appearance must have seemed extravagant to some when the supply for bakeries ran low. Gold lace scrolls were embroidered on cuffs, sleeves, shoulders, and hats. Officers also wore on their chests a silver gorget or miniature breastplate suspended from ribbons which were colored like the regimental facing.

Officer training was largely nil. Britain then had no military schools. Although the Ecole Militaire opened in 1751 to train officers, its graduates contributed little to France's war effort. What knowledge an officer received came from campaign experience or the few books on the subject. Literate officers could improve their skills by studying the ancient classics and numerous contemporary books on the art of leadership and war. During the French and Indian War, many an English or American officer packed in his haversack tattered volumes of Oliver Peabody's *An Essay to Revive and Encourage Military Exercises, Skills and Valour among the Sons of God's People in New-England* (1732), William Breton's *Militia Discipline, the Words of Command, and Directions for Exercising the Musket, Bayonet, & Carthidge* (1733), William Brattle's *Sundry Rules and Directions for Drawing up a Regiment* (1733), or Humphrey Bland's *An Abstract of Military Discipline; More Particularly with Regards to the Manuel Exercise, Evolutions, and Firings of the Foot, from Col. Bland* (1743). He might even have found an earlier work such as Robert Baret's *The Theorike and Practike of Moderne Warres, Discoursed in Dialoque* (1598), William Barriffe's *Military Discipline, or the Young Artillery-Man* (1643), Richard Elton's *The Compleat Body of the Art Military* (1659), James Fitzroy Scott, the Duke of Monmouth's *Abridgement of the English Military Discipline* (1690), and Nicholas Boone's *Military Discipline, The Compleat Souldier, or Expert Artillery-Man* (1701).[22] French officers could find inspiration in Vauban's *Projet de Tactique* and *L'Attaque et la Defense des Places* (1740), *L'Art de la Guerre Pratique* and *Traite de la Petite Guerre*, de Crisse's *Essay on the Art of War* (1754), or Marshall Saxe's *Reveries* (1756). However insightful or insipid such works were, in the end, leadership depended on experience, valor, initiative, intelligence, and fortune.

Purchasing a commission and living an officer's often extravagant lifestyle frequently consumed much of an aristocrat's disposable wealth. Officers boosted their income through both legal and illegal means. In both armies, officers received extra rations in proportion to their rank. British colonels, for example, got six times the daily food of a private. An officer could make a handsome profit selling the excess. A widespread practice was for officers to pocket the pay of nonexistent soldiers in their ranks. Official statistics on regimental strength thus often exaggerated a unit's true numbers.

Garnering new recruits for the regiment was an endless task. Disease, desertion, and combat annually cost the average regiment one of every five men. For France, this meant finding over 50,000 new recruits every year to maintain its 330,000-man army. Recruiting was most common in winter after the regiments had gone into cantonments and officers were free to scour the towns and villages for new cannon-fodder. Recruiters looked for men between 16 and 40 years old and over five foot, one inch in height. During the war, one in eleven French men with those qualifications donned a uniform. In beleaguered Brunswick, Hesse, Hanover, and Prussia, one in five men served. Soldiers volunteered for six-year enlistments. While hundreds of thousands of Britons and millions of French met this qualification, there were only so many willing men available. All regiments welcomed a certain number of enemy deserters in their ranks. Recruiters often filled their quotas by getting men befuddled with drink to take the king's enlistment shilling or livre, often found at a tankard's bottom. Ideally, recruits made up only one in three men in a regiment. A regiment's combat effectiveness is diluted as its proportion of green troops rises.[23] By the war's end, all the belligerents had drained their kingdoms of viable recruits.

Once a recruit had been nabbed, the officers had to uniform, arm, train, and feed him. By the mid-18th century, the French and British armies were approaching the imposition of standard uniforms. Although colored differently, the French and British uniforms sported similar patterns. Each regiment, however, had different-colored facings and cuffs. In both armies, drummers and flag-bearers wore uniforms with colors the reverse of their regiments. Thus did a drummer or flag-bearer wear a blue uniform with white facings and cuffs if his regimental uniform was white with blue facings and cuffs. The standard French marine or army uniform was a light grey coat, white shirt, and blue knee breeches and leggings. Line and grenadier troops alike wore cocked hats. Some regiments like the Berry, Guienne, or La Reine had red facings.

When the war broke out, British regulars wore red wool coats, vests, knee breeches, and leggings. Line troops wore cocked hats; grenadiers were decked with tall, pointed mitre caps with insignia and scrolls embroidered in silk, silver, and gold. Royal regiments had blue rather than red trousers. Three highlanders' regiments, the 42nd Black Watch, 77th, and 78th, fought with great distinction in North America. All wore red jackets and navy blue kilts, although they were issued pants for the harsh winter months. Although most American provincial troops wore uniforms cut from the same pattern as those of regular troops, the colors differed widely. Those from Massachusetts, Pennsylvania, New Jersey, and Virginia mostly wore blue uniforms faced with red; a few Pennsylvanian units wore green faced with red. Some regiments from various colonies favored red uniforms. Each soldier wore a buff leather belt that held his bayonet and short sword, and another belt over his left shoulder holding a cartridge box. By 1760, commanders had modified their troops' uniforms. Knee breeches were now dyed cream rather than red. Leggings ended just above the knee rather than midway up the thigh. Bearskin rather than embroidery encased a grenadier's mitre. Cartridge boxes now had holes for 36 rather than 18 rounds. Fully dressed, armed, equipped, and supplied with six days' rations, the British or French soldier groaned under 60 pounds of weight. In 1768, Whitehall issued its Clothing Warrant that standardized these changes already made by many regiments.[24]

With but one yearly change of uniform, the troops could look quite bedraggled, particularly after a long, hard stint on fatigue or patrol. Knox described a returning wood party from his regiment "as droll and grotesque an appearance as a detachment of Hungarian or Croatian irregulars, occasioned by the length of their beards, the disordered shape of their hats, and the raggedness of their partly-coloured cloathing; for some had brown, other blue watch-coats (buckled around their waists with a cartouch-box strap) and some were in their threadbare uniforms; in short they had very little of the British regular in them . . . troops long stationed in this province, who must in a great measure lay aside the uniformity of the clean, smart soldier, and substitute . . . the slovenly, undisciplined, wood-hewer, sand-digger and hod-carrier."[25]

Upon the annual receipt of a new coat, a soldier might pay a tailor a shilling to convert his old ragged uniform into a waistcoat or breeches, and the scraps into a forage cap. Soldiers garrisoned or campaigning on the frontier often supplemented their uniforms with articles adapted for a rugged, harsh wilderness. Boots were exchanged for moccasins "made of the skin of beaver, elk, calf, sheep, or other pliant leather, half-dressed: each moggosan is of one intire piece, joined or sewed up in the middle . . . and closed behind . . . they have no additional sole or heel . . . and must be used with three or four . . . socks, or folds of thick flannel wrapt round the foot; they are tied on the instep with thongs of the same leather, which are fastened to the joining behind, and run through the upper part . . . they are exceedingly warm, and much fitter for the winters of this country than our European shoe, as a person may walk over sheets of ice without the least danger of falling; the meaner sort of French and Indians make them of a tougher and thicker leather, but the heads of tribes, and better kind of French, affect a more gay, dressy sort, with very broad quarters to them, that turn over like the . . . neck of a shirt; and this part, as well as the vamp from the toe upwards, is curiously ornamented with narrow slips of red cloath, covered with white, green, and blue beads sewed on in various whimsical figures." Leggings were "made of frize or other coarse woollen cloth; they should be at least three quarters of a yard in length . . . then double it, and sew it . . . fitting this long, narrow bag to the shape of the leg . . . tied round under the knee and above the ankle with garters of the same colour; by which the legs are preserved from many fatal accidents that may happen by briars, stumps of trees, or under-wood, etc in marching through a close, woody country."[26] The Enlightenment's obsession with symmetry apparently even extended to shoes. Soldiers daily had to change their shoes between feet so that they "did not run croocked."[27]

Troops were armed with smoothbore muskets. The French regular musket or fusil was the 1754 .69 caliber, 11-pound model manufactured in Charleville or Saint Etienne. Some troops carried a much earlier but not much different 1717 version. Most marines shouldered a lighter 1729 musket made in Tulle, although during the 1740s, these were gradually replaced with Saint Etienne muskets. British muskets were affectionately known as the Brown Bess, a .75 caliber, 14-pound smoothbore, first designed in 1717 like the fusil. French and British muskets were mostly handmade with non-interchangeable parts. Bayonets fitted both the fusil and Brown Bess.

Loading was relatively simple. Charges of powder and ball were packed in paper cartridges which were stuffed in black leather–covered wooden boxes drilled to hold 18 or 36 rounds. To arm his musket, a soldier half-cocked the hammer, opened the pan, lifted his cartridge box flap, pulled a cartridge, bit off the tip, poured some powder in the pan and snapped it shut, dumped the rest of the powder down the musket barrel, stuffed the ball and paper in the barrel, rammed it to the bottom, and full-cocked the hammer. The musket was then ready to fire.

Good soldiers could get off three or even four shots a minute. Accuracy for the unsighted smoothbores, however, was a different matter—muskets shot wide beyond 50 or so yards. Troops were taught not to even bother aiming but simply to level their muskets in the enemy's direction and pull the trigger. At times, commanders ordered their troops to stuff a double charge and two balls down their musket barrels, as Wolfe did on the Plains of Abraham, or load their weapons with buckshot as well as a ball. The discharge had a better chance of hitting the enemy. In both armies, regiments lined across a field fired by platoons. Ideally, the first platoon had reloaded by the time the last along the line had emptied its muskets, thus presenting a continuous rolling barrage of lead toward the enemy.

There was a scattering of other weapons in both armies. Line officers were armed with largely ceremonial spontoons and swords. In battle, many wisely discarded their ponderous spontoons and carried muskets instead. A few rifle companies were distributed through both the French and British armies, but never enough to change the nature of the era's massed musket-and-horse warfare. Rifles were rare even among Americans. Most rangers slipped through the forest armed with muskets. A rifle's accuracy was offset by its expense and longer loading time.

In all, musket balls accounted for about 80 percent of deaths and wounds, and cannon shot and shell about 10 percent. Bayonets were rarely used and accounted for only 9 percent of casualties. Each weapon produced horribly gruesome wounds. Cannon balls and grape tore men apart; musket balls shattered bones and organs; bayonets ripped triangular wounds that could not be sewn back together. Even minor wounds usually brought infections and often gangrene. Men died lingering, excruciatingly painful deaths.[28]

The opportunity for soldiers to use their weapons was actually quite rare. In any army, soldiers mostly spent their time battling mind-numbing monotony, vermin, sickness, and extremes of heat, cold, snow, ice, and rain. Life consisted of long stretches of idle boredom broken by nauseating spats of combat terrors, disease, and harsh discipline. Many longed for faraway homes and rued the day they ever palmed the king's shilling or livre. Word from home was tenuous at best. Mail service was erratic. A letter might not catch up to its target until months or even years after it was originally sent.

British privates lived off 20 shillings a month; French privates on five sous, eight deniers. The pay of soldiers from both armies was docked for their uniforms. Troops were paid for woodcutting at a rate of two shillings a cord and a gill of rum every day. Lodging and food was free. Wedge tents were the soldiers' usual abode on or off campaign. Barracks were rare even in the home country. Troops were billeted among country peasants and town burghers, a practice that incensed most Americans. Soldiers were provided rations, although the amount and quality was usually dismal. Army rations, of course, varied with the relative abundance or scarcity of available food. French soldiers generally received daily rations of a half pound each of peas and salt pork, and a pound and a half of bread.[29] According to Knox, a British "soldier's allowance per week is seven pounds of beef, or, in lieu thereof, four pounds of pork, which is thought to be an equivilent; seven pounds of biscuit bread, or the same weight of flour; six onces of butter, three pints of pease, half a pound of rice; and this is called seven rations."[30] Soldiers and sailors at sea supplemented their rations by fish dragged from the depths with nets or hooks.

Winter was the most miserable season. Soldiers from both sides spent winters cutting and hauling wood, and huddling before smokey fires. Frost-bite was a near-constant enemy, blackening toes, fingers, nose-tips, and ears. If a snow-pack did not revive the deadened extremity it had to be amputated before gangrene developed and spread. Scurvy was a much more insidious form of slow death for many more troops. The disease was caused by bodies starved for the vitamins that come from fresh vegetables. The army's anti-dote to scruvy was spruce-beer, "made of the tops and branches of the Spruce-tree, boiled for three hours, then strained into casks, with a certain quantity of molasses; and, as soon as cold, it is fit for use."[31] Those who did not survive a winter were stacked like logs in sheds or beneath brush piles that kept away the wolves until the spring thaw allowed them to be interred in the earth.

Summer was not much better, bringing with it diseases and mosquitoes that caused "fevers by their virulence, and a person's head, face, and neck so swelled and inflamed as not to have a feature distinguishable; for this cause we always wore long linen trowsers, with crape or green gauze nets sewed to our hats, which hung down loose before and behind, with a running string at the bottom to gather it round the neck."[32]

Germs killed far more troops than bullets. Battle casualties generally ranged from 2 percent to 10 percent among troops engaged; disease killed four times more soldiers than battle. Disease festered in the reeking army camps with human and slaughtered animal waste piled just beyond the neat rows of tents or the palisade wall. Whether the troops drew their water from wells or streams, the source was invariably an open sewer clogged with the vilest sights, diseases, and odors imaginable. Ignorance and sloth kept regular and colonial soldiers alike from practicing even the most rudimentary sanitation precautions. Medical care was rudimentary at best in both armies. Without any real knowledge of sanitation or infection, hospitals became charnel houses whose stench was unbearable. Whether it was a wound or disease that dragged them to a hospital, 40 in 100 troops never survived the experience.

For that era's warfare, officers trained soldiers to be unbreakable machines that would obey a command amidst the worst fire and carnage.[33] One way they tried to achieve this was through incessant training in close-order drill, a practice useful for European battlefields but disastrous in the American wilderness. The other was by inflicting punishments before the assembled troops on soldiers who had made even the slightest of infractions. These punishments were cruel and sometimes murderous. Miscreants could run a gauntlet of their comrades armed with steel ramrods, ride a wooden horse with weights attached to their legs, or have their naked backs whipped. Desertion, theft, insult to an officer, and other crimes could result in the offender being lashed literally to within an inch of death with a cat-o'-nine-tails, a multi-stranded, lead-tipped whip. Floggings of a dozen or so strokes were common, but hundreds or even a thousand strokes were at times inflicted. Each stroke ripped skin from the man's back; several hundred strokes could gouge away flesh to the rib cage and backbone. Yet, somehow, despite the gruesome consequences, soldiers kept breaking the rules. Inhumane as it was, such vicious punishments did foster some benefits. Regular troops rarely broke and ran under fire—all that drilling and the threat of the lash literally kept them in line.

THE ART OF NAVAL WARFARE

By comparison, France rather than Britain should have become the world's greatest seapower. New France could have supplied all the masts, pitch, planks, yardarms, and tar necessary to build a huge war fleet. French warships were generally considered superior to their British counterparts in construction and maneuverability. With four times Britain's population, France should never have lacked for seamen. Indeed, tens of thousands of Frenchmen annually sailed on merchant ships to the world's far corners.

Yet France chose not to exploit these ample resources to challenge Britain on the high seas and defend the empire it had committed such treasury to create. More than anything else, France's failure is explained by a lack of will and imagination. French leaders refused to throw off the dead weight of tradition's shackles that bowed their vision to Europe. The repeated failure of Louis XIV's armies to retain the Netherlands or Rhineland let alone overrun more distant lands should have convinced Versailles that Europe's power balance was too great to break. Empire for France lay not on the continent, but around the world. France could have been defended with three-quarters the number of battalions, with the savings diverted to matching the British fleet in numbers, audacity, and skill. But that did not happen.

Perhaps the most important reason was that the French had earlier actually succeeded in achieving naval superiority, yet they failed to sweep the British navy from the seas. French naval power had peaked in the late 1670s when Jean-Baptiste Colbert increased the fleet from 20 ships in 1661 to 250 by 1677, a number then equivalent to the combined English and Dutch fleets. The French failed to exploit or maintain this advantage. No great French naval victories accompanied the enlarged fleet. Funding for maintenance failed to keep pace with that for building new ships, causing much of the fleet to rot away. Considerable patronage died with the French defeat at La Hogue in 1692. Despite the defeat, France's warship building continued for another decade, until 1702, when the fleet numbered 281 compared to 271 British ships. But Versailles refused to commit its warships to a decisive battle. During the first half of the 18th century, the French fleet eroded while the British fleet steadily rose in numbers. The Navy Minister from 1723 to 1749, Jean Frederic Phelippeaux, believed that France should maintain a large fleet, but was overruled by Louis XV and his ministers, Guillaume Dubois and Andre-Hercule de Fleury, who kept the naval budget low to avoid antagonizing the British.[34]

Although Britain too was wedded to Europe via its entangling alliance with Hanover, it also had the luxury of being surrounded by water. That and a pervasive fear of standing armies inspired by Oliver Cromwell's dictatorship led London to concentrate on building up its fleet in the late 17th century and throughout the 18th century. During that time, no one contributed more to ensuring British naval superiority than Admiral George Anson, who was appointed to the admiralty board in 1745, and served as First Lord from 1751 to 1762. A range of serious problems plagued the British navy when Anson took office, and he systematically confronted and overcame nearly all of them. A hodgepodge of ship sizes and designs composed the navy. Anson imposed new, streamlined standards so that each warship class was superior in design, construction, and firepower to its French counterpart, and ensured that recent innovations in rigging and sailplans were incorporated into Britain's latest ships. He alleviated a worsening timber shortage in Britain by encouraging merchant ships to be constructed in the American colonies, thus easing the pressure for what was considered to be superior quality English oak. America was already the primary source for the tall white pines used for masts and the elms used for keels. In 1748, he deepened the navy's pride by issuing uniforms to all officers, from admiral to midshipman. In 1755, he organized the marines into three divisions that enabled them to be more effectively dispersed through the fleets. Through Anson's tenure, promotion more than ever depended on a candidate's skills and successes.[35]

As a result of these different polices of Whitehall and Versailles, throughout the Seven Years' War the British fleet not only held twice as many ships as did the French fleet, but handled them with greater skill and audacity. In 1755, the English fleet of 116 ships-of-the-line and 113 smaller ships afloat, and 21 being built, was nearly three times larger than France's 38 ships-of-the-line and 32 afloat, with 22 being built. As can be seen below, English ships not only numbered more, but outgunned the French:[36]

1755 Comparison:

Guns	110	100	90	80	74	72	70	64	60	54	50	smaller
English	1	5	13	8	5	0	29	0	39	3	28	112
French	0	0	0	6	21	1	4	31	2	0	6	32

Throughout the war, Whitehall steadily increased its naval appropriations. The British navy's budget doubled between 1755 and 1758. By 1758, the British navy included 238 ships, of which 98 were ships-of-the-line compared to only 72 French ships-of-the-line. In 1759, the British sailed 107 ships-of-the-line to France's 50. In November 1762, the navy consisted of 305 ships and 85,665 seamen and marines.[37]

As if being outgunned and outsailed by a two-to-one ratio was not discouraging enough, French naval commanders faced additional challenges. Although French ports along the English Channel could harbor troop transports, they were too shallow for the massive warships that could convoy them for an invasion of Britain. The navy's two best ports, Brest and Toulon, were at opposite ends of France. Combining the fleets was difficult enough during peacetime and nearly impossible in the face of a British blockade.

Only less daunting was the annual challenge of resupplying New France. Once again, British naval superiority and the nearly constant blockade turned the dispatch of every supply convoy into a roll of the dice. The French fleet commander at Brest glued his eye to the weather gauge. If an Atlantic storm was severe enough, the British admiral commanding the blockade fleet might order his ships to run for shelter at Plymouth. Once the storm passed, the French would have a several days' jump on sailing into the Atlantic. Versailles could never decide whether it was better to send the ships all at once or in smaller numbers. The French Marine Minister expressed the dilemma: "To send succors in divisions is to run the risk of losing all in detail; to send them together, is to expose ourselves to a general action and to lose all at once."[38] Regardless of which method was tried, throughout the war, Canada suffered chronic shortages of munitions, Indian trade goods, and, above all, food.

The British admiralty faced its own challenges. Despite its greater ship numbers, the navy was hard-pressed to fulfill all the strategic demands placed upon it. The navy's primary objective was defensive—to prevent an invasion of Britain. To this end, the admiralty kept a squadron on patrol at the English Channel's western end, based at Plymouth, where it was ready to pounce on any invasion fleet setting sail from French ports. Before 1759, the blockade extended far from shore and frequently disappeared altogether as the squadron returned to port to refit; thus it was relatively easy for French ships to evade. Admiral Edward Hawke solved this problem in 1759 when he anchored his ships within miles of the French coast and staggered their relief, thereby cutting French blockade runners from many to a few.

Britain had strategic naval worries that extended far beyond the Brittany coastline. Throughout the 17th and 18th centuries, Britain fought a series of wars at least partly to ensure that no great power could take over the Netherlands and thus enjoy the potential to send an invasion fleet across the North Sea, or to intercept a French fleet that slipped past the fleet in the western English Channel. To counter this threat, Whitehall maintained a fleet in the eastern English Channel based at Portsmouth.

A much greater fear was that France and Spain would combine their fleets and send them into the Channel. In the 17th century, Britain fought to win and maintain Portugal's independence to sever that kingdom's fine harbors from Spain. A British squadron based at Lisbon watched Spain's naval base at Cadiz. The 1704 conquest of Gilbraltar allowed the British fleet stationed there to plug the Mediterranean Sea. Gibraltar, however, lacked a sheltered anchorage. In 1708, Britain conquered Minorca for the deep, landlocked port of Mahon. It was now much quicker for the fleet to rush to Gilbraltar from Mahon than Lisbon, when frigates brought word that the Toulon French fleet had set sail. From Minorca the British navy dominated both the western Mediterranean and Iberian west coast. The French upset this strategy when they captured Minorca in 1756, causing the British to rely once again on Gibraltar and Lisbon. British naval commanders fulfilled their mission despite the disadvantage. In 1758, Sir Henry's Osbourne's squadron prevented the Toulon fleet from sailing to Louisbourg's relief. In 1759, Admiral Boscawen's fleet sailed north from Gibraltar to attack Admiral de la Clue's invasion fleet at Quiberon Bay.

Britain maintained squadrons at strategic points around the world to guard its far-flung and growing empire. The naval base at Halifax was as strategically important to protecting the American colonies as Gibraltar was to patroling southwestern Europe's coasts. From Halifax, fleets could block-ade Louisbourg and the St. Lawrence, and convoy merchant ships to and from British ports. In the West Indies, naval superiority depended more on who owned the Windward Islands than superior numbers of ships. Ships setting sail from the French ports at Fort Royale, Martinique and Cape Francois, Haiti, or the Spanish port at Havana, Cuba enjoyed the easterly trade winds that carried them past the leeward British ports at Kingstown, Jamaica. Every year when the hurricane season started in June, Britain's West Indian fleet sailed from its vulnerable ports out of the Caribbean and up America's East Coast to shelter at New York, Boston, or Halifax. The fleet would return in October to patrol the Caribbean for another eight months. The British were also disadvantaged in India. French ships enjoyed fine harbors at Port Louis, Maritius, and Trincomalee, the best natural bay in the Indian Ocean, while all of the British towns on the Coromandel lacked good anchorage.

As if the British fleet were not stretched far enough, English merchants continually pressured the Cabinet to concentrate the navy's operations to "guarding convoys, chasing after privateers, and otherwise promoting British commerce. Important as these tasks might be, their priority was not justified by the total demands of an imperial struggle across half the world."[39]

With far fewer ships, the French tended to use them mostly to supplement the defense of fortresses. Cowed by an inferiority complex, French admirals rarely committed their fleets to battle, even when they enjoyed superior numbers, thus literally letting the wind blow away dazzling chances for victory. During the Seven Years' War, the French lost not one but three chances off Louisbourg and another off Quebec to strike what might have been crippling blows against the British. The first of these occurred in July 1757, when La Motte's combined fleet far outnumbered Hardy's nearby squadron. A successful attack on Hardy followed up by a sortie against Halifax might have intimidated the British into delaying an attack on Louisbourg not only that year, which happened anyway, but perhaps even the next. Yet, the French fleet remained anchored safely within Louisbourg's harbor. Two even greater chances arose to destroy British squadrons led by Holbourne in September 1757 and Boscawen in June 1758, when storms battered the British ships so severely they were virtually indefensible. Likewise at Quebec, a more aggressive use of French ships might have saved that city. The five frigates anchored up the St. Lawrence outgunned the few British ships that had sailed past the fortress's batteries in July. A well-planned and executed attack that destroyed those enemy ships might have prevented the British from sailing any more past Quebec, thus delaying Quebec's conquest that year and perhaps the next. The only use the French made of their flotilla at Quebec was to convert most of them into fireboats which, in the two separate nights they were launched, failed spectacularly to harm any British ships.

When French and British captains did close their ships for battle, their ability to act was limited by the "Permanent Instructions" that each side's admiralty had issued a half century earlier. Tactics were straightjacketed to each side advancing toward the other in rigid lines of ships. Nonetheless, once a British and French warship squared off, they did use different gunnery tactics. The French tried to disable enemy ships by firing chain and dumbbell shot toward the masts, sails, and rigging, and then sailing away. The British preferred to pound enemy ships with cannon shot aimed toward the waterline, before closing and boarding.

Despite Anson's reforms, the French still enjoyed an overall advantage over the British in ship design and construction. But while the French may have made better ships, the British were better sailors. Whether at sea or in port, the British were much more adept at handling ships. For example, after capturing Louisbourg in 1758, the British managed to cram 33 warships and 90 transports in a harbor where the French previously had trouble anchoring any more than 25 ships.[40] Hawke's victory at Quiberon Bay in 1759 depended as much on the ability to boldly pursue Conflans' ships into shallow waters as it did on superior firepower.

Better seamanship depended partly on taking advantage of technological advances like Hadley's Mirror Quadrant (1731) and the chronometer (1735), which allowed for a far more accurate understanding of one's position. The British also developed a sophisticated signaling method that enabled a fleet commander to coordinate his ships' movement. Captains could tap into the latest innovations in navigation and seamanship by reading such works as Joshua Kelly's *The Modern Navigator's Compleat Tutor* (1724), Captain Daniel Newhouse's *The Whole Art of Navigation* (1727), N. Colson's *The Mariner's Kalender* (1746), and John Robertson's *Elements of Navigation* (1754).

Yet another British advantage was its greater intelligence-gathering ability. Although both nations' assorted diplomats, courtesans, and letter-openers were probably equally as effective in gleaning important, trivial, and wrong information alike about the war, France lacked something that Britain enjoyed—Lloyd's of London. Since its founding in 1686, Lloyd's had built up an elaborate global information network to assist its insurance business, which, of course, proved a wonderful supplement to the government's spy network.

On sea as on land, the presence of skilled and bold officers often meant the difference between victory and defeat. To greatly varying degrees, both navies rewarded initiative and daring. Although their tactics were limited, officers enjoyed considerable freedom of action, including the powers to make war and diplomacy as seemed most appropriate to unique situations. Boldness led not only to promotion but to wealth. Prize money was split in thirds among the captain, petty officers, and crew.

Yet, British and French officers formed distinct institutions, which McLennan contrasts with only slight exaggeration: "One which was starved in money, men, and equipment, had to meet in conflict another on which were lavished the resources of a country constantly growing in wealth. The commanders of one were drawn from a single class, of the other, from a whole nation. Officers, whose experience led them to expect defeat, were opposed to others flushed with victory, or desirous of emulating the exploits of their colleagues; those knowing neither victory nor defeat made a vital difference in their careers; those assured of all the rewards of success, speedy professional advancement, rank, wealth, and glory."[41]

Perhaps no British institution rewarded genius more readily than the navy. For over two centuries before the Seven Years' War, English seadogs had stolen glory and treasure for Britain, and its officers had been rewarded no matter what their origins. As Peter Warren's career illustrates, through courage, skill, and luck, a lad who joined the navy as an ordinary seaman could not only become an officer but even an admiral and peer. Yet, while Whitehall encouraged initiative, its 1731 "Regulations and Admiralty Instructions" imposed uniform rules, standards, and behaviors on ships or fleet commanders.

What to British officers was a career, was to most French officers a sinecure. Aristocracy and gerontocracy ruled the French navy. Nobility rather than daring and skill filled officer's berths. Once in, officers stayed at the helm for decades after most of their British counterparts would have retired with small pensions. The French navy rewarded timidity. Officers advanced by avoiding defeat rather than tempting victory. The fleet's purpose was to preserve itself by anchoring in safe harbors or sailing away from the enemy. The ministry punished brilliant captains like Jean Vauquelin, Jean Joseph Rosier, or Beaussier de l'Isle by letting mediocrities leapfrog them into squadron commands.

If most talented officers, particularly in the British navy, could arise from any class, most seamen were dragged into the service from society's muck. Perhaps only one in five men aboard a British or French warship were there by choice. The rest were kidnapped from grog shops and alleys by press gangs armed with muskets, swords, and clubs. Impressment was legal as a draft for almost anyone from 18 to 55 years old. The admiralty issued press warrants to ship captains to fill their manpower needs. Other means were used to fill British ships. A 1755 law allowed foreign sailors to compose up to three-quarters of an English ship's crew. Another 1755 law recalled all British subjects from service in foreign ships. Even prisoners of war were recruited for service.[42]

The British navy resorted to the press gang far more frequently than did the French, for the simple reason that the former increased in ships while the latter diminished. From 1755 to 1763, 184,893 men served in the British fleet, of which about 145,000 were sailors and 40,000 were marines. As in land war, disease claimed far more seamen's lives than battle. During the war, only 1,512 were killed in battle or accidents while disease either killed or crippled an estimated 60,000 sailors, or one of every three men! Perhaps as many as 40,000 other sailors deserted. Of those who served in the British fleet, only about 35,000 had volunteered. Discounting the 40,000 marines, over 110,000 sailors had to be impressed. The navy's manpower needs rose steadily throughout the war. In 1756, the navy needed 50,000 men to operate its fleet, a number that rose to 70,000 by 1760. Fortunately for Britain, it had a vast pool of over 300,000 experienced seamen from its merchant, smuggling, and fishing fleets in Britain and America.[43]

From the very first times that British press gangs roamed America's ports, beating and hauling away unfortunates for the king's navy, the colonial populations and their leaders bitterly protested the practice. In 1693, Massachusetts governor William Phips actually got in a fist fight with the HMS *Nonesuch*'s Captain Richard Short for his impressment of Boston men. In 1702, the gunners manning Boston's Castle Island cannon fired on the HMS *Swift*, which was setting sail with impressed seamen. Yet the British navy continued to disembark its press gangs in American ports whenever it needed more hands. The impressments and tendency of seamen to hide or flee whenever British ships were in port disrupted merchant shipping. Franklin complained that impressment damaged colonial trade "more than the Enemy hurts it."[44]

Once aboard, a sailor's life was as grim as that of the landlubber soldiers. Winston Churchill's quip that the British navy's tradition was rooted in "rum, sodomy, and the lash" was not far off the mark. Those who broke the rules could suffer "gagging" with an iron bar, "running the gauntlet" of crew armed with sticks, and "flogging" with a cat-o'-nine-tails. The most horrible fate was to be "flogged through the fleet," a sentence that usually ended in death. The accused was tied in a whaleboat and flogged repeatedly before every anchored ship. The flogging might be suspended if he suffered too much blood loss only to be resumed after he recovered. Still, such floggings were rare and executions rarer still. Of the 40,000 sailors who deserted during the war, thousands were recaptured and severely punished. Yet only 26 of the most incorrigible were sentenced to be hanged for their offense, and probably no more than five actually went to the gallows.

While most seamen could dodge the lash, few escaped the diseases that ravaged fleets, of which scurvy, yellow fever, malaria, typhus, dysentery, smallpox, and venereal diseases were the most common afflictions. Scurvy remained a severe problem despite the publication of Dr. Richard Mead's *Discourse on Scurvy* (1749), and James Lind's *A Treatise on Scury* (1753) and *An Essay on Preserving the Health of Seamen in the Royal Navy* (1757), all of which pointed to fresh vegetables and fruits as a likely cure. It would not be until 1795 that the admiralty required all ship captains to provide lime and lemon juice to their crews.

While most sailors tried to avoid the navy, they flocked to privateers, whose officers were less harsh and rewards of victory much greater. Lord Loudoun explained why: "Privateering is so much in fashion and so beneficial . . . New York alone has above 3000 Men employed in it. Their situation is this: the Owner of the Vessel fits her out . . . for which he has but one third of the Prizes, the other two thirds go to the Crews; and as they have been extreamly successful they all make fortunes."[45] Every port served as a nest for privateers; none contributed more than Newport in which one of every three able-bodied men embarked to loot the wealth of enemy and neutral merchant ships alike.[46]

Privateers supplemented the efforts of both the French and British fleets. French privateers were more than three times more successful than their British rivals. In the four years from June 1756 to June 1760, French privateers took 2,539 British ships while the British captured 944 French ships.[47] These numbers are misleading. The British losses are greater because the French merchant marine had fewer ships to start with, and most remained rotting in port as the blockade tightened.

As the number of French merchant ships on the high seas diminished, British warships and privateers alike increasingly preyed on neutral ships. Foreign ships eventually carried two-thirds of French trade as Versailles temporarily dropped its Navigation Acts and allowed anyone to trade at its home or colonial ports. To counter this practice, Whitehall issued its "Rule of the War of 1756" based on the "Doctrine of Continuous Voyage" that argued that trade with a belligerent was not neutral but an act of alliance, and thus could be intercepted. Those ships seized came mostly from Holland followed by Denmark, Russia, and Sweden. These nations flirted with but never consummated the idea of deterring British predation by forming a League of Armed Neutrality.

Privateering caused insurance rates for shipping to soar until only the richest merchants could afford it. Although shipowners could diminish the threat from privateers by sailing together, convoys were costly; they took considerable time to gather and sailed only at the slowest ship's speed. Upon anchoring at a port, the convoy's ships then dumped their goods on local markets. The flood of goods and competition among merchants often meant that they were sold at a loss.

Ironically, while the British navy and privateers swept the seas of enemy and neutral ships sailing to New France, they never succeeded in ending American smuggling to the enemy. As supplies reaching New France plummeted, prices soared, along with the potential fortune for anyone who could successfully run the blockade. Whitehall was well aware that Americans committed the most smuggling to New France. The Board of Trade pressured but did not order the colonial governments to impose and enforce stricter laws against smuggling. However odious trading with the enemy may have seemed to most colonial leaders, vested interests prevented any serious attempts to curtail it. Many an assembly man had gained his wealth through smuggling. Even when a governor managed to convince the assembly to enact tougher laws and enforcement, such efforts were undercut by the lack of laws in other colonies. New York governor Charles Hardy explained that

"It is to no purpose for one Colony to lay a prohibition, if the others are not obliged to do the same."[48]

Only a concerted effort of colonial governments and the navy could have seriously dented the trade. That never occurred. Lord Loudoun did temporarily impose an export embargo in 1757 by preventing any American ships from sailing. The embargo merely delayed the trade while alienating prominent American merchants and their dependents.

How much did smuggling undercut Britain's war effort? Probably not much. Historian George Beer exaggerated when he argued that "the colonies neutralized the advantages arising from British naval activity, both supplying the French colonies with the sorely needed provisions, and also furnishing a market for their produce . . . [Smuggling] frustrated the policy of the British government, and prolonged the war; it aroused intense indignation and was unquestionably a potent factor in the subsequent alienation."[49] Certainly, British authorities viewed smuggling as treasonous and their attempts to stamp out the trade alienated those enriched by its profits. The amount of supplies reaching Canada was miniscule, however, compared to the need.

Although the British blockade was decisive in bringing New France to its knees, only the army could administer the coup de grace. No battle during the war was ever decided by a dearth of supplies; no garrison ever held out to the last bullet or biscuit. Victory ultimately depended on the ability of British commanders to defeat French forces in the field.[50]

THE FRENCH ARMY

At mid-century, France lacked leaders of the vigor, brilliance, and daring of earlier and later epochs.[51] King Louis XV seemingly cared more for the fate of his hunts than France. The King's Council decided overall strategy. The War Minister then devised and submitted campaign plans to his field marshalls or generals, who enjoyed considerable freedom in fulfilling those plans.

Unfortunately, France's generals were as mediocre as its ministers. Other than capturing Minorca in 1755 and Cumberland's entire army at Kloster-Zeven in 1757, the French generals led their armies to several minor field victories and a string of major and minor defeats. Louis Francois-Armand de Plesis, the Duc de Richelieu did capture Minorca (June 1755), although given his overwhelming numbers and local French naval superiority it could hardly have turned out otherwise. He also presided over Cumberland's surrender, although militarily he did little to bring it about. Marshall Victor Marie d'Estrees defeated Cumberland at Hastenbeck (July 1756) but failed to follow up his victory and was replaced by Richelieu. Charles de Rohan, Prince de Soubise was routed at Rosbach (November 1756), won a skirmish at Sondershausen (October 1758), and was routed again at Fillingshausen

(July 1761). Louis de Bourbon-Conde, Count of Clermont was defeated at Krefeldt (June 1758). Louis George Erasmas, Marquis de Contades lost at Minden (August 1759). Marshall Victor Francois, Duc de Broglie was perhaps the best French general, winning at Bergen (April 1759) and Corbach (July 1759), and he might have won at Fillingshausen (July 1761) as well had his command not been split with Soubise. Fortunately, the French had allied generals that more than once defeated Frederick II and Ferdinand. Austrian Marshall Leopold Joseph Maria Daun was perhaps the finest general allied with France. Russian General Peter Soltykov crushed Frederick at Kundersdorf.

French armies had not one but two leaders, the general and the intendant, each of which was appointed by the king. There were four ranks of generals, with marshalls the highest followed by lieutenant generals, camp marshalls, and brigadier generals. The commanding general was responsible for gathering intelligence and planning campaigns and battles. Intendants massed and dispensed the food, equipment, transportation, and munitions upon which armies subsisted—and attempted to pay for all this with money dispensed by the Treasury. To fulfill their respective functions, the general and intendant had to collect their own staffs. Although intendants were supposedly subordinate to generals, in practice the two jointly ran their army.

All other officer ranks below that of general were bought. The ranks from captain to colonel were purchased from a regiment with the War Minister's approval. The offices of lieutenant, cornet, and ensign could be bought from a regiment without higher approval. Most officers were aristocrats. In 1758, the army's 181 general officers included 3 royal princes, 5 other princes, 11 dukes, 44 counts, 38 marquis, 14 chevaliers, and 6 barons. The king and the regiments were happy to sell positions to the nouveaux riche, despite their common blood. Anywhere from one-third to one-half of officers were bourgeois. A handful of officers had risen through the ranks by displaying exemplary heroism and leadership. Most regiments limited the number of such officers in their ranks to a half dozen.

The French army was top-heavy with officers, with a ratio of one officer for every eleven enlisted men, compared to a much leaner Prussian officer corps with one for every 29 troops. In January 1758, the French army included 16 marshalls, 172 lieutenant generals, 176 camp marshalls, and 389 brigadier generals. Over 900 colonels overshadowed 163 regiments. Those too many chiefs were as much a financial as administrative burden. Officers were allotted rations in proportion to their rank. A lieutenant general, or example, drew 80 times more rations than a private. Officers sold their surplus rations to civilians and soldiers alike.[52]

The problems of incompetence, aristocracy, and corruption that plagued France also characterized New France's leadership. At first glance, New France would seem to have a leadership advantage over the American colonies. In contrast to the squabbling, jealous governors and assemblies of the thirteen English provinces, New France enjoyed a mostly unified, authoritarian government beholden only to Versailles. While the English governors largely reigned, New France's governor ruled. With an annual defense budget granted by Versailles, the governor-general commanded all French troops in the province and held sweeping powers to mobilize the country for war.

Unfortunately, New France's administration was hopelessly corrupt and inefficient. In a 1759 letter to the War Minister, General Montcalm accused Canada's officials of defeatism and even treason: "They . . . were all hastening to make their fortunes before the loss of the colony; which many of them perhaps desire as a veil to their conduct. . . . I have often spoken of these expenditures to M. de Vaudreiul and M. Bigot; and each throws the blame on the other."[53] Montcalm was not the only high ranking official to complain about the corruption rotting New France. The corruption appalled all the French officers assigned to the province. Indignation fills their letters and journals. Doreil, for example, bluntly warned that "ineptness, intrigue, lies, cupidity, will in a short time destroy this Colony, which costs the King so dearly."[54]

Pierre Rigaud de Vaudreuil de Cavagnial, Marquis de Vaudreuil served as governor from 1755 through 1760. At best he was a mediocrity. By most accounts Vaudreuil was not as corrupt as his subordinates in the administration. Canadian-born, he knew and sympathized with the plight of his realm. Yet Vaudreuil did nothing to curb the corruption all around him. His constant criticism of his field commanders' actions only weakened morale and decisiveness among the leaders. When Vaudreuil finally took direct command of the army after Montcalm's defeat on the Plains of Abraham, he ordered Quebec's mayor to surrender at first chance rather than hold out. That decision doomed Quebec. Bougainville offers this assessment of Vaudreuil as "a man, limited, without talent, perhaps free from vice, but having all the faults of a petty spirit, filled with Canadian prejudices, which are of all the most foolish, jealous, glorious, wishing to take all credit to themselves. He no more confides in M. de Montcalm than in the lowest lieutenant."[55]

Beneath Vaudreuil were three successive field generals. Jean-Armand Dieskau, Baron de Dieskau served from his arrival in 1754 until his capture at the Battle of Lake George in September 1755. He was replaced by Louis-Joseph de Montcalm, Marquis de Montcalm who led the French army until his death at Quebec in September 1759. Francois-Gaston de Levis, Duc de Levis served as commander from Montcalm's death until New France's surrender in September 1760. Dieskau and Montcalm were opposites in temperament, with the former daring to the point of recklessness and the latter prudent to the point of timidity. Levis was the most competent of the three commanders, carefully marshalling his outnumbered forces yet not hesitating to strike when the enemy appeared vulnerable. Of his three field commanders, Vaudreuil had the stormiest relationship with Montcalm. The governor continually harped on what he called the general's "defeatism and laggard action."

The various troops mustered to defend New France were far superior to its leadership. When the war began, New France had a trained, equipped standing army. Those troops were all members of the Compagnies Franches de la Marine commanded by the Ministry of Marine via New France's governor. Marine companies were first sent to Canada in 1683. They were organized as independent companies, with each ideally numbering 50 troops and four officers. Their uniforms were light grey leggings and coats with blue facings, linings, cuffs, and trousers. At first, the marine companies were composed solely of French officers and enlisted men. Over time, Canadians fleshed out the enlisted and officers' ranks until nearly all marines were born in the New World.

In 1754, there were 90 marine companies scattered in towns and posts across France's North American empire, including 30 in Canada, 24 in Isle Royale, and 36 in Louisiana. On March 14, 1756, company strength was boosted to 65 troops, giving those 30 Canadian companies 1,950 men. On March 15, 1757, Versailles sent ten more marine companies to Canada, raising the number to 40. In July 1757, eight companies were formed into the first marine battalion. In 1760, a second battalion was made from another eight companies. During the war, several Louisiana companies fought at Fort Duquesne and along the Canadian frontier.[56]

The marines were organized to garrison forts and fight in the forest, not engage in European-style battles. Man for man, however, these marine companies were superior to most British companies. Marine officers understood the land and native peoples. Skilled in wilderness survival and warfare, the marines were excellent light infantrymen, displaying continually the ability to fight, march, and subsist like Indians. In all, they displayed superior "mobility, deadly marksmanship, skillful use of surprise and forest cover, high morale, and . . . a tradition of victory."[57]

They also had a reputation for ill-discipline. Shortly after arriving in 1751, Governor Duquesne imposed a strict regimen of drill and punishments for infractions that gradually transformed the marines from an armed mob into professional soldiers. This transformation, however, was not occurring fast enough for the French regular officers who served in Canada during the war. Montcalm remarked that the marines were "a troop knowing neither discipline nor subordination. Within six months I would make grenadiers of them, and now I would carefully abstain from placing as much dependence on them as the unfortunate M. de Dieskau did, by having given too much ear to the confident talk of Canadians."[58]

The enlisted men's ill-discipline reflected the rudimentary military skills of their officers. The French officers complained that the "Canadian officers, though courageous, knew hardly anything of their profession. . . . They hardly knew their own troops, who were always billeted with the habitants. Even if they were together in their postings, they all thought of their own petty interests, which created conflicts between officers & soldiers. Isolation & their limited means for enforcing discipline rendered the latter insubordinate. Often they were not in the wrong."[59] As if slack discipline and aloof officers were not bad enough problems, Captain Pierre Pouchot also found the marines "were extremely ill armed, because they sent to the country all the rejects from the King's magazines."[60]

Although the War Ministry was in charge of all army or "troupe de terres" forces, it placed the battalions it sent to Canada under the Marine Ministry to avoid a split command. In all, Versailles committed twelve battalions from French regular regiments to Canada. In May 1755, four battalions from the La Reine, Guyenne, Bearn, and Languedoc arrived in Quebec, while two battalions from the Bourgogne and Artois regiments spilled ashore at Louisbourg. In 1756, the second battalions of the Royal Rousillon and La Sarre regiments disembarked with Montcalm at Quebec. Two battalions from the Berry regiments reached Quebec in 1757. Two battalions from the Volontaires Etrangers and Cambis regiments arrived at Louisbourg in 1758. A battalion's official strength was 31 officers and 525 enlisted men divided among twelve fusilier and one grenadier company.

These army troops were inferior to the marines in training, motivation, morale, and combat prowess. Officers bought their commissions; the enlisted were mostly society's castoffs. Nonetheless, as Frenchmen serving overseas they were paid twice what the marines received. As the war ground on, wounds, disease, and desertion depleted the ranks of the regular battalions. Versailles sent some reinforcements to fill this worsening gap, but most were replaced with some of Canada's best militia. Mixing veteran regulars with militia proved disastrous. Montcalm's attack on Wolfe before Quebec's walls dissolved as the regulars continued to march and fire steadily while the Canadians in their midst rushed ahead, fired, and dropped to the ground to reload.

In New France, all able-bodied men from 16 to 60, except members of religious orders and seigneurs, were required to serve in the militia (milice).[61] Each parish had at least one company; more populous parishes had two or more. Captains headed each company. The parishes were included in one of the three military districts headquartered at Quebec, Trois-Rivieres, or Montreal. Each district had a governor-general, colonel, lieutenant colonel, and major to command its troops. In 1750, there were 11,687 militia in 165 companies; by 1758, the militia's ranks had swelled to 15,000. Like militia elsewhere the Canadians were poorly equipped, trained, motivated, and led. Yet Montcalm skillfully made the best of the militia, using "them with good effect, though not in places exposed to the enemy's fire. They know neither discipline nor subordination, and think themselves in all respects the first nation on earth."[62]

New France's first cannoneers came from the ranks of marine companies, each of which sent a man to the artillery school at Quebec established in 1698. Those men then returned to their units to man its own cannon. It was not until 1750 that the first specialized artillery company of cannoneer-bombardiers was established in Quebec; a second company was raised in 1757. The gunners wore blue coats with red cuffs, facings, and trousers, and were armed with muskets, bayonets, and sabres. When not servicing cannon, they were used as grenadiers. Captain Francois Marc Antoine Le Mercier was New France's artillery commander.

No French regular cavalry units served in North America. In June 1759, the French did create a mounted squadron of 200 Canadians led by French officers. The troops wore blue uniforms with red facings while the officers wore their whitish-grey uniforms. They joined no battles but mostly scouted and occasionally skirmished with enemy patrols.

There was enormous rivalry and contempt among the marines, regulars, and militia, as antagonistic as that among similar British and American units. The French and Canadians generally despised each other. The French troops apparently saw their Canadian counterparts as savages or even beasts of burden. Vaudreuil wrote that the "troops from France are not on very good terms with our Canadians. What can our soldiers think of them when they see their officers threaten them with sticks or swords? The Canadians are obliged to carry these gentry on their shoulders, through the cold war, over rocks that cut their feet; and if they make a false step they are abused."[63] In retaliation, the resentful Canadians, however, "had an unfortunate habit of tripping in mid-stream."[64]

A chain of forts and fortified missions guarded New France's frontier, but it proved to be as vulnerable as it was slender. Fortresses gave their defenders an illusion of security. Pargellis reminds us that "of the twelve great French fortresses in America toward which British strategy was directed, eight fell with scarcely a shot fired as soon as the British managed to reach them. If Wolfe's exploits at Louisbourg and Quebec are excluded, the conquest of Canada sheds but faint glory on British arms."[65]

Why were New France's forts so vulnerable? Vauban's intricate, vast, seemingly impregnable fortification designs shape the popular image of French fortresses during this era. Vauban apparently had little influence on French forts in North America. To Bougainville's skilled engineer's eye and mind, the frontier forts were abominably constructed, maintained, defended, and supplied. In September 1756, he traveled from Montreal to Fort Carillon via Forts La Prairie, St. Jean, and Frederic. Even the roads and forts a day or so from Montreal he found wretched, describing La Prairie as "a badly made stockaded fort. . . . Reached St. Jean. . . . The Road across the flat land is very bad. It is necessary to rebuild it entirely, drying it out by [drainage] ditches on both sides and by raising the road surface . . . St. Jean is a fort built of squared posts with four bastions. The fort is badly built, cost 96,000 francs, and is in bad condition. There is normally a garrison of a captain of colony troops and fifty men. In the port there is a vessel which goes back and forth as convoy to St. Frederic and Carillon." Bougainville found Fort St. Frederic on Lake Champlain built "of stone with a great redoubt, also of stone, inside it. It is badly located, there being several heights which command it. Within musket range on their heights they have built a redoubt and defensive works of horizontal timbers, works badly made and more harmful than useful." Fort Carrillon "is square with four bastions of which three are in a defensible state. It is of horizontal timbers. The position is well chosen on a rugged rock formation, but the fort is badly oriented and is not far enough out on the north point of the lake, which has obliged them to make a redoubt at the place where the fort should have been. As for the rest of it, they would have done better to take advantage of the rock, breaking it up with a pickaxe and using it for the parapets."[66] Food was often execrable at the posts; soldiers subsisted for months on mouldy flour and rancid salt pork.

New France had a military resource that the American colonies lacked. In New France as elsewhere, priests formed a fifth column as much for Versailles as for Rome. The first priests to arrive in the wilderness amused, puzzled, and often provoked the Indians with their piety, austerity, and rigid morality. Over a century and a half, the trickle of converts became a flood as entire villages embraced Catholicism. Versailles had no better instrument of native manipulation than the priests who got their charges to supply the colony with furs, corn, and warriors.

A certain proportion of priests in the Catholic Church have always been worldly to varying degrees. In New France, some priests were actually warriors, not only provoking their minions to take up the hatchet but actually leading them on the warpath. Perhaps the most famous of these warrior priests were Abbe Jean Louis Le Loutre of Acadia, and Sulpician Abbe Francois Piquet, who founded a mission and fort at the Iroquois village of La Presentation in 1749 and over the subsequent years marched off with six war parties. Bougainville observed that Piquet "actually teaches them and drills them in the French military exercises. His assistant is Abbe Chevalier Terley, called Chevalier Terley because of his warlike disposition. There is in the fort a captain of colonial troops as commander, but all real control is ecclesiastical. They plan to transplant here all of the Five Nations that can be won over to France."[67]

THE BRITISH ARMY

Ideally, England needed no professional army; it was protected from foreign invasion by the navy and from civil unrest by the militia.[68] This happy geographical advantage was reinforced by the memories of Oliver Cromwell's dictatorship (1649–1660), kept vividly alive. Fear of military rule prompted Parliament to curtail peacetime army appropriations to skeletal proportions.

That traditional aversion to standing armies began to erode in mid-century. The wars Britain fought between Cromwell and Bonnie Prince Charles made glaringly obvious the conflict between the need to curb the political ambitions of generals and the need to organize, equip, and lead armies against the king's enemies, both foreign and domestic. The Jacobite Rebellion of 1745 broke out when Britain was already at war on the continent. The difficulty in mobilizing enough troops and supplies to crush Prince Charles' Jacobites and stave off defeat on the continent prompted King George II to revive the post of captain general of the army, and convince the Cabinet to give it to the victorious general at Culloden, his son, the Duke of Cumberland.

The captain general did not control the army, he was merely its most forceful advocate. The duties for governing the army were judiciously divided among several important posts. The Secretary at War was responsible for the army's financing and relations with civil authorities and populations, including recruiting, quartering, and requisitioning. Beneath the War Secretary was the Adjutant General, who was responsible for discipline and drill. The Ordnance Board was in charge of dividing up the Royal Artillery Regiment's cannons, mortars, howitzers, munitions, wagons, draft animals, and other equipment to garrison and field forces. The Judge Advocate General reviewed court martials. The men occupying these positions all had access to the king and Parliament alike.

As captain general, Cumberland did improve the army's fighting abilities by helping to propose and implement more drills and harsher discipline. Yet he had many critics. Among Cumberland's flaws were, his "appreciation of sea power was elementary; to him the navy was a convoy service, and its sole use in operations was the blocking of the St. Lawrence, as one ran a line of forts across Flanders to keep out the French. And Cumberland had no power to stir into action sluggish London departments."[69]

Whatever Cumberland's strengths and weaknesses, in all, Britain was ill-prepared for the global war it plunged into in 1756. With one-third France's manpower, Britain was hard-pressed to fill all its commitments and ambitions around the world. At the war's height, Britain's manpower was stretched so thin that at various times it helped deter a French invasion by deploying from Europe Hessian, Hanoverian, and Danish troops in the home islands. Although British redcoats were committed to the Army of Observation protecting King George II's German principalities, England's battles on the continent were waged largely by subsidizing its allies with one-year renewable infusions of pounds sterling—more than 10.8 million pounds to help Prussia and other German allies keep their armies afloat.[70]

At least two targets of these subsidies paid off handsomely. Prussia's King Frederick II and Brunswick's Prince Ferdinand kept a coalition of French,

Austrian, Russian, Swedish, and other troops at bay for a half dozen years. The *Annual Register* insightfully contrasted these two greatest generals among Britain's allies: "The king of Prussia rapid, vehement, impatient often gives decisive blows; but he often misses his stroke and wounds himself. Prince Ferdinand is cool, deliberate, exact and guarded; he sees every possible advantage, he takes it at the moment, pursues it as far as it will go, but never attempts to push it further. . . . Prince Ferdinand is famous for never committing a fault. The king of Prussia is above all the world in repairing those he has committed. . . . He commits an error, he repairs it; he errs again, and again admonishes us by his manner of escaping. We should often condemn the commander, but we are always forced to admire the hero."[71]

The more troops and treasury Versailles committed to the bloodbath in central Europe, the less were available for defending New France. Britain needed every advantage it could take for its war in North America. Mismanagement hampered its war effort more than anything else. Neither Whitehall nor the colonial governments were capable of rapidly and efficiently mobilizing and supplying troops. Each colony organized, financed, equipped, supplied, and transported its own troops. The war-waging abilities of each colony varied considerably according to their respective leaders, resources, and experiences. Lacking professional military and supply staffs, colonial governors had to improvise everything. Each colony formed its own "committee of war" to oversee its strategy, recruitment, and supply. Assemblies worsened matters by refusing to grant enough funds. Even then the appropriations often came with strings attached, designed to advance the assembly's side of long-standing political battles. To finance their war efforts, the assemblies stamped out paper credit and its accompanying inflation.[72]

During the war's early years, relations between Whitehall and the colonies were strained almost to the breaking point by differences over command, finance, and supply. In the summer of 1756, Lord Loudoun tried to alleviate the crippling problem of each colony having its own requisition and supply system by unifying them under his own command.[73] Although the new system was far more efficient, the colonial governments resented the usurpation of their power. Loudoun replied that as commander in chief he held a viceroy's supreme powers to mobilize colonial manpower, supplies, and finance in any way he deemed fit. The colonies insisted that the British commander's powers be limited to his troops and that the Crown pay for the war. Loudoun was the most arrogant and authoritarian of the commanders, imposing embargos on colonial trade, quartering redcoats in American homes, and issuing thinly veiled threats to force the provincial and town assemblies to comply if they failed to provide his demands.

In 1758, William Pitt helped resolve these conflicts. Henceforth, he, rather than the ranking field general, would serve as commander in chief. Unlike the British generals sent to America, Pitt always tried to base his relations with the colonists on cooperation rather than coercion. He won over many Americans when he promised that London would reimburse the colonies for most of their expenditures. Pitt would annually write each governor, informing him of that year's strategy and requesting that his colony make a specific military, supply, and financial contribution. The governor would then lay Pitt's request before the assembly which in turn could chose to fulfill it in part or whole, or reject it altogether. Britain eventually reimbursed 1,544,830 pounds to its colonies, or about 40 percent of their wartime appropriations. No province spent more than Massachusetts' 818,000 pounds, of which Parliament reimbursed 352,000 pounds.[74]

Relations among the colonies were often just as strained as between them and London. Cooperation among the colonies was as rare as it was fleeting. Each American colony was "a loose confederation of mutually suspicious towns, held together by a distrust of outsiders that was even more intense than their suspicion of each other and united by a narrow provincial culture."[75] New York governor Charles Hardy complained that "Our measures are slow; one Colony will not begin to raise their Men in an early time, doubting whether their Neighbors will not deceive them, in compleating their Levies so largely as they promised; By this Means we get late in the field; Our Magazines are not filled so soon as they ought";[76] New Jersey's William Livingstone lamented that the "colonies are nearly exhausted, and their funds already anticipated by expensive unexecuted projects. Jealous are they of each other; some ill-constituted, others shaken with intestine divisions, and, if I may be allowed the expression, parsimonious even to prodigality. Our assemblies are different of their governors, governors despise their assemblies; and both mutually misrepresent each other to the Court of Great Britain."[77]

The inability to cooperate cost the colonies dearly. While traveling through the colonies, Peter Kalm remarked that not only was the "opinion of one province . . . sometimes directly opposite to that of another, but frequently the views of the governor and those of the assembly of the same province are quite different; so that it is easy to see that while the people are quarrelling about the best and cheapest manner of carrying on the war, an enemy has it in his power to take one place after another. It has usually happened that while some provinces have been suffering from their enemies, the neighboring ones have been quiet and inactive, as if it did not in the least concern them. They have frequently taken up two or three years in considering whether or not they should give assistance to an oppressed sister colony, and sometimes they have expressly declared themselves against it. There are instances of provinces which were not only neutral in such circumstances, but which even carry on a great trade with the power which at that very time is attacking and laying waste some other province."[78]

As in every war, contractors got rich as they played off colonial procurement agents against each other, bidding up prices to exorbitant levels. Prices soared with the demand for relatively scarce or abundant products alike, supplied by a limited range of producers and merchants. The demands of war also caused severe labor shortages. Every British commander complained of the greed of colonial merchants. General Braddock's quartermaster, Sir John St. Clair, vilified the Americans for their want "of Scruple to make as great an Advantage as they can of the Forces that are sent to protect them."[79] During his 1758 campaign across Pennsylvania, General Forbes remarked acidly of the "villany and Rascality of the Inhabitants, who to a man seem rather bent upon our ruin . . . than give the smallest assistance, which if at last extorted is so infamously charged as shews the disposition of the people in its full Glare."[80] General Abercromby heartily concurred, writing Forbes that the colonials were "a Sett of people whose Sole pleasure seems to be that of thwarting every Measure of Government, tho ever So beneficial to themselves."[81]

If any party had the greatest cause for complaint, it was the Americans, who lost thousands of lives because a succession of grossly inept British generals were unable swiftly and decisively to defeat the French and Indians. North America was truly the "graveyard of British military reputations" for several English generals who had made their reputations fighting in Europe.[82] The American wilderness and its savages spooked Britain's generals. Even after a half dozen years of war, they failed to adapt tactics appropriate for wilderness fighting. Braddock's 1755 defeat haunted the British for the war's duration. Generals, officers, and troops alike were terrified by a wilderness which swallowed them and, when least expected, disgorged hordes of screaming Indians and their French commanders. In North America, generals tended "to be hesitant and cautious because they were operating at such great distances from the center of power. Lines of supply usually were stretched very thin, and the commander knew that if he took a risk and suffered heavy losses there was no likelihood of rapid support and reinforcement. One bad mistake could mean total failure, even disaster. . . . It is easy in retrospect to assume that more aggressiveness would have produced more and better victories. It might also have caused some terrible defeats."[83]

Incompetence ruined the careers of Braddock, Loudoun, Webb, Abercromby, and Murray, along with the lives of thousands of their men. The worst of the lot was Abercromby, whose decision to shatter his best regiments against that breastwork before Fort Carillon when a standard siege would have probably succeeded after severals days in bagging Montcalm's entire army, was nothing short of criminal. Braddock was ultimately responsible for the failure of Colonel Thomas Gage, who commanded his advanced guard, to send scouts far enough ahead to detect any ambush. After the French and British forces collided on that trail, Braddock remained too straightjacketed by military convention to allow his troops to take cover and return an accurate fire. Instead, he had his troops fire volleys that either shot above the enemy or even into the backs of redcoats standing rigidly before them. A fine line divides boldness from recklessness. Murray plunged over that line at St. Foy in 1760 when he ordered a poorly coordinated attack that dissolved into a rout when Levis skillfully parried it and counterattacked. Webb and Loudoun dishonored themselves because they shied from battle. Webb's refusal to march to Monro's relief at Fort William Henry was murderously disastrous.

Not all the British generals serving in North America were inept butchers. William Pitt chose commanders who could at least win battles and campaigns, men like George Howe, Jeffrey Amherst, John Forbes, and James Wolfe. Yet even these generals lacked the imagination, flexibility, and grit vital for military genius. Amherst and Forbes were ploddingly efficient. Each took his objective by simply and slowly marching huge armies against the inferior French and Indian forces before them. Howe enjoyed an ample gift for inspiring his troops with his bravery and good cheer. Yet if Howe also harbored that spark of battlefield genius, a French bullet destroyed his life before he could reveal it. Even Wolfe, the best remembered of the war's generals, was at best inconsistent. He excelled at leading his regiments into battle at Louisbourg and on the plains of Abraham. However, at Quebec, Wolfe was largely myopic to the grand tactical vision needed to win. It was his brigadiers who urged him to concentrate his badly scattered forces above the city and cut off the French army's supply line. His attack on Beauport was as stupid as Abercromby's at Fort Carillon.

Of the colonial leaders, few were given independent commands of campaigns. George Washington proved to be inept if fearless in an independent command but a competent enough aide and regimental colonel. The future founding father aside, the other two most prominent colonial commanders proved to be far more adept than their English counterparts. Although he never fought a field or wilderness battle, John Winslow proved his leadership mettle on the campaign up the Kennebec River (1754), at Fort Beausejour's siege (1755), and commanding the provincial army at Lake George (1756). Although William Johnson took the office with the greatest reluctance, he proved as skilled a general at the Lake George battle (1755) and Fort Niagara's siege (1759) as he was an Indian Superintendent. Another able colonial commander was John Bradstreet, who never rose beyond colonel. Whatever the assignment, Bradstreet plunged into it with energy, organization, and drive. The French attack on his bateauxmen at the Great Carrying Place (1756) would have routed most of his colleagues. Bradstreet cooly rallied his troops and then led them in a daring counterattack that routed the enemy. After lobbying for two years to attack Fort Frontenac, Bradstreet finally received permission to do so in 1758, then proceeded to skillfully invest, besiege, and take it. With better intelligence, he could have followed up his raid on Frontenac with an attack on Fort Niagara. Yet these were minor victories.

Unlike in previous French and Indian wars, when only token amounts of British regulars fought in North America, Whitehall sent over more than a score of regiments to serve in North America between 1755 and 1765.[84] Although they usually marched to victory or defeat with great bravery, colonists tended to complain that the redcoats warred far more effectively against their fellow subjects. Franklin reports how the British troops "in their first march . . . from their landing till they got beyond the settlements . . . had plundered and stripped the inhabitants, totally ruining some poor families, besides insulting, abusing, and confining the people if they remonstrated. This was enough to put us out of conceit of such defenders if we had really wanted any."[85] Pillage and rape were not uncommon alongside the regulars' camp and march since the army's "ranks were filled in great measure by professional criminals, who passed from regiment to regiment, spreading everywhere the infection of discontent, debauchery, and insubordination."[86] Wolfe had little faith in his own regulars: "I know their discipline to be bad and their valour precarious. They are easily put into disorder and hard to recover out of it. They frequently kill their officers through fear, and murder one another in confusion."[87]

During the war, over 11,000 Americans joined British regiments or independent companies or regiments raised in colonies.[88] The Crown began the practice in 1696 and thereafter periodically tried to leaven regular troops posted in the colonies with local recruits. In 1737, the 42nd became the first English regiment raised in the colonies and the first nearly all-American regular regiment—its officers were mostly English. King George II commissioned Georgia governor James Oglethorpe to recruit and command the 42nd to defend that colony's frontier with Spain. In 1740, the Crown authorized the raising of a second colonial regiment, the American Foot commanded by Virginia governor William Gooch. The American Foot was an all-American regiment that eventually included 36 companies from eleven colonies. Like all the units serving in the Cartegena campaign, the American Foot suffered terrible losses from disease. The regiment was disbanded in 1742.

Three regiments were raised during the final French and Indian War. The ranks of William Shirley's 50th and William Pepperell's 51st regiments were filled mostly by Massachusetts men. Those two regiments never had a chance to prove their mettle. They were surrendered and dissolved with Oswego's fall in 1756. The Royal American 60th regiment had a distinquished career, with its four battalions fighting in most of the war's campaigns. While Americans filled most of its ranks, the 60th was the only British unit in which any nationality could be an officer; many of its officers were Germans or Swiss, along with soldiers of fortune from a dozen other nations.

The attempts of English or American regular regiments to recruit invariably provoked heated protests from the colonial population and assemblies. While people were happy to see the local criminals, shiftless, and malcontents take the king's shilling, don redcoats, and march away, the wealthier among them resented it when their servants joined up. Pennsylvania governor Robert Morris went so far as to issue a proclamation, in February 1756, that forbade recruiters to enlist servants. Whitehall reacted with uncharacteristic swiftness to Pennsylvania's affront to its recruiters; in July 1756, Parliament amended the Mutiny Act to colonial governments, thus making any interference with recruitment a capital offense. It softened its law by promising to compensate the masters of servants and slaves for their losses.

Every colony raised one or more ranger companies which served as scouts and light infantry. Ranger companies and their commanders varied considerably in combat and wilderness prowess. No ranger leader was more dauntless or skilled than Robert Rogers, who harried the French and Indians in the Lake George region all year round.

Rogers was first offered the command of a ranger company in the fall of 1755. That company would be the first of ten independent regular companies paid and equipped by the Crown rather than a province. Each of Rogers' 50 or so successful scouts and battles boosted him in the eyes of his men and most officers. In February 1757, Loudoun gave Rogers command of the four then independent ranger companies at Fort William Henry. Later that year he ordered Rogers and three ranger companies to join his army at Halifax. In January 1758, Loudoun approved Rogers' plan to expand the rangers to 1,000 men in ten companies, and authorized him to select the officers and train the troops.

Captain John Knox observed the operations of the "rangers, under the command of Captain Rodgers, who . . . march out every day to scour the country; these light troops have, at present, no particular uniform, only they wear their cloaths short, and are armed with a firelock, tomahock or small hatchet, and a scalping knive; a bullock's horn full of powder hangs under their right arm, by a belt from the left shoulder; and a leathern, or seal's skin bag, buckled round their waist, which hangs down before, contains bullets and a smaller shot of the size of full-grown peas; six or seven of which, with a ball, they generally load; and their officers usually carry a small compass fixed in the bottom of their powder horns, by which to direct them when they happen to lose themselves in the woods."[89]

Despite Loudoun's promotion of Rogers and expansion of the rangers, he apparently retained mixed feelings about their worth and reliability. Among the advice Cumberland wrote Loudoun in 1757 was to "Teach your troops to go out upon Scouting Parties: for 'till Regular Officers with men that they can trust, learn to beat the woods & act as Irregulars, you will never gain any certain Intelligence of the Enemy, as I fear, by this time you are convinced Indians Intelligence & that of Rangers is not at all to be depended upon."[90]

Cumberland's suggestion coincided with a proposal by Lieutenant Colonel Thomas Gage of the 44th regiment. Gage had been with Braddock at the Monongahela and recognized that the battle might have been celebrated as a great victory rather than an ignominious disaster if the troops had been trained in irregular warfare. At Halifax, Loudoun approved Gage's proposal to finance and lead at his own expense the British army's first light infantry regiment, the 80th. The following year near Fort Carillon, Gage led the 80th into battle. To blend in with the forest, these light troops wore brown jackets without facings and even carried muskets with the steel barrels browned.

In addition to the regular regiments sent over or recruited in America, each colony raised its own regiments. None of the provincial regiments were permanent organizations. After receiving their annual quota of expected troop contributions from London, governors had to build regiments with volunteers and then dissolve the units when the enlistments ran out by year's end. Recruiting usually began in February when the governor appointed the colonels to each of that year's regiments. Along with their own commissions, colonels received blank commissions to hand out to lower ranking officers under his command. Ambitious and popular men could receive a commission according to the number of troops they raised, such as a captain for 50 men, a lieutenant for 25, and an ensign for 15. Officers were closely knit to their men since they often included relatives, friends, and neighbors. The various units usually assembled into their regiments by May, received the remainder of their enlistment bonus and equipment, and then marched or sailed off together to the front.

Strong incentives induced Americans to join a provincial rather than regular regiment. A provincial private generally earned twice that of his regular army counterpart, as well as an enlistment bounty, bonuses for work details, and, if he were lucky, enemy plunder. Strict contracts bound men to their units. Enlistments were usually for nine months, and none for more than a year. Many contracts bound the troops to serve in a particular campaign under particular officers. If for any reason, including military necessity, the army broke its contract, troops could and did pack up and walk home.[91]

If the number of volunteers did not reach the province's quota, governors were empowered to draft the remainder under Parliament's 1754 Act for Levying Soldiers. Governors used the militia as pools from which to fish for volunteers for regular units. County and town militia were assigned a quota of recruitments based on population that were cajoled into signing up. If volunteers did not fill the quota, officials did not hesitate to press others, usually the village riffraff, into service. Those drafted could hire a substitute if they paid a fine to the province, which could cost anywhere from five to twenty pounds. Otherwise, they were herded into a provincial regiment under the same contract as the volunteers.

The popular image of the war has it won by British redcoats and sailors, with provincial troops playing an undistinquished secondary role largely as teamsters and guards. In fact, aside from the triumphs at Louisbourg and

Quebec, provincial troops won Britain's most important victories. It was mostly Americans who captured Forts Beausejour, Frontenac, and Duquesne, and defeated the French at the battles of Lake George and the Carrying Place. In all, the provincials proved far more capable than the English in fighting the French. Winslow was openly proud of the provincial soldiers he used to take Fort Beausejour in 1755: "The Troops in General have behaved Well and I Cant but be of opinion Equal to any New raised Forces in the World. . . . and for Fatiques better then the regulars or at Least put to More Duty of that Kinde perticularly in Drawing the Cannon in all our removes and Solely ussed in advance Guards. . . . All Parties behave well."[92] As unsung a group of heros as those Americans shouldering muskets were those rowing bateaux and hauling supplies. Jennings even argues that the bateaux men "accomplished vastly more than the glamorized rangers who went on scalp-bounty hunts when in the mood. They fought with more success than the troops for whom they were supposed to be merely auxiliary provisioners."[93]

And then there were the militia.[94] From the first English settlements, the threat from hostile Indians and Europeans alike forced the new Americans to be amateur soldiers. Each colony had laws requiring all able-bodied, free men to join the militia. The militia, however, was not an American invention. Militias had been an integral if rarely tested part of English life since the Tudor Age. That tradition, however, differed sharply between the Americans and English. While the English mustered as a duty to the Crown, the Americans believed their service was as much a natural right as a freeman as a prop to a distant authority. A 1758 Massachusetts proclamation captured the close ties that Americans drew between freedom and military service: "As it is the essential Property of a free Government to depend on no other Soldiery but it's own Citizens for it's Defense; so in all such Governments, every Freeman and every Freeholder should be a Soldier. . . . Every Man therefore that wishes to secure his own Freedom, and thinks it his Duty to defend that of his Country, should, as he prides himself in being a Free Citizen, think it his truest Honour to be a Soldier Citizen."[95]

Although the requirements varied among the colonies, usually all males between 16 and 60 were called to muster, and each was required to keep a firearm, ammunition, gunpowder, and hatchet ready for instant use. Exemptions were common for such professions like legislators, judges, ministers, constables, owners of four or more slaves, college professors and students, and sailors. Some colonies required free blacks to serve alongside whites. Most colonies, however, shunned the practice. Even when invasion was imminent, few colonial assemblies would consider mustering slaves. The fear of armed slaves turning guns on their masters was simply too great. The frequency of militia drills varied largely with the potential threat facing a colony. The meetings ranged anywhere from once a week, to once a month, to several times a year. Laws also might require prominent towns to maintain military storehouses and forts.

The governor usually served as the colony's commander in chief, with colonels presiding over regiments, and captains over companies. A company might contain anywhere from 50 to 75 officers and troops. Ten to twelve companies were organized into regiments. A 1752 survey counted 45,000 militia in New England and Nova Scotia, 18,000 in New York and New Jersey, 14,000 in Virginia, and 13,000 in North Carolina. The militia mostly defended their own communities and were rarely mobilized for far away campaigns. Once or twice a year, the regiment might gather for close-order drill and volleys, often followed by a massive drinking bout—to build morale, of course.

Whether they were officers or enlisted men, relations between British and American soldiers usually burned with deep mutual contempt. Most British army officers hailed from the petty aristocracy and haughtily carried with them all that class's arrogance, conceits, and privileges. British officers and enlisted men alike never forgot for whom they were fighting—the king. No one else was of much concern. Thus, most looked down their noses at Americans whom they considered at best semi-barbarians. British military and government officials alike complained about the colonial willingness to finance and ability to fight a war against the French. Yet, the British could be rather hamfisted in trying to motivate their colonial charges. In a statement to George Washington, Governor Dinwiddie echoed the prevailing British attitude when he arrogantly sniffed, "The idle argument which is often used, namely, you are defending your Country and property, is justly look'd upon as inapplicable and absurd. We are defending part of the Domain of Great Britain."[96] Of course, most Americans saw things quite differently. Among the litany of complaints, they angrily pointed out that the British confiscated their property, used their men for cannon-fodder, and berated their efforts and loyalty.

Of all the colonial military practices that dumbfounded the British, the American practice of electing their leaders was probably the most striking to those of an army that auctioned off its officers' ranks to "gentlemen." In dealing with their American counterparts, British officers often found themselves forced to associate with the commonest of people. Their distaste was palpable. Colonel Henry Bouquet complained that colonial officers "haven't an idea of service, and one cannot depend on them to carry out an order."[97]

To resolve such complaints, in 1754, Whitehall issued its Rules and Articles of War that, among other things, subordinated American officers to British officers, and American troops to British army discipline. In August, War Secretary Henry Fox decreed that "no officer who has the Honour to bear The King's Commission can be required, or ought, to Act under the

Orders of a person who does not bear the King's Commission."[98] Since colonial officers received commissions from their respective governors rather than the king, the new law meant that colonial generals could theoretically be outranked by the lowest lieutenant. The Americans bitterly protested the new law. On November 12, 1754, King George II somewhat softened this subordination by proclaiming that henceforth provincial officers were subservient to any regular officer of the same rank but could command officers below their rank.[99] Colonial protests subsided to perpetual grumbles.

A few British generals like George Howe and John Forbes recognized the need for good relations between the English and Americans, whether they were officers or enlisted men. Howe was a soldier's soldier, joining officers and men alike around campfires or stalking alongside the rangers on patrol. Forbes issued an order to his army on September 28, 1758 that "Every one must be Sensible that a good Understanding and a Mutual Cement of Hands and Hearts will most Certainly be the most surest means of a Completion to all our wishes, that is success over our Enemys and the support prosperity of these Provinces."[100]

The vast majority of British officers lacked the good sense and sensitivity of a Howe or Forbes. Loudoun called the American soldiers "the lowest dregs of the People, on which no dependence can be had, for the defense of any particular Post by themselves." Braddock described the provincials as "slothful and languid" whose "Disposition renders them very unfit for Military Service." Most blistering of all was James Wolfe's assessment: "The Americans are in general the dirtiest most contemptable cowardly dogs that you can conceive. There is no depending on them in action. They fall down dead in their own dirt and desert by battalions, officers and all. Such rascals as those are rather an encumbrance than any real strength to an army." Wolfe held American troops in utter contempt: "there never was people collected together so unfit for the business they were set upon—dilatory, ignorant, irresolute, and some grains of a very unmanly quality and very unsoldier-like or unsailor-like."[101]

In all, regulars dismissed colonial troops as undisciplined, slovenly, and cowardly. The first two charges were largely true. For Americans discipline and training were rudimentary at best. At march, camp, and battle, provincial troops resembled armed mobs more than military units. The lack of training and sanitation among provincial troops caused heavy casualties under fire and tent alike. Commodore Charles Knowles, commanding Louisbourg's garrison in 1746, might not have been exaggerating when he wrote Newcastle that "these New England Folks were so lazy, that they not only pulled one End of the House down to burn which they lived in, but even buried their dead under the Floors and did their Filth in the Other corners of the House rather than go out of Doors in the Cold: They were of so Obstinate and licentious a disposition that not being properly under Military Discipline there was no keeping them in any Order."[102]

The word "cowardly," however, is nothing more than an unfair British smear on the Americans. Much like the regulars, the colonial combat record was mixed, with incidents of steadfast courage alternating with those of unbridled panic. Despite all the complaints about the ill-disciplined colonial troops, they proved to be not only as brave but generally more effective fighters than the redcoated regulars. In fact, the first two British field victories—at Lake George and the Great Carrying Place—were won not by British regulars but by American colonials. British regulars would not win a field battle before the Plains of Abraham in 1759.

Americans fought just as fiercely as the British; they just preferred sheltering behind trees and rocks when they did so. In the forest, this "American style" of warfare certainly made more sense than prevailing European standards. One recruit, Private David Perry, expressed his bewilderment over what he had been trained to do: "The whistling of the balls and the roar of the musquetry terrified me not a little. At length our regiment formed among the trees, behind which the men kept stepping from their ranks for shelter. Col. Preble, who, I remember, was a harsh man, swore he would knock the first man down who should step out of his first ranks which greatly surprised me, to think that I must stand still to be shot at."[103]

Volunteers made up the regiments that marched away to battle the French and Indians. A covenant bound enlisted men and officers in which the troops would elect and serve under those they respected. The respect was mutual. Provincial officers tended to use reason rather than coercion to induce their troops to follow army orders. Nonetheless, the militia practice of electing their officers served democratic principles at the expense of military effectiveness. Any general could have echoed William Johnson's complaint that: "A Popular Choice in Military Life & that by new Levies is founded in Ignorance & will be guided by Caprice, such officers in all probability be like the heads of a Mob, who must support their preeminence by unworthy Condensensions, & Indulgences subversive of order & the very existence of an army." Elsewhere, Johnson characterized his fellow Americans as "Naturally an Obstinate and Ungovernable People, and Utterly Unaquainted with the Nature of Subordination in Generall."[104]

For British and American officers alike the militia often seemed far more trouble than they were worth. Pennsylvania governor William Denny harped on the militia's want "of any kind of Discipline, each Man was humoured by his Officer, scarce two in a Company were of one Opinion and the Men could not be got to march against the Indians, and if the Savages by any accident came upon them they did not stand to their Arms but fled and increased the Panick amongst the Inhabitant which thereby became general."[105] Washington frequently expressed his own exasperations with the militia which "will never answer your expectation—No dependence is to be placed on them: They are obstinate and perverse; they are often egged on by the Officers, who lead them to acts of disobedience. And, when they are ordered to certain posts for . . . the protection of the Inhabitants, [they] will, on a sudden, resolve to leave them, and the united vigilance of their Officers can not prevent them."[106]

The Americans harbored their worst complaints for the British, remarking bitterly that the redcoats used them as laborers, cannon-fodder, and, quite literally, whipping boys. The British unhesitantly expressed their belief that colonials were merely "sufficient to work our Boats, drive our Waggons, to fell Trees, and do the Works that in inhabited Countrys are performed by peasants."[107] The redcoats would unashamedly sacrifice the Americans in battle while hogging all the glory of victory for themselves, a tendency that did not escape the notice of Americans. Franklin pointed out how the British regulars would, when joined with colonial troops, "claim all the Honor of any Success, and charge them with the Blame of every Miscarriage."[108] Colonel Israel Williams captured the dilemma of provincial troops accompanying British regulars: "We run a great Resk if we go on without em for if we should then not succeed we shall never be paid from [England] and if we go on with em it seams we shall loose the Glory if we Do succeed."[109]

The Americans were just as aghast at British army practices, particularly the hundreds of lashes on a soldier accused of a crime, which sliced through his flesh to the bone and often killed him. The British army and navy alike were well-known for viciously whipping those who committed high crimes and misdemeanors. Soldiers in Lord Loudoun's army could expect 1,000 lashes for being drunk and asleep on guard duty, stealing a pound of butter, a shirt, or a greatcoat from an officer, or refusing to go on guard duty; 2,000 lashes for stealing from a sutler.[110] Knox records a typical crime and punishment: "the wagoneers of the provincials were tried for stealing his majesty's arms and working tools; one was sentenced to receive four hundred lashes, the others three hundred each: the general [Amherst] made a public example of the principal, by ordering him first to be punished at the head of every regiment, and then to be turned out of camp and deemed unworthy to serve in the army; the other delinquents his excellency was pleased to pardon, but ordered that they should be marched prisoners to see the punishment inflicted on the chief transgressor. . . . Two others of these provincial teamsters, with three negros, were also tried as parties concerned and were acquitted."[111] Jennings points out that such lashings, "If done by Indians . . . would be called torture, and rightly. In this respect, torture functioned in oddly distinct ways in the two cultures. Both regarded it as punishment, but Indians tortured only their enemies. To make the analogy complete, we should have to assume that British upper-class officers conceived lower-class enlisted men as enemies. In a society as rigidly conceived as Britain's by social class, the assumption seems reasonable."[112]

Beginning in 1757, the Rules and Articles of War and Mutiny Act applied to provincial as well as regular troops. In ordering Loudoun to extend those laws to the Americans, Secretary of State Sir Thomas Robinson asserted that "all Officers and Soldiers of any Troops being mustered and in Pay, which are, or shall be, raised in any of the British Provinces in America, by Authority of the respective Governors or Governments thereof, shall, at all Times and in all Places, when they happen to join, or act in Conjunction with, his Majesty's British Forces, be liable to martial Law and Discipline, in like manner, to all Intents and Purposes as the British Forces are; and shall be subject to the same Trial, Penalties, and Punishments."[113] This decree and subsequent amendments caused endless squabbles between the English and Americans.

When British arrogance, regulations, and demands grew too onerous, the Americans simply deserted, sometimes en masse. Perhaps the most prominent mass desertion occurred in the summer of 1758 from Fort Herkimer, whose commander, Colonel John Stanwix, reported that 662 men had disappeared from the various American regiments under his command.[114] Washington explained the widespread desertions plaguing his regiment as natural to the love of freedom among Americans: "Our People were not calculated to be confined in Garrisons or kept in any particular Service; they soon grow troublesome & uneasy by reflecting upon the[i]r Folly in bringing themselves into a State of Subjection when they might have continued free and independent."[115] Although Washington understood why Americans deserted, he by no means condoned it. In 1757, he tried to deal with the mass desertions plaguing his regiment by ordering the execution of two particularly criminal offenders. The example deterred few from slipping away.

At times, the grievances of American troops grew so great that they took one huge step beyond desertion—mutiny. American mutinies never involved violence, but were more like strikes in which the troops would assemble, sometimes with lower ranking officers leading them, and present a petition of complaints to the commanding officer. The essence of any mutiny involved the troops' assertion that their contract had been violated, and they would refuse to serve until their rights and privileges had been restored. To try to get their troops to return to their barracks, commanders would use reason, often leavened by promises of reform and appeals to patriotism. None of these mutinies ended in bloodshed; most were resolved through compromise and better conditions.[116]

American civilians as well as soldiers grew to despise the British troops in their midst. The Mutiny Act authorized commanders to billet troops in private homes, but only at a fixed daily rate of compensation and only with the owner's permission. The procedure was for commanders to address their needs to the local magistrate, who in turn would appeal for volunteers among the populace. In practice, commanders frequently forced the locals to supply shelter, food, and firewood for their troops, a clear violation of the Mutiny Act and the 1628 Petition of Right. Even when compensation was provided, it often did not meet the expenses of the American colonies, whose cost of living was higher than England's. Americans were well aware that the British were violating their rights, and those violated complained loudly, if ineffectively. Specific clauses against quartering were later written into both the Declaration of Independence and Constitution.

The redcoats at times treated the American colonists as if they were the enemy, to be humiliated and exploited into submission. During one meeting with Pennsylvanian officials, St. Clair blustered that he would "march his Army into Cumberland County to cut the Roads, press Horses, Wagons, &ca.; that he would not suffer a Soldier to handle an Axe, but by Fire and Sword oblige the Inhabitants to do it, and take every man that refused to the Ohio . . . ; that he would kill all kind of Cattle and carry away the Horses, burn the Houses . . . that if the French defeated them by the Delays of this Province that he would with his Sword drawn pass through the Province and treat the Inhabitants as a Parcel of Traitors."[117]

Such attitudes fired ever more Americans to resent deeply British rule. As Jennings put it, increasing numbers of Americans saw the British troops as an occupying army—"corrupt police rather than liberating heros."[118] The rage sparked by British arrogance and looting during the war would boil over in the dozen following years marked by debilitating taxes, contempt for the colonial assemblies, atrocities, and Boston's occupation by the British army. The seeds of nationalism sown by British oppression would blossom into American independence and revolution.[119]

THE INDIANS

Indian allies were at once indispensable and burdensome to commanders.[120] While they were rarely decisive in any large battle, Indians were nearly always an effective and terrifying presence. Yet, rallying Indians onto the warpath was never an easy task. The French and British alike heaped upon erstwhile allies small mountains of munitions, guns, food, blankets, and trinkets, all the while inciting them with prolonged and nuanced diplomacy. Frontier commanders reasoned that all the expense, time, and frustration of buying their allegiance was but a fraction of what it cost to deploy regulars or even militia.

Indians tended to ally with the side that could dispense the most gifts and win the most victories. Yet, even with gifts and victories in abundance, getting the Indians on the warpath required the patience of Job. Indian councils followed a standard etiquette that the British or French had to strictly and respectfully follow or forego enlisting any warriors. Gifts were given to "cover the dead" lost in previous battles or epidemics. Long successions of eloquent speakers took the floor at length with no interruptions tolerated. One side usually spoke one day followed by replies and counter-replies day after day. Councils could last for weeks before a consensus was reached. Bougainville describes the process as taking a "long time to get them to make up their minds. It requires authority, brandy, equipment, food and such. The job never ends and is very irksome."[121] Pennsylvania's secretary, Richard Peters, recognized the vital importance of gifts to Indian diplomacy, remarking to Governor Shirley that "Bribery, among the Indians no more than among the French, is not deemed a crime, but a mark of respect and a Proof that you know their Importance, and whoever neglects it is impolitik and will suffer."[122]

Progressive French colonial policies helped offset the material advantages offered by the English. In 1755, an Iroquois chief pointed out a commonly observed difference between the English and French: "Brethern, are you ignorant of the difference between our Father [the French] and the English? Go and see the forts our father has created, and you will see that the land beneath their walls is still hunting ground, having fixed himself in those places we frequent only to supply our wants; whilst the English, on the contrary, no sooner get possession of a country than the game is forced to leave; the trees fall down before them, the earth becomes bare."[123]

Wampum belts were an important medium of diplomacy. Made from strings of patterned purple and white beads, they were exchanged to seal peace, alliances, or friendships. Diplomats traveled with wampum prominently displayed to enhance their immunity from scalp-hunters. Diplomats would solicit allies by tossing a war wampum belt at their feet during a council. The other side's chief would then indicate the choice for war by picking it up with a triumphant shout from the other Indians in council, or reject it by turning his head or even grinding the belt beneath his heel.

Among upper Mississippi valley tribes, the pipe or calumet served a purpose similar to that of wampum. The pipe was smoked or exchanged to secure an agreement, swear a solemn oath, or confer an honor. Scalps also could substitute for wampum belts as a diplomatic gift. Another symbolic gesture for war or peace was to "raise" or "bury" the hatchet.

The British and French enjoyed at least one negotiation advantage—the Indians could only trade for guns and gunpowder, they could not manufacture them. Indian power diminished with the supply of their weapons. Reversion to warring with bows and arrows was impractical. The Indians had largely lost their skill in making and wielding such weapons. Yet, as General Amherst found out in 1763, it did not pay to press this advantage too far. Amherst's decision to cut back arms and gifts to the Indians prompted a bloody revolt among a coalition of Great Lakes tribes.

A decision for war brought a new round of ceremonies. After the elderly sachems made a succession of eloquent war speeches, "they proceeded to nominate the war chiefs. As soon as one was named he rose and took the head of some animal that had been butchered for the feast. He raised it aloft so that all the company could see it, and cried: 'Behold the head of the enemy!' Applause and cries of joy rose from all parts of the assembly. The chief, with the head in his hand, passed down between the lines, singing his war-song, bragging of his exploits, taunting and defying the enemy, and glorifying himself beyond all measure. To hear his self-laudation in these moments of martial transport one would think him a conquering hero ready to sweep everything before him. As he passed in front of the other savages, they would respond by dull broken cries jerked up from the depths of their stomachs, and accompanied by movements of their bodies so odd that one must be well used to keep countenance. In the course of his song the chief would utter from time to time some grotesque witticism; then he would stop, as if pleased with himself, or rather to listen to the thousand confused cries of applause that greeted his ears. He kept up his martial promenade as long as he liked the sport; and when he had had enough, ended by flinging down the head of the animal with an air of contempt, to show that his warlike appetite craved meat of another sort."[124]

Once on the warpath, the French and British alike found themselves dependent on the Indians, who "determine the route, the halts, the scouts, and the speed to make, and in this sort of warfare it is necessary to adjust to their ways."[125] On a September 1756 raid, Bougainville complained that "the Iroquois, who being the greatest in number took the lead without even learning the wishes of the French commander. The chiefs, blankets on their backs and lance in hand, gravely advanced, took their places, and smoked the council pipe. The orator explained the purpose of the detachment, the reports of the scout, and on these matters they deliberated for a long time in the constant presence of a French interpreter. . . . As for the rest of it, the Indians treated us imperiously, made rules for us to which they did not conform, and one suspected that the Iroquois were not acting in good faith."[126] As General Braddock proved so glaringly, commanders who rejected their Indians' advice, strategy, and needs jeopardized their campaigns.

For the Indians, what the Europeans saw as an endless tangle of forests, mountains, marshes, and streams was not wilderness but home. Bougainville marveled at the Indians' ability "of finding tracks in the woods and of following them without losing them. . . . They see in tracks the number that have passed, whether they are Indians or Europeans, if the tracks are fresh or old, if they are of healthy or sick people, dragging feet or hurrying ones, marks of sticks used as supports. It is rarely that they are deceived or mistaken. . . . As regards their sense of direction in the woods, it is of a complete sureness. If they have left a place where they put their canoes, whatever distance they may have gone, whatever turns they may have made, crossing the rivers, mountains, they come directly back to the place where their canoes are left. Observation of the sun, the inclination of trees and of leaves . . . and finally an instinct superior to all reasons, these are their guides and these guides never lead them astray."[127]

Indians could be notoriously fickle. Even with the enemy at hand, the enthusiasm of an Indian war party could shrivel as fast as it flared. A prolonged siege, the loss of comrades, or even a bad omen or dream could demoralize a war party just as the taking of a few scalps or hostages could satiate its bloodlust and honor. Any of these experiences could prompt the Indians to turn for home.

As Captain Pierre Pouchot recounts, the Indians had perfected wilderness tactics: "At the very instant they surprise the enemy, they fire & very rarely fail to shoot their men down. They immediately rush forward, axe in hand, throw themselves on their adversary & . . . give him an axe blow to the head. If he flees, they throw it at him so that it sticks in his back, at which they are very skilled. As soon as the man is felled, they run up to him, thrust their knee in between his shoulder blades, seize a tuft of his hair in one hand &, with their knife in the other, cut around the skin of the head & pull the whole piece away. . . . Then, brandishing the scalp, they utter a whoop which they call the 'death whoop.' When fighting, they utter the most frightful yells they can manage, in order to give themselves courage & to intimidate the enemy. If they are not under pressure & the victory has cost them lives, they disembowel [the dead enemy] and smear the blood over themselves. Although they find these atrocities repugnant, they none-theless commit them in order to steel themselves to the slaughter & induce themselves in a kind of rage."[128]

Prisoners may well have envied the dead: "Until they arrive back at the village, the prisoners are treated well & without ill-will. On the retreat of the party . . . the man holding the scalps heads up the procession. . . . Then comes the prisoners . . . singing, although they do not feel like doing so. All the warriors are silent. The man holding the pole with the scalps first utters several shouts to indicate the number of men they have lost. It is a lugu-brious cry which gradually dies away. After these he utters a number of more lively shouts to express the number of scalps or prisoners taken. They all shout together . . . until they arrive at the chief's hut . . . the adolescents, women, and children rush up to greet them . . . [The prisoners] are lucky if they are steady on their legs for they are then assailed with a hail of stones & blows with sticks; the village folk compete in striking them the most. Then all join in except the warriors who calmly let them do it. . . . When one of these unfortunates falls, he is ill-treated even more harshly, especially if he screams, because that amuses them. It is rare for them not to arrive covered in bruises at the hut, where the chiefs & elders are assembled. The leader of the war party recounts the details of the journey & the operation, renders justice to each man & praises his warriors, mentioning their exploits. After that they present to the gathering the prisoners, each of whom is compelled to dance in turn. . . . Once the ceremony is over, the war chief disposes of the scalps & prisoners. . . . Normally, among the Iroquois, the prisoner destined to replace a dead man occupies the latter's place in the family. The entire nation regards him as one of its members & his new relatives remove the belt of slavery from his neck. If they do not want to adopt him & say that they are too upset to replace the dead man, the prisoner is handed over to the young men so that they may amuse themselves with him. This verdict is irrevocable and the unfortunate man is burned. . . . In other nations prisoners are even more to be pitied, because they are treated like dogs. They kill them with impunity when in a drunken state & in periods of food shortage do not hesitate to eat them."[129]

Throughout the war, most tribes allied with the French. There were good reasons for this. For 150 years, French missionaries and traders alike had lived among the Indians, gaining fluency in their languages and customs. The French largely understood the Indians far better than did the British, and thus tended to be more sensitive to Indian culture and needs. The French intermarried far more with the Indians than did the British, thus cementing formal alliances with kinship ties. Frequently, the missionaries were as frenzied as anyone in urging their Indian charges to take up the tomahawk against the infidel Protestants of the British colonies. While British settlers shoved out the Indians and took their lands, often through trickery and warfare, French settlers were fewer and mostly confined to the St. Lawrence valley between Quebec and Montreal. New France's centralized rule enabled the governor to distribute gifts as they were needed. Yet these diplomatic advantages were offset by the poor quality and higher prices of French goods, and, after the war broke out, by the dwindling supply of those gifts as the British blockade tightened.

France's Indian allies naturally tended to raid those enemy regions closest to their homes—the Micmac against Acadia, the Abenaki against New England, and the Iroquois and Ohio valley tribes, their ranks leavened by warriors from upper Great Lake tribes, against the frontiers of New York, Pennsylvania, Maryland, and Virginia. The strength of the French alliances with the Indians varied considerably from one tribe to the next. Bougainville observed that the "nations of the Far West are, in general, easier to lead than our domesticated Indians. They have greater respect for the French whom they see less often, moreover their great distance from home is a reason why they do not relax everytime they make a strike."[130]

Three missions in the Canadian heartland—Huron Lorette, Abenaki St. Francis, and Mohawk Caughnawaga—supplied most of the raiders who terrorized the English settlements. Yet, the Caughnawaga Mohawk were often loath to war against their British cousins to the south. Also loyal were the Ottawa, Objibwa, Mississauga, Potawatomi, and other tribes from the upper Great Lakes whose inhabitants knew only French merchants and priests and thus depended on the annual trade canoes from Montreal. Likewise, most Ohio valley tribes sided with the French despite their awareness that British goods were better made and lower priced. The bloody defeat of Braddock's army and subsequent French victories in the war's early years rallied Ohio valley Indians to the fleur de lis. Another attribute of a French alliance was possibly easing the still heavy yoke of Iroquois domination from their shoulders. The Micmac and Abenaki of upper New England and Acadia also sided exclusively with the French.[131]

The Iroquois were the most ambiguous toward the French. Like the Ohio tribes, the Iroquois wanted above all to be neutral, but failing that to be on the winning side. The Iroquois had not forgotten that not-so-distant past when they ruled supreme over most other Indian tribes from the Atlantic to the Mississippi and from well above the Great Lakes and St. Lawrence to far down in what is now Tennessee and the Carolinas. The French and British had gradually destroyed that vast empire through trade, war, missions, and disease. Ideally, the Iroquois wanted all white forts, whether British or French, to be removed from their territory.

French diplomacy toward the western-most of the Iroquois, the Seneca and Cayuga, was especially effective in enticing warriors to harass English settlements and join French forces. The French offered both gifts of trade goods and the threat to burn the villages of those who aided the British. Governor Vaudreuil spread word among the Iroquois that "should any of the Five Nations be found next spring among the English, I will let loose all our Upper and domiciliated Nations on them; cause their villages to be laid waste and never pardon them."[132]

British diplomacy was undercut not only because it lacked the sophistication of the French, but also as each colony pursued its own interests with the Indians. For example, it is interesting to speculate over the deployment of Iroquois power and the course of the war without William Johnson whose diplomacy prevented the Six Nations from joining the French en masse.[133] Yet, despite Johnson's strenuous efforts, only the Mohawk significantly aided the British during the first three years of war. All along Johnson had to compete for the Iroquois alliance, not only with the French but with fellow Americans like Governor William Shirley's agent Henry Lydius, or Pennsylvania's agent Conrad Weiser. While Johnson blasted Lydius' machinations, he and Weiser "were polite to each other; but, committed to opposing interests, they tried to move the Six Nations in different directions. Weiser wanted them to oppose the French at the Ohio. Johnson wanted them to attack the French at Montreal."[134] Regardless of whether the rivalry among colonial officers for Iroquois loyalties was acrimonious or collegial, it split the Longhouse and pushed many warriors into French arms. To varying extents, this colonial rivalry existed for any tribes whose villages straddled the claimed territories of two or more colonies. Each colony persisted in conducting its own interests and diplomacy with the Indians even after Johnson was named the Crown's Indian Superintendent in 1755, or the duty divided between a Northern Superintendent under Johnson and a Southern Superintendent under Edmund Atkins in 1756.

The French and Indian War occurred during the height of the "Age of Reason." The Indian warfare of slaughter, torture, and enslavement of soldiers and civilians alike clashed with that era's European warfare of limited campaigns and open field battles in which professional soldiers fought each other while sparing civilians. Did the French or British suffer any moral qualms about unleashing such Indian mayhem on their enemies?

For over a century, Canadian governors had been dispatching French-led Indian raids on the American frontier to torture, kill, scalp, and drag back into captivity as many colonists as possible. Not all French were nonchalant about the moral questions raised by the tactics of France's Indian allies. Jean-Nicolas Desandrouins rued the "misfortune to make war with such people, especially when they are drunk—a condition in which nothing stays their fury."[135] Bougainville confided to his diary the moral dilemma both the French and British faced when employing Indians: "The cruelties and the insolence of these barbarians is horrible, their souls are black as pitch. It is an abominable way to make war; the retaliation is frightening and the air one breathes here is contagious of making one accustomed to calousness ...What a scourge! Humanity shudders at being obliged to make use of such monsters. But without them the match would be too much against us. ... What can one do against invisible enemies who strike and flee with the rapidity of light. It is the destroying angel."[136]

Bougainville believed that another dilemma was the question of who should be the French liaison with the Indians. He condemned the practice of naming voyageurs to the post, arguing that "this function, which gives the greatest control over the Indians, is given to vile souls, mercenaries, cruel men, who are occupied only in retaining their control over the Indians, from which they draw a great profit in contenancing all their vices and even in furnishing the means of satisfying them."[137] Here Bougainville displays uncharacteristic naivete. The British tried to control Indians with regular officers and failed miserably. Only the toughest of men inured to the wilderness; those who spoke the Indian languages, and not only understood but sympathized with Indian culture and needs, were suited to being their liaison with France.

The best moral argument for Indian allies was that it was better to unleash them on one's enemies than have them wield the scalping knife against oneself. The strategy of divide and conquer proved the most effective way to manage the Indians. By exploiting long-smoldering Indian rivalries with arms, goods, and exhortation to war, the French and English could divert animosities against themselves, deepen the Indian dependence on European products, and garner more fur wealth. South Carolina Governor Robert Johnson succinctly captured this strategy: "It is always the maxim of our Government upon the Continent to promote war between Indians of different Nations with whom we Trade and are at peace with ourselves for in that consists our safety, being at War with one another prevents their uniting against us."[138]

In the end, just what impact did Indians have on the war? Without Indian support, the French would have been unable to stave off defeat for as long as they did. Jennings notes that "Britain's forces triumphed only in battles where Indians abandoned the French, were opposed by Indians allied to Britain, or where they played a negligible role."[139] The most decisive Indian impact was at the Monongahela, where over 600 Indians joined the relative handful of French regulars and Canadians in slaughtering Braddock's troops. Without them, the French would have had to abandon Fort Duquesne and perhaps their three forts leading to Lake Erie. The capture of those forts along with Fort Beausejour and Johnson's defeat of Dieskau at Lake George might have ended the war in 1755 with a limited British victory rather than the conquest of 1760.

While varying numbers of Indians could be found alongside the French in every battle against the British army, they more commonly launched scalp raids against American frontier settlements. Just beyond the British colonial frontiers, the French supplied Indian raiders from seven forts—Fort Toulouse on the Alabama River, Fort Duquesne at the Ohio River forks, Fort Niagara below the falls, Fort Presentation on the St. Lawrence, Forts Frederic and Carillon on Lake Champlain, and Fort St. Jean on the St. John's River. Those raids were nearly always bloody successes since the American "Settlements are Vag[u]e without Design, scattered, Independent, they are so settled, that from their Situation 'tis not easy for them to unite in a System of Mutual Defense, nor does their Interest lead them to such a System, & even if both did, Yet thro' the Want of a Police to form Themselves together are Helpless & Defenseless & thus have the English of this Sort for many Hundreds of Miles a long indefensible Line of Frontiers. . . . The French can collect in a short Warning at any Time, in any of their advanced Posts a Force sufficient to break up the Settlements & return again within their Lines before any Force can be collected to attack them. . . . The English are settled up to Mountains the very Mouth of the Denns of these Savages; in which Situation the Building a Line of Forts as a Barrier against them would be as little effectual as building a Line of Forts to prevent the Bears Wolves & Foxes from coming within them."[140]

Colonists tried to defend themselves by erecting stockades within their communities and fortifying their homes. But a static defense was no real defense at all. In an Indian war, the front line was wherever a raid happened to fall. Indian raiders could slip around forts and militia camps to slaughter, burn, and then disappear back into the wilderness. Even if a family succeeded in defending their home, they had to watch in impotent fury as the Indians slaughtered their livestock and burned their fields. If they fled to a stockade, they often returned to the smoldering ruins of their house.

The effectiveness of French and Indian raids was considerable. They tied down enemy troops, destroyed their sustenance, treasury, and morale, and crimped their ability to counterattack. The terror they reaped along the frontier destroyed crops, killed workers and soldiers, sent floods of refugees into the towns and cities, and diverted countless militia to defend their homes rather than march against the enemy. Evaluating the impact of Indian raids on the frontier, Jennings argues that "the quality of such casualties multiplied their impact far beyond comparable losses in set battles. Men lost in combat were, almost by definition, nonessential to the economy: they had become soldiers because they could be spared from production. But the destruction of whole families and their working farms eliminated a substantial component of British production beside providing plunder to alleviate Canadian scarcity. . . . The refugess rushed to the safety of towns, where they became consuming liabilities instead of producing assets. Their flight created panic and demoralization, and their natural fury created new political situations that troubled government and handicapped efforts to cope with the raids. The atrocities roused undiscriminating race hatred that played into the French hand by frightening off the remaining Indian allies capable of resisting guerrilla war. . . . [T]he French instigators faded off behind the screen of monsters of a race other than human. Refugees did not want to hear of proposals to solve problems or negotiate agreements with the Indians whose land many of the refugees had been occupying. Reasoned discussion became irrelevant to the emotions of people who had fled from the storm. Government understood the necessity of negotiation to win tribes away from French alliance, but refugees wanted hot revenge."[141]

While Indians were essential to the French war effort, they as much hindered as helped the British. In no British victory did Indians play more than an auxiliary role, and commanders usually complained that they were far more trouble than was worth the enormous expense of gifts and diplomacy in bringing them into the field. American rangers eventually performed all the scouting and fighting expected of the Indians, at a fraction of the cost and all year long. Perhaps the most important service that Britain's Indian allies made was to deny their bloody contribution to the French.

Yet, even the French at times questioned whether their Indian allies were worth all the treasury and effort to get them into the field. Bougainville complained that "they gather together in mobs, argue among themselves, deliberate slowly and all want to go together to make a strike and at the same place, because they prefer big war parties. Between the resolution made and the action taken there passes considerable time, sometimes one nation stops the march, sometimes another. Everybody must have time to get drunk, and their food consumption is enormous. At last they get started, and once they have struck, have they taken only a single scalp or one prisoner, back they come and are off again for their villages. Then for a considerable time the army is without Indians. Each one does well for himself, but the operation of war suffers, for in the end they are a necessary evil. It would be better to have on hand only a specified number of these mosquitoes, who would be relieved by others, so that we would always have some on hand. In general it does not seem to me that we are getting all the use we can out of these Indians."[142] It was that kind of war.

NOTES

1. Lawrence Henry Gipson, *The Great War for Empire: The Years of Defeat, 1754–1757* (New York: Alfred A. Knopf, 1959), 6:393, 401; Lee Kennett, *The French Armies in the Seven Years' War: A Study in Military Organization and Administration* (Durham, N.C.: Duke University Press, 1967), 77; James Pritchard, *Louis XV's Navy, 1748–1762: A Study of Organization and Administration* (Kingston, Ont.: McGill–Queens University Press, 1987), 137, 140; H. C. B. Rogers, *The British Army of the Eighteenth Century* (London: Allen & Unwin, 1977); Christopher Duffy, *The Fortress in the Age of Vauban and Frederick the Great* (London: Routledge and Kegan Paul, 1985); Christopher Duffy, *The Military Experience in the Age of Reason, 1715–1789* (New York: Barnes & Noble Books, 1987).

2. Don Miquelon, *New France, 1701–1744: "A Supplement to Europe"* (Toronto: McClelland and Stewart, 1987); Rene Chartrand, *Canadian Military Heritage 1000–1754*, vol. 1 (Montreal: Art Global, 1993); Rene Chartrand, *Canadian Military Heritage, 1755–1871*, vol. 2 (Montreal: Art Global, 1995); Ian K. Steele, *Guerrillas and Grenadiers: The Struggle for Canada, 1698–1760* (Toronto: Ryerson, 1969); Rene Chartrand, *The French Soldier in Colonial America* (Ottawa: Museum Restoration Service, 1984).

3. Adolphe B. Benson, ed., *Peter Kalm's Travels in North America: The Version of 1770* (New York: Dover Publications, 1987), 589.

4. Edward Hamilton, ed., *Adventure in the Wilderness: The American Journals of Louis Antoine de Bougainville, 1756–60* (hereafter cited as Hamilton, *Bougainville Journal*) (Norman: University of Oklahoma Press, 1964), 58.

5. Sir Julian S. Corbett, *England in the Seven Years' War: A Study in Combined Strategy*, 2nd ed., 2 vols. (London: Longmans, Green, 1907); Richard Middleton, *The Bells of Victory: The Pitt-Newcastle Ministry and the Conduct of the Seven Years' War 1757–1762* (Cambridge: Cambridge University Press, 1985).

6. Montcalm to Le Normand, April 12, 1759, in E. B. O'Callaghan and Berthold Fernow, eds., *Documents Relative to the Colonial History of the State of New York*, 15 vols. (hereafter cited as NYCD) (Albany, N.Y.: Weed, Parsons, and Co., 1853–1887), 10:926–65.

7. Hamilton, *Bougainville Journal*, 252–53. For an excellent account of fortress building and seige warfare, see "Memoir on the Defense of the Fort of Carillon," *The Bulletin of the Fort Ticonderoga Museum* 8, no. 3 (1972), 196–226.

8. Wolfe to Major Rickson, November 5, 1757, in Beckles Willson, ed., *The Life and Letters of James Wolfe* (hereafter cited as Willson, *Wolfe Letters*) (London: Heineman, 1909), 339.

9. Brian Connell, ed., *The Siege of Quebec and the Campaigns in North America, 1757–1760, by Captain John Knox* (hereafter cited as Connell, *Knox Memoir*) (Mississauga, Ont.: Pendragon, 1980), 189–90.

10. E. Wayne Carp, "Early American Military History: A Review of Recent Work," *Virginia Magazine of History and Biography* 94 (1986), 259–84; Don Higginbotham, "Early American Way of War: Reconnaissance and Appraisal," *William and Mary Quarterly* 44 (1987), 226–41.

11. Ian K. Steele, *Warpaths: Invasions of North America* (New York: Oxford University Press, 1994), 189–90; Peter E. Russell, "Redcoats in the Wilderness: Brit-

ish Officers and Irregular Warfare in Europe and America, 1740–1760," *William and Mary Quarterly* 35 (1978), 629–52.

12. Daniel J. Beattie, "The Adaptation of the British Army to Wilderness Warfare, 1755–1763," in Maarten Ultee, ed., *Adapting to Conditions: War and Society in the Eighteenth Century* (Tuscaloosa: University of Alabama Press, 1986), 56–83.

13. Amherst to Gage, June 6, 1759, Amherst Letters, vol. 4, Clements Library, quoted in Daniel J. Beattie, "The Adaptation of the British Army to Wilderness Warfare, 1755–1763," in Ultree, *Adapting to Conditions,* 78.

14. Howard H. Peckham, ed., *Journals of Major Robert Rogers* (hereafter cited as Peckham, *Rogers Journal*) (New York: Corinth Books, 1961), 43–51; John R. Cuneo, *Robert Rogers of the Rangers* (Ticonderoga, N.Y.: Fort Ticonderoga Museum, 1988); "Robert Rogers," "Rogers' Rangers," "Regulations for the Rangers Drawn Up by Robert Rogers," "The Rangers," *The Bulletin of the Fort Ticonderoga Museum* 4, no. 31 (January 1941), 1–19.

15. Peckham, *Rogers Journal,* 11.

16. Cornelius J. Jaenen, *The French Relationship with the Indian Peoples of New France and Acadia* (Ottawa: Research Branch, Indian and Northern Affairs, 1984), 168.

17. Connell, *Knox Memoir,* 135.

18. Ibid., 153.

19. Douglas Edward Leach, *Arms for Empire: A Military History of the British Colonies in North America, 1607–1763* (New York: Macmillan, 1973), 254.

20. Samuel P. Huntington, *The Soldier and the State: The Theory and Politics of Civil-Military Relations* (Cambridge, Mass.: Harvard University Press, 1957), 26–27.

21. Quoted in Lawrence Henry Gipson, *The Great War for Empire: The Victorious Years* (New York: Alfred Knopf, 1949), 7:175 n.28.

22. For James Wolfe's reading list, see his July 18, 1756 letter to Thomas Townsend in Willson, *Wolfe Letters.*

23. Kennett, *French Armies,* 76.

24. Sir John W. Fortescue, *A History of the British Army,* 13 vols. (1910–1935) (reprint, New York: AMS Press, 1976), 2:592 n.; Stuart Reid, *King George's Army, 1740–93,* vols. 1–2 (London: Osprey Books, 1995); J. A. Houlding, *Fit for Service: The Training of the British Army, 1715–1795* (Oxford: Oxford University Press, 1980).

25. Connell, *Knox Memoir,* 53.

26. Ibid., 54, 98.

27. Robin May, and G. A. Embleton, *Wolfe's Army* (London: Osprey Military Men at Arms Series, 1974), 42.

28. Kennett, *French Armies,* 116; Harold L. Peterson, *Arms and Armour in Colonial America, 1526–1783* (New York: Bramball House, 1956); M. L. Brown, *Firearms in Colonial America: The Impact of History and Technolgoy, 1492–1792* (Washington, D.C.: Smithsonian Institute, 1980).

29. Edward P. Hamilton, *The French Army in America* (Ottawa: Museum Restoration Service, 1967), 13.

30. Connell, *Knox Memoir,* 27.

31. Ibid., 38.

32. Ibid., 110.

33. Houlding, *Fit for Service.*

34. Pritchard, *Louis XV's Navy*; A. T. Mahan, *The Influence of Sea Power Upon History, 1660–1783* (1890) (reprint, Boston: Little, and Company, 1928); Michel Verge-Franceshi, *La Marine Francaise au XVIIIe Siecle* (Paris: Sedes, 1996).

35. G. J. Marcus, *Heart of Oak: A Survey of British Sea Power in the Georgian Era* (London: Oxford University Press, 1975); N. A. M. Rodgers, *The Wooden World: An Anatomy of the Georgian Navy* (Annapolis, Md.: Naval Institute Press, 1982); Ian K. Steele, *The English Atlantic, 1675–1740* (New York: Oxford University Press, 1986); Robert G. Albion, *Forests and Sea Power: The Timber Problem of the Royal Navy, 1652–1862* (Cambridge, Mass.: Harvard University Press, 1926); Daniel A. Baugh, *British Naval Administration in the Age of Walpole* (Princeton, N.J.: Princeton University Press, 1965); Sir William Laird Clowes, *The Royal Navy: A History from the Earliest Times to the Present*, 7 vols. (London: S. Low Martson and Company, 1897–1903); Sir Robert Beatson, *Naval and Military Memoirs of Great Britain, from 1727 to 1783*, 2 vols. (Boston: Gregg Press, 1972).

36. Richard Middleton, *The Bells of Victory: The Pitt-Newcastle Ministry and the Conduct of the Seven Years' War, 1757–1762* (Cambridge: Cambridge University Press, 1985), 24–25.

37. Stephen F. Gradish, *The Manning of the British Navy during the Seven Years' War* (London: Royal Historical Society, 1980), 46.

38. Memoir on Canada, January 1759, NYCD 10:934.

39. Leach, *Arms for Empire*, 197.

40. J. S. McLennan, *Louisbourg from Its Foundation to Its Fall, 1713–1758* (1918) (reprint, Halifax, N.S.: The Book Room Limited, 1994), 296.

41. Ibid., 309.

42. Gradish, *Manning of the British Navy*, 111.

43. Ibid., 111, 120; Marcus, *Heart of Oak*, 130.

44. Franklin to Galloway, London, April 7, 1759, in Leonard W. Labaree, ed., *The Papers of Benjamin Franklin* (New Haven, Conn.: Yale University Press, 1962), 8:315–16; see also Jess Lemisch, "Jack Tar in the Streets: Merchant Seamen in the Politics of Revolutionary America," *William and Mary Quarterly* 3rd ser., 25, no. 3 (1968), 371–407; William Pencak, "Thomas Hutchinson's Fight against Naval Impressment," *New England Historical and Genealogical Register* 132 (1978), 25–36; William Pencak, "Warfare and Political Change in Mid-Eighteenth Century Massachusetts," in Peter Marshall and Glyn Williams, eds., *The British Atlantic Empire Before the American Revolution* (London: Frank Cass, 1980).

45. Loudoun to Cumberland, June 22, 1757, in Stanley Pargellis, ed., *Military Affairs in North America, 1748–1763: Selected Documents from the Cumberland Papers in Windsor Castle* (1936) (reprint, Hamden, Conn.: Archon Books, 1969), 376.

46. John Alden, *General Gage in America* (Baton Rouge: University of Louisiana Press, 1948), 253; Sheila L. Skemp, "A World Uncertain and Strongly Checker'd," in Ultree, *Adapting to Conditions*, 84–103.

47. Lawrence Henry Gipson, *The Great War for Empire: The Culmination, 1760–1763* (New York: Alfred A. Knopf, 1964), 8:71.

48. Hardy to Board of Trade, October 13, 1756, NYCD, 7:163; see also Emory R. Johnson et al., *History of Domestic and Foreign Commerce of the United States*, vol. 1 (Washington, D.C.: Carnegie Institute, 1915); Richard Pares, *Colonial Blockade and Neutral Rights, 1739–1763* (Oxford: Oxford University Press, 1938); Rich-

ard Pares, *War and Trade in the West Indes, 1739–1763* (1936) (reprint, London: F. Cass, 1963).

49. George Louis Beer, *British Colonial Policy* (1922) (reprint, Gloucester, Mass.: Peter Smith, 1958), 87–88, 127–28.

50. Gerald S. Graham, "The Naval Defense of British North America, 1739–1763," *Royal Historical Society Transactions* 4th ser., 30 (1948), 95–110.

51. Kennett, *French Armies;* J. A. Houlding, *French Arms Drill of the 18th Century* (Bloomfield, Ont.: Museum Restoration, 1988); Douglas Clark Baxter, "Pension Expectations of the French Military Commis," in Ultree, *Adapting to Conditions,* 177–234; Clive H. Church, *Revolution and Red Tape: The French Ministerial Bureaucracy, 1770–1850* (Oxford: Clarendon Press, 1981); Roland Mousnier, "La Fonction publique en France du debut du seizieme siecle a la fin du dix-huitieme siecle. Des officiers aux commissaires puis aux commis, puis aux fonctionnaires," *Revue Historique* 530 (April–June 1979), 321–35; Rene Mousnier, *Institutions de la France sous la Monarchie Absolue,* 2 vols. Les Organes de l'Etat et la Societe (Paris: Universataires de France, 1974, 1980); Jean-Pierre Samoyault, *Les Bureaux du Secretariat d'Etat des Affaires Etrangeres sous Louis XV* (Paris: Editions A. Pedrone, 1971); Michael Antoine, "L'Entourage des ministres aux XVIIe et XVIIIe siecles," in Michael Antoine et al., eds., *Origines et Histories des Cabinets des Ministres en France* (Geneva: Librarie Droz, 1975); Anne Buot de l'Epine, "Les Bureaux de la Guerre a la fin de l'Ancien Regime," *Revue d'Historique de Droit Francais et Etrangere* 54 (1976); Louis Andre, *Michel le Tellier et l'Organization de l'Armee Monarchique* (Paris: Felix Alcan, 1906); Douglas Clark Baxter, "Premier Commis in the War Department in the Latter Part of the Reign of Louis XIV," in *Proceedings of the Western Society for French History* 8 (1981), 81–89; John Rule, "The Commis of the Department of Foreign Affairs Under the Administration of Colbert de Croissey and Colbert de Torcy, 1680–1715," ibid., 69–80; Andre Corvisier, "Clientales et fidelites dans l'armee francaise aux XVIIe et XVIIIe siecles," in Yves Durand, ed., *Homage a Roland Mousnier, Clienteles et Fidelities en Europe a l'Epoque Moderne* (Paris: Presses Universitaires de France, 1981), 217–18; "Memoire historiques concernant l'ordre royale de militaire de Saint-Louis et l'institution du merite militaire" (Paris: Imprimerie Royale, 1785).

52. Kennet, *French Armies,* 57, 65–66.

53. Montcalm to Belle-Isle, April 12, 1759, NYCD, 10:960–62.

54. Doreil to Belle-Isle, July 31, 1758, NYCD, 10:769.

55. Hamilton, *Bougainville Journal,* 331.

56. Chartrand, *French Soldier,* 9–14, 16–19; see also W. J. Eccles, "The French Forces in North America During the Seven Years' War," *Dictionary of Canadian Biography* (Toronto: University of Toronto Press, 1966–), xv–xxii; George F. G. Stanley, *Canada's Soldiers;* Edward P. Hamilton, *The French Army in America* (Ottawa: Museum Restoration Service, 1967).

57. W. J. Eccles, "The French Forces in North America during the Seven Years' War," *Dictionary of Canadian Biography* 3:xvii.

58. Montcalm to Argenson, August 28, 1756, NYCD, 10:463.

59. Dunnigan, *Pouchot Memoirs,* 78.

60. Ibid.

61. Francis Back and Rene Chartrand, "Canadian Militia, 1750–1760," *Military Collector and Historian* 34, no. 1 (Spring 1984), 18–21.

62. Montcalm to Paulmy, September 18, 1757, NYCD, 10:635–36.

63. Vaudreuil to minister, October 23, 1756, MG 1 Serie, C11A, Canadian Public Archives.

64. Eccles, "French Forces," xix–xx.

65. Pargellis, *Military Affairs*, xx.

66. Hamilton, *Bougainville Journal*, 31, 33–34.

67. Ibid., 17.

68. Caroline Robbins, *The Eighteenth Century Commonwealman: Studies in the Transmission, Development, and Circumstances of English Liberal Thought From the Restoration of Charles II until the War with the Thirteen Colonies* (Cambridge, Mass.: Harvard University Press, 1959).

69. Pargellis, *Military Affairs*, xx.

70. Gipson, *Great War*, 8:30.

71. Ibid., 8:42–43.

72. William Pencak, "Warfare and Political Change in Mid-Eighteenth Century Massachusetts," *Journal of Imperial and Commonwealth History* 8 (1980), 51–73; William Pencak, *War, Politics, & Revolution in Provincial Massachusetts* (Boston: Northeastern University Press, 1981); Harold E. Selesky, *War and Society in Colonial Connecticut* (New Haven, Conn.: Yale University Press, 1990).

73. Stanley McCrory Pargellis, *Lord Loudoun in America* (New Haven, Conn.: Yale University Press, 1933).

74. Julian Gywn, "British Government Spending and the North American Colonies, 1740–1755," *Journal of Imperial and Commonwealth History* 8 (1980), 74–84; Pencak, *War, Politics, & Revolution*, 135, 154.

75. Labaree, *The Papers of Benjamin Franklin*, 5:400.

76. Hardy to Halifax, May 7, 1755, in Pargellis, *Military Affairs*, 171.

77. Quoted in Parkman, *Montcalm and Wolfe*, 244.

78. Adolph B. Benson, ed., *Peter Kalm's Travels in North America: The Version of 1770* (1937) (reprint, New York: Dover Publications, 1987), 138–39.

79. Pennsylvania Colonial Records, 6:415.

80. Alfred P. James, ed., *Writings of General John Forbes Relating to His Service in North America* (Menasha, Wis.: Collegiate Press, 1938), 224–25.

81. Abercromby to Forbes, April 24, 1758, AB 189, Huntington Library.

82. Lawrence Henry Gipson, *The Great War for the Empire: The Years of Defeat, 1754–1757* (New York: Alfred A. Knopf, 1959), 193. For excellent accounts of daily life for British and Americans on campaign, see "Captain Moneypenny's Orderly Book, June 30 to July 7, 1758," *The Bulletin of the Fort Ticonderoga Museum* 2, no. 8, (July 1930), 54–67; "Captain Moneypenny Orderly Book, June 30 to August 7, 1758," ibid., 434–61; "Captain Moneypenny's Orderly Book, July 15 to August 3, 1759," ibid., 2, no. 10 (July 1932), 219–53; "Robert Webster Journal, April 5 to November 23, 1759," ibid., 2, no. 10 (July 1931), 120–153; "Life of David Perry," ibid., 14, no. 1 (Summer 1981), 4–8; "Journal of Captain Cobb," ibid., 12–31; "Josiah Goodrich Orderbook," ibid., 39–61.

83. Douglas Leach, *Arms for Empire* (New York: Macmillan, 1973), 253.

84. Sylvia R. Frey, *The British Soldier in America: A Social History of Military Life in the Revolutionary Period* (Austin: University of Texas Press, 1981); Alastair MacLennan, "Highland Regiments in North America," *The Bulletin of the Fort Ticonderoga Museum* 12, no. 2 (September 1966), 118–25.

85. Nathan G. Goodman, ed., *A Benjamin Franklin Reader* (New York: Thomas Y. Crowell, 1945), 175.

86. John W. Fortescue, *A History of the British Army*, 13 vols. (London, 1889–1930), 2:32.

87. Quoted in Francis Jennings, *Empire of Fortune: Crowns, Colonies, & Tribes in the Seven Years War in America* (New York: W. W. Norton, 1988), 221.

88. William A. Foote, "The Pennsylvania Men of the American Regiment," *Pennsylvania Magazine of History and Biography* 87 (1963), 31–38; William A. Foote, "The South Carolina Independents," *South Carolina Historical Magazine* 62 (1961), 195–99; Douglas Leach, *Roots of Conflict: British Armed Forces and Colonial Americans, 1677–1763* (Chapel Hill: University of North Carolina Press, 1986).

89. Connell, *Knox Memoir*, 22.

90. Cumberland to Loudoun, 1757, quoted in Cuneo, *Rogers*, 54–55.

91. F. W. Anderson, "Why Did Colonial New Englanders Make Bad Soldiers? Contractual Principles and Military Conduct during the Seven Years' War," *William and Mary Quarterly* 38 (1981), 395–417.

92. John Winslow to Charles Gould, June 27, 1755, in *Collections of the Nova Scotia Historical Society for the Years 1878–1884* (Belleville, Ont.: Mika Publishing Company, 1976), 4:181.

93. Jennings, *Empire of Fortune*, 292.

94. John W. Shy, ed., *A People Numerous and Armed* (New York: Oxford University Press, 1976); Lawrence D. Cress, *Citizens in Arms: The Army and Militia in American Society to the War of 1812* (Chapel Hill: University of North Carolina Press, 1982).

95. John W. Shy, "A New Look at Colonial Militia," *William and Mary Quarterly* 3rd ser., 20 (1963).

96. John C. Fitzpatrick, ed., *The Writings of George Washington*, 39 vols. (Washington, D.C.: U.S. Government Printing Office, 1931–1944), 2:26.

97. Sylvester K. Stevens et al., eds., *The Papers of Henry Bouquet* (hereafter cited as Stevens, *Bouquet Papers*), 6 vols. (Harrisburg: Pennsylvania Historical and Museum Commission, 1972–1984), 2:72.

98. Henry Fox to Demere, August 25, 1754, State Papers, 41/21, Colonial Office, 324/28, f. 428.

99. Sketch of Regulations & Orders Proposed Relating to Affairs of North America, November 1754, in Pargellis, *Military Affairs*, 34–36; Sketch of an Order About the Rank of the Provincial Troops in North America, 1754, ibid., 43–44.

100. Forbes orders to Captain Wrightson, July 24, 1758, AB 941, Huntington Library.

101. Loudoun to Holderness, August 16, 1757, LO 4239, Huntington Library (HL); Braddock to Robinson, June 5, 1755, LO 581, HL; Wolfe to Sackville, August 7, 1758, Willson, *Wolfe's Letters*, 392; Leach, *Roots of Conflict*, 130–31.

102. Knowles to Newcastle, July 9, 1746, Colonial Office Papers, 5/44 ff. 136–41, quoted in Leach, *Roots of Conflict*, 74.

103. "Life of David Perry," *The Bulletin of the Fort Ticonderoga Museum* 14, no. 1 (Summer 1981), 5–6.

104. Johnson to Spencer Phips, October 10, 1755, in James Sullivan and A. C. Flick, eds., *The Papers of Sir William Johnson* (Albany: University of the State of New York, 1922), 2:164; William Johnson to Loudoun, December 20, 1756, LO 2371, Huntington Library.

105. Denny to Loudoun, November 12, 1757, LO 4793, Huntington Library.

106. Washington to Stanwix, July 15, 1757, in W. W. Abbott, ed., *The Papers of George Washington* (hereafter cited as Abbott, *Washington Papers*) (Charlottesville: University Press of Virginia, 1984), 4:306; F. W. Anderson, "Why Did Colonial New Englanders Make Bad Soldiers?: Contractual Principles and Military Conduct During the Seven Years' War," *William and Mary Quarterly* 38 (1981), 395–417.

107. John Shy, *Toward Lexington: The Role of the British Army in the Coming of the American Revolution* (Princeton, N.J.: Princeton University Press, 1965), 100.

108. Franklin to Fawkener, July 27, 1756, in Pargellis, *Military Affairs*, 185.

109. Israel Williams to Joseph Dwight, July 7, 1756, Massachusetts Historical Society, Hutchinson Papers, Misc. Bound, cs Mass., pub. 24:441.

110. Leach, *Roots of Conflict*, 112.

111. Connell, *Knox Memoir*, 164–65.

112. Jennings, *Empire of Fortune*, 209.

113. R. C. Simmons and P. D. G. Thomas, eds., *Proceedings and Debates of the British Parliaments Respecting North America, 1754–1783*, vol. 1, 1754–1764 (Millwood, N.Y.: Kraus International Publications, 1982), 1:28.

114. Stanwix to Abercromby, August 6, 1758, AB 948, Huntington Library.

115. Washington to Dinwiddie, August 4, 1756, in Abbott, *Washington Papers*, 3:312–18.

116. Anderson, *People's Army*, 191–92.

117. St. Clair to Robert Napier, June 13, 1755, in Pargellis, *Military Affairs*, 93.

118. Jennings, *Empire of Fortune*, 207.

119. Shy, *Toward Lexington*; Alan Rodgers, *Empire and Liberty: American Resistance to British Authority, 1755–1763* (Berkeley: University of California Press, 1965); John Philip Reid, *In Defiance of the Law: The Standing Army Controversy, the Two Constitutions, and the Coming of the American Revolution* (Chapel Hill: University of North Carolina Press, 1981); Stephen Saunders Webb, "Army and Empire: English Garrison Government in Britain and America, 1569–1763," *William and Mary Quarterly* 34 (1977), 1–31.

120. Stephen H. Cutcliffe, "Colonial Indian Policy as a Measure of Rising Imperialism: New York and Pennsylvania, 1700–1755," *Western Pennsylvania Historical Magazine* 64 (1981), 237–268; James Axtell, *The European and the Indian: Essays in the Ethnohistory of Colonial North America* (New York: Oxford University Press, 1981); James Axtell, *The Invasion Within: The Contest of Cultures in Colonial North America* (New York: Oxford University Press, 1985); Robert Berkhofer, "The French and Indians at Carillon," *The Bulletin of Fort Ticonderoga Museum* 9, no. 6 (1956), 134–69.

121. Hamilton, *Bougainville Journal*, 36.

122. Peters to Shirley, May 12, 1755, mss., Huntington Library; Wilbur R. Jacobs, *Diplomacy and Indian Gifts: Anglo-French Rivalry along the Ohio and Northwest Frontiers, 1748–1763* (Stanford, Calif.: Stanford University Press, 1950).

123. Secret Conference with Indians at Montreal, October 23, 1754, NYCD 10: 269.

124. Lettre du pere (Roubaud), Missionaire chez les Abenakis, October 21, 1757, in *Lettres Edifiante et Curiesuse*, 1810, 6:189.

125. Hamilton, *Bougainville Journal*, 37.

126. Ibid., 38–39.

127. Ibid., 55.

128. Dunnigan, *Pouchot Memoirs*, 476–77; Leroy V. Eid, " 'A Kind of Running Fight': Indian Battlefield Tactics in the Late Eighteenth Century," *Western Pennsylvania Historical Magazine* 71 (1988), 147–71; Leroy V. Eid, " 'National' War Among Indians of Northeastern North America," *Canadian Review of North American Studies* 16, no. 22 (Summer 1985), 125–54.

129. Dunnigan, *Pouchot Memoirs*, 479–80.

130. Hamilton, *Bougainville Journal*, 45.

131. Gordon M. Day, *The Identity of the St. Francis Indians* (Ottawa: National Museum of Man Mercury Series, Canadian Ethnology Service Paper 71, 1981); Cornelius J. Jansen, *The Relationship with the Native People of New France and Acadia* (Ottawa: Research Branch, Indian and Northern Affairs Canada, 1984); Kenneth M. Morrison, *The Embattled Northeast: The Elusive Ideal of Alliance in Abenaki-EuroAmerican Relations* (Berkeley: University of California Press, 1984).

132. Vaudreuil to Machault, September 31, 1755, NYCD, 10:378.

133. Milton W. Hamilton, *Sir William Johnson: Colonial America, 1715–1763* (Port Washington, N.Y.: Kennikat Press, 1976); Alan Eckert, *Wilderness Empire: A Narrative* (Boston: Little, Brown, 1969).

134. Jennings, *Empire of Fortune*, 79; Paul A. W. Wallace, *Conrad Weiser, 1696–1760* (Chapell Hill: University of North Carolina Press, 1959).

135. Jean-Nicolas Desandrouins, August 28, 1756, NYCD, 10:466.

136. Hamilton, *Bougainville Journal*, 41, 191.

137. Ibid., 243.

138. Quoted in Richard P. Sherman, *Robert Johnson: Proprietary & Royal Governor of South Carolina* (Columbia: University of South Carolina Press, 1966), 98.

139. Jennings, *Empire of Fortune*, 214.

140. "Considerations Upon the Scite, Interests, and Service of North America," by Thomas Pownall, 1755, in Pargellis, *Military Affairs*, 165.

141. Jennings, *Empire of Fortune*, 194–95.

142. Hamilton, *Bougainville Journal*, 60.

4

1754

I heard the bullets whistle, and, believe me, there is something charming
in the sound.
>   —George Washington, 1754

We would like very much to go to Virginia. We understand there are a
great many pretty mademoiselles there.
>   —A French officer to Major Adam Stephen
>   after Fort Necessity's surrender, 1754

I wou'd Die ten thousand Deaths to have the pleasure of possessing this
Fort but one Day, they are so vain of their success at the Meadows it's
worse than Death to hear them.
>   —Excerpt from an intelligence report secreted to the British
>   by Hostage Robert Strobo in Fort Duquesne, 1754

In 1754, France and England would begin their fourth war in North America, a war neither side wanted. After all, both kingdoms were still recovering financially and emotionally from their latest war, which had ended a mere six years earlier. The bewhigged ministers of Versailles and Whitehall certainly would have rejected war if they had known that it would destroy France's North American empire in the short run and much of Britain's North American empire within a generation. No one, of course, expected those results. The previous wars had all ended in stalemate. It was assumed that another war would end as inconclusively as the others, with the only gains deeper national debts and more crowded cemeteries.

Yet the British and French alike refused to back down from the crises smoldering in the upper Ohio valley and Acadia. War merely brought with it tragedy. Accompanying retreat was something far worse—dishonor. With fixed and leveled bayonets, the French and British marched steadily toward each other in hopes the other would back down. Neither did. Both saw their own acts as purely defensive and the other's as naked aggression. Newcastle, for one, maintained that the French would not declare war if the English solely asserted "our rights and possessions in North America, by either building Forts on our boundaries to render theirs useless, or else by demolishing such as may have been clearly and notoriously built upon our ground."[1] The French, of course, saw their own actions in the same light. The crisis escalated as one side's aggressive act led the other to retaliate more harshly, which in turn elicited even tougher measures from the first side.

Diplomacy might have defused the crisis. Article IV of the 1749 Aix-la-Chapelle Treaty called for an Anglo-French commission to resolve the plethora of territorial disputes that stretched back to the 1713 Treaty of Utrecht. In 1750, London dispatched William Mildmay and William Shirley as commissioners to Paris to join French commissioners de La Galissoniere and de Sihouette. Instead of overcoming their differences, those diplomats spent four years engaged in a dialogue of the deaf.[2]

It is often said that future wars are sown by the treaties "settling" past wars. Few treaties have been written as vaguely as that of Utrecht. The Aix-la-Chapelle Treaty not only failed to clarify Utrecht's lingering ambiguities, but added more to the list. British and French commissioners spent years trying to define the boundaries alluded to by Utrecht and Aix-la-Chapelle. To that end they prepared lengthy legal briefs asserting their respective claims to the disputed territory. But it was all to no avail.

The French maintained a watershed theory of empire that allowed possession of all lands from a river's mouth to its source. The theory conveniently assigned to France the St. Lawrence, Ohio, and Mississippi river valleys east to the Appalachian Mountains watershed, since they had discovered and exploited those regions. This confined the British to those lands draining from streams in the Appalachian Mountains east to the Atlantic Ocean. In a letter to Governor Duquesne, Minister Rouille captured the essence of France's claim: "The river Ohio and the rivers which fall into it unquestionably belong to France. It was discovered by M. de la Salle; since then we have always had trading posts there, and our possession of it has been all the more continuous since it is the most used communication between Canada and Louisiana. It is only for a few years that the English have undertaken to trade there; and today they wish to exclude us from it. However, up to now they have not claimed that these rivers belong to them. Their claim is that the Iroquois are lords over them and that being sovereign of those Indians, they can exercise these rights. But it is certain that the Iroquois have no claim there and that moreover this pretended sovereignty of the English over them is a myth. . . . However it is of the greatest importance to check the progress of the claims and enterprises of the English on that side. Were they to succeed there, they would cut the communications of the two colonies of Canada and Louisiana."[3]

At first glance, the French claim seemed unassailable. First claims and possession then as now are thought to be the most sound legal defense. In the 17th century, the French indeed had systematically explored and established trading posts throughout the Great Lakes, Mississippi, and lower Ohio River valleys. The trouble was that although London might concede France's prior discovery and claim, by the mid-18th century, British traders had supplanted their French rivals throughout the Ohio River valley. The British further argued correctly that the French had never truly explored the upper Ohio River valley. But these counterarguments too had loopholes. The British hold on the region's trade was tenuous at best. Celoron's vigorous military and commercial effort had driven away the British traders. The establishment of permanent French trade and military posts in the upper Ohio could permanently lock out the British.

But the British had yet another card to play in the game for the region. They argued that Britain's claim to the Ohio country was reinforced by the Utrecht and Aix-la-Chapelle treaties, both of which contained clauses designating the Iroquois as British "subjects." When the French had conceded that designation they had no idea that Whitehall would use it to claim all lands whose inhabitants the Iroquois deemed vassals. Since the Iroquois had earlier conquered the Ohio River tribes, Whitehall asserted ownership over those lands as well. The British pointed to 1701 and 1726 treaties they had signed with the Iroquois who had deeded them lands in the Great Lakes, and the Ottawa, Ohio, and Illinois River valleys. If Versailles accepted this assertion, it would have conceded to the British virtually all of New France west of Montreal.

Versailles naturally rejected this argument's legal logic. The French pointed out that they and their Indian allies had subsequently driven the Iroquois from those lands. They further argued that the British lacked the power to possess the lands they claimed, while the French did. Finally, the French maintained that the Iroquois lands were confined to where they actually lived, somewhere between the Hudson River and Lake Chautauqua. This was a strong counterargument. Even Iroquois agent William Johnson privately admitted that "in a political Sense our claims . . . in several Colonies include lands we never saw, and over which we could not Exercise full Dominion with 10,000 of the best Troops in Europe, but these claims are kept up by European powers to prevent the Enchroachments or pretensions of each other."[4]

The Iroquois further muddied London's claim by declaring themselves the "subjects" or "children" of both their "fathers," Britain and France. "Fathers" acquired the title by supplying presents to "children," something

France and Britain alike did for the Iroquois and other tribes. If another tribe was not one's child or father, it was likely one's enemy. The Iroquois gladly accepted the British as the more generous of its two patrons, but remained fiercely independent of both, bristling at the claim that they were anyone's "subject."

Another stalemate arose over Utrecht's bequeathal of Acadia to England. The French and British disagreed over where Acadia began and ended. The English insisted that Acadia included all lands east and south from the St. Lawrence River to New England, a realm which would have included all of present-day Nova Scotia and New Brunswick and a strip of Quebec. The French dismissed the English claim, and instead maintained that Acadia was confined to what is now Nova Scotia without Cape Breton. This assertion was undermined by the fact that before Utrecht, Versailles itself had delimited Acadia as the English now did.

These seemingly unbridgeable positions were cemented by the personalities and interests of the diplomats. Shirley and La Galissoniere were each side's hardliners.[5] It was La Galissoniere who had designed the French strategy for retaking the Ohio River valley. Shirley had organized the successful campaign to take Fort Louisburg in 1745 and complained bitterly when it was returned to France in 1748. Thus did both men personalize the conflicts between their two countries. In focusing on endlessly debating the Ohio valley and Acadia disputes, the commissioners devoted little effort to resolving a host of other festering conflicts over the four Neutral Islands in the Caribbean, freedom of the seas, the status of ships taken after Aix-la-Chapelle was signed, fishing rights off Canada, and respective claims in India. Conflicts over substantial problems worsened with squabbles over more petty disputes such as the language to be used, the negotiation agenda, the frequency of meetings, and so on. Each side accused the other of cunning and deceit. In this last accusation, at least, both sides were correct.

But the British commissioners were as divided between themselves as from the French. Conflicting strategies and egos caused Shirley and Mildmay to dispise each other. Mildmay denounced Shirley as "a slow mule that understands neither french or english and yet is obstinate in his way." In November 1750, Shirley wrote up a legal brief to submit to the French. Mildmay complained that "when the foul draft was produced, I found it dressed in so mean a stile, in so confused an Order & with so many improper observations, that I was forced immediately to take pen in hand & draw up one in a different form."[6]

While the positions simply hardened over the five years of negotiations, some faces and places changed. Shirley was recalled in 1751. William Anne Keppel, Earl of Albemarle, took his seat. Direct talks between ambassadors commenced in 1752. Negotiations shifted from Paris to London in 1753. The Ambassador to Britain, Charles Pierre Gaston Francois de Levis, Duc de Mirepoix, led the French effort against his counterpart Sir Thomas Robinson, Secretary of State for the Southern Department.

No matter who was involved, the diplomats spent most of their time either endlessly repeating their respective positions or indulging in equally endless rounds of parties. Newcastle wrote in June 1754 that "I am quite sick of Commissaries, Tho' I don't well know how to get rid of Them. I am sure, They will do no Good; and Therefore hope, We shall not be so far amuse'd by Their Conferences, as To suspend or delay, taking The Proper Measures to defend Ourselves, or recover our Lost Possessions."[7]

After the first year of meetings it was obvious to both sides that they would remain deadlocked because their respective demands were irreconcilable. Yet neither the French nor British wanted to break off negotiations. The hope was that they could stave off war with endless talk; the fear was that war would commence when they stopped talking. These beliefs were wrong. The diplomacy would continue for a year even after French and British subjects began killing each other in the Ohio valley, Acadia, and elsewhere. In the end, negotiations failed. Only conquest would settle the conflicting claims.

WASHINGTON'S CAMPAIGN

It would be a dangerous and humiliating year for George Washington. En route back to Williamsburg, Washington almost died, not once but twice. Impatient to carry word to Dinwiddie, Washington opted to head straight home rather than back to speak before the Logstown Council as etiquette demanded. Washington insulted Tanaghrisson and his followers when he announced that he and Gist would head back alone on December 26, leaving behind the Indians, the four English packers, and Van Braam. Washington was far more concerned with getting home in the teeth of fierce winter storms: "the Cold increas'd very fast, & the Roads were geting much worse by a deep Snow continually Freezing. . . . I took my necessary Papers, pull'd off my Cloths, tied My Self up in a Match Coat; & with my Pack at my back, with my Papers & Provisions in it, & a Gun, set out with Mr. Gist."[8]

The two men almost did not make it. Meeting a lone Indian, they employed him as a guide. Gist grew increasingly wary of their guide as the Indian gradually took them northeast rather than southeast. Suddenly, the Indian whirled and fired his musket at them. The shot missed. Gist tackled the Indian and was about to kill him when Washington restrained him. They let him go unharmed, then hurried away in fear that he would bring back a war party to kill them. Washington came to believe that the French had hired the Indian to assassinate them. That belief would influence his own attack in June on Captain Jumonville and his men.[9]

A day later, while crossing the Allegheny River on a crudely built raft, Washington toppled into the freezing water. Gist managed to drag him out on an island where he built a bonfire and they passed a miserable night. The next morning the river had frozen over and they managed to cross on the ice and logjams. They finally reached John Frazier's trading post on the Monongahela River where they rested several days. On New Year's Day, they resumed their journey. They were heartened on January 6 when they passed an Ohio Company party leading seventeen pack horses toward the Ohio forks to build a trading post. A day later they met a group of settlers heading toward the forks. Perhaps the Virginians had won the race after all, Washington hoped. The major reached Williamsburg on January 16 where he handed Dinwiddie a 6,000-word report on the French presence and Indian attitudes.

Dinwiddie responded by accelerating Virginia's race for the Ohio forks. On January 26, 1754, he commissioned Ohio Company field leader William Trent a captain, and ordered him to form a 100-man company of recruits from among the frontiersmen "west of the mountains" and to march them to the Ohio forks where they would build a fort. Trent's orders specifically authorized him to "keep possession of his majesty's lands on the Ohio, and the waters thereof, and to dislodge and drive away, and in case of refusal and resistance to kill and destroy or take prisoners all and every person and persons whatsoever, not subjects of the king of Great Britain."[10]

As one of the region's toughest and most experienced frontiersmen, Trent was a good choice. In 1746, he had joined a raid against Canada. For several years thereafter he had served as a Pennsylvania militia captain as well as a business associate of Indian trader George Croghan. In 1752, as Ohio Company agent, Trent had supervised the building of a road from the trading post at Wills Creek to the confluence of Redstone Creek and the Monongahela where he erected a storehouse. From there it was only 37 miles to the Ohio River. Upon receiving his commission and orders, Trent sprang into action. On February 14, he arrived at the Ohio forks with 42 troops and immediately set them to work building Fort Prince George. Satisfied with the progress, Trent left Ensign Edward Ward in charge and hurried back to Wills Creek to recruit more men and supplies.

Meanwhile, Dinwiddie knew that he would need far more than a company of frontiersmen to drive off the French. Acting on the principle that strength increases with numbers, on January 29, he sent letters to governors William Shirley of Massachusetts, James De Lancey of New York, Jonathan Belcher of New Jersey, James Hamilton of Pennsylvania, Horatio Sharpe of Maryland, Matthew Rowan of North Carolina, and James Glen of South Carolina, as well as the Oneida Chief Scarouady, the Iroquois, the Catawba, and the Cherokee, asking them to join Virginia in sending troops to Wills Creek by March 1754 and expelling the French from the upper Ohio country.[11]

Although his entreaties to the Indians and governors alike went largely unheeded, Dinwiddie's correspondence represented an unprecedented attempt to coordinate policies among the American colonies. This effort would inspire the "committees of correspondence" among the colonies in the years preceding the American Revolution. He also had Washington's report published as a pamphlet and sent it to the other colonial governors and to newspapers in America and Britain with pleas for unity against the French menace. In England, the *London Magazine* and *Gentleman's Quarterly* printed the report in full, thus alerting the English public to the crisis brewing in the Ohio valley. It was also Washington's first flash of public fame. Unfortunately, that fame would quickly sour when the press got wind of what happened at Great Meadows.

Dinwiddie had as much trouble raising funds from Virginia's tightfisted assembly as he did garnering aid from other colonies. The assemblymen had good reason to be skeptical of Dinwiddie's requests. From the time he took office, two of Dinwiddie's private interests got thoroughly entangled with his public policies and at once helped precipitate and inhibit British attempts to repel the French from the Ohio country. Dinwiddie had invested in the Ohio Company and championed its cause throughout his administration. He also insisted on his "right" to pocket a "pistole fee" from each land claim application for a hundred or more acres. When applicants refused to pay the pistole (a currency unit worth about five dollars today), Dinwiddie refused to affix his seal to their deed. The assembly bitterly criticized this tax, even though Virginia's council had approved it on April 22, 1752, although that action was not legally binding until the Board of Trade approved. The Board, however, refused to act, despite receiving several letters from Dinwiddie asking for a decision; they preferred to rule only after a complaintant sued.

On February 14, 1754, in a speech before the council and House of Burgesses, Dinwiddie explained in detail the results of Washington's mission and the threat posed by France to Britain's claims to the upper Ohio country. The speech brilliantly mixed appeals to the representatives "on every point upon which men have been vulnerable to war since time immemorial—their honor, their safety, their freedom, the protection of their homes and families, and finally, a masterly touch, the century-old hatred and distrust of the English for the French."[12] He then asked the assembly for a 20,000-pound defense appropriation.

Despite the pistole fee deadlock, the assembly did appropriate 10,000 pounds to raise six 50-man companies of the Virginia Provincial regiment that would repel the French from the Ohio country. The appropriation was only half of what Dinwiddie had requested, but hefty nonetheless. The assembly, however, attached a rider to the bill that would allocate 2,500 pounds to send their representative, Peyton Randolph, to London to plead their case before the Board of Trade. Although Dinwiddie was certainly pleased to receive any money, he bitterly denounced the strings attached to it. He also regretted that they had not acted earlier: "if our Assembly had voted the money in November which they did in February, it's more than probable that the fort would have been built and garrisoned before the French had approached. . . . I am in hopes that the eyes of the other colonies will be opened; and if they grant a proper supply of men, I hope we shall be able to dislodge the French or build a fort on that river."[13] As if Dinwiddie was not insulted enough by the way the assembly appropriated the money, in May the Burgesses sharply tugged again in their war over power and rights with the governor—they set up a committee to supervise the allocation of the 10,000-pound defense appropriation.

Meanwhile, on February 23, 1754, Dinwiddie sent out yet another urgent appeal to the other colonial governors for help against the French. In his letter he revealed that Virginia's assembly had only appropriated 10,000 pounds for the efforts.[14] This paltry sum dampened the willingness of the other governors to contribute. After all, if the colony with the most at stake in the struggle was so niggardly, why should any other colony mount a major financial and military effort?

No governor faced a more difficult task of financing a war effort than Pennsylvania's James Hamilton. Throughout Pennsylvania's history, the Quaker-dominated assembly had not approved a shilling for defense. Hamilton received Dinwiddie's request the day after the assembly had adjourned. He reckoned that Virginia's 10,000-pound appropriation would not supply a 400-man unit for more than seven months. Such a force would barely be adequate for guarding the frontier, let alone seizing the forks of the Ohio River and driving the French from the region. Hopeless as any appeal to the Pennsylvanians to help Virginia's cause might seem, Hamilton reconvened the assembly. Before them, he pointed out that "unless we are able to make a good and secure Lodgment against the Enemy this Summer it is clear that the whole Expense of the Armament will be thrown away and perhaps the lives of many of his Majestye's Subjects sacrificed to little or no Purpose."[15] Surprisingly, Hamilton's appeal moved the assembly, which voted to match Virginia's 10,000-pound appropriation. But then the assembly failed to agree on just how to raise that amount, and the appropriation died. Other assemblies also rejected aiding Virginia. In the end, only North Carolina contributed anything—12,000 pounds.[16]

As if his squabbles with the Burgesses were not infuriating enough, Dinwiddie had a devilish time raising troops. When he tried to call out the militia, the counties refused to send their men beyond their districts. He then called for volunteers to join the newly designated Virginia Provincial Regiment. Few men stepped forward. On February 14, he sweetened the appeal by promising volunteers shares of the 200,000 acres of Ohio Company lands in the Ohio valley. A handful more entered the ranks.

The governor gave overall command to militia Colonel Joshua Fry. Fry was certainly a learned man, having attended Oxford University, taught mathematics and natural history at William and Mary College, and, in 1751, collaborated with Peter Jefferson, Thomas' father, in drafting a map of Virginia. Politically, he had an impressive resume, having served as a surveyor, justice of the peace, and assemblyman. But other than enjoying the sinecure of peacetime militia captain, he had no military experience. Fry would die before he could honor or disgrace himself in battle.

Washington's star of destiny continued to burn bright. On March 15, Dinwiddie sent Washington a lieutenant colonel's commission and orders to march his troops toward the Ohio River when he was ready. Washington was already at Alexandria trying to raise troops when the commission arrived. Being named lieutenant colonel of the 1st Virginia Regiment was an immense responsibility for a headstrong, hot-tempered 22-year-old. It would also be a continual frustration. By March 8, a mere 23 of 170,000 white Virginian men had gathered to Washington's side at Alexandria. The "self-willed and ungovernable" recruits proved an endless frustration for Washington and the other officers. Washington complained to Dinwiddie that most recruits are "loose, idle persons that are quite destitute of house. . . . There is many of them without shoes, other's want stockings, some are without shirts, and not a few that have scarce a coat or waistcoat to their backs."[17]

By April 2, Washington had gathered into two companies 139 officers and men, most of whom lacked uniforms, arms, munitions, and rations. On that day he led his troops out of Alexandria on the long march west to the Ohio forks. He paused for several days at Winchester to recruit more men and supplies. On April 18, he marched northwest with 159 men and eleven officers for Wills Creek, where he arrived five days later. Dinwiddie ordered Washington "to act on the defensive, but in case any attempts are made to obstruct the works by any persons whatsoever, to restrain all such offenders, and, in case of resistance, to make prisoners of, or kill and destroy them."[18]

Washington was to be the wedge of what Dinwiddie hoped was an offensive against the French throughout the Ohio valley. Colonel Fry would remain at Winchester to recruit more men before marching to join Washington. Meanwhile, Dinwiddie sent more messages to the Iroquois, Catawba, Cherokee, and Chickasaw, urging them to attack the French wherever they could be found.

The French got to Fort Prince George before Washington. On April 17, Ensign Ward and his 41 men were astonished to see a flotilla of 60 bateaux and 30 canoes filled with 600 troops and 18 artillery pieces commanded by Captain Claude-Pierre Pecaudy de Contrecoeur. The French disembarked a mere 150 yards from the fort. Contrecoeur quickly massed his artillery and troops before the fort, just beyond musket shot. He then sent Captain Francois Le Mercier, two drummers, and an Indian toward the fort to demand that Ward surrender within an hour or perish.

Perplexed at what to do, Ward asked Tanaghrisson's advice. The chief told him to announce he lacked the authority to make so momentous a decision. Ward agreed and together with a French interpreter and an Indian they marched from the fort under a truce flag to negotiate with Contrecoeur. The French captain rejected Ward's claim that he had no power to capitulate. He offered to postpone the actual handover until noon the next day and allow the English to take away all their equipment and weapons. Faced with insurmountable odds and a generous offer, Ward sensibly surrendered. Tanaghrisson erupted in rage at Contrecoeur, pointing out that he had invited the British to build a fort there and the French had no right to determine the fate of Indian lands. Contrecoeur ignored Tanaghrisson and treated Ward to an elaborate feast. On April 18, Ward and his men marched out of the fort between the French ranks with full honors of war. Tanaghrisson and his followers stalked away. Contrecoeur renamed the fort Duquesne, after Canada's resolute governor-general.[19]

Ward and his men hurried back to Wills Creek where he briefed Washington on all that had happened. He also conveyed a message from Tanaghrisson to the governors of Virginia and Pennsylvania: "Have good courage and come as soon as possible; you will find us as ready to fight as you are yourselves. If you do not come to our assistance now, we are entirely undone, and I think we shall never meet together again. I speak with a heart full of grief."[20] Washington sent Ward on to Williamsburg to report and solicit instructions.

Despite the distressing lack of volunteers capped by Fort Prince George's surrender, Virginia's war effort seemed to pick up in May. Early that month, Colonel Fry and Governor Dinwiddie met in Winchester. Shortly thereafter, Colonel James Innes arrived with 300 North Carolina troops. Ever sensitive to Indian affairs, Dinwiddie realized that adroit diplomacy was as important as massed troops in winning the contest for the Ohio valley, and eagerly awaited a council of all the tribes he had called to Winchester.

Dinwiddie was further heartened when George Croghan and Andrew Montour arrived, having earlier received a Dinwiddie summons to aid Virginia's Indian diplomacy and recruitment. In accepting Dinwiddie's offer, Croghan and Montour now worked for Virginia as well as Pennsylvania. Croghan did not let the two colonies' conflicting interests complicate his efforts; all along that canny trader acted largely in ways that advanced his own business interests. Like Croghan, the half-Seneca Montour, who spoke English, French, and a half dozen Indian languages, found that generally his own interests coincided with those of the two colonies; when they clashed, he too put his own interests first. Dinwiddie commissioned Montour a captain and ordered him to recruit a company of Indian scouts. By May 26, Montour had instead mustered eighteen frontiersmen to serve with him as scouts for the campaign and, ideally, as traders afterward.

Despite his strenuous efforts, Dinwiddie's Indian diplomacy failed. He waited sixteen days before finally realizing that no Indians would attend his council. The Iroquois sent runners with a message stating that they would only attend their traditional council at Onondaga. Tanaghrisson sent word that he would not come when his own people were imperiled by the French presence. The Catawba, Chickasaw, and Cherokee did not even bother to reply to the wampum belts he had sent them.

Governor James Glen was responsible for the southern Indians' silence. In a March 14 letter, he had urged Dinwiddie that "the surest way to have any effectual Assistance from the Catawbas or Cherokees is by the Intervention of this Government; they have been under our direction for upwards of thirty years, and there is not a Headman or warrior of any Note among them that I do not personally know."[21] That advice seems to have pricked Dinwiddie's ample ego. Spurning it, he had tried to negotiate directly with those tribes, alienating them in the process. Learning of Dinwiddie's entreaties, Glen urged those tribes to stay home and remain mute to the Virginia governor's pleas. He later angrily explained his action in a letter to Dinwiddie: "The person who has been sent from [Virginia] to the Cherokees and Catawbas, to invite (and I must add to press) them to go thither to get Presents, has spoken very disrespectively of this Province to the Indians."[22]

The result of this ego clash was to deprive Washington of desperately needed Indian scouts and warriors. The presence of several hundred southern Indians at Great Meadow could have prevented the humiliating fiasco that eventually occurred. Then again, Washington alienated Tanaghrisson and the 100 Indians who actually did join him. Lacking in diplomatic skills, gifts, and food, Washington more probably would have driven off any Cherokee and Catawba who might have appeared, just as he did Tanaghrisson's followers.

By late May, Washington's small force was encamped at Great Meadows, 65 miles southeast of Fort Duquesne and 51 miles northwest of Wills Creek. Rather than fortify his position and await reinforcements, Washington marched his men forward to the Ohio Company storehouse at Redstone Creek on the Monongahela. Receiving reports that the French had over 800 men, Washington then retreated his force back to Great Meadows.

On May 25, Colonel Fry began a march toward Great Meadows at the head of three companies totaling five officers and 110 troops. Accompanying Fry was Croghan with a wagonload of gifts to sway the Indians toward Virginia. Along the way, Fry's horse bolted and threw him. Fry died of the injuries on May 31. A runner sent word of the tragedy to Dinwiddie in Winchester. On June 4, Dinwiddie informed Washington that he was now in charge of the entire regiment until Colonel James Innes assumed command.[23]

Fresh on the heels of this message, Gist arrived with word that a 50-man French force led by Commissary Michel Pepin La Force had captured his home thirteen miles away on the road to the forks. Washington ordered

Captain Hogg to take 75 men and recapture Gist's home. La Force withdrew before Hogg arrived. After resting there several days, Hogg retired to Great Meadows.

Meanwhile, an Indian dispatched by Tanaghrisson arrived with word that his scouts had located another French patrol. Washington immediately sallied forth with the Indian and 75 troops, half his total command. Six miles north of Great Meadows, Washington joined with Tanaghrisson, Scarouady, and ten other Indians. There he left half his force and embarked into the forest with 40 troops guided by the Indians toward the French. In a hollow were encamped Ensign Joseph Coulon de Villiers, the Sieur de Jumonville, and 33 French soldiers.

What happened next? All accounts agree that firing broke out that left Jumonville and nine other French dead and 22 captured, while one escaped to carry word of the attack to Fort Duquesne. Bullets killed one of Washington's men and wounded two others. The Indians scalped the French dead and later sent the trophies to other tribes to enlist their participation in the war.

But the accounts differ widely over the details of the shoot-out. According to Washington, "having held a Council with the Half-King, it was concluded that we should fall on them together; so we sent out two Men to discover where they were, . . . after which we formed ourselves for an Engagement, marching one after another in the Indian Manner: We were advanced pretty near to them, as we thought, when they discovered us; whereupon I ordered my Company to fire. . . . [We] received the whole Fire of the French, during the greatest Part of the Action, which only lasted a Quarter of an Hour, before the Enemy was routed. We killed Mr. de Jumonvilles . . . as also nine others; we wounded one, and made Twenty-one Prisoners. . . . The Indians scalped the Dead."[24]

Another account has Washington and Tanaghrisson differing "much in judgement, and on the Colonel's refusing to his advice, the English and Indians separated. After which the Indians discovered the French in a hollow and hid themselves, lying on their bellies behind a hill; afterward they discovered Col. Washington on the opposite side of the hollow in the gray of the morning, and when the English came out of their cover and closed with the French [the Indians] killed them with their tomahawks, on which the French surrendered."[25]

Strikingly different from Washington's account is the official French report: Jumonville "set out with an escourt of thirty men, and the next morning found himself surrounded by a number of English and Indians: The English quickly fired two vollies which killed some soldiers. M. de Jumonville made a sign that he had a letter from his commander; hereupon the fire ceased, and they surrounded the French officer, in order to hear it. He immediately ordered the summons to be read, and as it was reading the second time, the English assasinated him. The rest of the French that escorted him, were, upon the spot made prisoners of war . . . the Indians who were with the English, had not fired a gun; and that in the instant M. de Jumonville was assasinated, they threw themselves in between the French and their enemies."[26]

Washington heatedly dismissed the French claims that they were on a diplomatic mission: "instead of coming as an Embassador, publickly, and in an open Manner, they came secretly, and sought after the most hidden Retreats . . . incamped, and remained hid for whole Days together, and that, no more than five miles from our camp. . . . They say they called to us as soon as they had discovered us; which is an absolute Falsehood for I was then marching at the Head of the Company going towards them and can positively affirm, that, when they saw us, they ran to their Arms, without calling; as I must have heard them had they done so."[27]

John Shaw provides perhaps the most reliable version, even though he was not at Great Meadows at the time and built his account from statements by those who were with Washington: "one of the them [The French] fired a Gun upon which Col. Washington gave the Word for all his Men to fire. Several of them being killed, the Rest betook themselves to flight, but our Indians haveing gone round, the French when they saw them immediately fled back to the English and delivered up their Arms desireing Quarter which was accordingly promised them. Some Time after the Indians came up the Half King [Tanaghrisson] took his Tomahawk and split the Head of the French Captain haveing first asked if he was an Englishman and haveing been told he was a French Man. He then took out his Brains and washed his Hands with them and then scalped him. All this he [Shaw] has heard and never heard it contradicted but knows nothing of it from his own Knowledge only he has seen the Bones of the frenchmen who were killed in Number about 13 or 14 and the Head of one stuck upon a Stick for none of them were buried."[28] This account was reinforced by a *Pennsylvania Gazette* article on June 27, 1754, which stated, "One of the those Five [Frenchmen] which were killed and scalped by the Indians, was Monsieur Jumonville, an Ensign, whom the Half King himself dispatched with his Tomahawk."[29]

During their interrogation, the surviving French officers, Ensign Pierre Jacques Druillon and La Force insisted that their party was simply a peace mission sent by Contrecoeur warning the British to abandon French territory. They demanded their release as diplomats. Washington in turn asked them to explain why a diplomatic mission would hide in the woods rather than advance boldly to the British camp. A search of Jumonville's body, however, revealed Contrecoeur's letter. Perhaps deeply torn over his decision to open fire, Washington herded his prisoners back to Great Meadows.

Was Washington's attack on Jumonville justified? Dinwiddie's instructions authorizing him to use force if necessary and the French seizure of the British fort certainly gave Washington ample reason to believe that war had already broken out. Washington would not learn of Jumonville's diplomatic credentials until after they were found on the dead captain. Jumonville's furtive lurking nearby Great Meadows certainly seemed to make him more a spy than a diplomat in Washington's eyes. If Shaw's version is correct that a French sentry fired first, then Washington's volleys were justified. But we will never know exactly what happened.

The day after the attack, Washington sent a courier with a report of the skirmish to Dinwiddie in Winchester. Dinwiddie then promptly sent orders to Major George Muse at Wills Creek to hurry the two companies encamped there to Great Meadows. Muse arrived at Great Meadows on June 9. Washington now commanded five companies of 293 Virginia troops, along with a dozen Indians.

Less welcome was the arrival of about 100 more Indian warriors, wives, and children. Washington complained that the Indian horde ate up his provisions. Tanaghrisson had his own complaints, later remarking bitterly to Conrad Weiser that Washington was "a good-natured man but had no experience . . . [He] would by no means take Advice from the Indians . . . he lay at one Place from one full Moon to the other and made no Fortifications at all, but that little thing in the Meadow, where he thought the French would come up to him in open Field; . . . had he taken the Half King's advice and made Fortifications as the Half King advised him to make he would certainly have beat the French off; . . . the French had acted as great Cowards, and the English as Fools in that Engagement; . . . Half King had carried off his Wife and Children, so did other Indians before the Battle begun, because Col. Washington would never listen to them, but was always driving them on to fight by his directions."[30]

As if the Indians were not trouble enough, on June 14, Captain Mackay arrived with 100 regular troops of the South Carolina Independent Company, 60 cattle, and five days' supply of flour. A dispute immediately arose when Mackay claimed for himself the position of commander, arguing that a regular captain outranked a militia lieutenant colonel. Washington rejected the claim. Mackay's attitude is understandable. After all, the captain had eighteen years of military experience while Washington was a young novice. When neither man would give in, the captain announced he would take no orders from Washington nor would he allow his troops to do so. The regular troops lounged around while the colonials improved the road and makeshift defense.

Since receiving his commission, Washington had felt overwhelmed by the duties, his inexperience, the frustrations of raising and leading an armed mob, the disputes with the Indians, and the deaths of Jumonville and his men, capped by Mackay's refusal to submit to his command. He threatened to resign in several letters to Dinwiddie. The governor talked him into remaining and tried to resolve the dispute by placing Mackay under his own command.[31]

On paper, Washington's force seemed formidable. All told, the muster rolls named around 400 men of whom 300 were Virginians and 100 in Mackay's regular company. Washington's actual fighting strength was much less. Fevers had laid up many of the men while others had deserted. Undeterred by all this, to free himself from Mackay and force a battle with the French, Washington marched his troops and Indian allies to Gist's home. Arriving there on June 18, they found another 40 Indians. For three days, Washington tried to woo the mixed Shawnee, Mingo, and Delaware into joining him by sharing with them his dwindling supplies of food and gifts. Washington's diplomacy failed. The Indians drifted away, followed by increasing numbers of Tanaghrisson's people.

As desertion and illness diminished Washington's command, reinforcements swelled the French force. On June 26, Captain Louis Coulon Ecuyer, Sieur de Villiers, arrived at Fort Duquesne with 20 soldiers and 130 Indians including Huron, Canadian Iroquois, Ottawa, Algonquians, Abenaki, and Nipissing. Villiers was a veteran frontier war leader who had led raids throughout King George's War and accompanied the 1749 Celoron expedition. He reached Fort Duquesne just when Le Mercier was about to push south with 500 troops and eleven Indians to attack Washington. Villiers urged his friend and subordinate to delay his campaign a day while the reinforcements rested, then together they could march against the British. Revenge was as important as duty and military necessity in prompting Villiers' request. Villiers was the dead Jumonville's older half-brother.

That night Villiers harangued the assembled Indians with stirring words: "The English have murdered my children; my heart is sick; tomorrow I shall send my French soldiers to take revenge. And now, men of the Saut St. Louis, men of the Lake of Two Mountains, Hurons, Abenakis, Iroquois of La Presentation, Nipissings, Algonquins, and Ottawas,—I invite you all by this belt of wampum to join your French father and help him to crush the assassins."[32] The next morning Villiers strode from Fort Duquesne down the path to Great Meadows at the head of over 700 hundred French and Indians.

As this was happening, a council of war among Washington and his officers at Gist's agreed to concentrate their troops there for a showdown with the French. Washington himself leaned toward marching on Fort Duquesne. Indian scouts had convinced him that "the Fort may be surprised, as the French are encamped outside, and cannot keep a strict Guard."[33] Washington sent a letter to Mackay requesting that he bring up his South Carolina regulars.

Perhaps to Washington's surprise, Mackay complied, arriving the afternoon of June 29. Around the same time, an Indian trotted into camp with news of Villiers' reinforcements and approach. Washington again gathered his officers and sought their advice. Fearing that the French could easily bypass them and sever their supply line, Washington and his officers prudently agreed to retreat all the way back to Wills Creek. Washington's force made it to Great Meadows by July 1. There his men collapsed, exhausted from malnutrition and overwork.

Great Meadows is a shallow grassy bowl of a valley surrounded by forest-covered hills. Every inch of that bowl was within musket shot of the forest. Washington's defense consisted of a small circular stockade 53 feet in diameter in the meadow's center. One small hut which served as a storehouse stood within the stockade. At best only about 50 men or a company could cram into the stockade which, with a touch of irony, Washington named Fort Necessity. The rest of his men lay exposed outside, crouched behind makeshift log breastworks or in shallow pits. Washington described the setting as "a charming field for an encounter."[34] Once the firing began, his men would use much harsher words for it and their youthful commander.

Washington had hoped to find reinforcements and supplies at Fort Necessity that would have arrived when he was at Gist's. Instead, Great Meadows was nearly deserted but for the forlorn little fort in its center. Disgusted with the indecisiveness and arrogance of the British, Tanaghrisson and his Indians disappeared. Washington deployed his troops around the fort and mounted six of his nine swivel guns on the walls. He sent a message to Captain Innes at Wills Creek, urging him to hurry forward with men and supplies.

On July 2, the French and Indians reached Gist's where they bedded down for the night. Villiers had hoped to advance swiftly the thirteen miles to Great Meadows, starting at dawn the next morning. His plan, however, was delayed when the Nipissing and Algonquians refused to go further. Villiers' pleas and promises convinced most of the Nipissing to continue; the Algonquians returned to Fort Duquesne. En route to Great Meadows, Villiers briefly detoured to visit Jumonville's camp. The sight and stench of the rotting corpses must have enraged him and the others. Two and a half miles from Great Meadows, Villiers divided his force into three columns to encircle Great Meadows and cut off any possible escape. By late morning on July 3, the French and Indians slowly crept down through the forest until they reached the meadow's edge.

Although he did not yet know it, Washington was outnumbered three to one. Only 284 of his men reported fit for duty. Sickness had downed another 100, most of whom were crammed within Fort Necessity. Scores of other men had deserted since the campaign began. A steady rain had turned the meadow into a quagmire. Morale had plunged with the miserable weather, rations, sickness, and dark surrounding wilderness.

Musket shots suddenly exploded from the forest. Screaming that the enemy were attacking, a wounded sentinel rushed back to the fort. Washington ordered the men to assemble. Officers shouted their men into ragged lines. Gunners lit punks and manned the swivels. From the forested southwest hills, the French and Indians suddenly emerged screaming taunts and war cries. They advanced in three columns and then deployed in a long line around 600 yards from the fort and then advanced toward it. As the French and Indians strode within range, with a nod from Washington, Major Adam Stephens ordered the swivel guns to open fire. Washington then commanded his troops to fire at will. The French and Indians fired and surged forward to within 60 yards of the entrenchments. Then, unwilling to risk the battle in one assault, Villiers ordered his men to withdraw into the forest. From behind trees and rocks the French and Indians peppered the fort and trenches with musket shot.

As the day wore on, morale among Washington's troops dropped to rock-bottom. Enemy fire killed or wounded one man after another, and cut down the horses and cattle. Food and ammunition were nearly exhausted. The downpour continued, filling the trenches with ankle-deep water and soaking the powder. They had but two screw-rods to pull the sodden charges from their muskets. To lighten the men's misery, Washington ordered his rum casks tapped. Most of his troops were soon drunk. In his journal, Washington claimed that as evening descended, twelve Virginians lay dead and 43 were wounded. Dinwiddie later reported that the total losses were 30 dead and 70 wounded, a figure which presumably included Mackay's regulars with the Virginians.[35]

Although Villiers had cut off and shot up the enemy, he faced his own problems. His men were exhausted from the march and rain. Wet powder and fouling had silenced many muskets. Ammunition was running out. He had no cannon to blow apart the stockade. His troops had little stomach for a direct assault on the Americans. Musket balls had killed at least two French and an Indian and wounded about 70 others.[36] It was feared that British reinforcements could suddenly appear. Worst of all, the Indians threatened to scatter to their homes the next morning.

At dusk, Villiers sent word to the British for a parley. Washington declined, fearing it was just a ruse to inspect his defense. The French then said that an American officer could visit their lines. Washington agreed and sent out Captain Van Braam and wounded Ensign Peyroney who both spoke some French. Not long after disappearing into the forests, Van Braam and Peyroney returned with Villiers' proposal for the British surrender.

Washington and his officers gathered around as Van Braam translated the terms scrawled on two sheets of paper. Either Van Braam's French was not as good as he claimed or, eager to end the siege, he deliberately mistranslated some passages that otherwise might have prompted the officers to carry on the fight. The most controversial of these was to interpret "l'assassinat du Sieur de Jumonville" as the death rather than murder of that officer. In return for two hostages, to ensure that the 21 French prisoners taken in the Jumonville fight would be returned along with a promise that they not return to the region for a year, Villiers promised Washington that he and his troops would be allowed the honors of war, the retention of their arms, supplies, and personal effects, and repatriation. He even allowed the British to keep some men on the site to guard supplies that could not be hauled away for want of enough draft animals. Having displayed generosity, Villiers then played his trump card. If the British refused to surrender, Villiers warned that 400 Indian reinforcements were expected the next morning and he could not be responsible for their conduct should an assault overwhelm the defenders. That threat of Indian massacre if a British garrison refused to surrender would become a standard French negotiation tactic.

Washington and his officers pondered their options. They were already outnumbered three to one, odds that might worsen to five to one in the morning. There was little chance of reinforcements. They had fought valiantly and had expended most of their ammunition. And the terms seemed quite generous, all except the clause that they surrender their munitions. Lacking that, the Indians could massacre them. La Peyroney had collapsed from his wound so only Van Braam returned to the French lines with Washington's request that his troops be allowed to retain their ammunition. Villiers granted permission and had the surrender document rewritten accordingly and returned.

With his officers' approval, Washington then unwittingly signed the document which named him as Jumonville's murderer. He later reported that "we were willfully, or ignorantly, deceived by our interpreter in regard to the word assassination. . . . The interpreter was a Dutchman, little acquainted with the English tongue, therefore might not advert to the tone and meaning of the word in English; but, whatever his motives were for so doing, certain it is, he called it the death, or the loss, of the Sieur Jumonville. So we received and so we understood it, until, to our great surprise and mortification, we found it otherwise in a literal translation."[37]

The next morning, which ironically was July 4, Washington turned over Van Braam and Captain Robert Stobo as hostages and ordered his troops to march away. Without draft animals, Washington had to leave eleven badly wounded men at Fort Necessity. The retreat must have been miserable. As the troops dragged away the wounded and sick and what possessions they could carry, haughty Indians strode along side terrifying them by shaking their scalping knives and, in broken English, gleefully boasting of the tortures they would inflict. When Washington ordered the men to camp a few miles from the fort, the Indians spilled among them to loot and bash in the brains of two wounded men before raised American muskets stopped them from murdering others. A muster revealed that some men were missing. Washington sent an armed company back to Great Meadows where they discovered the men in Indian hands.

After receiving Washington's protest, Villiers ordered the Indians to release the men. Villiers later wrote that the "Number of their Dead and Wounded, moved me to Pity, notwithstanding my Resentment for their having in such a Manner, taken away my Brother's Life. The Indians, who had obeyed my Orders in every Thing, claimed a right to the Plunder; but I opposed it; However, the English being frightened, fled and left their Tents, and one of their Colours."[38]

It would be a grueling four-day, 52-mile trudge back to Wills Creek, where Washington's troops arrived on July 9. A roll call revealed only 165 men fit for duty, 55 wounded, 29 exhausted men who had dropped out along the road, and 19 missing or deserted, along with the 11 wounded left behind at Fort Necessity. Within days, two-thirds of the Virginians would disappear into the surrounding forests; the lucky ones would eventually return home.

Washington almost disappeared as well—into disgrace. He arrived back at Williamsburg on July 17 to receive Dinwiddie's restrained criticism. His attack on Jumonville and humiliating surrender at Fort Necessity had provoked the wrath of the governor and many other British on both sides of the Atlantic. Dinwiddie heatedly pointed out that his "orders from me, were by no means to attack the Enemy till the whole Forces were join'd."[39] William Johnson offered a more scathing assessment of the Virginian's actions: "I wish Washington had acted with prudence & Circumspection requisite in an officer of his Rank, and the trust at that time reposed in him, but (on considering the affair) I cant help Saying he was wrong in many respects, and I doubt his being too ambitious of acquiring all the honour, or as much as he could, before the rest joined him, and giving too much Credit to the reports . . . given by the French deserters . . . was the rock on which he Splitt. He should rather have avoided an engagement until our Troops were all assembled, for Marching by detachments in such a close country and against such an Enemy, will never do."[40]

Yet, instead of cashiering Washington, the governor sent him back to the scraps of his regiment. Dinwiddie still hoped that the other colonies would send sufficient troops, supplies, and money to the combined forces of Washington and Innes. Innes would then march the army against Fort Duquesne.

In contrast to the British plight, Villiers and his men returned triumphantly to Fort Duquesne. In a letter to Governor Duquesne, Villiers explained his victory: "We made the English agree to give us in their own hands, that they had committed an assassination on us, in the camp of my brother. We had hostages as sureties for the French whom they had in their power: we compelled them to evacuate the country as belonging to the most Christian King. We obliged them to leave us their cannon, which consisted of nine pieces. We had already destroyed all their horses and cattle, and further we made them give in their own hand that the favor we showed them was only to prove to them how greatly we desire to treat them as friends."[41] Villiers was correct about all but his last point—friendship between the French and British was no longer an option.

ALBANY CONGRESS

While British and French troops squared off in the upper Ohio valley, a drama was unfolding in Albany that was in many ways as important as that engulfing Washington and his ragged troops. On June 19, 1754, 23 commissioners from six colonies—New York, Massachusetts, New Hampshire, Connecticut, Rhode Island, and Maryland—convened a Congress in Albany to forge a common front on Indian and other policies. Each colony's assembly had conferred different powers and goals on its commissioners to the Congress. Some assemblies had pointedly rejected the invitation. Virginia and New Jersey refused to attend on the grounds that they had no treaties with the Iroquois and did not want to contribute to the expense of a common treaty.

While the Congress's main purpose was to forge a united Indian policy, some delegates promoted an even more important issue—colonial union. Benjamin Franklin brought with him his "Short Hints toward a Scheme for Uniting the Northern Colonies," which he had been promoting since 1751. Franklin's plan called for each colony to send representatives and taxes in proportion to its population to an assembly which, along with a governor general appointed by the king and Grand Council elected by the assembly, would determine the collective defense and Indian policies. To implement this plan, Franklin called first for an act by Parliament and only then approval by the colonial assemblies. Franklin justified the submission to Parliament as the best way to finesse bitter divisions among the provinces because "the colonies were seldom all in equal danger at the same time, or equally near the danger, or equally sensible of it; that some of them had particular interests to manage, with which a union might interfere; and that they were extremely jealous of each other."[42] Colonies could withdraw from a voluntary union, but not one decreed by Parliament. In a May 9 edition of his *Pennsylvania Gazette*, Franklin had published a long essay justifying a voluntary union of the colonies to best counter the French threat. Accompanying the essay was a woodcut of a severed snake with each segment labeled a different colony. The woodcut warned the reader to "Join or Die."

Franklin's was not the only union proposal. Richard Peters submitted the much weaker "A Plan for a General Union of the British Colonies of North America" that involved a "Committee of Union" whose members were elected annually by the assemblies and would debate, reach a consensus, and then propose specific military plans, and troop and revenue contributions to each colony. The king rather than Parliament would approve the arrangement and its subsequent plans. Thomas Hutchinson's plan envisioned two unions, one of northern and the other of southern colonies. Each union would have an assembly of delegates elected for three-year terms, a Grand Council elected by the assembly, and a governor. Thomas Pownall called not for a permanent institution, but simply for a temporary Congress to agree on and implement a grand strategy to defeat the French.

Those who favored colonial union faced powerful opposition. New York's newly appointed governor James De Lancey led those commissioners who feared any union would be led by Massachusetts governor Shirley. New York and Massachusetts were estranged from a festering border dispute and Boston's determination to negotiate its own treaties with the Iroquois. Although De Lancey was the only governor at the Congress, ironically, his official power was limited; the Board of Trade had given him no other duty but to call and host but not run the Congress. De Lancey was not only opposed to a union, he was disinterested in even forging a common Indian policy. He used the Congress to divert attention from his faction's trade with Montreal and land grabs from the Iroquois.

When most of the Indians failed to show up on the appointed date, those favoring a union quickly forged a consensus around the idea. The consensus was not hard to achieve. Adherents simply pointed to the sentence in Lord Halifax's September 18, 1753 letter that stated the "hearty Desire of acting in Concert with Us against his Majestie's enemies, concur in Sentiment with His Majestie's Ministers of the Necessity of a general Union of all the Provinces both in Councils and Forces."[43] The Congress voted unanimously to form a committee with one member from each delegation to consider the various union proposals. On June 28, the committee agreed to make Franklin's plan the basis for debate before the entire Congress. On July 2, the Congress voted in favor of seeking Parliament's approval for a colonial union plan. On July 9, the committee on plans submitted the final version. On July 10, the Congress approved the final draft of the "Plan of Union" and sent it to Parliament for its approval.

The Union would include all the colonies except the buffers of Georgia and Nova Scotia. The king would appoint a president-general while the colonial assemblies would elect members to three-year terms in a House of Representatives which in turn would elect Grand Council members. Each colony would have two members in the Grand Council. Membership in the House of Representatives, however, would be based on population—seven members each for Virginia and Massachusetts, six for Pennsylvania, five for Connecticut, four each for New York, Maryland, North Carolina, and South Carolina, three for New Jersey, and two each for Rhode Island and New Hampshire. The Union would meet at least once a year; more if the president-general or seven colonies called for emergency sessions. The plan defined the British colonial empire as including not only all fourteen American colonies, but all land west to the Pacific Ocean. Within that vast realm, the Union would have the power and revenues to negotiate with Indians, declare war, build forts, mobilize troops, launch warships, buy land, judge conflicting territorial claims, and divide all lands west of the Appalachian

Mountains into new colonies. Union revenues would come from tariffs and excise taxes.

It was a breathtakingly sweeping plan that would have dramatically shifted the course of American and world history had it been adopted. The "Union Plan" would have created a federal government far stronger than the Continental Congress and Articles of Confederation assembled during the American Revolution, and not that different from the 1787 Constitution. The only significant difference was that the Union would not have enjoyed sovereignty, which would have remained in the firm hands of Parliament and the king. Looking back from 1789, Franklin reflected that "if the . . . Plan or some thing like it, had been adopted . . . the subsequent Separation of the Colonies from the Mother Country might not so soon have happened, nor the Mischiefs suffered on both sides have occurred, perhaps during another Century. For the Colonies, if so united, would have . . . been . . . sufficient for their own Defense, and . . . an Army from Britain . . . would have been unnecessary" along with the series of taxes imposed on the Americans to support that army.[44] Of course, it was for those very reasons that American patriots were relieved that the "Union Plan" failed.

The delegates took the plan back to their respective colonial assemblies. On July 22, De Lancey sent the plan and other congressional papers to the Board of Trade. For varying reasons, no assembly approved the Albany Plan of Union. The Board of Trade refused even to consider it. The plan died. The last thing London wanted was a colonial union—even then it feared the possibility of American independence.[45]

Ironically, on June 14, while the Albany Congress was meeting, the Board of Trade agreed to formulate its own plan for colonial union. On August 9, it submitted a "Draught of a Plan or Project for a General Concert" that called for union by mutual consent of the colonies. The Privy Council rejected the Board of Trade's plan. As Jennings points out, the Board of Trade called for a colonial concert rather than union, in which London would be the conductor: "Under the board's plan the colonies were not to be consulted except to determine how money was to be raised from their own peoples after the commander in chief had decided how much each was to be assessed."[46]

While the Congress debated plans for union, Indians began appearing in Albany. Most of the Iroquois who attended were Mohawks. The Iroquois were as split as the colonies, with the Mohawk intriguing against the Onondaga for supremacy in the League. To retain New York's authority over the tribe, De Lancey excluded the other colonial commissioners from his first two meetings with the Iroquois. Only after De Lancey promised the Iroquois justice for their grievances in return for their re-acknowledging their "covenant chain" with New York did he open the council to all the colonial representatives.

On July 2, the conference opened with all participants present. De Lancey delivered a speech calling on the Iroquois to resist French enticements. The Iroquois replied with a litany of complaints about the miserly presents they had received, encroachments on their land by various colonies, and the trade with Montreal by Albany merchants. The latter complaint was a direct swipe at De Lancey and his faction. They also renewed a call they had made three years earlier for William Johnson to be charged with Indian affairs.[47] Participant Thomas Pownall explained that the Iroquois were "in good earnest afraid of the French, and having no confidence or trust in any measures or promises we enter into, and finding that by our measures we are neither able nor willing to defend them, they were sensible that such a declaration (drawing the French upon them) must be the ruin of them. Their Resolution therefore was to observe a neutrality."[48]

No Iroquois chief was more loyal to the British than the Mohawk sachem Theyanoquin, or Chief Hendrick, a scarred veteran of dozens of raids, many of which had taken scalps from the French or their Indian allies. Hendrick's reply must have first heartened and then disturbed the assembled colonial leaders, as his initial promise of alliance gave way to bitter criticism of the British policy of weakness toward the French and neglect of the Iroquois. Perhaps most stunning of all was his prediction that the war would inevitably lead to the Iroquois' destruction.

Reverently taking the wampum belt, Hendrick asserted that the Iroquois "solemnly renew and brighten the covenant chain. We shall take the chain-belt back to Onondaga where our council-fire always burns. . . . It is true that we live disunited. We have tried to bring back our brethen, but in vain; for the Government of Canada is like a wicked, deluding spirit. You ask why we are so dispersed. The reason is that you have neglected us for these three years past. You have thus thrown us behind your back; whereas the French are a subtle and vigilant people, always using their utmost endeavors to seduce and bring us over to them. . . . The Governor of Virginia and the Governor of Canada are quarrelling about lands which belong to us, and their quarrell may destroy us. . . . Look at the French: they are men; they are fortifying themselves everywhere. But you are all like women, bare and open, without fortifications."[49] He ended by asking that "Coll. Johnson may be reinstated and have the Management of Indian Affairs, for we all lived happy, whilst they were under his Management, for we love him, and he is us, and he has always been our good and trusty Friend."

The colonial commissioners agreed to all these demands. The Indian council ended on July 9 with the Iroquois pleased by all the promises and 30 wagonloads of presents given them by the Congress.

A few Iroquois were to receive even more. Connecticut's delegates were also members of the Susquehanna Land Company which had long claimed the upper Susquehanna River valley. On July 11, Connecticut's negotiators, trader John Lydius and missionary Timothy Woodbridge, finalized an agreement with some Iroquois in which the colony would pay 2,000 pounds sterling for "rights" to five million acres of the Wyoming valley of the Sus-quehanna River. Unfortunately for Connecticut, several chiefs had earlier sold part of that same parcel to Pennsylvania. The overlapping claims became a bitter conflict between the two colonies that persisted for a decade until the Continental Congress settled it in 1775. Even worse, the sale further splintered relations among the Iroquois. Although not even members of the League Council at Onondaga, the Mohawk chiefs figured prominently in a deal whose land was in Onondaga territory whose inhabitants were mostly Delaware. The League Council later disavowed the sale.[50]

The Albany Congress broke up with its delegates pleased at having forged union with each other and the Iroquois. To their bitterness, they would soon learn that they would remain as estranged from each other and the Iroquois as ever.

WILLIAM JOHNSON

Who was that man, William Johnson, whom Hendrick and the other Ir-oquois called to represent them?[51] It would be difficult to find a character at once as colorful and decisive as Johnson in shaping events during the French and Indian War. Born around 1715 in County Meath, Ireland, from an early age he revealed an agile intelligence and ambition that strained the limits of what he could achieve as an Irish Catholic. Fortunately, Johnson found a powerful patron in his uncle, naval Captain Peter Warren, who had already become wealthy by marrying into the De Lancey family and would later gain fame by commanding the fleet that helped capture Louisbourg. Aware of his nephew's abilities, Warren invited Johnson to gather Irish fam-ilies and bring them as tenants to his estate in the Mohawk River valley, which he then would manage. In 1737, Johnson arrived in the Mohawk valley with a dozen families.

During the next two decades, Johnson amassed a land empire across the valley by skillfully diverting much of the region's Indian, settler, and land trade from Albany merchants to himself. Through fair and amiable dealings he gained the respect and the business of the valley's mishmash of inhabi-tants—Dutch, Indians, English, Germans, and others. Johnson was a stocky six foot tall, brave, quick-witted, and gregarious, at once a "man's man," and a "ladies' man," a prodigious eater, drinker, and fornicator who may well have fathered hundreds of Indian children, who was plagued by syphilis and would die in 1774 of cirrhosis of the liver. With his wealth he built a magnificent Georgian home, outbuildings, Indian council house, and, later, a stockade on the Mohawk River's north bank across from Fort Hunter. Mount Johnson became the valley's diplomatic as well as economic and cultural center.

From his first arrival in the valley, the Indians, particularly the Iroqouis, had fascinated him. He acquired their trust through fair dealings and immersing himself in their customs and languages. The Mohawk called him "Warraghiyagey" or "Doer of Great Things" and made him a sachem in their confederation, which allowed him to sit and vote in their council at Onondaga. Johnson rose just as steadily in New York civil affairs. During King George's War, Governor George Clinton named Johnson the district's justice of the peace in 1745 and militia colonel and Commissioner of Indian Affairs in 1746.

Johnson played his role as intermediary brilliantly, convincing the Iroquois and English alike that he worked unceasingly for their respective interests. His role as Iroquois sachem must have startled the colonists. When Johnson and the Iroquois arrived at the 1746 Albany conference, Warraghiyagey "put himself at the Head of the Mohawks, dressed and painted after the Manner of an Indian War-Captain; and the Indians who followed him, were likewise dressed and painted as . . . when they set out for War. The Indians saluted the Governor as they passed the Fort, by a running Fire; which his Excellency ordered to be answered by a Discharge of some Cannon from the Fort; he afterwards received the Sachems in the Fort Hall, bid them Welcome, and treated them to a Glass of Wine."[52] Governor Clinton ordered Johnson to "send out as many Party's of . . . Indians as you possibly can against the French & their Indians in Canada to harass and Alarm their Quarters in all Parts and to take Prisoners for Intelligence . . . likewise Scalps, and for every such Prisoner or Scalp . . . the Person Producing . . . shall Receive the Reward."[53] Johnson led a war party north but got no further than Lac Sacrament, which he would later rename Lake George. Not encountering any hostile French or Indians, he and his followers returned home.

At the time, Johnson could not have realized that his uneventful journey to Lac Sacrament would mark the start of a fifteen-year struggle to retain the alliance of as many Iroquois as possible. The duty was an enormous and mostly thankless burden. The obstinacy of colonial and Indian leaders alike, the miserliness with which the New York assembly granted goods with which to buy the Indians' friendship, and the constant danger of assassination continually drained Johnson's physical and emotional health.

He spent most of King George's War at Fort Johnson paying Indians for scalps they had taken on the warpath, although the nationality of the victims was impossible to determine. In 1748, he made an impassioned speech for an alliance between the English and Iroquois before the Onondaga Council, but before any warriors took the warpath, word arrived that a peace treaty had been signed. When Johnson attempted to resign as Indian Commissioner in 1750, Mohawk Chief Hendrick led a delegation to Albany to protest to Governor Clinton. Hendrick explained: "We were very much shocked when Coll. Johnson sent a Belt of Wampum through the Six Nations, to Inform us that he declined acting any more with us, and it was the more Terrible, because he was well acquainted with our publick Affairs.

. . . In War time he was like a Tree, that grew for our use, which now seems to be falling down, tho it has many roots; his knowledge of our affairs made us think him one of us (an Indian) and we are greatly afraid, as he has declined, your Excellency will appoint some other person, a stranger both to us and our Affairs; and we give your Excellency this Belt of Wampum in order to raise up the falling Tree."[54]

With bitterly mixed feelings, Johnson resumed his office only to resign it again the following year in protest at New York's refusal to fulfill its promises to the Indians or to repay him for all the trade goods he had dispersed to keep the peace. Hoping to entice Johnson back as Indian Commissioner, Clinton named him to the Provincial Council. Instead, Johnson used his infrequent journeys to the council in New York City to press it to redeem his expense and land claims. The issue was not resolved until December 1754 when Shirley and De Lancey promised compensation to Johnson in return for his agreeing to serve as Indian Commissioner, this time not just for New York but as the Crown's Superintendent for its North American colonies.

KENNEBEC CAMPAIGN

William Shirley was as vigorous and skilled a governor for Massachusetts as Dinwiddie was for Virginia.[55] Born in England in 1694, he received a law degree at Cambridge University and practiced at the Inner Temple before sailing to Boston in 1731. There Shirley acquired a reputation for intelligence and judiciousness while traveling the circuit. He was appointed an admiralty court judge when a position opened in 1733. His professionalism and devotion to the king's interest on the bench, along with his wife's constant lobbying in London, secured him an appointment as governor of Massachusetts in 1741. Shirley proved to be a decisive, visionary war leader during King George's War when he sent troops to Annapolis Royal which repulsed a French siege in 1744, erected forts and mustered troops across New England's frontier, tried to interest other governors in a grand plan for Canada's conquest, and, most importantly, in 1745, planned and mobilized the 3,600-troop expedition that took Louisbourg. Shirley remained in Boston during the Louisbourg campaign, while Peter Warren commanded the fleet and William Pepperell the army. To Shirley's disappointment, knighthoods for the victory went to Warren and Pepperell but not to himself. He did receive, along with Pepperell, a colonelcy for one of the two new regular regiments to be raised in America. In 1749, Shirley was asked to join the joint commission in Paris to draw the boundaries between the British and French empires in North America and the Caribbean. There he would remain in fruitless, endless negotiation rounds until he returned to Boston in August 1753.

Throughout 1754, amidst the brewing crisis, Shirley boosted New England's defense through several measures. In May, he received reports of a

French threat to settlements on the lower Kennebec River in Maine. The governor promptly sought and received his council's approval to mobilize six militia companies and send them to the Kennebec. To command the 800 troops he had mustered for the campaign, Shirley chose John Winslow. It was a good choice. Winslow was an esteemed veteran of King George's War, having served as a captain in the disastrous 1745 attempt to take Cartegena and the triumphant 1746 seizure of Louisbourg. Shirley ordered Winslow to erect one fort at the head of the Kennebec's navigation 43 miles from the sea and another fort 20 miles further upstream at the seventeen-foot Taconnett Falls. Beyond that the Kennebec River was largely terra incognita to all but a few English fur traders. In a letter to Halifax, Shirley explained that erecting forts high up both the Kennebec and Hudson Rivers would, "by continually hanging over Canada, like two Thunder-Clouds, keep the French and their Indians in a proper Respect and awe of the English Colonies."[56]

Winslow established Fort Western at the head of navigation and Fort Halifax at the falls. Leaving 100 men at Fort Western and 200 at Fort Halifax, he ascended the Kennebec with 500 men to determine its practicality as an invasion route in either direction. He found nothing but a primeval wilderness crossed by an occasional Indian path. From that quarter New England clearly faced no threat greater than an occasional Indian raid. In a letter recounting his successful expedition, Winslow poetically concludes: "Thus I have led you a Wild Goose Chase in a Wild Wilderness & like the Moose & Bears the Native Inhabitants, and the more savage Aboriginals the Indians, Made Mother Earth our Bed, and the Canopoly of Heaven our Covering, yet thro Gods goodness lost but three Men only."[57]

As a reconnaissance in force, Winslow's campaign was a success, if only in exploding the myth that the Kennebec River was an invasion route to and from Quebec comparable to the Lake Champlain corridor. A chain of navigable rivers and lakes, scattered settlements, and broad trails united Montreal and Albany; nothing like that existed between Fort Western and Quebec. That route was even less significant for the French than the British. While a British army moving up the Kennebec would at least be stumbling slowly and arduously toward Quebec, a French army coming down river had no significant towns or even forts before it. Yet, by sending an occasional raiding party down the Kennebec, the French could scare New Englanders into diverting vital men, munitions, and supplies away from the important campaigns.

THE POLITICAL AND FRONTIER WAR

With the summer barely half over, there remained several months of campaign weather. Dinwiddie tried heroically to elicit from his own assembly and from other colonies enough troops and supplies to allow one more campaign against Fort Duquesne before the season's end. Although his fellow governors were sympathetic, like Dinwiddie their assemblies had tied their fiscal hands. The political standoff between each colony's governor and assembly would continually stymie the war effort.

Dinwiddie pleaded with Virginia's assembly to appropriate more military funds. The assembly granted 20,000 pounds but attached a rider which required Dinwiddie to renounce the pistole fee. Dinwiddie refused and the bill died. In a September 1754 letter to Pennsylvania's governor Hamilton, Dinwiddie sourly complained that a "Governor is really to be pitied in the discharge of his duty to his King and Country, in having to do with such obstinate, self-conceited people. . . . I cannot satisfy the burgesses unless I prostitute the rules of government."[58]

Hamilton must have grimaced knowingly; he had encountered similar obstructions from his own assembly. Perhaps no colony was more divided on ethnic and religious lines than Pennsylvania.[59] The Quakers dominated the state's eastern region, the Germans the south central region, a melange of Scots, Irish, and English the western frontier, while Anglicans were scattered across the province. Each group had its own specific needs, values, and interests, and pushed hard to realize them in the assembly.

William Penn and his Quakers had founded Pennsylvania and controlled the colony for its first half century. By the 1750s, however, the Quakers had lost their majority in the assembly and a power balance emerged between them and the German and frontier settlers. A coalition emerged between the Quakers and Germans based on numerous shared interests, the most important of which was a sincere pacifism and an unflinching determination to preserve their religious and political liberties.

Pennsylvania's defense had traditionally relied on buying the allegiance of neighboring Indian tribes with generous annual presents. This low-cost strategy had successfully defended Pennsylvania from attack during earlier wars with the French. All along, the Quaker-dominated assembly had rejected repeated appeals by the proprietors and their Anglican supporters for a militia. The most the Quakers were willing to concede was for volunteers to serve. Besides the violation of their pacifism that compulsory militia service would bring, they feared the power a provincial militia could give to the governor, particularly by handing out officer commissions as patronage and using soldiers to bully voters during elections. Unsurprisingly, the frontier settlers fought the hardest for military aid and a voluntary militia. They bitterly resented the gridlock between the assembly and governor over military appropriations. The Anglican representatives in the assembly were a swing vote. Although they rejected pacifism and fought hard to pass a militia law and aggressive policy toward the Indians, the Anglicans did cooperate with the Quakers on conflicts over political rights with the proprietors and governor.

In trying to retain their privileges, the proprietors targeted the Quakers as the leaders of their opponents. Although Pennsylvania's founder, William Penn, had himself been a devout Quaker, his progeny's faith had been largely shelved for more worldly pursuits. Proprietor Thomas Penn had converted from the Friends to the Anglicans as a vital step in setting up a political machine in London and Philadelphia. Penn unsuccessfully used a variety of means to undercut Quaker power, the most blatant of which was to try to disqualify Quakers by requiring them to make an oath of allegiance that would have violated their vow of pacifism. Quakers lobbying in London and Philadelphia succeeded in killing his proposal. His attempt only heightened their solidarity and opposition to him.

Penn's only real power depended on appointing governors with the skills to check Quaker excesses and subtly undermine their power. Hamilton lacked those requisite skills. The assembly rejected his call in July for appropriations, arguing that it was "composed of a majority who are constitutionally principled against war, and represent a well-meaning peaceable people."[60] The next month, the governor tried again to extract 20,000 pounds from the assembly. The Quakers issued a compromise 10,000-pound appropriation for the "king's use," which washed their hands of the "blood money," and insisted that it be financed partly by taxing the proprietor's lands. The governor vetoed the bill.

In all, contributions from the colonies ranged from niggardly to nonexistent, a result worsened by news of Washington's defeat. Pennsylvania and New Jersey sent nothing but regrets to Dinwiddie's appeals. South Carolina and New York sent their regular infantry companies but contributed nothing thereafter that year. In July, Maryland's assembly granted 10,000 pounds and a company of 100 men in aid to Virginia. North Carolina's assembly was the most generous, appropriating 12,000 pounds to raise and dispatch to Virginia a 750-man regiment. There it was expected that Virginia would pay for the regiment's maintenance. When an exchange of letters between the two colonies revealed this misconception, North Carolina reduced the number of troops to 450. Those troops did make it to Virginia. Of Virginia's 230,000 people, 27,000 were enrolled in militia companies. Yet, only several hundred of those men volunteered to defend their dominion's frontier.

The troops that did assemble around Winchester were little more than an armed mob. The men were undisciplined, slothful, and inclined to desert. Each man had his own particular reasons for desertion, but all would revile the dearth of pay, food, shelter, clothing, munitions, arms, and even purpose. When the Virginians learned that the North Carolinians received three shillings a day while they were only getting eightpence, and that even that pittance would be reduced, most headed home. The North Carolina troops then mutinied at Augusta Court House when their paymaster ran out of money. The unit was disbanded on August 11. Washington complained to Dinwiddie that the "Soldiers are deserting constantly, and yesterday . . . 25 of them collected and were going off in Face of their Officers, but were stop'd and Imprison'd before the Plot came to its full height. . . . There is scare a Night, or opportunity, but what some or other are deserting, often two, or three, or 4 at a time."[61]

The animosity between royal and colonial officers continued. The captains of the two Independent Companies of New York and one of South Carolina refused to obey the orders of Colonel Innes, who sported merely a colonial commission. To finesse the problem, Dinwiddie revamped his Virginia regiment into eight companies each led by a captain. He then recalled all his commissions and reissued them as captains or lower. When Washington received his demotion to captain, the future "father of his country" angrily resigned and retired to Mt. Vernon. Dinwiddie tried to placate Washington by writing him a promise that he could both keep his honorary title as colonel and his troops separate from Sharpe's, although his real rank of captain would be retained. To this offer, Washington replied: "if you think me capable of holding a Commission that has neither rank nor emolument annexed to it; you must entertain a very contemptible opinion of my weakness, and believe me more empty than the Commission itself."[62]

Dinwiddie's one uplifting bit of news was a spy report from the hostage Robert Strobo at Fort Duquesne. Strobo proved to be a false insurance policy for France and a boon for British intelligence then, and for historians ever since. Hostage officers taken in peacetime had a different status than civilian captives or war prisoners. Strobo was allowed to roam freely throughout Fort Duquesne. Throughout July he sketched a plan of Fort Duquesne and wrote an 800-word explanation of the garrison's strengths and weakness on an 8 ¾" by 14 ¾" sheet of paper. Only 400 troops remained after Le Mercier left with 1,000 troops and most Indians had returned to their villages. He urged a "Strike this fall as soon as possible . . . one hundred trusty Indians might Surprise this fort. They have access all Day & might lodge themselves so that they might secure the Guard with their tomahawks shut the Salley gate & the Fort's ours. None but the Guard & Contracure stay in the Fort at night. The guard never exceeds 50, all the rest are in the cabines round the Fort."[63] Strobo managed to convey it to the British camp at Wills Creek via a sympathetic Delaware Indian. Fearing the report might be lost, he then wrote and forwarded a second. Perhaps to bolster the report's credibility, Strobo signed his name to it. That decision would return to haunt him.

Strobo's report reached Croghan at Wills Creek on August 16. Croghan promptly made and forwarded copies to governors Dinwiddie and Hamilton. The reports galvanized the two leaders. Dinwiddie sent an order to the officer escorting the 21 French prisoners back toward Fort Duquesne that they instead be incarcerated in Williamsburg. The governor had decided on an even exchange in which Strobo and Van Braam would be returned for the three French officers while the remaining prisoners would be retained for future negotiation leverage. Dinwiddie ordered Innes to forward word of the new terms to Fort Duquesne. Contrecoeur received the message and promptly rejected it. In a letter to Innes, he demanded that all the French be released or he would retain the hostages indefinitely.

In September, newly appointed North Carolina governor Arthur Dobbs arrived from London in Virginia with a royal commission naming Maryland governor Horatio Sharpe as commander in chief and lieutenant colonel of all colonial troops, and granting him 20,000 pounds for another campaign against Fort Duquesne. Sharpe had been a regular army officer and held the respect of the Independent Company captains. Promising as all this seemed, the season was now too advanced for a campaign, even if the troops had been available.

That autumn, the Board of Trade finally resolved the deadlock between Dinwiddie and the House of Burgesses by granting the governor the right to collect a pistole fee unless it was for less than 100 acres, for undelineated land "westward of the mountains," or for land sold before April 22, 1752. In November 1754, the assembly appropriated 20,000 more pounds for defense. Even without the pistole fee conflict, it is questionable whether the assembly would have granted more defense money.

WHITEHALL'S GRAND STRATEGY

The death of Henry Pelham on March 4, 1754 shook up the Cabinet. Pelham's half-brother, the Duke of Newcastle, became de facto Cabinet head and first lord of the Treasury. Walpole's description of Newcastle was scathing: "A borrowed importance and real insignificance gave him the perpetual air of a solicitor. . . . He had no pride, though infinite self-love. He loved business immoderately. . . . When left to himself, he always plunged into difficulties, and then shuddered for the consequences."[64]

Newcastle stood a middle ground between the hawks like Halifax, Cumberland, and Fox who sought a showdown with France, and the rest of the Cabinet, who favored conciliation. On June 26, 1754, he assembled the leading Cabinet members to debate just what should be done about the French "invasion." Newcastle succeeded in pressing his argument that a show of strength was the most prudent means of deterring the French. The Cabinet agreed to send Dinwiddie 10,000 pounds to bolster his military forces and buy the Indians' allegiance. An additional 10,000 pounds of credit was made available to Dinwiddie from Ohio Company partner John Hanbury.[65] To address the crisis, Newcastle had seemingly struck a sensible compromise between "toughness" and fiscal restraint. But the policy debate had only begun.

The leading "hawk," William Augustus, the Duke of Cumberland, was King George II's younger and favorite son.[66] Although then only 33 years old, Cumberland had acquired a reputation for toughness and decisiveness during his short career. He had served in Europe in 1745 and brutally destroyed the Jacobite rebellion in Scotland with the 1746 battle of Culloden and subsequent atrocities. Cumberland pushed a hard line toward the French and Americans alike, stressing the vital need to forcefully keep the French at bay and colonial assemblies down. Only British regulars could crush the French on the Ohio, Cumberland argued, and advocated sending two regiments to do so.

King George II joined Newcastle and most ministers in rejecting Cumberland's plan as needlessly expensive, provocative, and, perhaps more worrisome, a diversion of vital resources from the real French threat to British interests—in Europe. To the king, the French threat loomed most menacingly over his birthplace, Hanover, rather than across the Atlantic to his North American empire. George II was unwilling to divert any regulars to the New World. Nor was there any precedent to do so. The previous wars between the French and English in North America had been fought predominantly with colonial militia or volunteer troops.

In August, Charles Lawrence, Nova Scotia's newly appointed lieutenant-governor, joined the debate over British military plans for 1755. Lawrence was a career officer who had entered the army as an ensign in 1727, had worked his way up to lieutenant colonel of the 45th infantry in 1750, and since then had served in Nova Scotia through 1754 when he was named lieutenant-governor. In an August 1, 1754 letter to Halifax, Lawrence advocated Fort Beausejour's destruction, after which "the French Inhabitants on that side must either be removed to this, or driven totally away by Fire and Sword; for if all the villages beyond Beau-Sejour are not destroyed, and some of the Dykes cut, The French . . . would immediately return to take possession of their habitations and rebuild their forts." To Lawrence, the immediate threat to Nova Scotia was from the French settlers rather than the distant French army or navy. He went on to report that many Acadians had refused to take the loyalty oath and have "Incendiary French Priests among them" urging them to revolt against British rule. As the Acadians "possess the best and largest Tracts of land in this province it cannot be settled with any effect while they remain in this situation, and tho I would be very far from attempting such a step without your Lordships approbation, yet I cannot help being of the opinion that it would be much better, if they refuse the oaths, that they were away."[67]

Lawrence's plan would not arrive in London for another six weeks, shortly after the policy debate was rekindled by news of Washington's surrender. But the humiliating surrender at Great Meadows prompted Newcastle to adopt Cumberland's plan of sending two regiments to North America and trying to convince the Cabinet to go along. The Cabinet split over the plan between confrontationists and conciliators. The most significant stumbling block to Newcastle's plan was the king. To gain the king's approval, Newcastle appealed to Cumberland who promised to work on his father, but at the price of his joining the Cabinet. Newcastle conceded.

As captain general, the king's son, and now an informal Cabinet member, Cumberland soon dominated policy toward North America. It was Cumberland who would transform the brush war between small colonial armies into a grand war eventually dominated by European regiments. Lord Shelburne later asserted that "the war was contrived by the Duke of Cumberland underhand. . . . The Duke of Newcastle was frightened, bullied and betrayed into it."[68]

Cumberland prevailed upon his father to send two Irish regiments and Major General Edward Braddock to North America to retake the forks of the Ohio. The choice of Braddock was not surprising. The two men had a friendship going back a decade, culminating when Braddock took command of Cumberland's own Coldstream Guards. Cumberland and his war faction then worked on the Cabinet to convert a confrontation at the Ohio forks into a four-pronged campaign against the French across North America. Campaigns would be launched not only against Fort Duquesne but also Fort Frederic on Lake Champlain, Fort Niagara on Lake Ontario, and Fort Beausejour in Acadia.

At first, Newcastle and a Cabinet majority rejected any attacks on those other forts for fear they would provoke a general war with France. But by constantly harping on the news of Washington's surrender and Lawrence's dire report of a French threat to Acadia, the Cumberland faction eventually bent the reluctant majority to its will. On September 26, the inner Cabinet of Newcastle, Anson, Halifax, Robinson, and Fox met with King George II and Cumberland at St. James Palace to endorse the grand plan.

Shortly thereafter, to ensure that the decision for war was irrevocable, Cumberland and Fox announced their troop movements in the court *Gazette*; other newspapers in London, the British Isles, and the American colonies soon picked up the startling news. Ambassador Mirepoix demanded an explanation of the expedition from Sir Thomas Robinson, who blandly replied that the reinforcements were solely to bolster the colonies' defenses. Ironically, the British ambassador to France, the Earl of Albemarle, "happened to be colonel of Braddock's regiment, father of the commodore of the fleet that took Braddock to Virginia, titular governor for seventeen years of a Virginia he had never visited, [and] a member of the inconclusive boundary commision that had failed to delineate the Ohio or Nova Scotia boundaries."[69] When Louis XV demanded from him an explanation of British reinforcements, Albemarle echoed the claim that they were merely defensive.

Seeking to prevent a war, Versailles chose to avoid rather than confront the British provocation. Minister of Marine Jean Baptiste de Machault d'Arnouville ordered Governor Duquesne to restrain his troops and Indians.

The only offensive Machault authorized was the seizure of Fort Halifax on the Kennebec River, an order that would not be implemented.[70]

Would Parliament agree to fund the Cabinet's ambitious plan? King George II opened Parliament on November 14 with an account of the worsening crisis in North America and an urgent appeal to its members to rally to their imperiled nation. He then submitted the bill. Parliament complied, voting unanimously to appropriate for next year's army and navy budget one million pounds, of which 50,000 pounds would underwrite the North American operations.

The actual campaign details developed through a series of meetings, intelligence reports, and policy papers from the leading military planners. British intelligence on French North America was actually quite good.[71] Two October 1754 reports to Cumberland compiled from accounts by Washington, traders, and Indians gave specific French troops numbers in their forts across the Great Lakes, St. Lawrence, and Lake Champlain empires.[72]

On November 25, 1754, the Cabinet issued Braddock his formal "Secret Instructions." The commander in chief's objective was "to recover the Territories belonging to His [Majesty's] Colonies there & to His Subjects & allies the Indians, which the French (most unjustly & contrary to Solemn Treaties subsisting between the two Crowns of Great Britain and France) invaded & possessed themselves of & raised Fortifications."[73] To this end, the British forces would drive the French from their forts at Duquesne, Niagara, Frederic, and Beausejour, and assert control over the surrounding regions. More specifically, the plan included sending Colonel Peter Halket's 44th and Colonel Dunbar's 48th regiments to Virginia. There, those regiments' ranks would be augmented to full strength by recruits from the American colonies. Two colonial regular regiments, the 51st and 52nd, would be reactivated by William Shirley and William Pepperell, respectively. Shirley would recruit his 50th regiment from Boston and Pepperell his 51st regiment from New York and Philadelphia. Secretary of State Robinson wrote the colonial governors to ask that they assist in recruiting those four regiments up to strength and cooperating with Braddock. As for logistics, Whitehall authorized adequate supplies of cannon, munitions, muskets, food, and uniforms, and named Sir John St. Clair Deputy Quartermaster-General. London even worked out an exchange rate between the pound sterling and the various colonial currencies to limit any overcharging of British forces. One chief engineer and four subordinate engineers were appointed for assignment with the various forces. Provincial officers would be subordinate to someone of equal rank in the regular army, but superior to all below their own rank. All commanders were ordered to nurture Indian alliances as essential auxiliaries to their campaigns. Support from the Iroquois confederation was considered essential for the strategy's success.

The Crown did agree to a unification of the colonies under one head, but it was quite different from the Albany Plan of Union. When Major

General Braddock was named commander in chief of all British regular and colonial forces in North America, he was empowered to supply, quarter, and maneuver his forces as he saw fit. To aid Braddock, Robinson ordered the colonial governors to supply and quarter at their colonys' own expense the British troops sent into their midst, as well as to chip in to a "common fund" for the North American commander in chief's disposal.[74] The presence of those redcoated officers and enlisted men would quickly wear thin on Americans. Jennings points out that the British troops dispatched to America soon became an "army of occupation . . . the same soldiers whose primary mission was to conquer Canada became the instrument of royal authority for disciplining the colonies."[75]

Admiral Augustus Keppel was given command of all naval forces in North American waters, which would include two ships of the line, two frigates, and 13 transports. After transporting the reinforcements to Virginia, Keppel would attempt to sever the communications between France and Canada, and the smuggling between Acadia and New England.

As Whitehall finished up its campaign planning for 1755, there was a trans-Atlantic meeting of minds over Acadia that went beyond merely seizing Fort Beausejour. A December 1753 Board of Trade report to King George II warned that "should the French continue in possession of any Settlement on the River St. Johns, the direct communication between Your Majesty's other American Colonies and Nova Scotia will be intercepted and broken, and that Province, instead of being a barrier to the rest of Your Majesty's Dominion on the Continent of America, will be itself a separate Colony, exposed to the French encompassing it on every side; the force of Canada and Cape Breton will be united . . . the extensive and very beneficial Trade to those parts for Lumber and Furrs . . . will be left open to the French . . . the Attainment & Security of which so large Sums have from time to time been chearfully expended by this Nation in the settling of Nova Scotia, will be lost not only to Great Britain, but transferred to the Power of France."[76]

In December, still not having heard from London, Lawrence dispatched captains Robert Monckton and George Scott to explain his plan to Shirley, who had just received details of the 1755 campaign from Whitehall. Shirley enthusiastically embraced the grand plan. He and Pepperell immediately began mustering their two regiments of regulars and raising other volunteer regiments. Shirley hoped that taking Acadia would be the first step before reconquering Louisbourg and Isle Royale. Yet the written instructions from Earl Holderness, the Secretary of State, did inhibit Shirley: "as it's His Majesty's determination not to be the aggressor, I have the King's commands, most strictly to enjoin you, not to make use of the armed force under your direction, excepting within the undoubted limits of His Majesty's dominions."[77] Those "undoubted limits" were subject to considerable doubt.

CONSEQUENCES

Did the volley of musket balls which tore through Jumonville's patrol start the French and Indian War? Francis Parkman states unequivocally that "this obscure skirmish began the war that set the world on fire."[78] Parkman exaggerates wildly. London and Paris would not formally exchange war declarations until two years later in 1756, and even then for reasons unconnected with events in North America—the French invasion of British Minorca.

Nonetheless, George Washington's aggressive blunderings on the Pennsylvania frontier did move Whitehall and Versailles closer to a global war that neither wanted, was prepared to fight, nor even understood until years after it began. Washington's signature on a surrender document naming him Jumonville's murderer was a brilliant propaganda coup for the French. The French printed and distributed the document throughout Europe. The British were clearly the aggressors, trumpeted the French.

Yet, even at that late hour, war was not inevitable. Diplomacy could have averted it. The attack on Jumonville flared a crisis that had smoldered ever since the last war ended, and made its peaceful resolution ever more unlikely.

Which side, if either, was ultimately responsible for renewed war in North America?[79] Jennings points the finger directly at the war party in London: "The brawling at the forks of the Ohio was not the cause of the Seven Years War; rather it served as an excuse for powerful Englishmen who wanted to fight France. The 'bush war' could have been contained and settled somehow by negotiation as other conflicts at the periphery of empire had previously been eased. This was what George II and Louis XV wanted, and it was what their chief ministers wanted, but the English belligerents demanded what the French moderates could not concede, and the French hard-liners forced responses that the English moderates could not accept. Each side maneuvered for positions of strength that could not be abandoned. Having achieved strength, each side had to use it. The 'doves' lost control when they conceded the 'hawks' fundamental premise that the two countries' 'natural' enmity could only end by conquest."[80]

If Washington's "assassination" and surrender were important if not decisive in provoking the war, they certainly undermined British power. The surrender was a disaster for British relations with the Indians. Johnson's secretary Daniel Claus remarked that he had "never the like seen how quick the nations turned after Colonel Washington's defeat."[81] In December 1754, Johnson wrote: "Upon the News of the first Engagement at Ohio, Our friend Indians were in high spirits, but the last had a verry different Effect, of which . . . Soon after . . . the news of Washington's defeat, above two Hundred of the Six Nations went to Canada, as did also Severall of Both Mohawk Castles. . . . I fear many of them will be prevailed on to join the French & go to Ohio, as Severall of them have done last Summer, and those who may return will be so corrupted & poisoned that they Seduce the rest."[82]

In the minds of Britain's political and military elite, Washington's ineptness was characteristic of the colonists. Lord Albemarle, the British ambassador to France, maintained that "Washington and many such may have courage and resolution, but they have no knowledge or experience in our profession. Consequently, there can be no dependence on them."[83] A succession of British generals like Braddock, Webb, Loudoun, and Abercromby would cherish this stereotype, spurn most advice from colonial officers, and heap even greater disasters and accusations of ineptness upon their own shoulders. That anti-American prejudice was impregnable in the minds of most Englishmen, and would persist throughout the French and Indian War and even through the British surrender at Yorktown a generation later.

NOTES

1. Quoted in L. H. Gipson, "A French Project for Victory Short of a Declaration of War, 1755," *Canadian Historical Review* 26 (1945), 362.

2. Theodore Calvin Pease, ed., *Anglo-French Boundary Disputes in the West, 1749–1763* (Springfield: Collections of the Illinois State Historical Library 27, French Series 2, 1936); Max Savelle, "Diplomatic Preliminaries of the Seven Years' War in America," *Canadian Historical Review* 20 (1939), 1–43; Max Savelle, *The Diplomatic History of the Canadian Boundary, 1749–1763* (New Haven, Conn.: Yale University Press, 1940); Lawrence Henry Gipson, *Zones of International Friction: The Great Lakes Frontier, Canada, the West Indes, India, 1748–1754* (New York: Alfred A. Knopf, 1942), chap. 10.

3. Rouille to Duquesne, May 15, 1752, in Theodore Calvin Pease and Ernestine Jenison, eds., *Illinois on the Eve of the Seven Years' War, 1747–1755*, vol. 29 (Springfield: Collections of the Illinois State Historical Library, 1940), 631.

4. Johnson to John Tabor Kempe, September 7, 1765, in James Sullivan and A. C. Flick, eds., *The Papers of William Johnson* (hereafter cited as Sullivan, *Johnson Papers*), 14 vols. (Albany: State University of New York, 1921–1965), 11:925.

5. John A. Schutz, *William Shirley: King's Governor of Massachusetts* (Chapel Hill: University of North Carolina Press, 1961), chap. 8.

6. Mildmay to Fitzwalter, October 20, 1750, December 2, 1750, Mildmay, "Private Correspondance," quoted in Gipson, *Zones of Friction*, 309–10.

7. Quoted in Francis Jennings, *Empire of Fortune: Crowns, Colonies, & Tribes in the Seven Years War in America* (New York: W. W. Norton, 1988), 127.

8. Donald Jackson, ed., *The Diaries of George Washington, 1748–65* (hereafter cited as Jackson, *Washington Diaries*), vol. 1 (Charlottesville: University of Virginia Press, 1976), 155.

9. In his journal, Gist states unequivocally that there was only one Indian. Jackson, *Washington Diaries*, n.157. Washington said that "we fell in with a Party of French Indians, which had laid in wait for us, one of them fired at Mr. Gist or me, not 15 Steps, but fortunately missed. We took this Fellow into Custody, & kept him 'till about 9 o'Clock at Night, & then let him go, & then walked all the remaining

Part of the Night without Making any stop; that we might get the start, so far as to be out of the reach of their pursuit next Day." Ibid., p. 155.

The descrepancy between the two accounts cannot be resolved. If more than one Indian was involved in an ambush, why would not the others have opened fire as well, let alone allow the two Americans to subdue one of their comrades. I used Gist's account because it was the much more detailed and likely of the two.

10. Dinwiddie Commission of William Trent, January 27, 1754, in R. A. Brock, ed., *The Official Records of Robert Dinwiddie, Lieutenant Governor of the Colony of Virginia, 1751–1758* (1883) (hereafter cited as Brock, *Dinwiddie Papers*) (reprint, New York: AMS Press, 1971), 1:56–57.

11. Dinwiddie to Shirley, January 29, 1754, in Brock, *Dinwiddie Papers*, 1:69–71; Dinwiddie to De Lancey, ibid., 1:65–66; Dinwiddie to Belcher, ibid., 1:68–69; Dinwiddie to Hamilton, ibid. 1:63–64; Dinwiddie to Sharpe, ibid., 1:67–68; Dinwiddie to Rowan, ibid., 1:64–65; Dinwiddie to Glen, ibid., 1:61–63; Dinwiddie to Monacatoocha, ibid., 1:57, Dinwiddie to the Six Nations, ibid., 1:58; Dinwiddie to Catawba, ibid., 1:60; Dinwiddie to Cherokee, ibid., 1:61.

12. Louis Knott Koontz, *Robert Dinwiddie, His Career in American Colonial Government and Westward Expansion* (Glendale, Calif.: Arthur H. Clark, 1941), 259.

13. Dinwiddie to Hanbury, May 10, 1754, in Brock, *Dinwiddie Papers*, 1:153–55.

14. Dinwiddie to Hamilton, February 23, 1754, ibid., 1:81.

15. Votes and Proceedings of the House of Representatives for the Province of Pennsylvania, Pennsylvania Archives, 8th ser., 8 vols. paged continuously (Harrisburg, 1931–35) 5:3701–2, 3706.

16. Herbert L. Osgood, *The American Colonies in the Eighteenth Century*, 4 vols. (1924) (reprint, Gloucester, Mass.: Peter Smith, 1958), 4:336–37.

17. Washington to Dinwiddie, March 9, 1754, in W. W. Abbott, ed., *The Papers of George Washington* (hereafter cited as Abbott, *Washington Papers*) (Charlottesville: University Press of Virginia, 1984), 1:73.

18. Dinwiddie to Washington, January 1754, in Abbott, *Washington Papers*, 1:63.

19. A. T. Volwiler, ed., "William Trent's Journal at Fort Pitt," *Mississippi Valley Historical Review* 11 (1924), 408–10.

20. John C. Fitzpatrick, ed., *The Writings of George Washington* (hereafter cited as Fitzpatrick, *Washington Writings*), 39 vols. (Boston: Houghton Mifflin, 1931–1944), 1:76.

21. Glen to Dinwiddie, March 14, 1754, P.R.O., C.O. 5:14, 297.

22. Glen to Dinwiddie, August 15, 1754, P.R.O, C.O. 5:12, 475.

23. Washington to Dinwiddie, May 27, 1754, in Abbott, *Washington Papers*, 1:104; ibid., May 29, 1754; ibid., 1:107–15; Dinwiddie to Washington, ibid., May 25, 1:102–6; ibid, June 4, 1754, 1:126–28.

24. Jackson, *Washington Diaries*, 197; W. J. Eccles, "Coulon de Villers de Jumonville, Joseph," *Dictionary of Canadian Biography* (Toronto: University of Toronto Press, 1966–), 3:150–51.

25. George Washington to Dinwiddie, May 29, 1754, in Fitzpatrick, *Washington Writings*, 1:65–66.

26. Memoire Contenant le Precis des Faits, quoted in Charles H. Ambler, *George Washington and the West* (1936) (reprint, New York: Russell and Russell, 1971), 65.

27. Jackson, *Washington Diaries*, 197.

28. Sworn affidavit of John Shaw before South Carolina Governor James Glen, August 21, 1754, in William L. McDowell, Jr., ed., *Documents Relating to Indian Affairs, 1754–1765* (Columbia: University of South Carolina Press, 1970), 4–5.

29. Quoted in Ambler, *Washington and the West*, 67–68. Which account is to be believed? We can reasonably conclude with Jennings that "both sides smudged the facts for political and propaganda purposes." *Empire of Fortune*, 69.

30. "Conrad Weiser's Journal," *Minutes of the Provincial Council of Pennsylvania* (hereafter cited as Pa. *Council Minutes*) (1851) (reprint, New York: AMS Press, 1968), 6:151–52.

31. Washington to Dinwiddie, June 12, 1754, in Fitzpatrick, *Washington Writings*, 1:81–82.

32. Extract of Villier Journal in Varin Letter to Bigot, July 24, 1754, in E. B. O'Callaghan and Bertold Fernow, eds., *Documents Relative to the Colonial History of the State of New York* (hereafter cited as NYCD), 15 vols. (Albany, N.Y.: Weed, Parsons, and Co., 1853–1887), 10:261.

33. Jackson, *Washington Diaries*, 208.

34. Washington to Dinwiddie, May 27, 1754, in Abbott, *Washington Papers*, 1: 104.

35. Dinwiddie to Board of Trade, July 24, 1754, in Brock, *Dinwiddie Papers*, 1: 239–43.

36. Varin to Bigot, July 24, 1754, NYCD, 10:260–61.

37. Jackson, *Washington Diaries*, 170.

38. Ibid., 170.

39. Dinwiddie to Sharpe, July 31, 1754, in Brock, *Dinwiddie Papers*, 1: 258.

40. Johnson to Goldsbrow Banyar, July 29, 1754, in Sullivan, *Johnson Papers*, 1: 409–10.

41. Villiers to Duquesne, July 1754, in Fernand Grenier, ed., *Papier Contrecoeur et autres documents concernant le conflit Anglo-Francais sur l'Ohio de 1755 a 1756* (Quebec: Les Presses Universitaires Laval, 1952).

42. Reasons and Motives on which the Plan of Union was formed, July 1754, in Leonard W. Labaree, ed., *The Papers of Benjamin Franklin* (hereafter cited as Labaree, *Franklin Papers*) (New Haven Conn.: Yale University Press, 1962), 5:400, 397–416; see also To Alexander and Colden with Short Hints for Uniting the Northern Colonies, June 8, 1754, ibid., 5:337–38; Procceedings of the Albany Congress, June 19–July 11, 1754, ibid., 5:344–53; Albany Congress Committee, June 28, 1754, ibid., 5:357–64; Peters, Notes on Debate, July 1, 1754, ibid., 5:364–66; Albany Congress, July 9–10, 1754, ibid., 5:366–92.

43. Hamilton to Assembly, February 14, 1754, in Pa. *Council Minutes*, 5:721.

44. Franklin Remark, February 9, 1789, in Labaree, *Franklin Papers*, 5:417.

45. Gilbert Olson, "The British Government and Colonial Union, 1754," *William and Mary Quarterly* 3rd ser., 17, no. 1 (January 1960), 22–34; James A. Henretta, *"Salutary Neglect": Colonial Administration Under the Duke of Newcastle* (Princeton, N.J.: Princeton University Press, 1972).

46. Jennings, *Empire of Fortune*, 117.

47. John R. Alden, "The Albany Congress and the Creation of the Indian Superintendencies," *Mississippi Valley History Review* 27, no. 22 (September 1940), 193–210.

48. Thomas Pownall to My Lord [Halifax], in "Personal Accounts of the Albany Congress of 1754," ed. Beverly McAnear, *Mississippi Valley Historical Review* 39, no. 4 (March 1953), 740–41.

49. Proceedings of Albany Congress, Hendrick's Speech, July 2, 1754, NYCD, 6:869–70.

50. William Brewster, *The Pennsylvania and New York Frontier, 1700–1763* (Philadelphia: George S. McNanus Co., 1954).

51. James Thomas Flexner, *Mohawk Baronet: A Biography of Sir William Johnson* (1959) (reprint, Syracuse, N.Y.: Syracuse University Press, 1979); Allan W. Eckert, *Wilderness Empire: A Narrative* (New York: Bantam Books, 1989); Milton W. Hamilton, *Sir William Johnson: Colonial American, 1715–1763* (Port Washington, N.Y.: Kennikat Press, 1976).

52. Cadwallader Colden, *The History of the Five Indian Nations of Canada, Which Are Dependent Upon the Province of New York in North America* (1747) (reprint, New York: AMS Press, 1973), 3:164.

53. Clinton to Johnson, August 28, 1746, Sullivan, *Johnson Papers*, 1:60–61.

54. Six Nation Council, July 2, 1751, ibid., 1:340.

55. John Schutz, *William Shirley, King's Governor of Massachusetts* (Chapel Hill: University of North Carolina Press, 1961).

56. Shirley to Halifax, August 20, 1754, in Stanley Pargellis, ed., *Military Affairs in North America, 1748–1765: Selected Documents from the Cumberland Papers in Windsor Castle* (1936) (reprint, Hamden, Conn.: Archon Books, 1969), 23.

57. John Winslow to Charles Gould, December 30, 1754, in Pargellis, *Military Affairs*, 54–58.

58. Dinwiddie to J. Abercromby, September 1, 1754, in Brock, *Dinwiddie Papers*, 1:296–97; also Dinwiddie to Hamilton, September 6, 1754, ibid., 1:306–9.

59. Theodore Thayer, *Israel Pemberton: King of the Quakers* (Philadelphia: Historical Society of Pennsylvania, 1943); Theodore Thayer, *Pennsylvania Politics and the Growth of Democracy, 1740–1776* (Harrisburg: Pennsylvania Historical and Museum Commission, 1953); Dietmar Rothermund, "The German Problem of Colonial Pennsylvania,", *Pennsylvania Magazine of History and Biography* 84, no. 1 (January 1960), 10–13; Dietmar Rothermund, *The Layman's Progress: Religious and Political Experience in Colonial Pennsylvania, 1740–1770* (Philadelphia: University of Pennsylvania Press, 1961); Richard Bauman, *For the Reputation of Truth: Politics, Religion, and Conflict Among the Pennsylvania Quakers, 1750–1800* (Baltimore, Md.: Johns Hopkins University Press, 1971); Jack D. Marietta, "Conscience, the Quaker Community, and the French and Indian War," *Pennsylvania Magazine of History and Biography* 95, no. 1 (January 1971), 3–5, 19–21; James Hutson, *Pennsylvania, 1749–1770: The Movement for Royal Government and Its Consequences* (Princeton, N.J.: Princeton University Press, 1972).

60. Assembly to Hamilton, March 2, 1754, in Pa. *Council Minutes*, 5:748.

61. Washington to Dinwiddie, August 20, 1754, in Abbott, *Washington Papers*, 1:189.

62. Washington to William Fitzhugh, November 15, 1754, ibid., 1:226.

63. Robert C. Alberts, *The Most Extraordinary Adventures of Major Robert Strobo* (Boston: Houghton Mifflin, 1965), 103.

64. John Brooke, ed., *Horace Walpole, Memoirs of King George II*, 3 vols. (New Haven, Conn.: Yale University Press, 1985), 1:344.

65. Sir Lewis Namier, *The Structure of Politics at the Accession of George III*, 2nd ed. (London: Macmillan and Co., 1957); Jacob M. Price, "The Great Quaker Business Families of the Eighteenth Century," in Richard S. Dunn and Mary Maples Dunn, eds., *The World of William Penn* (Philadelphia: University of Pennsylvania Press, 1986), 363–99.

66. Bruce Lenman, *The Jacobite Risings in Britain, 1689–1746* (London: Eyre Methuen, 1980); John Prebble, *Culloden* (Harmondsworth: Penguin Books, 1967; E. M. Lloyd, "William Augustus, Duke of Cumberland," *Dictionary of National Biography* 61:341.

67. Lawrence to Halifax, August 23, 1754, in Pargellis, *Military Affairs*, 29.

68. Quoted in Philip C. Yorke, *The Life and Correspondance of Philip Yorke, Earl of Hardwicke, Lord High Chancellor of Great Britain*, 3 vols. (Cambridge: Cambridge University Press, 1913), 2:256–57.

69. Ian K. Steele, *Betrayals: Fort William Henry & the "Massacre"* (New York: Oxford University Press, 1990), 41.

70. Machault to Duquesne, February 17, 1754, NYCD, 10:275–78; L. H. Gipson, "A French Project for Victory Short of a Declaration of War," *Canadian Historical Review* 26 (1945).

71. For the development of the plan's details, see "Sketch of Regulations & Orders Proposed Relating to Affairs of North America, November 1754"; "Considerations Relating to Measures to Be Taken with Regard to Affairs in North America, November 1754"; Remarks on the Pass of Niagara, November 1754"; "Memorial and State of the Exchange with the British Colonies of North America 1754"; "Sketch of an Order About the Rank & Ca of the Provincial Troops in North America"; "Sketch for the Operations in North America, November 16, 1754"; "Instructions from the Lords of the Admiralty to Admiral Keppel"; "Private Instructions for Major-Gen. Braddock" (Cumberland Papers), in Pargellis, *Military Affairs*, 34–54.

72. "Account of the French Forts in Canada and Upon the Lakes, October 1754"; "Different Routes in North America, 1754"; ibid., 30–32.

73. "Sketch for the Operations in North America, November 16, 1754," ibid., 44–46.

74. Lawrence Henry Gipson, *The British Empire before the American Revolution* (New York: Alfred A. Knopf, 1958–1970), vol. 6, 57 n.48.

75. Jennings, *Empire of Fortune*, 112.

76. Board of Trade to the King, December 7, 1755, in Pargellis, *Military Affairs*, 17–18.

77. Holderness to Shirley, August 28, 1753, in Charles Henry Lincoln, ed., *The Correspondance of William Shirley*, 2 vols. (New York: Macmillan, 1912), 2: 13.

78. Francis Parkman, *Montcalm and Wolfe: The French and Indian War* (1886) (reprint, New York: Da Capo Press, 1995), 88.

79. Patrice Louis-Rene Higonnet, "The Origins of the Seven Years' War," *Journal of Military History* 40 (March 1968), 57–90; T. R. Clayton, "The Duke of Newcastle, the Earl of Halifax, and the American Origins of the Seven Years' War,"

The Historical Journal (Cambridge, England) 24, no. 3 (September 1981), 571–603.

   80. Jennings, *Empire of Fortune*, 123.
   81. Quoted in Flexner, *Mohawk Baronet*, 122.
   82. Johnson to Shirley, December 17, 1754, Sullivan, *Johnson Papers*, 1:430–31.
   83. Quoted in Jennings, *Empire of Fortune*, 123.

5

1755

A little more or a little less territory in North America should not cause a war. Each nation possesses more than she can use for a long time to come.
                              —Antoine-Louis Rouille, Comte de Jouy, 1755

How little credit is given to a Commander, who perhaps after a defeat, in relating the cause justly lays the blame on some individual whose cowardly behav'r betray'd the whole to ruin; how little does the World consider the Circumstances, and how apt are Mankind to level their vindictive Censures against the unfortunate Chief, who perhaps merited least of the blame.
                              —George Washington, 1755

Who would have thought it?
                              —General Edward Braddock's dying words, 1755

While French and British subjects killed each other in North America's wilderness, diplomats met to prevent the fighting from escalating into a general war.[1] During 1755's first three months, British diplomats issued several formal demands that the French withdraw from the disputed territories in the Ohio valley and Acadia. In January, Sir Thomas Robinson proposed to French ambassador to the Court of St. James, Charles Pierre Gaston Francois de Levis, Duc de Mirepoix, that the North American boundaries be restored to those following the 1713 Treaty of Utrecht. It was not until February 20, however, that Robinson conveyed to Mirepoix the specifics of such a withdrawal. Whitehall proposed that both sides demilitarize all lands between the Wabash River, Lake Erie, Lake Ontario, the Niagara River, and the Ohio River. All forts in that region would be dismantled and the troops withdrawn to undisputed territories. British and French alike would be allowed to trade freely throughout that region. The Cabinet left the east side of this region vague, not wanting to declare the Allegheny Mountains the boundary since it would chop off Pennsylvania's western claims. As for Acadia, the ancient French boundaries would become those for England. This meant that the British could legally extend their empire down the west side of the Bay of Fundy to the Penobscot River. While the French were mulling over their response to this proposal, in March Robinson attempted to bolster the British case by submitting cartographer John Mitchell's just published map, which gave Britain the Ohio River forks and created a neutral buffer zone from the Appalachian Mountains to the Wabash River. This claim was rooted in the Utrecht Treaty, which awarded the British sovereignty over the Iroquois, and thus by extension over any Iroquois lands.[2]

The French rejected all these proposals. Practically, they could not accept a plan which granted Britain the forks of the Ohio and allowed its traders access to the Ohio River country, thus putting at risk communications between Canada and Louisiana. Legally, they pointed out that the Iroquois had always considered themselves sovereign and refused to bow to the British or French, thus nullifying Whitehall's claim to their territory. Mirepoix further argued that the map's extension of Iroquois lands all the way to the Wabash River and into Ontario was simply wrong. Most of those tribes not only rejected any notion of Iroquois sovereignty over their lives, but continued to send out war parties against the League. For example, the map claimed the Iroquois had subdued and then allied with the Mississauga. Actually, the Mississauga had repelled the Iroquois in the early 1700s and remained at war with them. Summing up his argument, Mirepoix asserted that "The Indians in question are free and independent and none of them can be termed subjects of either crown. The statement of the Treaty of Utrecht is faulty in that respect and cannot change the nature of things. It is certain that no Englishman would dare, without running the risk of being murdered, to tell the Iroquois they were English subjects."[3]

Politely dismissing the British map, the French unfolded their own map which placed their Fort Duquesne and Fort Niagara and the British Fort Oswego in a neutral zone. They thus agreed to dismantle two of their forts if the British dismantled one of theirs. This was a stunning concession.

War could have been averted had the British accepted the French concessions and arguments about Iroquois independence. Lord Halifax led the hardliners in the British Cabinet to reject the French proposal. Whitehall asserted that four French forts violated British territory: Fort Beausejour, Fort St. Frederic, Fort Niagara, and Fort Duquesne, and demanded that they be dismantled. Once again, the British diplomats unrolled their map and repeated their position. That map was essentially an ultimatum to the

French to abandon their historic and economic stake throughout the Ohio River valley or else be prepared for war. This the French were unprepared to do. The gap between the two positions appeared unbridgeable. As one French minister put it, "War alone can end our differences. . . . If they are determined at London to kindle a war, all we can say to forestall that evil will not prevent it."[4]

ESCALATION

Neither side wanted an all-out war. The previous war that had ended a mere six years earlier had financially exhausted both kingdoms. Yet each side not only reinforced its forces in North America, it ordered them to take the offensive. And each was two-faced when the other demanded an explanation of such aggressive acts.

On December 22, 1754, Major General Edward Braddock set sail for Virginia from Cork, Ireland, aboard the *Norwich*, accompanied by his aide, Captain Robert Orme, and his secretary, William Shirley, the governor's son. Braddock was an uninspiring choice to command British forces in North America. For 43 of his 60 years he had laboriously made his way up the officer ranks of the Coldstream Guards, becoming its lieutenant colonel in 1745. He transferred to the 14th regiment to become its colonel in 1753. Before arriving in America, Braddock had never held an independent command, let alone responsibility for commanding forces scattered over half a continent. But he had faithfully served Cumberland in Europe, and that is what counted most in his appointment.[5]

Four weeks after Braddock sailed away to America, his troops were ready to follow. On January 15, 1755, Sir Peter Halkett's 44th and Thomas Dunbar's 48th regiments, each with around 500 men, accompanied by a Royal Artillery company with four twelve-pounders, six 6-pounders, four 8-inch howitzers, and fifteen cohorn mortars, and related supplies embarked at Cork in thirteen transports and three ordinance ships. Braddock reached Hampton Roads, Virginia on February 19, 1755. Four days later he arrived at Williamsburg to confer with Dinwiddie and correspond with other colonial governors. Throughout March, the troop transports straggled into anchor off Hampton Roads, Virginia. No French warships had tried to impede the British flotilla's passage.

Versailles, meanwhile, had dispatched its own general and troops to North America. Those reinforcements were not so lucky in getting there. For North America's defense, Versailles could spare only six of its 395 battalions. In January the 3,000 troops of those six battalions—La Reine, Bearn, Artois, Bourgogne, Guyenne, and Languedoc—gathered at Brest and Rochefort. The Artois and Bourgogne battalions were sent to Louisbourg and the other four to Quebec.

Sailing with the fleet was New France's new governor-general, Pierre-

Francois de Rigaud de Vaudreuil de Cavagnal, Marquis de Vaudreuil, who would serve as governor from June 23, 1755 when he arrived until September 8, 1760 when he surrendered New France. Vaudreuil was born in Quebec in 1698, the son of the man who was Canada's governor from 1703 to 1725. In 1733, he was named governor of Trois-Rivieres. In 1742, he was appointed Louisiana's governor, a post he held with distinction until 1753. King Louis XV named him governor of New France on January 1, 1755, following a brief sojourn at Versailles. Vaudreuil would be Canada's only native-born governor. Although he was commander in chief of Canada's military, Vaudreuil had no military experience. At most, he had once accompanied a bloodless campaign against the Fox Indians in 1728. Bougainville, who came to know intimately Vaudreuil's foibles during his four years in New France, described him as "a timid man . . . who neither knows how to make a resolution nor to keep one once made."[6]

To command his North American army, on March 1, King Louis XV chose Marechal de Camp (major general) Jean-Armand, Baron de Dieskau. The German had proven his bravery on numerous battles and was lieutenant colonel of the Bentheim Regiment, a German unit attached to the French army. Unfortunately, soon after arriving Dieskau aroused criticism by treating "the troops in the German manner. He was no longer willing to speak to common officers and only received representations from corps commanders whom he never consulted—a very great drawback in a small army. He listened only to the advice of Pean and Mercier. They alone were his eyes & ears and he no longer deferred to the opinions & feelings of M. de Vaudreuil who, being head of the colony & a native of it, necessarily had a more intimate knowledge of it than he did. The two officers in question [were] wholly inept except so far as their own interests were concerned. . . . M. Dieskau discovered the secret of displeasing the governor of the country and the troops."[7]

Responsibility for the war in North America was split between two ministries, the Marine and War, and their two respective commanders, Governor Vaudreuil and General Dieskau. While supreme commander, Vaudreuil also headed the Canadian troops or troups de la marine while Dieskau handled the regulars or troups de la terre. It was a system designed to appease bureaucratic jealousies rather than fight wars. Accompanying Vaudreuil and Dieskau was Andre Jean-Baptiste Doreil, the deputy commissary-general for New France.

The leaders and troops were conveyed to New France by a fleet of eighteen warships commanded by Admiral Dubois de La Motte. To squeeze in all those troops and supplies, La Motte had reluctantly ordered most of the cannons stripped from eleven of his ships. His fleet would be accompanied well into the Atlantic by nine other warships led by Admiral MacNemara. Although the combined fleet was supposed to sail on April 15, it remained at anchor until May 3. Five days after leaving France, La Motte signaled

MacNemara that they could separate. MacNemara sailed on to Lisbon while La Motte headed toward the St. Lawrence.

La Motte's fleet almost did not reach Quebec. From January 21, when the English Cabinet first received word of the French plans until the final decision on April 10, the leaders debated just how far to respond. On March 24, King George II did solicit and receive from Parliament additional funding for the military. Yet the question remained what, if anything, to do about the French reinforcements about to leave for Canada.

On April 10, the Cabinet agreed to dispatch Admiral Boscawen's naval squadron to "cruise off Louisbourg, with instructions to fall upon any French ships of war that shall be attempting to land troops in Nova Scotia or to go to Cape Breton, or through the St. Lawrence to Quebec . . . in Case any opposition shall be made . . . you will use the Means in your Power to take and destroy them."[8] On April 23, Boscawen sailed with eleven ships-of-the-line and one frigate to intercept the French convoy. Three weeks later, with similar instructions, Admiral Francis Holbourne followed with seven ships to join Boscawen.

Despite the British fleet's earlier start, Boscawen failed to intercept La Motte's fleet. However, on June 8, four warships from his fleet did catch up to three French ships—the *Alcide*, *Lys*, and the *Dauphin Royal*—which became separated from the others in a thick fog. Eight companies of regulars were crammed aboard the *Lys*, which mounted only 22 of its 62 guns, while nine companies crowded the *Dauphin Royal*, which had only 24 of its 74 guns. Only two companies were aboard the *Alcide*, whose 64 guns were ready for action.

The British took the French by a vicious trick. When the French captain of the *Alcide*, Hocquart, called out to the approaching British whether they were at peace or war, his British counterpart, Captain Howe, affirmed peace. But as his ship, the *Dunkirk*, drifted alongside the *Alcide*, Howe suddenly ordered his gunners to fire a broadside into the French ship, killing or wounding about 100 men. The sporadic return fire killed 7 and wounded 27 British sailors. As the other three British warships closed in with the *Dunkirk* for the kill, outgunned and battered, first the *Alcide* and then, after a chase and exchange of cannon fire, the *Lys*, struck their colors. The *Dauphin* escaped into the fog. The eight companies aboard the *Lys* and two on the *Alcide* would be sorely missed in the years ahead. Sixty-eight companies of regulars, however, along with the commanders did make it safely to New France aboard the other ships.[9]

When word reached Paris in July that Boscawen's fleet had attacked the French convoy, Versailles immediately called ambassadors Mirepoix and de Bussy home from London and Hanover, respectively. Despite the blatant attack on the high seas, France resisted declaring war on England. Versailles needed at least another year before it could ready fleets and alliances powerful enough to challenge England. To declare war now would mean watching helplessly as British warships emptied the seas of French merchant and naval vessels.

The British were no more eager to declare war. The naval victory complicated British diplomacy. In mid-July, when apprised of the victory, Newcastle's response was worried: "We have done either too little or too much."[10] Newcastle had hoped the massive show of strength along the frontier would deter the French from escalating the conflict into a general war. Instead, his coordinated offensives on four fronts precipitated the war that most in London and Paris wanted to avoid.

Ironically, Whitehall now had evidence that the French intentions were primarily defensive. Secret papers captured aboard the *Alcide* revealed French plans to harass the frontier with Indian raids while retaining the French regulars to defeat any British offensive.[11]

Although diplomatic relations were broken, neither the French nor the English would declare war on each other until nine months and thousands of lives later. Meanwhile, each side mobilized for what it hoped was a winning blow.

BRADDOCK

Braddock was but a few days in America before he began alienating virtually all of the colonial leaders and their constituents he had supposedly come to protect. Franklin later wrote that Braddock "was, I think, a brave man, and might probably have made a good figure in some European war. But he had too much self-confidence; too high an opinion of the validity of regular troops; too mean a one of both Americans and Indians."[12] Braddock's secretary, William Shirley, wrote that, "We have a general most judiciously chosen for being disqualified for the service he is employed in almost every respect. He may be brave for aught I know, and he is honest in pecuniary matters."[13] By one account, Braddock "was a Man of Sense and good nature'd too tho' Warm and a little uncooth in his manner—and Peevish—with all very indolent and seem'd glad for any body to take business off his hands, which may be one reason why he was so grossly imposed upon, by his favourite—who realy Dirrected every thing and may Justly be said to've Commanded the Expedition and the Army."[14] Washington wrote that Braddock "has lost all degree of patience, and . . . I fear, represents us in a light we little deserve; for instead of blaming the individuals as he ought, he charges all his disappointments to a public supineness, and looks upon the country . . . as void of both honor and honesty."[15] Pennsylvania Chief Justice William Allen described Braddock as "an improper man, of a mean Capacity, obstinate and self-sufficient, above taking advice, and laughed to scorn all such as represented to him that in our Wood Country war was to be carried on in a different manner from that in Europe."[16] In all, Whitehall would have been hard-pressed to find anyone else in the British army more inappropriate to command a North American campaign; it would have been easy, however, to appoint others just as incompetent—the British officer corps was filled with men as arrogant, ignorant, and closed-minded as Braddock.

His first salvo was against Pennsylvania. His quartermaster general, Sir John St. Clair, had, a week after arriving in America on January 7, written a letter to newly installed Governor Robert Morris asking him for the latest information on the war, and for 700 troops and appropriate supplies. In doing so, St. Clair merely repeated instructions that had been sent by Secretary of State Thomas Robinson and echoed by Governor Morris months earlier.[17] But Pennsylvania's assembly rejected any military appropriations. To St. Clair, Morris decried the "Infatuation and Obstinancy of the People I have to deal with, or at least their Representatives, that tho' their Country is invaded . . . I could not persuade them to act with vigour at this Juncture, or even to grant the Supplies expected by the Crown and recommended by the Secretary of State."[18] In fact, the assembly had voted for appropriations but Morris had vetoed them because they were tied to taxation of the proprietors' lands.

Braddock had arrived in America as eager to fight the Quakers as the French. Proprietor Thomas Penn had seen the war as a way to discredit the Quaker majority in the assembly. On November 7, 1754, he wrote Braddock, requesting a meeting before the latter sailed for America.[19] Eager for information about the colonies, Braddock agreed. In the meeting Penn painted a devastating portrait of Quaker duplicity and discouraged Braddock from trying to elicit aid from them. So when St. Clair angrily told Braddock of what Morris claimed was the Quaker refusal to grant appropriations, the general weighed into the dispute. In a February 28 letter to Morris, Braddock exploded in wrath against the "pusillanimous and improper Behavior in your Assembly, and to hear of Faction and Opposition where Liberty and Property are invaded, and an absolute Refusal to supply either Men, Money, or Provisions for their own Defense while they furnish the Enemy with Provisions." [20] Braddock actually threatened to "repair by unpleasant Methods" or quarter his troops on the inhabitants if they failed to send aid. Although Braddock would not live long enough to realize that threat, his successors would.

Morris promised to do what he could while continuing to blame the Quakers for the refusal to supply the British army. To Braddock, Morris all but accused Pennsylvania's assembly and population of treason: "The conduct . . . has been so very absurd that they have suffered the French to take quiet Possession of the most advantageous Places. . . . I am heartily sorry that a Province that I have the Honor to preside over should behave in so shocking a manner."[21] Perhaps hoping that Braddock's threat to send troops might intimidate his bulky assembly, he grossly exaggerated the colony's population and wealth to make the failure to send aid seem all the more miserly. At one point, Morris claimed that Pennsylvania had a population of 302,000 which could support an army of 100,000 soldiers, while 500 ships annually cleared Philadelphia's port. The actual figures were about half of that. Nor did Morris limit his criticism to Pennsylvanians. He blasted all the colonies for failing to mobilize enough troops and supplies for the war, and for turning a blind eye to the smuggling that strengthened the enemy.

Morris convened the assembly and read them Braddock's letter. The representatives were appalled by Braddock's insulting and threatening tone. Yet, under Franklin's guidance, the assembly eventually voted a 25,000-pound appropriation in military supplies. Although the amount was less than the 40,000 Franklin had proposed, it was far better than nothing. Morris promptly vetoed the appropriation, asserting that it would be all or nothing.

Franklin appealed to Governor Shirley for help in pressuring Morris to cooperate with the assembly. Shirley sent his own request to the Pennsylvania Assembly for contributions to his Fort Frederic campaign. The assembly voted Shirley 10,000 pounds. Morris vetoed that measure as well. In a series of letters to all concerned, Shirley's representative to Pennsylvania, Josiah Quincy, praised the assembly and condemned Morris.[22]

Franklin found a way to circumvent Morris. He talked the assembly into borrowing 15,000 pounds from the Loan Office, which it directly controlled. The Loan Office did not have that much money on hand, and had to issue bills of credit to raise the amount. Of the total, it forwarded 10,000 to Shirley and 5,000 to Braddock. Morris still had one more transparent trick up his sleeve. Rather than include it in the council minutes, he pocketed a letter from Shirley lauding the assembly's appropriation. The assembly found out about the letter, surreptitiously obtained a copy, and printed it along with a letter thanking Shirley.

Morris tried to get in the last word. In a letter to the Secretary of State, Sir Thomas Robinson, Morris viciously denounced "such Powers in the Hands of any Assembly, and especially of one annually chosen by a People, a great Part, if not a Majority of whom are Foreigners, unattached to an English Government, either by Birth or Education."[23] Two decades later, Americans would rise in revolt against such attitudes.

While Braddock jousted with various colonial leaders and assemblies, he waited impatiently at Williamsburg for his army. The ships conveying his troops and supplies arrived at nearby Hampton Roads between March 2 and 18. On March 10, he sent out letters to governors Sharpe, Morris, De Lancey, and Shirley to meet him in Annapolis in April. He then sailed with his troops up the Chesapeake Bay to Alexandria. On April 3, accompanied by Dinwiddie, he journeyed to Annapolis for his meeting with the governors. Only Sharpe awaited him. A snowstorm further north had buried the roads and delayed the others' arrival. Braddock returned with Dinwiddie to his army at Alexandria, leaving Sharpe to await the three northern governors and escort them to his headquarters.

There, on April 14, 1755, Braddock met with governors Robert Dinwiddie of Virginia, Robert Morris of Pennsylvania, James De Lancey of New York, William Shirley of Massachusetts, and Horatio Sharpe of Maryland, along with postmaster general Benjamin Franklin, William Johnson, and Admiral Augustus Keppel, the commander of British naval forces in North America.[24] The general opened the meeting by submitting his instructions to establish a common fund to which each colony would contribute a quota assessed by London. Stunned by the demand, the governors politely rejected it, arguing that it was difficult enough to extract appropriations from their recalcitrant assemblies for their own military efforts; their assemblies would never contribute money to any fund beyond their control. It was Braddock's turn to be stunned. Heatedly, Braddock insisted that they contribute. The governors promised to do what they could but could not guarantee the results. Any money the assemblies granted would undoubtedly be appropriated for very special purposes, never into a common fund which Braddock could use as he saw fit.

The governors judged correctly. Of all the money the assemblies appropriated later that year, only one colony did not earmark it for its own troops and campaigns. South Carolina donated 4,000 pounds directly to Braddock. Ironically, Braddock had excluded South Carolina's governor James Glen from his Alexandria Council. Dinwiddie had insisted that Glen be snubbed because he discouraged southern Indians from heading north to fight with the middle colonies against the French and because of his harsh measures against Virginians trading with the Cherokee.[25]

Braddock's bullying demeanor and demands had offended nearly every governor. Jennings goes so far as to state, "At this point began in earnest the colonial resistance to imperial rule that would culminate eventually in its overthrow. The resistance was not the choice of the governors, imperialists to a man; rather, they were obliged reluctantly to confess themselves powerless to fulfill the crown's demand because of their awareness of the resistance among their own peoples."[26]

Setting aside the common fund dispute, the governors enthusiastically greeted Braddock's explanation of the four-pronged strategy devised by the Cabinet. They had independently developed a similar plan over the preceding fall and winter. After announcing that he would march against Fort Duquesne, Braddock appointed Shirley to head the Fort Niagara campaign, William Johnson for the Fort Frederic campaign, and Brigadier General Robert Monckton for the Fort Beausejour campaign.

Braddock then handed William Shirley the Crown's commission naming him second in command of British forces in North America and authorizing him to draw bills on the British Treasury for his expenses. The general agreed with the governors that Johnson should also be made Iroquois Superintendent to keep them in the British fold. The commission Braddock issued to Johnson granted him "sole Management & direction of the Affairs of the Six Nations of Indians & their Allies with full Power & Authority to treat & confer with them as often and upon such matters as you shall judge necessary."[27] Accompanying the commission was 800 pounds with which to buy gifts for the Indians. Braddock then dismissed the council. Each member returned to his respective colony to carry out his duty, accompanied by a matrix of hopes and worries.

Although Braddock's troops were encamped all around his headquarters, they were hardly ready to march on Fort Duquesne.[28] The task of mobilizing supplies and transport for the army deeply frustrated Quartermaster-General John St. Clair, as it would anyone entrusted with that thankless but essential duty. As late as May, after four fruitless months of cajoling bulky governors and assemblies, St. Clair had gathered at Wills Creek, which had been renamed Fort Cumberland, only a few horses, wagons, and supplies. St. Clair complained that "the Inhabitants are totally ignorant of Military Affairs: Their Sloth & Ignorance is not to be discribed; I wish General Braddock may be able to make them shake it off."[29] When Braddock arrived with his two regiments at Fort Cumberland on May 10, he had little better luck. He bemoaned, "the difficulties and disappointments I have met with from the want of Honesty and Inclination to forward the Service in all Orders of people in these colonies."[30]

It was then that Ben Franklin came to the rescue. Franklin had attended the Alexandria Council because Braddock had requested a postal system to connect his army with the provincial capitals. Pennyslvania's assembly had dispatched Franklin, the American colonies' deputy postmaster general, to the council with a promise to help underwrite the entire system. Franklin accompanied Braddock to his next headquarters at Frederick, Maryland to help set up the postal system and ease the animosity that had boiled within Braddock and St. Clair over Pennyslvania's failure to contribute. In their daily meals together, Franklin used his wit and deft diplomacy for "removing all his prejudices, by the information of what the assembly had actually done before his arrival, and were still willing to do, to facilitate his operations."[31]

Franklin did more than explain the subtleties of Pennsylvania politics. When Braddock complained about his army's want of transport, Franklin maintained that Pennsylvania could supply to Braddock what Maryland and Virginia had refused. The general commissioned the postmaster to gather the necessary transport. Within days of arriving back in Philadelphia, Franklin had worked his charm on Quaker leaders Chief Justice William Allen and assemblyman James Wright, while distributing a broadside to the population to create support for lending transport to the army. The army would pay a driver, wagon, and four-horse team fifteen shillings a day and a horse with a pack-saddle two shillings a day, after they arrived at Fort Cumberland. But after this positive incentive in his broadside, Franklin warned that if Pennsylvania failed to provide enough transport within two weeks, Braddock would send troops to take them. Whatever their motivation for doing so, on May 20 teamsters led into Fort Cumberland 91 wagons. Franklin further endeared himself to Braddock and his officers by garnering and dispatching to them donations of brandy, wine, chocolate, cheese, coffee, tea, and other luxuries that filled eleven wagons. Unfortunately, while the officers nibbled and sipped, the over 600 horses gathered at Fort Cumberland weakened and died daily from want of forage. There was no grass; the teamsters had to feed the horses with leaves stripped from the trees.[32]

Franklin's intercession was vital to the campaign. St. Clair later wrote that "no magistrate in Virginia or I believe in Maryland gave themselves the least trouble to assist in collecting the Country people to work upon the Roads, and to provide us with Carriages: But on the Contrary every body laid themselves out to put what money they cou'd in their Pockets, without forwarding our Expedition. In this Situation we never cou'd have subsisted our little army at Wills Creek, far less carried on our Expedition had not General Braddock contracted with the People of Pennsylvania for a Number of Waggons."[33]

While Braddock eagerly took Franklin's supplies and transport, he rejected that sage's advise. Shortly before returning to Philadelphia, Franklin had warned the general that the "only danger I apprehend . . . to your march is from ambuscades of Indians, who by constant practice are dexterous in laying and executing them; and the slender line, near four miles long, which your army must make, may expose it to be attacked by surprise in its flanks, and to be like a thread into several pieces, which from their distance cannot come up in time to support each other." To this, Braddock arrogantly replied: "These savages may, indeed, be a formidable enemy to your raw American militia, but upon the King's regulars and disciplined troops, sir, it is impossible they should make any impression."[34] One wonders if Braddock recalled the exchange during his dying moments.

As his reply to Franklin made clear, Braddock was openly contemptuous of colonial soldiers and citizens alike. The general complained that he had assembled "about two thousand effectives, the greatest part Virginians, very indifferent Men, this Country affording no better; it has cost infinite pains and labour to bring them to any sort of Regularity and Discipline: Their officers are little better, and all complaining of the ill Usage of the Country, who employ'd them last Year without pay or provision."[35]

Braddock tried to alleviate these deficiencies by intermingling provincial and regular units. At Fort Cumberland on June 8, Braddock's army consisted of 2,233 men of whom 2,041 were fit for duty, including 685 men with Colonel Peter Halkett's 44th regiment, 645 men with Colonel Thomas Dunbar's 48th regiment, 317 from eight Virginia companies, 51 from Captain John Dagworthy's Maryland company, and 72 from Captain Brice Dobbs' North Carolina company, 82 men and 84 men from two New York independent companies commanded respectively by Captains John Rutherford and Horatio Gates, and 96 men from a South Carolina company commanded by Paul Demere. Braddock placed two Virginian and one Maryland company with Halkett's regiment while the rest of the provincial companies marched with Dunbar. Braddock also brought with him a large artillery train, including four 12-pounders, six 6-pounders, four 8-inch howitzers and fifteen cohorn motars, and nearly 200 wagons.[36]

Braddock's contempt for the provincials damaged their recruiting as well as their morale. He so grossly maligned the Virginia regiment that " 'no person of any property, family, or worth' had since enlisted in it." [37] One exception was George Washington who, after repeated requests by the general, finally agreed to serve as Braddock's aide. Washington would play a major role in the campaign, first in convincing Braddock to leave behind his wagons and march toward Fort Duquesne with a select body of infantry, and then helping extract the army from its bloody defeat on the Monongahela.

The campaign against Fort Duquesne would be unlikely to succeed without Indians as scouts and fighters. Almost everyone seemed to understand this except Braddock. His orders from London clearly spoke of the need for Indian allies, a warning echoed by all the colonial leaders. But Braddock rejected any advice from colonial or Indian leaders alike that conflicted with his belief that European-style tactics were suitable to America's wilderness.

Despite Braddock's disinterest, colonial leaders did what they could to gather Indians to his side. At the Alexandria Council, Dinwiddie had promised Braddock 400 Cherokee and Catawba warriors. His conflict with Glen, however, sealed off access by his agents to the southeastern tribes. In the end, Dinwiddie sent no Indians to Braddock's army. Johnson was a little more successful. Upon receiving his commission as Indian Agent, he sent word to George Croghan to join Braddock with the anti-French Mingo who had sought refuge at his farm at Aughwick near Carlisle, Pennsylvania.[38] In early May, Croghan, 50 warriors, and their families arrived at Braddock's camp.

Their arrival dismayed rather than pleased the general. Braddock found repulsive everything about the Indians—their appearance, demeanor, values, and tactics. As disgusting to that bachelor general were the liaisons between Indian women and his troops. When he ordered the Indian women to leave, they left accompanied by their men. Thus did Braddock blind himself tactically and strategically.

At some point after bidding the Mingo "good riddance," Braddock had second thoughts. He dispatched Croghan to rally the Delaware and Shawnee on the Ohio to his side. Mingo chief Tanaghrisson had died the previous October. Scarouady had taken his place, seconded by Delaware Chief Shingas. Those chiefs arrived with a mix of Delaware, Shawnee, and Mingo. When Shingas and the other elders pressed Braddock on the future of their lands, the general bluntly told them that not only were the lands English and would be settled, but that no Indians would be allowed to remain there.

Incensed, Shingas and the other chiefs replied that "if they might not have Liberty to Live on the Land they would not Fight for it. To which Genl Braddock answered that he did not need their Help and had no doubt of driving the French and their Indians away."[39]

Shingas and the other Indians dispersed, most to return to their villages, some to Fort Duquesne to help the French. That fall, Shingas himself would take the warpath against the British. Only Scarouady and seven other warriors accompanied Braddock to his death. Scarouady would later remark that Braddock "was a bad man when he was alive; he looked upon us as dogs, and would never hear anything what was said to him. We often endeavoured to advise him of the danger he was in with his Soldiers; but he never appeared pleased with us and that was the reason that a great many of our Warriors left him and would not be under his command."[40]

Braddock's confidence that he would capture Fort Duquesne without Indian help was not entirely fanciful. Stobo's spy report of the previous year and subsequent reports by Indian scouts had described Fort Duquesne's defenses as dilapidated and its garrison as understrength and demoralized. Strobo had advised taking the fort by ruse with Indians simply strolling in as they were normally allowed. That idea presented Braddock with a terrible dilemma; it at once offered him an easy victory and vindication of all those who trumpeted the vital need for Indian allies. Stobo's plan could not have been any more unorthodox by European standards. Braddock crumpled Stobo's plan in his mind. British regulars, not savages, would take Fort Duquesne.

On May 29, St. Clair led an advanced guard of 600 troops and axmen from Fort Cumberland onto the trail toward Fort Duquesne, along which they tediously chopped a narrow, stump-filled wagon road. It was not until June 10 that Halkett's regiment marched out, followed by the artillery and Dunbar's regiment.[41]

The army crawled less than three miles a day. Parkman paints a lyrical picture of Braddock's march: "The road was but twelve feet wide, and the line of march often extended four miles. It was like a thin, long party-colored snake, red, blue, and brown, trailing slowly through the depth of leaves, creeping around inaccessible heights, crawling over ridges, moving always in dampness and shadow, by rivulets and waterfalls, crags and chasms, gorges and shaggy steeps. In glimpses only, through jagged boughs and flickering leaves, did this wild primeval world reveal itself, with its dark green mountains, flecked with the morning mist, and its distant summits penciled in dreamy blue. The army passed the main Allegheny, Meadow Mountain, and Great Savage Mountain, and traversed the funeral pine-forest afterwards called the Shades of Death. No attempt was made to interrupt their march, though the commandant of Fort Duquesne had sent out parties for that purpose. A few French and Indians hovered about them, now and then scalping a straggler or inscribing filthy insults on trees; while others fell upon the border settlements which the advance of the troops had left defenseless. Here they were more successful, butchering about thirty persons, chiefly women and children."[42]

On June 18, the army encamped at Little Meadows, a mere 30 miles beyond Fort Cumberland. Here, at a council of war, Washington success-fully convinced Braddock to leave behind his wagons and most supplies and hurry to Fort Duquesne with picked troops supplied by pack-horse. His argument's linchpin was the latest Indian scout's report that 500 French troops were hurrying to Fort Duquesne. Braddock became determined to beat them there. He ordered Colonel Dunbar to command the teamsters and companies left to guard the supplies and wagons, while he pushed 1,600 men of his army forward. About 300 troops and axmen under Colonel Thomas Gage formed the advance guard.

As they neared Fort Duquesne, the troops and officers alike grew ever more hair-triggered. French Indians had killed and horribly mutilated a score of stragglers and pickets. Troops screamed and fired at shadows in the night. Braddock doubled the sentries and ordered his men to sleep on their arms. On July 5, French Indians killed three stragglers behind the advance guard. Spotting the enemy, Croghan and some Indian scouts dashed for-ward to overtake them. Shots broke out. The French Indians scattered. Vir-ginian troops rushed up and opened fire. A musket ball killed Scarouady's son. Now only Scarouady and six other Indian scouts remained and they threatened angrily to leave. Croghan urged Braddock to "cover the dead with gifts" to assuage Scarouady's mourning. For once, Braddock took an Indian expert's advice. Heavy with grief, Scarouady agreed to stay with the army.

Meanwhile, the French commander, Claude-Pierre Pecaudy de Contre-coeur, was having his own problems with Indians, most of whom were Ot-tawa and Potawatomi led by Charles Langlade, leavened by Ohio Indians rejected by Braddock and contingents of Abenaki, Caughnawaga Mohawk, Huron, and Mingo.[43] Contrecoeur had difficulty getting his Indians to take the warpath. Only after being showered with gifts would parties of Indians accompanied by Canadians slip out to harass Braddock's line of march, pick off stragglers, and bring back word on how far the British had advanced. While each British soldier lived in dread that the next hideous death would be his own, Contrecoeur complained that Braddock kept his troops "so constantly on guard, always marching in battle formation, that all the efforts that our detachments put forth against them are useless."[44]

As if the inability of Contrecoeur's Indians to kill large numbers of the enemy were not worrisome enough, Fort Duquesne's defenses were indeed as flimsy as spies had reported. The square fort had bastions at each corner and ten-foot-thick ramparts built of earth enclosed by logs with a twelve-foot palisade on top. Within the fort stood an officers quarters, barracks, storehouses, magazine, and guardhouse in various stages of completion.

There were, however, no bomb-proof casemates. Beyond the walls were ravelins, ditches, and glacis. The forest was cut back beyond musket shot. These defenses might defeat an infantry attack but would crumble under a sustained bombardment; that is, if Contrecoeur had enough troops to adequately man those defenses. By June 1755, the French had only 465 troops in the entire upper Ohio valley, including 258 at Fort Duquesne and 104 at Fort Le Boeuf, along with 102 at Fort Presque Isle.[45]

Well aware that Braddock's force outnumbered his own by three to one, Contrecoeur debated whether to stand and fight or burn the fort and retreat. That decision was made when Captain Daniel Hyacinthe Mary Lienard de Beaujeu arrived on July 7 to take command of the fort. Then 44 years old, Beaujeu was a veteran frontier officer, having commanded Forts Detroit and Niagara. Contrecoeur disputed Beaujeu's authority. Beaujeu agreed to remain temporarily subordinate if Contrecoeur allowed him to lead an attack on Braddock.

The following day, on July 8, a scouting party reported that Braddock's army was less than nine miles away. Beaujeu gathered the Indians and sang the war song. The Indians were split, with the Shawnee and Mingo eager to attack and the Potawatomi opposed, while the Ottawa, Huron, and others sat the fence. Beaujeu agreed to postpone the attack until the next morning. On July 9, Beaujeu again harangued the gathered Indians, chiding them for cowardice and insisting that they would win a great victory that day. An hour or so later, when Beaujeu strode from the fort, 637 Indian warriors accompanied his 36 officers and cadets, 72 regulars, and 146 marines.[46] Captain Jean-Daniel Dumas commanded the French troops while Charles Langlade led the Indians.

The sun burned down hotly under a sky void of cloud or wind. Along the forest path Braddock's troops stumbled along, sweating, straining, and cursing as they had daily for almost six weeks. But today the tension must have boiled within each man as the word passed that they were a mere half-day's march from Fort Duquesne. That morning, they had crossed the Monongahela twice, once above and once below where Turtle Creek flows from a gorge into the river. They did so to avoid a possible ambush in that gorge. At each ford Gage had deployed his troops to minimize the chance of ambush. To their relief, the handful of Indians lurking about the first ford fled and none appeared at the second ford. Having surmounted the worst possible battlegrounds without an attack, the troops must have pushed on to Fort Duquesne with renewed confidence.

Croghan, Scarouady, and the Indians scouted a hundred or so yards ahead of a small advanced guard of 20 men, followed by Gage's 300 troops. On either flank, 20-man patrols pushed through the woods. Trailing Gage's troops were St. Clair's axmen, the New York Independent Company, two cannon, and several supply wagons. A hundred or so yards behind them was the main body, led by Captain Robert Stewart's 29 horsemen. Braddock and his officers followed, and then Lieutenant Ralph Burton at the head of the 44th, the cattle, other cannon, and wagons, and finally Colonel Halkett commanding the rear guard of 400 American troops.

Shortly after one o'clock, one mile on the trail beyond the second ford, the scouts spotted Beaujeu's column and ran back to Gage's troops. Engineer Captain Harry Gordon stared past the scouts down the trail at a white man dressed like an Indian running toward him. The man was Beaujeu. When Beaujeu saw the British column, he turned and waved his hat. The French and Indians filed off to the left and right. Gage ordered his troops to form a line and open fire. A bullet from the third volley smashed through Beaujeu's skull, killing him instantly. Some Canadians panicked and fled. Dumas took command and rallied the remaining Indians and French regulars whose fire intensified. Rather than try to smash through the enemy or even stand firm, Gage ordered his men to withdraw back down the trail toward Braddock's main force. The retreat heartened the French and Indians who extended their lines around the British troops crowding the trail and shot down dozens in their crossfire.

Gage brought up his two cannon and had them fired through the forest. The cannon balls tore through the trees but probably hit no one. Gage then ordered some of his men to charge a hill on his right where the enemy fire was the most deadly. The British regulars advanced, but the thickets and enemy fire broke their ranks. Their panic spread to the rest of Gage's troops. Abandoning the cannon, they surged back through the woods until Gage rallied them a hundred yards down the trail.

A quarter mile behind Gage when the firing broke out, Braddock ordered Burton forward with 800 men and three 12-pounders. Braddock remained behind with Halkett and the troops guarding the wagon train. Burton's troops soon caught up to Gage's, and the two forces became entangled into a mob. As the firing intensified, Braddock and Washington rode forward to join the battle. Musket balls tore down hundreds of men. The Virginians broke ranks to shelter behind trees and fire at the French and Indians. Braddock and the other officers charged among the Virginians, swinging their swords flat against them to beat them back into line.

"Friendly fire" can occur in any battle, particularly when British regulars were massed among trees and ordered to fire volleys in different directions with no visible target. By one account of Braddock's defeat, "its the general opinion more were kill'd by our own Troops than by the Enemy."[47] Washington wrote bitterly that "Our poor Virginians behaved like men and died like soldiers; for I believe that out of 3 companies that were there that day, scarce 30 were left alive . . . the dastardly behavior of the English Soldiers . . . exposed all those who were inclin'd to do their duty to almost certain death. . . . It is supposed that we left 300 or more dead in the Field . . . and it is imagin'd (I believe with great justice too) that two-thirds . . . received their shots from our own cowardly dogs of Soldiers, who gathered themselves in a body contrary to orders 10 and 12 deep, would then level, Fire, & shoot down the Men before them."[48]

Many of these deaths occurred when Captain Thomas Waggoner led his Virginians against the knoll. Slaughtered by enemy and friendly fire, his troops broke and ran. Braddock ordered another charge against the hill, this time by Burton and his regulars. Burton pushed a hundred men into a broken line and led them forward. Dozens of men fell dead or wounded all around; others cowered trembling behind trees. A handful pushed forward through the undergrowth. A musket ball wounded Burton. He and those troops still on their feet retreated to the mob packed along the trail.

The battle had raged three hours. Hundreds of redcoats and colonials lay dead while the rest screamed in agony and terror or fired into the forest. Most officers, including the 44th regiment's Halkett, were dead or dying. Four or five horses had been killed beneath Braddock. The general finally ordered the remnants of his command to retreat. As the mob surged back down the path, a musket ball smashed through the general's arm, ribs, and into a lung. Braddock gasped out orders to make a stand behind the Monongahela but his officers could rally no more than a handful of troops. Braddock ordered Washington to ride to Dunbar and bring reinforcements and supplies.

The rout was unstoppable. The troops fled from a horrible scene of carnage and mayhem. British officers had made conspicuous targets as they strode and shouted up and down the broken ranks. Sixty-three of the 86 officers present were killed or wounded, along with 456 killed and 421 wounded among the 1,373 enlisted men. Although in the thick of battle, Washington escaped unscathed; musket balls had ripped through his clothes and killed two horses beneath him. In addition to destroying much of Braddock's army, the French captured four brass 12-pounders, four brass 6-pounders, four brass 8-inch howitzers, three "grenade mortars" (probably 42/5 inch cohorns), along with several hundred cattle and horses, and tons of supplies. The French paid little for their blood-drenched victory—the soldiers lost 28 killed and about the same wounded, and the Indians 11 killed and 29 wounded.[49]

Frenzied by the scalping and looting, the French and Indians did not pursue the British. That evening, the French dragged into Fort Duquesne Braddock's guns, ammunition, supplies, and livestock. They later transported the cannon to French forces on Lake Ontario where they would be used against the British at Fort Oswego. The French found among the captured loot Braddock's chest containing his secret papers, including Stobo's message. Fortunately for Stobo, the French were so elated over their victory that they did not execute him for espionage.

Another prisoner at the fort, James Smith, recalled that he "heard a number of scalp-hallos, and saw a company of Indians and French coming in. I observed that they had a great number of bloody scalps, grenadiers' caps, British canteens, bayonets, etc., with them. . . . Those that were coming in and those that had arrived kept a constant firing of small arms, and also the great guns in the fort, which were accompanied with the most hideous shouts and yells from all quarters, so that it appeared to me that the infernal regions had broke loose. About sundown I beheld a small party coming in with about a dozen prisoners stripped naked, with their hands tied behind their backs and their faces and parts of their bodies blacked; these prisoners they burned to death on the bank of the Allegheny River, opposite the fort. I stood on the fort wall until I beheld them begin to burn one of these men; they had him tied to a stake, and kept touching him with firebrands, redhot irons, etc., and he kept screaming in a most doleful manner, the Indians in the meantime yelling like infernal spirits."[50] In all, that night the Indians burned alive 12 of their 30 prisoners. With their bloodlust satiated, the Great Lake and Ohio valley warriors vanished over the next few days to their distant villages.

On July 13, 1755, Braddock died with the words, "Who would have thought it? We shall better know how to deal with them another time."[51] An anonymous eyewitness offered perhaps the best epitaph when he reported that Braddock "behaved with a great deal of Personal Courage . . . but that's all that Can be said . . . [he] Continued to give orders 'till he expired."[52] Washington offered this balanced assessment: "Thus died a man whose good and bad qualities were intimately blended. He was brave even to a fault, and in regular service would have done honor to his profession. His attachments were warm, his enmities were strong, and, having no disguise about him, both appeared in full force."[53]

Braddock "was buried on the high road, that the Army might march over, to deface any marks of a Grave."[54] Many soldiers must have felt a grim satisfaction at trampling the grave of the arrogant, ignorant man who had led them into a blood-soaked debacle. Whatever their feelings about Braddock, the officers certainly feared later learning that the Indians had dug up and scalped the general's corpse.

Braddock's defeat was largely his own fault. Had Braddock and his officers made several different choices, the campaign might have been a British triumph rather than disaster. If Braddock had marched westward across Pennsylvania, whose settlements stretched closer to Fort Duquesne, he might have gotten to the forks earlier when fewer Indians had joined the French. Presumably, Washington would have convinced Braddock to leave behind his wagon train and advance quickly on the Pennsylvania route just as he had on the historic route.

Even more serious was Braddock's rejection of Indian allies and wilderness tactics. He insulted the Indians with his arrogance and miserliness, driving many of them into the arms of the French. Those same Indians would gleefully butcher redcoats on the Monongahela. Croghan later argued that "if we had fifty Indians instead of Eight . . . we might in a great measure have prevented the Surprise that Day of our unhappy Defeat."[55]

In the forest numbers are far less important than tactics. Although the British had twice the men of the French, those massed redcoats proved to be nothing more than a huge target for French and Indian muskets. British officers actually used their swords to swat the Americans back into ranks when they took cover and aimed at the enemy.

Of course, even if Braddock had chosen the shorter route, befriended rather than insulted potential Indian allies, and dispersed his men behind cover when the fighting broke out (improbable at best given his rigid character), the French and Indians might still have caught Braddock in a bloody crossfire en route to Fort Duquense, which raises another possibility.

What if Gage had been as careful guarding his advance toward Fort Duquesne as he had covering his two crossings of the Monongahela? If Braddock blundered strategically, Gage did so tactically. Earlier that day he had skillfully deployed his troops at the two fords to guard against ambush. That success and lack of Indian sign made him complacent, overconfident. Beyond the second ford he failed to secure a knoll shadowing the trail that his troops would march along. After firing broke out, the French and Indians would swiftly take and use that knoll to murderous effect. Following the first exchange of musket shots a precious minute or two passed when the battle could have gone either way—the Canadians fled, the Indians and British hesitated. A succession of British volleys from that knoll might not have hit anything human but could have spooked the Indians into retreating.

Maybe. On the other hand, even if Gage had secured the knoll, the British would more probably still have suffered a bloodbath. The Indians and French deployed all around the British troops and decimated them. Even without enjoying the knoll's advantage, they would have still maintained that murderous crossfire. But the British were their own worst enemy; as many redcoats apparently died from "friendly" fire as from enemy fire.

The command fell on the shoulders of Colonel Thomas Dunbar. The colonel tried to impose order, but the defeat had shattered the army's morale and discipline. Dunbar was as eager to flee the wilderness as most of his officers and men. Throughout the campaign, he had complained of ill health and asked to be sent home. Now was his chance to scurry away to safety. He ordered the men to carry what supplies they could and destroy the remainder. Flames consumed a huge mountain of supplies and 150 wagons; dozens of gunpowder barrels and 1,500 artillery shells were smashed and dumped into streams. The dead and some wounded were abandoned: "the road was full of Dead and . . . dieing who with fatique or Wounds Could move on no further; but lay down to die."[56] Then the army fled to Fort Cumberland 60 miles away, arriving there on July 22.

The rout disgusted some officers: "Scandalous the action was, more Scandalous was the base and hurried retreat with the immense destruction and expense to the Nation—what was lost in the Action with what was destroy'd afterwards by ourselves, amounted . . . to near three hundred thousand pounds value besides the loss of Blood. . . . In nine days from the time we Retreated . . . we arrived at Wills Creek where we now are but Col. Dunbar soon proposes to move to Philadelphia with the King's Troops 'till he receives orders from England. Pity it was that . . . of destroying the valuable stores & provisions & makeing a shameful flight—notwithstanding their was not one Indian or french man in pursuite—did not determine on building a stockade . . . in which Case it would have Secured our Fronteers—and been a Cheque on the Enemy our being so far advanced in the Country; we destroy'd provisions enough, which, without any supply would have lasted us all, these six months."[57]

The defeat at the Monongahela crushed the British army's morale. Though the British troops still outnumbered the French forces at Fort Duquesne by 1,000 men, they and their officers had no stomach to fight. That Colonel Dunbar did not attempt to march again on Fort Duquesne is understandable. What he did, however, is inexplicable. On August 2, Dunbar ordered his 1,516 regulars to march from Fort Cumberland toward Philadelphia, leaving behind his heavy cannon, a melange of 160 provincials, supplies, and wounded, and leaving the Virginia and Maryland frontiers to the whims of fate.

Dunbar's action was scorned then and has been ever since. With a mixture of contempt and black humor, Franklin recollected that Colonel Dunbar "was requested to afford some protection to the inhabitants; but he continu'd his hasty march thro' all the country, not thinking himself safe till he arriv'd in Philadelphia, where the inhabitants could protect him."[58] In a long letter to Dunbar, Dinwiddie presented an in-depth argument for trying another campaign against Fort Duquesne later that summer; the governor's reaction when he learned of the colonel's flight was scathing: "he was to march to Phila'a for Winter q'rs . . . in the Middle of Summer . . . [leaving] the road to the Ohio open to facilitate the Invas'n of the Enemy, and left our Frontiers to be guarded by 400 Sick and wounded . . . he appears to have determin'd to leave our Frontiers as defenseless as possible. . . . I must confess the whole Conduct of Colo. Dunbar appears to me monstrous."[59]

The colonists feared more than Indian raiding parties. The news of the French victory spread through the slave cabins throughout the colonies, igniting hopes that a French army would soon appear to liberate them. The ever-present fear of a slave revolt reached panic levels, particularly in Virginia. Dinwiddie wrote Halifax that Virginia's defense was inhibited by fear of a revolt by "Negro Slaves, who have been very audacious on the Defeat on the Ohio. These poor Creatures imagine the French will give them their Freedom. We have too many here, but I hope we shall be able to defeat the Designs of our Enemies and keep these Slaves in proper Subject."[60]

FORT BEAUSEJOUR

Set atop a ridge, Fort Beausejour was a pentagon-shaped earth fort with brick casemates and stone barracks, garrisoned by 160 regular troops. Twenty-four cannon of various sizes and one mortar were mounted on the walls. Boscawen's victory had cut off Fort Beausejour from any hope of receiving reinforcements. Word of the sea battle plummeted morale among the defenders. From Fort Beausejour's ramparts, as the defenders ruminated on their fate, they could at least enjoy a spectacular panorama of the surrounding marshes, fields, and villages, the Bay of Fundy to the southwest, and British Fort Lawrence on a ridge four miles distant to the southeast. In the valley between the two forts meandered the Missaquash River.

Commanding Fort Beausejour was Captain Louis DePont Duchambon de Vergor. Vergor was a model of familial if not military stoicism; he got the position because his wife was one of Intendant Bigot's mistresses. If Vergor had any question about his priority in commanding the fort, Bigot dispelled them: "Profit by your place, my dear Vergot; clip and cut—you are free to do as you please—so that you can come soon to join me in France and buy an estate near me."[61]

As if having a leech for its commander were not debilitating enough to its defense, Fort Beausejour also had an English spy. Although born in France, Thomas Pichon seems to have favored the nation of his English mother. As the fort's commissary, Pichon probably knew as much about the Beausejour's strengths and weaknesses as the commander himself. Starting in September 1754, Pichon began sending to Fort Lawrence's commander, Captain George Scott, vital information on Fort Beausejour's defense, morale, supplies, strategy, and troop dispositions, the Acadian population, and copies of military reports.

Governor Shirley had named John Winslow to gather and lead New England troops to join Lieutenant Colonel Robert Monckton's command in Nova Scotia. By April, Winslow had assembled about 2,000 men in Boston and divided them into two battalions, of which he commanded one and George Scott the other. Winslow contracted with a motley collection of 40 sloops, fishing boats, and schooners to transport his army to Nova Scotia. On May 26, the flotilla departed, protected by three frigates. It arrived safely at Annapolis Royal late the next day. After gathering supplies and allowing the men a debauch ashore, the fleet set sail again and arrived at the beach below Fort Lawrence on June 2. There Monckton, commander of British forces in Nova Scotia, extended his authority over Winslow's army.[62]

Learning of the New England army's arrival, Vergor sent word to Le Loutre to march the local militia and Micmac to his aid. He also dispatched a courier to Louisbourg to request reinforcements. About 1,200 Acadians eventually gathered on the slopes surrounding the fort. However, few of the militia had weapons or the will to fight, nor did Vergor have enough

rations to feed them all. Le Loutre selected around 300 to join Fort Beausejour and dispersed the rest. Vergor sent the Micmac on scouting and
sniping attacks around the British camp.

On June 4, Monckton marched the 2,000 New England troops and his
280 regulars toward Fort Beausejour. The French had destroyed the Pont-a-
Buot bridge and, unbeknownst to the British, had packed about 400 regulars, militia, and Micmac in a blockhouse and breastwork a couple of
hundred yards from the river. When Monckton's column reached the destroyed bridge, the French opened fire. Monckton brought up his three
cannon to bombard and eventually drive away the French. The British
quickly repaired the bridge and marched across and up the ridge where they
pitched camp and dug entrenchments several miles east of Fort Beausejour.
That night Vergor burned the church and village just outside the fort to
deny the British those potential strongpoints.

On June 12, Captain Scott led his battalion along the ridge and entrenched it a quarter mile from Fort Beausejour. Lieutenant Vannes marched
out with 180 men to attack Scott's troops but retreated when he realized
the enemy was superior in numbers. The French cannon opened fire on
Scott's men, but to little effect. On June 13, Winslow's battalion relieved
Scott's. During a heavy rain the following day, he opened fire on the fort
with two small mortars. A French cannon shot knocked out one of them.
Winslow ordered two more mortars brought up and the firing continued.

The French cause seemed increasingly hopeless. Later that day a courier
sneaked through the British lines with a letter from Fort Louisbourg. Vergor
could expect no help from them. Two days later, a shell tore through a
casemate roof and killed an officer, two enlisted men, and an English prisoner. Although French casualties now totaled only nine dead and seven
wounded, the deaths in what was thought to be an indestructible casement
destroyed morale among the militia. French artillery lieutenant Jacau de
Fiedmont reported that this "disaster increased the disorder which reigned
in the fort. The settlers went in a body to the Commandant to demand that
he should capitulate, saying that, if there were any opposition to the decision
. . . they would no longer respect the garrison, whose threats they did not
fear in the least, and would turn their arms against the officers and the
soldiers, and deliver the fort to the English."[63]

In the face of this mutiny, Vergor had little choice but to surrender. On
June 16, a white flag was raised and Vannes dispatched to the British lines
to ask for terms. Monckton promised that the defenders could march out
with honors of war but could not participate in the war for six months.
Those Acadians who took part in the defense would be pardoned. Vergor
agreed and signed the surrender document. Le Loutre escaped with many
of his followers.

That evening Scott marched in with a contingent and took formal possession of Fort Beausejour, which later was renamed Fort Cumberland. In all, Fort Beausejour's capture was not a great feat of British arms. The British outnumbered the French ten to one. It was, however, a minor triumph for colonial forces which made up 2,000 of the 2,200-man British army.

The British followed up their victory by scouring the region of French land and sea forces. Winslow sent a letter to the French commander of Fort Gaspereau twelve miles away, demanding its capitulation. The commander, Benjamin Rouer de Villeray, quickly complied. Winslow's troops marched into Fort Gaspereau the following day on June 17. On June 21, Captain Rous appeared with several companies of troops crammed aboard three British warships off French Fort St. Jean. The French set fire to their fort and retreated. Meanwhile, British warships and privateers ravaged French shipping and burned villages around Isle Royale. That year, the British took 24 French vessels in addition to the two 64-gun warships, the *Alcide* and the *Lys*, of La Motte's fleet earlier that spring.[64] On September 15, Le Loutre was finally captured when a British frigate overtook the French schooner upon which he had sought refuge. The impassioned priest and partisan leader, who had instigated the Micmac against the British since 1738, was sent to England where he remained in prison for the next eight years. Of the French positions in the region, only Louisbourg remained secure, although its garrison and civilian population suffered from an increasingly severe food shortage.

SHIRLEY VERSUS JOHNSON: ROUND ONE

At a glance, it may seem strange that Braddock assigned Johnson to take Fort Frederic and Shirley to take Oswego. After all, Niagara is far closer to Fort Johnson than Boston. The decision, however, involved the types of troops assigned each campaign rather than geography. Regular troops were deemed necessary for the distant Niagara campaign while provincial volunteers were sufficient for the much closer Fort Frederic campaign. Shirley naturally wanted to command the campaign which would employ troops he himself had raised.

At first, the two men cooperated. Shirley supported Johnson's dual role as Indian Superintendent and commander. Johnson, however, doubted his own military abilities. Ever since Shirley and the other leaders had first proposed that he lead the Fort Frederic campaign, Johnson had rejected the notion, arguing that he lacked the expertise to fulfill that role successfully. He only reluctantly accepted that command when Braddock joined the others at the Alexandria Council to agree that he was the best man to lead it. In the month following that decision, Johnson's doubts were reinforced by all the frustrations of trying to organize, supply, train, and march a colonial army toward Lake Champlain. In May, he admitted to Braddock that "I am truly sensible of my own Inability to be at the head of this undertaking & I am afraid I shall have but few with me to assist & strengthen my Incapacity."[65]

Despite his lingering doubts, once he got his major general's commission, co-signed by Governors Shirley and Lawrence, Johnson tried to be as independent as possible in the exercise of his new powers. To dilute the command over him with as many conflicting voices as possible, Johnson also got Governor De Lancey to issue him a New York general's commission.

After Shirley's initial enthusiastic endorsement of Johnson, the friendly relations between the two steadily decayed into eventually open animosity. Fouling relations between them was the use of Albany as the base for both campaigns. Each commander dispatched hundreds of axmen into the surrounding forests to fell trees with which to build hundreds of bateaux and wagons for their respective armies. They sent agents through the countryside to buy up as much food as possible to feed their men. In July, without any prior consultation, Shirley diverted the Jersey Blues from Johnson's command to his own.

But the biggest rivalry between Johnson and Shirley was over the loyalty of the Iroquois. Throughout the summer and fall, Shirley intruded on Johnson's duties as Indian Superintendent, denouncing him before the Mohawk and sending his own agents among them and the other Iroquois. The Iroquois had become the rope in a tug-of-war between Shirley and Johnson, and they resented it. Johnson inevitably won. But the struggle divided the Iroquois and inhibited many of their warriors from taking the warpath. It was Shirley's interference in Indian affairs more than anything else that infuriated Johnson.

As in any war with the French, the Iroquois were essential to any British plans. The Six Nations stretched between Fort Oswego and Albany. At the very least, their neutrality had to be preserved at all costs. Ideally, however, the League could be induced to war against the French posts at Forts Frederic, Niagara, and Presque Isle. Yet, the British would be lucky to enlist more than a handful for either campaign. The Iroquois were bitterly divided over whether to support the French or English. Most sat the fence hoping the white enemies would destroy each other. Only Mohawk Chief Hendrick and Oneida Chief Red Head continued to give Johnson and the English their undivided loyalty.

Upon receiving his Indian Superintendent commission, Johnson sent out runners to the Six Nations and other tribes for a council in June. Meanwhile, he dispatched to the Iroquois such skilled frontiersmen as John Butler, Thomas Butler, Jonathan Stevens, and Benjamin Stoddert who would serve as advisors, diplomats, and war leaders. He made Daniel Claus one of several interpreters and chose Peter Wraxall to be his secretary.

In contrast, Shirley had little experience with, understanding of, or compassion for Indians. His plan for employing them as auxiliaries revealed these shortcomings. He hoped to organize the Indians into companies of 100 each, commanded by captains, lieutenants, and ensigns, and subject to military discipline. Those who knew anything about Indians ridiculed the plan. In a June 19 letter to Shirley, Johnson warned against forming Indians into companies, arguing that it "is impossible that sort of regularity can be obtained amongst those People. . . . [T]heir officers must be Interpreters and take Care of them in all respects besides doing their duties as officers."[66]

From June 21 to July 9, Johnson presided over a Grand Council with the Iroquois at his home, Fort Johnson. Over 1,106 Indians had gathered there to feast, split 800 pounds worth of presents, and make long eloquent speeches. Among the Indians were 408 Mohawk, 103 Cayuga, 200 Oneida, 100 Onondaga, 67 Seneca, 64 Tuscarora, 130 Delaware, and several score from other tribes.[67]

Things seemed to be going well until Colonel John Henry Lydius appeared. Shirley had employed Lydius to recruit Indians for his Oswego campaign. The governor thought he had made a good choice. Lydius had spent years with the Iroquois, spoke the language, and had even been inducted into the Turtle Clan. But Shirley's choice was poor on two counts. Johnson complained that Lydius and his agents were "working with Money and by every Kind of Artifice to destroy my Influence, to overset the Measures agreed upon at our Meeting & to turn the Indians from the Crown Point to the Niagara Expedition."[68] Johnson became furious at Shirley's seeming disregard for his commission as sole Iroquois agent, and the delicate diplomacy in which he was engaged to get warriors from the Six Nations to march with any British offensive. Even if the entire League agreed to ally with the British, there were only so many Iroquois to go around. Johnson needed them for his own Fort Frederic campaign. As if this were not bad enough, Lydius had previously used his connections to buy the upper Susquehanna region from the Iroquois for a company of Connecticut land speculators. To do so, however, he paid off only a few prominent leaders and thus split the Iroquois into factions bitter over the deal. Shirley was unaware that most Iroquois reviled Lydius.

Although Mohawk Chief Hendrick was the senior Indian head man, he had Red Head speak for him. Red Head rose and bitterly denounced Lydius. To Johnson, Red Head complained, "Brother. You promised us that you would keep this fireplace clean from all filth and that no snake should come into this Council Room. That Man sitting there (pointing at Coll. Lydius) is a Devil, and has stole our Lands, he takes Indians slyly by the Blanket one at a time, and when they are drunk, puts some money in their Bosums, and perswades them to sign deeds for our lands upon the Susquehana which we will not ratify nor suffer to be settled by any means."[69] Johnson replied by apologizing for Lydius' presence and promising that all injustices would be reversed. The council returned to its central issue, mustering warriors for the warpath against the French.

On June 25, Johnson felt the time was right to inspire the Iroquois to join Braddock's campaign. The appeal failed. The Iroquois had no desire to fight alongside their ancient enemies, the Cherokee, whom Dinwiddie had promised to Braddock. Word arrived from the Mingo expelled from Braddock's camp that the general had no use for them. Even had large numbers of Iroquois been willing to go, it would have taken weeks for them to travel from the Mohawk River to Fort Cumberland. They would never have reached Braddock before July 9.

Nor were the Iroquois in any mood to join any campaign against the French. Johnson found "most of the leading Men in the upper Nations of this confederacy, had entered into engagements with the French, and would speedily have effected a general defection from us to them and joined the French against us, and I fear their example would have produced a total destruction of our interest amongst the confederate Nations."[70] Little more than 300 Indians, mostly Mohawk, eventually marched with Johnson.

The strains of serving simultaneously as Indian agent and army commander were weighing Johnson down. During the conference he wrote Governor De Lancey that "I am in private working with the Sachems & leading men from morning to night. The Fatique I have undergone has been too much for me. It still continues & I am scarce able to support it. I am distress'd Where to get victuals for such Numbers, they have destroyed every Green thing upon my Estate, & destroyed all my meadows. I must humour them at this critical juncture."[71]

As if alienating Johnson were not folly enough, Shirley compounded it by attacking the livelihood of New York governor De Lancey by trying to sever the trade between the Albany merchants and Montreal. Shirley's effort certainly made military sense. Among other goods the Albany merchants gave the French and their Indian allies were muskets, powder, and shot for the furs they brought in. The French and Indians in turn used many of those same munitions in raids against the New York and New England frontiers. Among the many New Yorkers enriching themselves from the smuggling was Governor De Lancey.

De Lancey and his faction dismissed the strategic rationale behind Shirley's attempts to stop the smuggling. Instead they saw Shirley's efforts as part of a stratagem to fulfill his ill-concealed ambition to be named governor of New York. If Shirley could weaken the wealth and prestige of the De Lancey machine, he could possibly induce London to recall that corrupt governor and put Shirley in his place.

Johnson himself had long competed with the De Lancey machine, and was not eager to associate too closely with New York's governor. Yet De Lancey could tip the colony's resources toward either campaign or even retain them. By July, Johnson had united with De Lancey against their common enemy Shirley. Neither heeded Shirley's demands for them to forward supplies, cannon, troops, and Indians to Fort Oswego.

Yet another prominent colonial leader whom Shirley had alienated was Thomas Pownall, previously his secretary and currently New Jersey's lieutenant-governor. Although Pownall had traveled with Shirley to Alexandria where the conference with Braddock took place, he had not been invited to actually join the meeting, an affront that had embittered the proud man. Pownall would later join with Johnson and De Lancey to bring down Shirley.

Shirley arrived at Albany on July 10, and met Johnson on July 15. The commander in chief criticized the Indian agent for critical references to Shirley that appeared in an account of the Indian conference and for hoarding all the Indians for his own campaign. Johnson apologized, then asked for funds and supplies for his own campaign, and commissions for his officers. Shirley agreed to appropriate Johnson another 1,654 pounds and issued the requested commissions.

The settlement appeased neither man. Shirley still smoldered over what he thought were Johnson's slights and attempts to hog all the Indian allies for himself. Meanwhile, Johnson's anger soared as Lydius continued to hover about, undercutting his authority and alienating the Indians. Throughout the summer, animosities between Shirley and Johnson would rise to a feverish intensity.

The news of Braddock's defeat scuttled any attempts to recruit Indians. De Lancey feared that the news destroyed "our Powers . . . to prevail on the Indians to join us, nay I very much fear their self-Preservation may influence the greatest part of them to join our Enemies against us."[72] De Lancey was right.

VAUDREUIL

Not having been in Canada for thirteen years, Vaudreuil settled eagerly into his new role. As someone born and raised in Canada, he saw New France as more than a mere square on a global chessboard. Canada was his home, and he sought to defend it with an enthusiasm and single-mindedness rarely displayed by his predecessors and the legions of French officers and soldiers who were temporarily billeted there.

Vaudreuil undoubtedly soon became aware that Bigot's machine was sapping what little wealth and vitality New France produced. Yet, while no evidence proves that Bigot snared Vaudreuil within his corruption web, the governor did nothing to stop it. Vaudreuil dared not confront the establishment. While he was Louisiana's governor, he had learned well the price paid by the virtuous. When he had tried to curb the excesses of that province's officials, his own career suffered. A relatively old man of 56 when he arrived as governor in New France, he desired nothing more than a secure, untroubled tenure.

Turning his back on the rot consuming Canada, Vaudreuil concentrated his efforts on winning the frontier war with the British. His primary objective was to eliminate a long-standing thorn in New France's side—British Fort Oswego on Lake Ontario. The capture of Fort Oswego would not only eliminate Britain's ability to disrupt Quebec's long, tenuous trade, military, supply, and communications line through the Great Lakes to its western-most outposts, but it would destroy any immediate possibility that the British could march against Fort Niagara. A French fort at Oswego would provide a springboard for future French offensives into the Mohawk River valley. If the French could take Fort Oswego in 1755, they could seriously consider an offensive against Albany the following year. Albany's capture would provide a base for attacking east throughout New England or south to the gates of New York City itself.[73]

Amidst this planning arrived news of Braddock's defeat. New France celebrated the decisive victory on the Monongahela with feasts, Te Deums, and church bells. France won a great propaganda as well as military victory on the Monongahela. Braddock's papers offered "the most authentic proof of extensive plans, for long the principal occupation of the court of Great Britain, to surprise this colony and invade it at a time when, on the faith of the most respectable treaties of peace, it should be safe from any insult."[74] Vaudreuil forwarded the papers to Paris where they were studied by the ministers and, after their publication in the *Mercure de France*, by the public.

Although Vaudreuil now held the plans for Britain's four-pronged offensive, he wanted the men and supplies to counter them. Fortuitously, French forces had broken Braddock's prong while Monckton's had captured most of Acadia. As for the remaining two, there was little he could do but encourage his field commanders to fight on. Vaudreuil understood that the Monongahela battle could have been just as devastating a defeat for France. The French could not count on other British commanders performing as ineptly as Braddock.

Braddock's captured plans prompted Vaudreuil to alter his strategy. With the defeat of one of the four-pronged attacks on Canada, he decided to blunt the most threatening of the remaining three. With the immediate British threat to Fort Duquesne eliminated, Vaudreuil ordered most of its defenders and the captured cannon to march to Fort Niagara. He then diverted those troops designated for the attack on Fort Oswego to concentrate at Fort St. Frederic under Jean-Armand Dieskau. Dieskau would then launch an offensive down Lake George and the Hudson to defeat Johnson. Vaudreuil explicitly ordered Dieskau to march "with the entire of his army without ever dividing his forces."[75] Fort Oswego's conquest could await 1756.

Finally, Vaudreuil launched that staple of warfare in North America, Indian raids. In a letter to his son, Vaudreuil explained their utility: "I apply myself particularly to sending parties of Indians into the English colonies. . . . Nothing is more calculated to disgust the people of those colonies and to make them desire the return of people . . . the English have lost one hundred men for our one."[76]

OSWEGO

Throughout the summer, unit after unit had traversed the 217 miles between Albany and Oswego. By early August, Shirley's 50th and Pepperell's 51st regiments and Colonel Peter Schulyer's 500-man New Jersey battalion, named the "Jersey Blues" after their uniforms, had arrived at Oswego. En route, the 50th rankled local sentiments when it pressed into service Mohawk valley men, including some of Johnson's tenants and two of his slaves.

On August 4, Shirley was at Wood Creek just days from Oswego when he received word of Braddock's defeat and the death of his eldest son William. As if that news were not crushing enough, with Braddock's death the entire command of Britain's forces in North America now fell upon Shirley's shoulders. Shirley adjusted the grand strategy to accommodate Braddock's defeat. He decided that it was more than ever essential to take Fort Niagara. If Fort Duquesne could not be taken by direct assault, Shirley reasoned that he could induce its surrender with a successful British offensive from Fort Oswego against the French supply lines on Lake Ontario. He dispatched Captain John Bradstreet to Fort Oswego to build up a fleet and troops strong enough to dominate Lake Ontario.[77]

Shirley feared the army already concentrated at Oswego was not strong enough to take Fort Niagara. On August 6, he sent orders to Dunbar in Philadelphia to march his regulars to Albany for winter quarters. He planned to use those troops for the next year's campaign against the French on either Lake Champlain or Lake Ontario. Upon learning of Shirley's decision, Dinwiddie protested and promised that he could raise as many as 500 men to supplement a march by Dunbar against Fort Duquesne. Shirley agreed and sent word to Dunbar to cooperate with the governors of Virginia, Maryland, and Pennsylvania if the colonel thought that was practical. Dunbar and his officers rejected any notion of another try at Fort Duquesne that year or any other. They continued their march to Albany, arriving on October 21, too late, of course, to contribute to Shirley's campaign.

Meanwhile, on Lake Ontario's shore, Bradstreet organized a shipbuilding industry among his shipwrights and axmen. By the summer's end, the flotilla would include two 40-foot, 20-ton galleys, each armed with a dozen swivels, and two 60-ton schooners, each with eight 4-pounders and 30 swivels. With this flotilla, Shirley planned "to cut off the Return of the French from their Forts on the Ohio as well as at Niagara this year as also from being supply'd with Provisions from Montreal, and so starving their Garrisons there this winter."[78] It was a sensible plan that Shirley would never be able to implement.

Shirley demanded an Indian contingent to march with him to Oswego, and eventually convinced a score of Stockbridge and Mohawk to accompany him. He arrived at Oswego on August 17. On September 3, Colonel James Mercer appeared with the artillery. On September 8, the last of the expected troops arrived. Shirley now commanded about 1,700 men. He was eager to take the offensive.

Though the army seemed formidable, sickness left many unable to hold a musket and had killed hundreds of others. Morale had plummeted among the troops when word of Braddock's defeat reached them. Desertions increased. Training was minimal. Many of the troops did not even know how to properly care for and fire their muskets. Against Shirley's army, the French had massed 1,500 men at Frontenac and 1,200 at Niagara. If Shirley attacked one, the French could easily sail down Lake Ontario and capture Oswego, thus cutting off his retreat. Shirley's son, John, shared his father's deepening pessimism. In a letter to Governor Morris, John lamented that the Crown's troops did not "have much to boast; some are insolent and ignorant, others capable but rather aiming at shewing their own Abilities than making a proper use of them. . . . I am greatly disgusted at seeing an Expedition . . . so ill concerted originally in England and so ill appointed, so improperly conducted since in America, and so much Fatigue and Expense incurred for a Purpose which . . . might better have been let alone . . . when We were at Alexandria I look'd upon [it] to be very great and promising, thro' Delays and Disappointments which might have been prevented grown cloudy and in Danger of ending in little or nothing."[79]

Shirley's officers, however, began to question whether an offensive against Fort Niagara was feasible that year. Reports of French strength and grumblings among his officers prompted Shirley to call a war council on September 18. There Shirley proposed scenarios for attacking Niagara or Frontenac. His officers rejected both plans, citing the heavy, persistent rains that had made travel treacherous on Lake Ontario. They agreed to wait until the weather cleared before they decided. On September 27, Shirley convened another council. The weather remained as bad as ever. The officers were united behind delaying the campaign until the following spring. The 50th and 51st regiments would winter at Oswego while the Jersey Blues returned to Albany.

Shirley reluctantly agreed. Deeply depressed, he returned to Albany bearing the loss of one son and impotent to take revenge. At Albany, Shirley's travails deepened—his son John died of dysentery in November.[80]

LAKE GEORGE

That summer, Johnson suffered his own gauntlet of obstacles as he tried to build an army and march it north against the French. To aid the novice commander, Braddock had sent him words of encouragement and the multitalented Captain William Eyre. Arriving at Albany on June 13, Eyre proved to be an invaluable assistant, serving Johnson as engineer, quartermaster, and chief of staff.[81]

Johnson and Eyre had their work cut out for them. New England contingents dribbled into Albany throughout the summer. At first, the recruits were mostly "well & in heigh spiritts for marching, but are unhapaly detained for want of our stores."[82] Most volunteers were attired in homespun clothing and carried muskets of varying calibers and qualities. Their morals were as varied, with profane characters of all walks of life rubbing shoulders with strict puritans. Training was rudimentary at best, and even then puzzled most recruits. One Massachusetts man was "greatly suprised . . . to think that I must stand still to be shot at."[83] The army was short of food, ammunition, medicine, tents, blankets, kettles, cannon, rum, and, above all, pay. The lack of sanitation caused hundreds of men to sicken, and scores to die. The wretched conditions inspired hundreds eventually to desert.

Johnson tried to impose order on the soldiers but they remained more an armed mob than an army. Each province's troops had their own supply system, and everything—munitions, kettles, food, medicine, draft animals, tents—was scarce. With his assembled horde, Johnson experienced the same frustrations felt by any commander of colonial troops: "The Officers of this Army with very few Exceptions are utter Strangers to Military Life and most of them in no Respect superior to the Men they are put over. They are like the heads and indeed are the heads of a Mob. The Men are raw Country Men. They were flattered with an easy & a speedy Conquest; All Arts were used to hide future Difficulties and Dangers from them. . . . Most of them came with nothing more than a Wastecoat, 2 Shirts and one Blanket, Their Tents ill made, not Weather Proof."[84] Johnson described his officers as mostly "low weak People, who have neither the ability nor Inclination to maintain a necessary Superiority, some of them I believe are sorry Fellows & rather join with than restrain their men. . . . The Indians are perpetually Drunk, their Insolence . . . give me not a Moments rest or leisure. What with the trouble I have with the Indians & that disorderly management there is among the Troops, I . . . have neither rest night nor day, nor a comfortable thinking hour to myself. Our Sick increase our Men Impatient to have the affair ended. . . . I would exert Authority but I cannot be sufficiently seconded."[85]

The soldiers not only drilled but prayed en masse daily, and for many it was difficult to decide which practice they disliked more. All the praying seems to have been no more effective in making the men better Christians than all the drilling did in making them better soldiers. The looser morality of some of the troops appalled the more rigid New England men. Colonel Ephraim Williams wrote that "We are a wicked profane army, more especially the New York troops & Road Island, nothing to be heard among a great part of them but the language of Hell."[86]

It was not only language to which Williams referred. The New York and

Rhode Island troops brought women of various occupations with them while the other New England troops went without. The disparity fueled tensions. The presence of hundreds of women in camp caused "immoralities of all kinds" against which Johnson promised to "use my utmost power to suppress & chastize."[87] Eventually, Johnson ordered all the women—virtuous and otherwise—to return to Albany.

Despite his attempts to impose order, Johnson was popular in the ranks who knew a soldier's soldier when serving under one. The army surgeon, Thomas Williams, wrote that Johnson "is a complete gentleman, & willing to oblige & please all men, familiar & free of access to the lowest Centinel, a gentleman of uncommon smart sense & even temper; Never yet saw him in a ruffle, or use any bad language—in short . . . he is almost universally beloved & esteemed by officers & soldiers . . . for coolness of head and warmness of heart."[88]

By mid-July, Johnson had over 2,600 men scattered in camps near Albany. At least one contingent had arrived with strings attached. Connecticut's assembly only sent troops after Shirley promised that Phineas Lyman of that province could be second in command. Lyman arrived at Albany on June 30. On July 17, Johnson ordered Lyman to advance up the Hudson, building a road along the way. Johnson then had each new company that arrived, equipped, trained, and then marched north to join Lyman. At the 14-mile "Great Carrying Place" between the Hudson River and Lac Sacrament, the troops built a stockade which their commander named after himself. Axmen began a road north toward Wood Creek.

On August 15, Johnson reached Fort Lyman around which over 3,500 armed men were encamped, including several scores of Indians. To avoid tragedies, Johnson distributed red strips of cloth to the Indians to wear as headbands and had the army use his Indian name, Warraghiyagey, as the password. Like all commanders, he at times wondered whether his Indian allies were worth all the trouble they caused. To Thomas Pownall, Johnson wrote that "tho I have at present not quite 60 Inds. with me, yet that tendious particularity which is their Character at all times, & their insatiable thirst of Rum takes up more of my time & gives me more constant Uneasiness, than all the affairs of the army would otherside do. Imagine that you see my Tent from Morning to night crowded with Indians, with officers &c. all impatient to be heard, each thinking his own affairs more important than the others. I am obliged to hear all . . . this is the real Picture tho but faintly drawn of my Life every day, wch I assure you renders it miserable & almost intollerable & tis in no ones power to relieve me."[89]

Scouts returning from Canada reported that Dieskau had gathered an army of 8,000 men at Fort Frederic and was preparing to advance on Albany. At an August 22 war council, Johnson and his officers agreed to abandon the Wood Creek route since that stream was easily blocked by low water and trees felled across it. Instead, the army would cut a road along the trail to Lac Sacrament and embark there against Fort Frederic. On August 26, Johnson led 2,000 troops and Indians toward Lac Sacrament, while Colonel Blanchard remained with 500 men to finish Fort Lyman. Upon reaching the lake on August 28, Johnson renamed it Lake George and ordered his men into a fortified camp on its south shore. The following day, 200 more Iroquois arrived in camp. As soon as enough boats were built, his 2,200 man army would be ready to head north toward Fort Frederic.[90]

Meanwhile, what were the French plans?[91] By August 20, Dieskau had massed all available troops at Fort Frederic. In all, Dieskau had about 3,500 men in his army, including 1,000 regulars from the Languedoc and La Reine battalions, 1,600 militia, and between 500 and 700 Indians. Legardeur de Saint-Pierre, the same man who had warned away Washington, commanded the Indians. Like all frontier commanders, Dieskau would be quickly exhausted from the expense and sensitivity necessary to retain his Indian allies: "They drive us crazy from morning to night. There is no end to their demands. They have already eaten five oxen and as many hogs, without counting the kegs of brandy they have drunk. In short, one needs the patience of an angel to get on with these devils; and yet one must always force himself to be pleased with them."[92]

On August 24, Dieskau reached a bold decision based on a careful analysis of his scouts' reports, maps of the region, and the ideas of his veteran commanders. Rather than wait for the enemy to besiege Fort Frederic, he chose to move down Lake Champlain and build a fort at the portage to Lake George. From this forward position, he could command either the Lake George or Wood Creek approaches to Lake Champlain and strike against the enemy, should the opportunity present itself.

That opportunity came. Dieskau rested his army at Fort Frederic several more days before setting sail and oar down Lake Champlain. On September 2, his army reached the portage from Lake Champlain to Lake George which the Indians called Ticonderoga and Dieskau renamed Carillon. There Dieskau set his troops to work building Fort Carillon.

On September 4, Indians brought in a prisoner who claimed that Johnson's army had retreated to Albany, leaving exposed the 500 men at Fort Lyman. After a short council with his officers, Dieskau decided "to leave the main body of the army where I was [Fort Carillon], and to take with me a picked force, march rapidly, and surprise Fort [Lyman] and capture the 500 men encamped without its walls."[93] Dieskau's 1,500 men with him now consisted of 216 grenadiers from the Lanquedoc and La Reine battalions, 684 militia, and over 600 Indians from various tribes. By September 5, Dieskau's force had paddled down Wood Creek and up South Bay. He disembarked his army, left 200 men to guard the boats, and marched through the woods with the rest toward Fort Lyman.

Johnson's Indian scouts served him well. On the morning of September 7, several strode in to report that "when we first set out from hence we went to South Bay where we spied the Tracts of two men wch we followed & came to the Tracts of three more wch we pursued & in Journey towards Evening (3 nights ago) we heard 6 Guns fired & we proceeded on our Journey till Night & in the morning the day before Yesterday we heard so many Guns fired that we could not count them, up wch we counselled together & thought this Army must be proceeding by way of Wood Creek, but upon going that way we found we were mistaken for there were no tracts that way, upon wch we turned back towards South Bay in our road found three large Roads made by a great Body of Men Yesterday wch we judge were marching towards the Carrying Place & we returned as quickly as possible."[94]

After conferring with his officers, Johnson asked for volunteers to warn Colonel Blanchard at Fort Lyman of the enemy's approach. One man, Jacob Adams, stepped forward. Adams was given a dispatch, hopped atop Johnson's horse, and cantered off. A half hour later, two Indians and two soldiers strode off toward Fort Lyman. Johnson ordered more scouts sent out and the camp guards doubled.

Adams was less than two miles from Fort Lyman when "he found himself in the midst of the French army & was called to stop, but he depending on the Swiftness of his horse thought he would force his way thro' but was fired at, knocked off the horse & the Dispatches found upon him."[95] Dieskau now learned that Johnson's entire force was only a dozen miles away. As he pondered what to do, twelve supply wagons from Fort Lyman soon appeared. The Indians overwhelmed them, capturing most of the teamsters. Several escaped to alert Fort Lyman. The second group of messengers from Johnson's camp heard gunfire up the road. The group split up, with two slipping around the French to warn Blanchard and the other two hurrying back to Johnson's army.

Dieskau convened a council of his officers and chiefs that lasted most of that afternoon and into the night. He and most officers preferred attacking the weaker Fort Lyman and thus cutting off Johnson's supplies and retreat. The Indians refused to do so and urged Dieskau instead to turn and attack Johnson's camp on Lake George. The French commander had little choice but to agree to the change in strategy.

Upon receiving word that the enemy had cut off the road to Fort Lyman, Johnson called his officers to council. The assumption was that the Indians were simply a large raiding party. The meeting broke up in indecision. Early the next morning, Johnson reconvened his council. Upon listening carefully to his officers' advice, Johnson decided to send 500 troops to South Bay and inland to cut off the enemy's retreat. Protesting the division of forces, Chief Hendrick argued that "if they are to be killed, they are too many, and if they are to fight, they are too few."[96] He picked up a stick and snapped it. Then, picking up a handful of sticks, he demonstrated that it could not be broken. Johnson and his officers got the point. The entire force would march toward Fort Lyman.

Around eight o'clock on September 8, Colonel Emphraim Williams set off up the road with his 500 Massachusetts troops, followed by Lieutenant Colonel Nathan Whiting's 500 Connecticut troops. Hendrick and his Mohawk accompanied Williams' troops. The lessons of Braddock's defeat had not been learned. Inexplicably, Williams failed to send out advanced or flanking guards.

Meanwhile, Dieskau was reluctantly marching his army toward Lake George. His regulars took the road while the Indians and militia flanked them through the thick woods 30 paces on either side. Three miles from Lake George, French Indian scouts brought in a prisoner who confessed that troops were marching toward them. Dieskau deployed his regulars across the road and mixed forces of militia and Indians on either side. His plan was to allow the British to advance on his regulars while he double-enveloped them with his Indians and militia. The terrain could not have been worse for European-style warfare but was perfect for an ambush: "On the Left of the Road, all along the line they had placed themselves in, they had the advantage of being covered with a thick growth of Brush and Trees, such as is common to swampy Land as this was; On the Right, they were all along defended, as with a Breastwork, by a continued Eminence, filled with Rocks and Trees, and Shrubs as high as a Man's Breast."[97]

At a critical moment, the Indians once again determined events. Indian loyalties sprang the trap. Spotting Mohawk with Williams' advanced guard, Dieskau's Iroquois called out a warning. While the French and British stood by nervously, their respective Iroquois allies tried to convince each other to defect or retreat. An Abenaki musket shot broke the impasse. Ragged volleys exploded followed by continuous gunfire. Dieskau's left flank poured musket balls into Williams' troops, cutting down scores of men. Many of Williams' men ran toward the high ground, hoping to shelter there. As they approached, the French and Indians rose from behind their rocks and shrubs to open fire. Bullets cut down Williams and Chief Hendrick. The survivors scrambled back through the woods to the road. Whiting's troops ran up and joined the fight, saving Williams' command from complete annihilation. Firing and then dashing from one tree and rock to the next, the remnants of the colonial troops retreated back to camp.

A lucky shot saved the Americans from being annihilated. When a bullet killed Saint-Pierre, the fighting spirit of the Indians under his command died with him. When the Canadians saw the Indians hold back, they too hesitated to press the assault. The Indians scattered across the battlefield, carving scalps from dead and wounded alike, bashing in the skulls of those still living, dragging prisoners to their feet, and gathering armfuls of enemy clothes, munitions, and weapons. Rather than continue the pursuit with just his regulars, Dieskau ordered his men to regroup before marching on. The delay saved the remnants of the fleeing provincial troops.

After hearing the firing break out, Johnson ordered his entire army of 1,600 men into a huge half-circle with each flank anchored on the lake. Lyman's Connecticut troops were in the line's center facing the road, while the Massachusetts troops of Colonels Pomeroy, Titcomb, and Ruggles massed on the left. Five hundred men were kept in reserve on the right where a swamp and ravine protected the camp. Wagons, barrels, logs, and bateaux were formed into barricades. Men with hatchets desperately tried to chop and drag away some of the undergrowth beyond camp. Three cannon were placed with their barrels trained on the road and another was pulled atop a hill within the camp.

The hastily assembled defense was nearly too late, as Peter Wraxall, Johnson's secretary, revealed: "Our people run into Camp with all the Marks of Horror & Fear in their Contenances, exagerating the Number of the Enemy, this infected the Troops in Camp. The Enemy were advancing, Our General harangued & did all in his Power to animate our People, I rode along the line Regiment to Regiment, decreased the Enemy's Numbers, promised them a cheap Victory if they behaved with Spirit, begun a Huzza which took, & they planted themselves at the Breast-Work just as the Enemy appeared in Sight. The Enemy had been obliged to halt upon some Disputes among their Indians, this happy Halt, in all Probability saved Us, or the French General would have continued his Pursuit, & I am afraid entered with the last of our flying Men, before our Troops recovered from their consternation. Great Numbers of our Men hid themselves during the Engagement, and many pretended sickness. . . . I believe about 1700 Men stood to their duty."[98]

The French and Indian advance guards crept up and began firing. By noon, all of Dieskau's troops were massed in the woods. With the camp's south side protected by a swamp, Dieskau could only attack its east and north ends. He ordered his Languedoc and La Reine grenadiers in the center and his Canadians on his right to advance. The grenadiers advanced six abreast and then, just beyond musket shot, fanned out into long lines. The Canadians and Indians crouched, fired, and slipped forward from one rock and tree to the next.

Captain Eyre, commanding the cannon, ordered them to concentrate their fire on the grenadiers. As the French marched closer, the massed muskets of the troops behind the barricade opened fire. Scores of French crumpled. Dieskau ordered his grenadiers to retreat. The lull in the firing disappeared as Dieskau ordered his Canadians and Indians on the right to attack again. A bullet slammed into Johnson's thigh; he was dragged back into one of the tents. Lyman took command. The French and Indians again retreated under the persistent fire.

Dieskau ordered a third attack, this time through the swamp and ravine on his left flank. Shortly after issuing the order, a bullet tore into Dieskau's thigh followed by another into his knee. The attack sputtered out. Canadians and Indians began drifting away. After Dieskau fell he handed over command to his aide, Pierre-Andre Gohin, Comte de Montreuil. Montreuil ordered the army to retreat. By now, it was about four o'clock in the afternoon. But the battle was not yet finished.

Fortuitously for the British, earlier that day, Colonel Blanchard had sent Captain William Maginnis at the head of 120 New Hampshire and 90 New York troops to march toward Lake George and determine the enemy's strength. What could have been a disaster contributed to the British victory. Shortly after Montreuil ordered a retreat, Maginnis' troops appeared in the French rear and opened fire. Meanwhile, seeing the enemy disappear into the woods, Lyman ordered his men to advance. The troops pushed forward, firing and yelling. Caught between two fires, the French and Indians broke and fled.

The troops of Lyman and Maginnis joyfully linked but did not pursue the enemy far. Wraxall explained that "a Pursuit might have been dangerous to Us. The Day was declining—The Rout of the Enemy not Certain—The Country all a Wood—our Men greatly fatigued, provided neither with Bayonets or Swords, undisciplined, & not very high spirited. These Reasons . . . induce me to think we had better be content with the fortunate Repulse we had given the Enemy, and before Night put every thing in Order and Security, for the Prisoners said they had 1000 Men more who were expected on their March to reinforce them."[99]

It was a bloodly victory for the British and defeat for the French. The British lost 120 killed, 80 wounded, and 62 missing, and their Indians 38 killed or missing and 12 wounded. Colonels Williams and Titcomb and Chief Hendrick were among the dead. Most British losses occurred at the ambush on the road. The French officially recorded 107 dead and 130 wounded. Most French losses came from the regulars who had stood and fought on the road in the morning and then charged the camp that afternoon. As was their custom, both the French and British Indians disappeared to their homes shortly after the battle.[100]

The most serious French loss was that of their leader, Dieskau, whom the American soldiers found "resting on a stump abandoned and destitute of succor. Feeling for his watch, to surrender it, one of our men suspecting him in search of a pistol, poured a charge through his hips; of which wound he is not yet recovered."[101] Having nearly killed him, the soldiers dragged Dieskau into camp before the Mohawk could mutilate him in revenge for Hendrick's death. Johnson ordered 50 men to guard him from the enraged Mohawk. Wraxall reported that Johnson treated Dieskau "with the utmost Humanity & Generous delicacy, had him laid on his own Bed, and tho' the Doctor attended to dress his wound, had all the French General's first looked at & dressed. The Baron de Dieskau from first to last behaved with

Magnanimity, with the most decent Composure, & with a frank Politeness, in short, the Philosopher, the Soldier, and the Gentleman shone conspicuous through his whole behavior."[102]

Ian Steele notes the ironies of the Battle of Lake George: "A frontier trader and adopted Mohawk chief, who had absolutely no conventional military experience, struggled to conduct his campaign like a regular officer. A European-trained French general, in North America for only three months, adopted Amerindian ambush techniques successfully. A veteran Mohawk warrior was among forty who died after failing to scout adequately. American volunteers and Mohawk defended a makeshift breastwork against attack by bayonet-wielding French regulars, rather than scattering to fight a guerrilla war in the woods. Dieskau, in defeat, had stopped Johnson's offensive."[103]

Johnson was now in a strategic position similar to that of the French after Braddock's defeat. He had routed an enemy advance, inflicted numerous casualties, captured important documents relating plans and numbers, and even held their commanding general captive. But, short of supplies, ammunition, men, and, above all, will, Johnson and Lyman decided not to follow up their victory with an advance on Forts Carillon and Frederic. In fact, Lyman, Wraxall, and Eyre all reported that they feared another French attack. In a September 10 letter to Shirley, Eyre reported that "the Enemy by all Accounts are very formidable, & I think it not improbable, they will . . . Visit soon; if they can seize and take our Work at the Carrying Place . . . it would cut off our retreat and Communications with Albany, and totally stop our Reinforcements and Provisions from Joining us."[104] On September 14, Johnson dispatched three Connecticut companies to reinforce Fort Lyman, which he renamed Fort Edward.

Learning of Johnson's victory, on September 19, Shirley sent him a letter that studiously avoided any congratulations but instead blistered him for not directly writing of the affair and not immediately advancing on Fort Carillon. Johnson replied that his army was incapable of moving and cited discipline and supply shortages. Supplies and reinforcements arrived over the next few weeks, swelling Johnson's army to over 3,600 men. Shirley again urged Johnson to advance. On September 22, Johnson and Lyman presided over a war council which rejected an offensive.[105]

Their decision was probably the best under the circumstances. The army could not advance on Fort Carillon by land or water. No road followed Lake George north to Fort Carillon, only an Indian path. Even if a level road had existed there were not enough draft animals to carry the army's supplies; nor were there boats to convey the army up Lake George. As for the army, only 1,800 of the 3,600 troops were fit for duty. None of them were regulars; all were unskilled volunteers with rapidly diminishing enthusiasm and health. The New England and New York troops squabbled and even fought. Desertions increased. Mutiny was muttered through the ranks.

Tents, food, clothing, and other necessities were rationed. The Indians drifted away; and, the fierce Adirondack winter was just around the corner.[106]

The supply problem was alleviated shortly after the new governor, Charles Hardy, arrived at New York on September 2. As a formal naval officer, Hardy was not only interested but experienced in military affairs. He reached Albany on September 20 and immediately organized wagon trains to convey supplies up the Hudson. At a September 29 meeting, Johnson swung Hardy to the view that an advance that year was impossible. Although Johnson agreed with the chorus opposed to an army campaign, he did urge launching a large-scale raid against the enemy before snow blanketed the region. On October 30, Johnson called a war council to propose sending a large raiding expedition by bateaux up Lake George to attack the French camp at the north bay. The council voted it down as too risky.

The army lay entrenched at Lake George throughout November, its ranks steadily withering from desertion and disease. There Captain Eyre designed and supervised the construction of a fort which Johnson named William Henry, after the king's grandson. Few troops would defend Fort William Henry that winter. A November 20 council among Shirley, Hardy, De Lancey, and lesser officers decided to withdraw and discharge all but 750 troops from Johnson's army, composed of contingents from each New England province and New York. Of those troops, about 430 would remain at Fort William Henry and 320 at Fort Lyman, recently renamed Fort Edward. The order was carried out, and those troops lucky enough to be discharged returned happily to their homes.

William Johnson was among those who left. He submitted his resignation on December 2 and returned to his home to concentrate on fulfilling his duties as Indian Superintendent and militia colonel. Arriving home, he renamed Mount Johnson Fort Johnson and sent runners to the tribes for a council. Shirley sent Johnson a new commission which eliminated his power of "sole management" over the Indians.[107] Shirley hoped that Johnson would reject the limited role, whereupon he would appoint Conrad Weiser in his place. Johnson received the new commission while he was holding an Indian council. He almost did resign in anger, but Governor Hardy convinced him to carry on. Instead, Johnson hurried down to New York City to confront Shirley.

THE FRONTIER AND NAVAL WAR

At Fort Duquesne, Contrecoeur withdrew to Fort Niagara, leaving Captain Dumas in charge. Dumas followed up the French victory by sending warbelts to all villages throughout the upper Ohio valley. The message was either to become a French ally or face devastation. The crushing French victory sparked debates at Indian Council fires along the Appalachian frontier. Those who had always favored the French now bolstered their arguments with the logic of being on the winning side or else risking French retaliation.

Indian war parties flocked to Fort Duquesne where Dumas liberally supplied them with munition and gifts before sending them against the English settlements. In midsummer, Dumas reported that he had "six or seven different war-parties in the field at once, always accompanied by Frenchmen. Thus far, we have lost only two officers and a few soldiers; but the Indian villages are full of prisoners of every age and sex. The enemy has lost far more since the battle than on the day of his defeat."[108]

Braddock's defeat enabled the French and Indians to punch back the frontier to the Blue Ridge Mountains in Virginia and the Allegheny Mountains in Pennsylvania. Thousands of settlers abandoned their homes and fled to the safety of tidewater settlements. In all, the French estimated that by the year's end Indian raids had "disposed of more than 700 people in the Provinces of Pennsylvania, Virginia, and Carolina, including those killed and taken prisoner."[109]

The English were largely impotent before these French and Indian raids. After Dunbar had fled to Philadelphia with his regulars, Washington remained to command the frontier's defense. On August 14, 1755, Dinwiddie commissioned Washington a "colonel of the Virginia regiment and commander-in-chief of all the forces now raised and to be raised for the defense of this his majesty's colony."[110] The House of Burgesses voted a 40,000-pound appropriation for a 1,000-man Virginia volunteer regiment, and 200 rangers in four companies.

Eventually, Washington gathered about 1,500 men around his headquarters at Winchester, but they were more a mob than an army. Discipline and training were virtually nonexistent. A steady stream of desertions offset any new recruits. Washington could do little to repel the Indian raids but scatter small detachments at towns across the frontiers, and dispatch patrols to gather intelligence. Washington wrote that daily "we have accounts of such cruelties and barbarities as are shocking to human nature. It is not possible to conceive the situation and danger of this miserable country. Such numbers of French and Indians are all around that no road is safe."[111]

At times it seemed the British fought each other more fiercely than the enemy. At Fort Cumberland, regular Captain John Dagworthy not only refused to take orders from either George Washington or Colonel Adam Stephen, but even tried to submit those two Virginians to his own orders. Dagworthy impounded supplies sent by Virginia's assembly to its own troops. Washington wrote Dinwiddie that he would resign if Dagworthy did not submit to him. Dinwiddie replied that he could do nothing. Maryland governor Sharpe backed Dagworthy. Washington received permission to journey to Boston and make his case directly to the commander in chief himself, William Shirley. After listening to the Virginian's arguments, Shirley wrote an order making Dagworthy a Maryland rather than regular captain, and sent orders to Sharpe to force Dagworthy to accept Washington's authority.

Meanwhile, Braddock's defeat had not intimidated all of the Ohio valley Indians into joining the French. While British officers dickered and their troops caroused or deserted, Scarouady led a delegation to an August council at Philadelphia. In his speech before Governor Morris, Scarouady indirectly criticized him and his government for failing to rally sympathetic tribes to the British side: "We let you know that our Cousins the Delawares, as well as our Brethren the Nanticokes, have assured me that they were never asked to go to war against the French in the late Expedition." He left unspoken the disastrous results for the British of that neglect. Scarouady and the others were willing to put that behind them, promising "in the strongest Terms that if their Brethren the English (especially those of Pennsylvania) will give them their Hatchet they would make use of it, and would join with their Uncles [the Six Nations] against the French. So we assure you by this belt of Wampum that we will gather all our Allies to assist the English in another Expedition. One word of Yours will bring the Delawares to join you."[112]

Morris failed to provide that word. He thanked Scarouady and the other representatives "for their generous offer of engaging in another Expedition if this Government will put the Hatchet into their hands," but then told them to delay any action until the Iroquois had decided. Morris had little choice. He could not promise the Indians something that the assembly probably would not provide. Yet his refusal's consequences were severe. Unable to obtain munitions and food from the English, the Indians could only turn to the French.

Quakers were not the only religious group to suffer suspicion and discrimination during the war. At that time, Catholics numbered only about 1 percent of Pennsylvania's population, included peoples of German, Irish, and English ancestry, and had no representatives in the assembly. Despite or perhaps because of their lack of power, they became pawns in the political struggle between the assembly and the proprietors. In July 1755, Conrad Weiser, a close ally of Penn and Smith, reported that Catholic settlers on the Susquehanna River were conspiring with the French and Indians. An assembly investigation found no basis for the charge. Jennings called the charge politically motivated, noting that it came from Conrad about the time Governor Morris was trying to get the assembly to approve a regular militia.[113]

In October 1755, a series of Indian raids devastated settlements in western Pennsylvania and the Susquehanna River valley. On October 16, Shingas led an attack on a settlement on Penn's Creek that killed thirteen and captured eleven settlers. An October 31 raid on Great Cove wiped out half the population. Nearly all the settlers beyond the Susquehanna had either fled or been killed.

The frontier settlements sent petitions to the assembly pleading for it to send them arms, munitions, and other supplies with which to better defend themselves. Morris used the reports of destruction and massacres to shame the Quaker-dominated assembly into appropriating the necessary funds for a militia and presents to the Indians. He presented a bill to the assembly that empowered the governor to appoint militia officers and use funds as he saw fit; pacifists would be excluded from service. The assembly voted down Morris' militia bill.

Franklin and Evan Morgan did succeed in mustering a majority in the assembly to approve 1,000 pounds for the "King's Use" which would go to the besieged settlers for munitions and food.[114] Unfortunately, the money was distributed through merchants who charged exhorbitant prices for the badly needed goods. The corruption gave Governor Morris and Thomas Penn ammunition for their fight against the assembly majority, charging them with both corruption and allocating that appropriation outside the proper channel through the governor's office.[115]

Morris stepped up his support for a regular "militia" whose finances and commissions he would control. The majority rejected his proposal. Although Franklin favored a militia, he opposed allowing the governor to control it. Following Franklin's lead, on November 25, the assembly voted for a volunteer militia whose finances and officers' commissions would be controlled by the assembly. It named Franklin the militia's colonel. Companies were formed across the colony and officers elected.

News of the massacre of the Moravians and Christian Indians at Gnadenhutten galvanized the assembly into appropriating 60,000 pounds for the war effort on November 27, but stipulated that it and not the governor would control its spending. The assembly authorized the building of four forts at strategic points along the frontier, including Forts Lyttleton, Shirley, Granville, and Castle.

Although Morris signed both bills, he condemned the assembly's power over the militia and spending bills. In London, Thomas Penn unsuccessfully lobbied Parliament, the Board of Trade, and the Privy Council for the militia's repeal. When Morris threatened to incorporate the militia as regular troops and ship them off to New York, the companies refused to be sent and even withheld the names of their officers.

Meanwhile, a trade rather than military war preoccupied the southern colonies. South Carolina governor Glen sought to retain the monopoly for his province's merchants with the Cherokee and Catawba, which ambitious traders from Virginia and North Carolina tried to enter. Glen threatened to confiscate the goods of any outsiders found trading in territory claimed by South Carolina. Glen also tried, ineptly, it turned out, to wean the Choctaw away from the French alliance. The southern frontier remained at peace, but tensions were bubbling among the tribes, especially the Cherokee, that eventually would explode over into war.[116]

That year, aside from Acadia, the only unqualified success for British arms was on the high seas. By October 1755, the British fleet had taken 110 French ships worth six million pounds as prizes.[117] Much of the rest of France's merchant and war fleet were anchored in safe harbors. Having accomplished one mission, Admiral Keppel received orders from Whitehall for another related problem—to stamp out the colonial smuggling with the enemy: "It having been represented to His Majesty, that an Illegal Correspondance and Trade is frequently carried on, between the French and King's Subjects in the several Colonies, You are to take all possible Measures to prevent the Continuance of such dangerous Practices, and more particularly to hinder the French from being supplied, on any Accout whatsoever, with Provisions, or Naval or Warlike Stores."[118] This mission would be far more difficult and politically if not militarily costly.

THE ACADIAN DIASPORA

By midsummer, the British now held most of inhabited Acadia, leaving Fort Louisbourg on Cape Breton more isolated than ever. But the British ruled over a sullen, armed enemy populace. Acadians had begun leaving well before the infamous explusion of 1755. Two thousand left in 1751 and another thousand the following year. When the war broke out, 8,850 Acadians remained split among six large parishes in Nova Scotia, while perhaps as many as 8,000 more were in New Brunswick. Although the French army and Le Loutre were gone, they left behind a legacy of inciting the Acadians to fight against the British. If a French fleet suddenly appeared in the Bay of Fundy, the British might well find themselves besieged from all sides.

The Acadians' eventual expulsion had been set in motion over eighteen months before it actually took place. On March 4, 1754, the Board of Trade drafted a letter to Nova Scotia governor Lawrence, denying the Acadians any right to their lands "but upon condition of taking the Oath of Allegiance absolute and unqualified with any Reservation whatever."[119] In October 1754, the Board asked Nova Scotia chief justice Jonathan Belcher to render an opinion on the questions of loyalty and property. Belcher ruled in favor of the Board's assertion that no Acadians had a right to the land he tilled unless he unconditionally declared himself a British subject.

Acadian security disappeared with the British conquest of all of Nova Scotia in June 1755. Shortly thereafter, Governor Lawrence began to take steps that would eventually result in the Acadian diaspora. On July 18, 1755, he expressed to the Board of Trade his determination "to bring the inhabitants to a compliance, or rid the province of such perfidious subjects."[120] In an August 11 reply, Secretary of State Sir Thomas Robinson expressed his concern that word of the expulsion might provoke an insurrection and called on Lawrence to allow the neutral Acadians to "remain in quiet possession of their settlements, under proper regulations."[121] The Board of Trade had previously responded ambiguously to Lawrence's explusion plan but essentially granted him permission to carry it out as justified by their treason and refusal to take an unqualified loyalty oath.[122]

Perhaps afraid that his plan would be rejected, Lawrence acted before receiving any response. On July 28, 1755, Nova Scotia's Provincial Council unanimously agreed Lawrence's plan to expel the Acadians and confiscate all their property that could not be carried away. On July 31, Lawrence wrote Monckton at Fort Cumberland, informing him of the council's decision and ordering him to have his commanders round up the Acadians. Transport ships were ordered to gather at Fort Cumberland, Grand Pre, Fort Edward, and Annapolis to embark the Acadians for exile to other British colonies. The Acadians would not be allowed to flee to Canada or other French territories for fear they would simply aid France's military effort.

Over the next month, detachments of soldiers marched through the countryside burning dwellings and herding the Acadians to Fort Edward, Fort Cumberland, Grand Pre, and Annapolis. On October 13, British ships crammed with 1,100 Acadians set sail to other British colonies. Over the next four months more than 4,000 other Acadians were expelled. Thereafter, as the British overran other areas of Acadia they deported the inhabitants. Between 1755 and 1762, 11,000 of 15,000 Acadians were expelled.[123] The money to transport the Acadians came from wealth confiscated from them. Few Acadians escaped imprisonment and eventual exile. Hundreds died of sickness and heartbreak whether hiding in the woods or crammed aboard ships.

The best account of the Acadian expulsion comes from John Winslow. On August 6, he first learned of the decision from Monckton. On August 15, Winslow left Fort Cumberland with 300 troops for Fort Edward. There he received orders from the council enpowering him: "If you find that fair means will not do with them, you must proceed by the most vigorous measures possible, not only in compelling them to embark, but in depriving those who shall escape of all means of shelter or support, by burning their houses and by destroying everything that may afford them the means of subsistence in the country."[124]

On August 19, Winslow arrived at Grand Pre on Minas Basin whereupon he reluctantly ordered all Acadian males of ten years and older to gather at Grand Pre on September 5, 1755. Four hundred and eighteen males did obey the summons that fateful day. Winslow posted troops around the Acadians. Then, with bitterly mixed emotions, he first explained that he was acting solely on the "King's instructions," then sadly admitted that the "duty I am now upon, though necessary, is very disagreeable to my natural make and temper, as I know it must be grevious to you. . . . But it is not my business to animadvert on the orders I have received; and therefore without hesitation I shall deliver you His Majesty's instructions and commands, which are that your lands and tenements and cattle and livestock of all kinds are forfeited to the Crown, with all your other effects, except money and household goods, and that you yourselves are to be removed from this province."[125] Upon pronouncing them the king's prisoners, he had them locked in the church. He did allow them to chose 20 among them to carry word of the order to all other Acadians.

In an October 19 letter to the Board of Trade, Lawrence explained the benefits that would follow the Acadians' expulsion. Loyalists would replace traitors. Hostile Indians would no longer receive provisions and intelligence from sympathetic inhabitants with which to raid British loyalists. The vast expense of maintaining Nova Scotia—between 1751 and 1758, the province imported 96,735 pounds worth of goods and exported only 550 pounds worth—would disappear as that province eventually became self-sufficient and prosperous.[126]

Lawrence's grand plan was imposed not only at expense of the Acadians but at that of the American colonies as well. To the anger of the Americans, the ships dumped the Acadians in ports along the Atlantic Coast. No one wanted bitter enemies in their midst. Southern colonies like South Carolina, Georgia, and Virginia, obsessed with the fear of slave revolt, forced the wretched exiles back to sea. Colonies from Maryland north grudgingly accepted the Acadians as indentured servants and dispersed them widely across the land, but kept them far from the frontier.[127]

SHIRLEY VERSUS JOHNSON: ROUND TWO

On December 12, Shirley convened a council of war in New York with Governors Hardy, Sharpe, Morris, and Thomas Fitch of Connecticut, and Colonels Dunbar and St. Clair. There Shirley unveiled his four-pronged strategy for 1756. Campaigns would be launched up Lake Champlain against Fort Carillon and Fort Frederic, across Lake Ontario against Fort Galette, Fort Frontenac, and then Fort Niagara, up Braddock's road against Fort Duquesne, and up the Kennebec River toward Quebec.

Unbeknownst to Shirley, by September 6 the Cabinet had agreed on a similar strategy that involved preliminary campaigns against Forts Frederic and Niagara, and from there on to Montreal, accompanied by yet another attempt to take Fort Duquesne. One thousand reinforcements would be sent across the Atlantic to Albany to refill the shattered ranks of the 44th and 48th regiments. London feared a French diversion from the Mississippi against the southern colonies, but felt that local troops would serve as an adequate defense.[128]

But while Shirley wanted to discuss strategy, his enemies sought to topple him. Over the previous year, Shirley's blunderings and arrogance had created a powerful coalition of enemies, including De Lancey, Hardy, Clinton, Morris, Johnson, Pownall, Dinwiddie, and Banyar. Throughout the summer and autumn, most of Shirley's enemies wrote harsh letters to various ministers in London detailing their charges of corruption and mismanagement by the governor and commander in chief. On September 3, Johnson wrote the Board of Trade a blistering complaint against Shirley, accusing him of undermining his military campaign and Indian diplomacy, and acting as "my inveterate Enemy . . . the whole weight of his power, his influence, his craft and abilities, will be exerted to blast my character . . . Gross falsehoods (such as he has already asserted, both in his speeches to the Indians and in his letters to me) artful misrepresentations—deliberate malice . . . worked up by his people . . . whose very livelihood depends upon inflaming him against me."[129] New York governor Charles Hardy's letter sizzled with rage and contempt for Shirley: "I never met his equal. . . . I fear he is no better than an artful Deceiver ready to advance anything in his Representations of Things as Facts, when he is perhaps more a Stranger to the Facts he asserts. . . . The scene of Confusion I left him in at Albany, is hardly to be Credited."[130]

As if such accusations were not bad enough, the interception of anonymous letters from someone in Pennsylvania to French Ambassador Mirepoix in London cast further doubts on Shirley's competence. The letters were from someone well-placed in colonial affairs. Of this affair, Fox wrote, "I don't suspect Shirley of Treachery, but I have no doubt of his having great Schemes, and that he Trusts the execution to Traitors, and that he ought not to stay in North America."[131]

In December 1756, the anti-Shirley cabal gathered in New York to resolve to drag Shirley down once and for all. Both sides sought a showdown in London. On Christmas day, Shirley dispatched his agents, Major John Rutherford and Captain Staats Morris, to London to present his case. Thomas Pownall set sail on February 8, 1756 to present the anti-Shirley side.

How valid were the charges against Shirley?[132] The assertion that Shirley stole Johnson's Indians from him was perhaps true but hardly an impeachable offense. Shirley was, after all, the commander in chief. He needed Indian allies for his campaign as much as Johnson did at Lake George. Shirley's agents did manage to cull a few Indians to their ranks. But the tug-of-war between Shirley and Johnson alienated far more Iroquois than it won for either side. Johnson vigorously denied Shirley's counter-charge that he had hoarded all the Indians for his own campaign. Johnson's case was severely damaged when one of his officers, Daniel Claus, admitted that he had discouraged the Indians from joining Shirley.[133]

Far more serious, however, were the charges that he had grossly enriched himself from public funds. Indeed, Shirley practiced the usually modest colonial corruption on a grand, almost French Canadian scale. He ran a vast political machine with branches not only throughout Massachusetts but all New England and New York, which liberally dispensed offices, licenses, and pardons to influential followers. The charges against Shirley came not just from "the prejudiced tales of his political enemies in Massachusetts and New York, but rather on the impartial and more damning indictment to be found in ledgers, returns, and accounts."[134]

Shirley would lose the power struggle with those against him. In June 1756, Shirley would receive a humiliating recall to London on corruption charges. Jennings writes that when "Johnson and his friends brought Shirley down, they knowingly toppled the most powerful man in British America, governor of one of the richest colonies and commander in chief over all."[135]

William Johnson's rise from frontier trader to military hero paralleled Shirley's fall, and was almost as controversial. After a year and a half of humiliating defeats, British officials and subjects everywhere were starved for any success. Monckton's conquest of Acadia was strategically important but hardly the stuff to ignite the popular imagination. Much more colorful was the bloody battle of Lake George in which the provincials fought three separate actions before finally routing the French and capturing their commander, Dieskau. Propagandists and wishful thinkers on both sides of the Atlantic transformed it into a brilliant victory and the British leader, William Johnson, into a dazzling hero.

Not everyone saw Johnson as a hero. By some accounts of the Lake George battle, Johnson skulked in his tent while Lyman conducted the defense. William Livingstone declared that "If any man obtained laurels without earning them, it was the fortunate general; who, by the splendid representations of his secretary, and the sovereign decree of his patron, is exalted into an eminent hero."[136] Even Johnson's friends could criticize his leadership, especially his tendency to try to conciliate everyone. New York Council Deputy Secretary Goldsbrow Banyar wrote Johnson that he was "certainly right to consult in all ocassions, but perhaps it had been better for the Common cause if you had been guided by Your own Judgement, or at least have try'd your authority early."[137] To his credit, Johnson himself admitted his shortcomings as a commander and gave Lyman full credit for his leadership.

Johnson's generalship aside, no one can deny him his skill at Indian diplomacy or bravery in battle. However, political patronage and the public need for a hero were perhaps even more important in elevating Johnson to stardom. Johnson had powerful patrons in London like Lord Halifax and the Pownalls, whom he served well. The king named Johnson a baronet and awarded him 5,000 pounds on November 27, 1755. The honors arrived with General Webb in June 1756.

CONSEQUENCES

The year brought limited victories and bitter defeats to the French and British alike. The British somewhat offset the bloody disaster on the Monongahela with the capture of the Chignecto Isthmus and Dieskau's defeat and capture on Lake George. Shirley's planned offensives against Frontenac and Niagara, however, lay stillborn. Much money there was spent with nothing gained but Oswego's fortification.

Mostly American men and English money supplied Britain's 1755 campaigns: "The four major operations involved some eleven thousand men, about ninety-four hundred of whom were either Americans recruited into British regiments, American volunteers, or Amerindians. Britain assumed all the costs of the two most expensive expeditions, those under Braddock and Shirley. Colonial assemblies paid all expenses connected with Johnson's expedition, but the British Parliament granted them a 'bounty and recompense' of 120,000 [pounds] in 1756. Robert Monckton's expedition, manned almost entirely by colonials, was entirely financed by Britain. In addition to paying expenses, the British paid the wages of six thousand of the eleven thousand soldiers in the field, and the costs of the naval fleets and convoys."[138]

The French could at best muster about half that number, although 3,000 of their men were well-trained regulars. The descrepancy in numbers of British and French troops was not terribly important. Defenders need fewer troops than attackers. Versailles underwrote nearly all the expenses of supplying and defending New France.

The British strategy for 1755 had very misplaced priorities. Ironically, of the year's four offensives, the British poured the most men and supplies into the least significant route to strike New France. Taking Fort Duquesne would have, at best, won a disputed territory. The choice to take Fort Duquesne makes political if not military sense. After all, the fighting had broken out over the control of the upper Ohio River valley whose drainage was claimed by both kingdoms. Formal war had not been declared. London could and did claim that Braddock's campaign was simply an attempt to remove French trespassers from British territory.

The battle of the Monongahela could have gone either way. After all, most of the Canadians fled at the first shots. Gage would have had plenty of time to deploy his men had he followed such standard precautions as sending scouts out a mile or so rather than several hundred yards before his advance guard and securing that ominous hill on his right flank. With a British victory on the Monongahela, most Indians would have deserted the French and Braddock would have easily taken Fort Duquesne and probably Forts Machault, Le Boeuf, and Presque Isle as well before the winter. The brush war would have ended with the British strategically placed for the official Seven Years' War that followed—or perhap even kept the French and British from crossing swords in it altogether. Braddock's army on Lake Ontario might have intimidated Versailles into not declaring war against Britain in May 1756 or thereafter, for fear of quickly losing all of New France.

The campaign against Forts Beausejour, Gaspereau, and St. Jean did remove thorns from Nova Scotia's side. Like the Fort Duquesne campaign, the thrust against the French forts on the Chignecto Isthmus made political sense. Britain claimed those lands under the Utrecht Treaty and thus could justify an attack as simply retaking its own land illegally occupied by the French. Yet, if Lawrence had chosen to simply stand firm on the Chignecto's east side, at worst the English settlers would have suffered bloody Indian and French raids as they had during King George's War.

The campaign against Fort Niagara made little more strategic sense. The Niagara campaign would have unrolled along a thin, vulnerable supply line from Albany up the Mohawk, over the Great Carrying Place, and down the Onondaga River to Oswego, and from there by a fleet of bateaux to the western end of Lake Ontario. Taking Fort Niagara would have been difficult enough; holding it tougher still. And after all that, the rewards of success would not have been decisive. True, one route between France's Great Lakes posts and Montreal would indeed have been severed. But the annual fur wealth brought down the Great Lakes could have simply been diverted to the Ottawa River route to Montreal, or even the Mississippi River and New Orleans. Likewise, the annual supply of gifts and trade goods to the Indians could have reached the Great Lakes by sending it up the Ottawa River or, if the St. Lawrence was blockaded, the Mississippi River route.

In 1755, the Hudson-Champlain-Richelieu corridor was the only available decisive route to victory. That corridor provided the shortest route for British forces to the heart of New France, or for French forces to the heart of the northern colonies. French forces defending Forts Frederic, Isle aux Noix, St. Jean, and Chambly would undoubtedly mount formidable resistance, and victory was certainly not guaranteed, even to the most skilled British commander. A British campaign up that corridor would demand vast supplies of bateaux, provisions, munitions, well-trained troops, and Indian allies, along with an able commander. But, of course, any campaign against the French anywhere in North America would demand the same.

The British had the capability to hold the line with minimal forces at either Fort Lyman or Fort Oswego, and launch a powerful offensive from the other. But they lacked enough strength to attack simultaneously on both fronts. Yet, that is exactly what they tried to do. The Albany-Montreal corridor strategically outweighed all others. The war could be won or lost by what happened in that region. The Lake Ontario campaign diverted essential men and supplies from Johnson's army. Had Shirley's troops and supplies been massed with Johnson's army, would it have taken Fort Frederic? The chance of success certainly would have increased, but was not guaranteed. After all, in 1758, Abercromby's army outnumbered Montcalm's four to one before Fort Carillon, yet suffered a devastating defeat.

The other dagger to New France's heart was, of course, to send a British fleet and army up the St. Lawrence to take first Quebec and then Montreal. This option was not available to the British in 1755. The fleet remained scattered and the army was undermanned. It would be another two years before the British fleet could muster enough warships and troop ships to launch such a campaign.

Yet another possibility should be considered. What course would history have taken if Boscawen had bagged the entire French fleet on June 8, an event that might well have happened had La Motte's other ships not escaped into a fog bank? Without 3,000 regular troops and that year's munition, food, and trade good supplies, New France would have had to remain strictly on the defensive. Only enough trade goods would have been on hand to entice hundreds rather than thousands of Indians to the warpath. And the French stigma of losing an army and fleet at sea might well have limited their Indian allies to scores rather than hundreds.

Yet, the word of Boscawen's victory would have arrived too late to the Monongahela—Braddock's army would have still been defeated. Likewise, Monckton's easy victories on the Chignecto Isthmus would have been un-altered while the presence of Forts Niagara and Frontenac would probably have still inhibited Shirley from marching against either one. The only significant change might have occurred on Lake Champlain. Without Dieskau and his regulars before him, Johnson's army, despite his late start, might well have reached and taken a weakly defended Fort Frederic. If that happened, the following year, a British army would have been well-placed to advance on Montreal. If that were combined with a British fleet blockading the St. Lawrence, Versailles might well have agreed to a treaty ceding the upper Ohio valley and all of Acadia to Britain.

Another interesting "what if" involves the Indians agreeing to Dieskau's plan for a surprise attack against Fort Lyman, thus cutting off Johnson's retreat from Lake George. Over 900 American troops had massed at Fort Lyman. Yet most lacked more than rudimentary discipline and training, and sat in an unfortified makeshift camp beyond the fort. Only one cannon had been mounted on Fort Lyman's walls. A surprise attack by Dieskau and his Indians might have routed that entire army and taken the fort. With luck his audacious plan could have bagged Johnson's entire army. From there, Dieskau could have marched uncontested into Albany, cutting off Shirley at Oswego. With Albany and the armies of Johnson and Shirley taken, London would have had to sue for peace.

Interesting as these scenarios are, neither a Boscawen nor a Dieskau victory would have drastically changed history's course. A limited war and peace in 1755 would not have prevented the Seven Years' War from engulfing Europe in 1756. A victory by Boscawen might have advanced while a Dieskau victory would have merely delayed the probably inevitable British conquest of New France. And, even if New France survived beyond 1763, it probably would not have lasted long after 1789. As for the Americans, the heavy British taxation, repression, and arrogance that provoked the 1776 Revolution might well have been delayed for another generation.

If the British stumbled or held the line on three of four fronts, how did the French perform? French corruption, incompetence, and neglect lost Acadia as much as British audacity. Vergor's venality epitomized the spoils system that exploited New France. Yet, a less greedy officer might not have held out any longer. Reinforcements from Louisbourg might have held the line or simply swelled the ranks of prisoners captured by the British.

The French, however, did prove superior in the complementary efforts of wilderness tactics and Indian diplomacy. Getting to the decisive battlefield with the decisive numbers of troops and supplies was, of course, only half the struggle. Proper tactics were as essential to victory as proper strategy. Although most Americans understood the nature of Indian warfare, their British overlords would never truly accommodate themselves to that reality. Reflecting on Braddock's defeat, Colonel Dunbar expressed the exasperation the British felt when fighting "an invisible enemy . . . this Manner of fighting confounded the people; they saw and heard fireing and the fatal consequences but few saw an Enemy."[139] During that battle, Braddock and his officers beat back into line those Americans who sheltered behind trees and fought Indian style.

The ability of European commanders to adapt to Indian-style wilderness warfare varied considerably from one commander to the next. Braddock failed to do so; Dieskau quickly grasped what was necessary. Ideally, the leap from one mode of warfare to the other should not have been that difficult for either man. Guerrilla warfare was actually quite common in Europe—both Braddock and Dieskau had confronted it. Psychology explains their different responses to warfare in North America. By all accounts, Braddock was a rigid, unimaginative, and authoritarian personality who contemptuously disdained most advice given him. In contrast, Dieskau listened carefully to his veteran bush-fighters like Legardeur de Saint-Pierre and Louis Legardeur de Repentigny, and incorporated their experience into his strategy. In the end, of course, their similarity exceeded their differences—both generals were defeated.

The failure of either side to win decisively meant that the war would continue. In 1756, however, the war's nature would be transformed from frontier struggle between France and Britain into a global struggle that would include a half dozen great powers and a host of minor allies. That conflagration and its results will be explored in this book's companion volume, *The First Global War: Britain, France, and the Imperial Struggle for North America, 1607–1755.*

NOTES

1. Theodore Calvin Pease, ed., *Anglo-French Boundary Disputes in the West, 1749–1763* (Springfield: Collections of the Illinois State Historical Library 27, French Series 2, 1936); Max Savelle, "Diplomatic Preliminaries of the Seven Years' War in America," *Canadian Historical Review* 20 (1939), 1–45; Lawrence Henry Gipson,

"A French Project for Victory Short of a Declaration of War," *Canadian Historical Review*, 26 (December 1945), 361–71.

2. Edmund Berkeley and Dorothy Smith Berkeley, *Dr. John Mitchell: The Man Who Made the Map of North America* (Chapel Hill: University of North Carolina Press, 1974), 176; Walter Klinefelter, *Lewis Evans and His Maps* (Philadelphia: American Philosophical Society, new ser. 61:7 [July 1971]), 49.

3. Quoted in Pease, *Anglo-French Boundary*, 223–24.

4. Ibid., 161–62.

5. Lee McCardell, *Ill-Starred General: Braddock of the Coldstream Guards* (1958) (reprint, Pittsburgh: University of Pennsylvania Press, 1986).

6. Edward P. Hamilton, *Adventure in the Wilderness: The American Journals of Louis Antoine de Bougainville, 1756–1760* (1964) (reprint, Norman: University of Oklahoma Press, 1990), 193.

7. Brian Leigh Dunnigan, ed., *Memoirs on the Late War in North America Between France and England by Captain Pierre Pouchot* (Youngstown, N.Y.: Old Niagara Association, 1994), 76; J. R. Turnbull, "Jean-Armand Dieskau," *Dictionary of Canadian Biography* (Toronto: University of Toronto Press, 1966–), 3:185–86.

8. Quoted in Lawrence Henry Gipson, *The Great War for Empire: The Years of Defeat, 1754–1757* (New York: Alfred A. Knopf, 1959), 6:103, 109.

9. Versailles Instructions to Vaudreuil, April 1, 1755, in E. B. O'Callaghan and Berthold Fernow, eds., *Documents Relative to the Colonial History of the State of New York* (hereafter cited as NYCD), 15 vols. (Albany, N.Y.: Weeds, Parsons, and Co., 1853–1887), 10:290–94.

10. Gipson, *Great War for Empire*, 6:107–17.

11. Vaudreuil to Machault, July 10, 1755, NYCD, 10:305–9.

12. Nathan G. Goodman, ed., *A Benjamin Franklin Reader* (New York: Thomas Y. Crowell, 1945), 173.

13. William Shirley the younger to Robert Morris, May 23, 1755, *Minutes of the Provincial Council of Pennsylvania* (hereafter known as Pa. *Council Minutes* (New York: AMS Press, 1968), 6:405.

14. Anonymous letter on Braddock's Campaign, July 25, 1755, in Stanley Pargellis, ed., *Military Affairs in North America, 1748–1765: Selected Documents from the Cumberland Papers in Windsor Castle* (New York: Archon Books, 1969), 119.

15. Washington to Fairfax, June 7, 1755, in John C. Fitzpartick, ed., *The Writings of George Washington*, 39 vols. (Washington, D.C.: U.S. Government Printing Office, 1931–1944), 1:133.

16. Allen to Barclays, July 21, 1755, in Lewis Burd Walker, ed., *The Burd Papers: Extract from Chief Justice William Allen's Letter Book . . . Together with an Appendix Containing Pamphlets in the Controversy with Franklin* (Pottsville, Pa.: Standard Publishing Company, 1897), 23.

17. John St. Clair to Robert Morris, January 14, 1755, in Pa. *Council Minutes*, 6:298–99; Robinson to Morris, October 26, 1754, ibid., 6:200–202; Morris to Assembly, December 19, 1754, ibid., 6:202–3.

18. Morris to St. Clair, February 10, 1755, ibid., 6:299.

19. Francis Jennings, *Empire of Fortune: Crowns, Colonies, & Tribes in the Seven Years War in America* (New York: W. W. Norton, 1988), 141–46.

20. Braddock to Morris, February 28, 1755, in Pa *Council Minutes*, 6:307–8; see also Braddock to Morris, March 10, 1755, ibid., 6:332–34.

21. Morris to Braddock, March 12, 1755, ibid., 6:335–38; Robert V. Wells, *The Population of the British Colonies in America before 1776: A Survey of Census Data* (Princeton, N.J.: Princeton University Press, 1975), 143; Theodore Thayer, *Pennsylvania's Politics and the Growth of Democracy, 1740–1776* (Harrisburg: Pennsylvania Historical and Museum Commission, 1953).

22. Quincy to Morris, March 21, 1755, in Pa. *Council Minutes*, 6:329–30; Quincy to Morris, March 31, 1755, ibid., 6:340; Quincy to Morris, April 1, 1755, ibid., 6:353–53.

23. Morris to Sir Thomas Robinson, April 9, 1755, quoted in Gipson, *Great War for Empire*, 6:69–70.

24. Minutes of the Alexandria Conference, April 14, 1755, in Pa. *Council Minutes*, 6:365–69.

25. Gipson, *Great War for Empire*, 6:71–72.

26. Jennings, *Empire of Fortune*, 146.

27. Commission from Braddock to Johnson, April 15, 1755, in James Sullivan and A. C. Flick, eds., *The Papers of Sir William Johnson* (hereafter cited as Sullivan, *Johnson Papers*), 14 vols. (Albany: State University of New York, 1921–1965), 1: 465–66.

28. Franklin Thayer Nichols, "The Organization of Braddock's Army," *William and Mary Quarterly* 4 (1947), 125–47.

29. St. Clair to Braddock, February 10, 1754, in Pargellis, *Military Affairs*, 64.

30. Braddock to Adjutant General Robert Napier, June 8, 1755, in Pargellis, *Military Affairs*, 84–85.

31. Goodman, *Franklin Reader*, 168.

32. Ibid., 168–72; Whitfield J. Bell and Leonard Labaree, "Franklin and the 'Wagon Affair,'" *Proceedings of the American Philosophical Society* 101 (1957), 551–58.

33. St. Clair to Robert Napier, June 13, 1755, in Pargellis, *Military Affairs*, 93.

34. Goodman, *Franklin Reader*, 173–74.

35. Braddock to Napier, March 17, 1755, in Pargellis, *Military Affairs*, 77–80.

36. "A Return of His Majesty's Troops Encamped at Will's Creek, June 8, 1755"; "A Return of the Virginia, Maryland, & North Carolina Troops, Encamped at Will's Creek, June 8, 1755"; "A Return of the Detachment of the Royal Artillery Regiment, Encamped at Will's Creek, June 8, 1755"; ibid., 86–91.

37. Richard L. Morton, *Colonial Virginia*, 2 vols. (Chapel Hill: University of North Carolina Press, 1960), 2:687–88.

38. Johnson to Croghan, April 23, 1755, in Sullivan, *Johnson Papers*, 1:475–76.

39. Beverley W. Bond, ed., "The Captivity of Charles Stuart, 1755–57," *Mississippi Valley Historical Review* 13 (1926–1927), 58–81; William A. Hunter, "Documented Subdivisions of the Delaware Indians," *Bulletin of the Archeological Society of New Jersey* 20 (1978).

40. Indian Council at Philadelphia, August 22, 1755, in Pa. *Council Minutes*, 6: 589.

41. For an excellent reconstruction of the battle that succeeds in making sense of the often contradictory accounts, see Paul E. Kopperman, *Braddock at the Monongahela* (Pittsburgh: University of Pennsylvania Press, 1977). The book includes copies of the battle's 22 firsthand accounts. Many of these accounts are also in Pargellis, *Military Affairs*, 98–129.

42. Francis Parkman, *Montcalm and Wolfe: The French and Indian War* (1886) (reprint, New York: Da Capo Press, 1995), 120.

43. David R. Edmunds, *The Potawatomis: Keepers of the Fire* (Norman: University of Oklahoma Press, 1978), 50–51; George F. G. Stanley, *New France: The Last Phase, 1744–1760* (Toronto: McClelland and Stewart, 1968), 98.

44. French Battle Account, August 8, 1755, in Pargellis, *Military Affairs*, 129.

45. Duquesne to Minister of Marine, June 25, 1755, in Sylvester K. Stevens and Donald H. Kent, eds., *Wilderness Chronicles of Northwestern Pennsylvania* (Harrisburg: Pennsylvania Historical Commission, 1941), 64–65.

46. "Journal of Operations, July 22 to September 30, 1755," NYCD, 10:337–40.

47. Anonymous letter on Braddock's campaign, July 25, 1755, in Pargellis, *Military Affairs*, 117.

48. Washington to Dinwiddie, July 18, 1755, in W. W. Abbott, ed., *The Papers of George Washington* (Charlottesville: University Press of Virginia, 1983), 1:339–40.

49. For these and other estimates, see Pargellis, *Military Affairs*, 97, 131–32; Account of the Battle of the Monongahela, July 9, 1755, NYCD 10:303–4; Dieskau to Doreil, August 16, 1755, ibid., 10:311–12.

50. Quoted in Kopperman, *Braddock at the Monongahela*, 92.

51. Goodman, *Franklin Reader*, 175.

52. Anonymous letter on Braddock's Campaign, July 25, 1755," in Pargellis, *Military Affairs*, 120.

53. Washington to Dinwiddie, July 18, 1755, in Abbott, *Washington Papers*, 1: 340.

54. Anonymous Letter on Braddock's Campaign, July 25, 1755, in Pargellis, *Military Affairs*, 120.

55. Council Minutes, January 13, 1756, in Pa. *Council Minutes*, 6:781–82; Council Minutes, January 14, 1756, ibid., 6:783–84.

56. Anonymous letter on Braddock's Campaign, July 25, 1755, in Pargellis, *Military Affairs*, 124.

57. Ibid., 123.

58. Goodman, *Franklin Reader*, 175.

59. Dinwiddie to Dunbar, July 26, 1755, in R. A. Brock, ed., *The Official Records of Robert Dinwiddie, Lieutenant-Governor of the Colony of Virginia, 1751–1758* (1883) (reprint, New York: AMS Press, 1971), 2:11820; Dinwiddie to Sharpe, August 25, 1755, ibid., 2:170.

60. Dinwiddie to Halifax, July 23, 1755, in Brock, *Dinwiddie Papers*, 2:114.

61. Quoted in Gipson, *Great War for Empire*, 6:233; See J. Clarence Webster, ed., *Journals of Beausejour: Diary of John Thomas; Journal of Louis de Courville* (Sackville, N.B.: The Tribune Press, 1937); J. Clarence Webster and Alice Webster, eds., *The Siege of Beausejour in 1755: A Journal of the Attack on Beausejour Written by Jacau de Fiedmont* (St. John, N.B.: New Brunswick Museum, 1936).

62. Dominick Graham, "The Planning of the Beausejour Operation and the Approaches to War in 1755," *New England Quarterly* 41 (1968), 551–66; "Journal of Colonel John Winslow of the Provincial Troops," Massachusetts Historical Society.

63. Fiedmont, *Siege of Beausejour*, 31.

64. J. S. McLennan, *Louisbourg from Its Foundation to Its Fall: 1713–1758* (1918) (reprint, Halifax, N.S.: The Book Room Limited, 1994), 205.

65. Johnson to Braddock, May 1755, in Sullivan, *Johnson Papers*, 1:5–14.

66. Johnson to Shirley, June 19, 1755, in Charles Henry Lincoln, ed., *The Correspondance of William Shirley, Governor of Massachusetts and Military Commander in America, 1731–1760* (hereafter cited as Lincoln, *Shirley Correspondance*), 2 vols. (New York: Macmillan, 1912), 2:193.

67. Johnson to Hopkins, June 26, 1755, in Sullivan, *Johnson Papers*, 1:655–56; Johnson to Braddock, June 27, 1755, ibid., 1:662–65.

68. Johnson to De Lancey, July 30, 1755, NYCD, 6:794–97.

69. Mt. Johnson Council, July 3, 1755, NYCD, 6:984.

70. Johnson to Lords of Trade, July 21, 1755, NYCD, 6:962.

71. Johnson to De Lancey, June 27, 1755, in Edmund O'Callaghan and Berthold Fernow, eds., *Documentary History of the State of New York* (DHNY), 4 vols. (Albany, N.Y.: Weed, Parsons, and Co., 1850–1851), 2:665–66.

72. Sullivan, *Johnson Papers*, 1:736, 795.

73. Vaudreuil to Machault, July 24, 1755, NYCD, 10:306–9.

74. Guy Fregault, *Canada: The War of the Conquest, 1754–1760* (trans. Margaret M. Cameron) (Toronto: Oxford University Press, 1969), 97.

75. Vaudreuil to Dieskau, September 25, 1755, NYCD 10:328; Vaudreuil to Machault, September 15, 1755, ibid., 10: 325–26; Dieskau to Doreil, August 16, 1755, ibid., 10: 311–12; Herbert L. Osgood, *The American Colonies in the Eighteenth Century*, 4 vols. (1924) (reprint, Gloucester, Mass.: Peter Smith, 1958), 4: 367.

76. Vaudreuil to Machault, June 8, 1756, NYCD, 10: 413.

77. William G. Godfrey, *Pursuit of a Profit and Preferment in Colonial North America: John Bradstreet's Quest* (Waterloo, Ont.: Wilfred Laurier University Press, 1982).

78. Shirley to Sir Thomas Robinson, August 11, 1755, in Lincoln, *Shirley Correspondance*, 2:219–20.

79. Shirley to Morris, May 23, 1755, in Pa. *Council Minutes*, 6:405–6.

80. Shirley to Robinson, September 19 and 28, and October 5, 1755, in Lincoln, *Shirley Correspondance*, 2: 261–70, 289–300, 309–10.

81. For first-person accounts of the campaign, battle, and aftermath, see Peter Wraxall to Henry Fox, September 27, 1755, in Pargellis, *Military Affairs*, 137–45.

82. Wyllis E. Wright, *Colonial Emphraim Williams, A Documentary Life* (Pittsfield, Mass.: Berkshire County Historical Society, 1970), 106–7.

. 83. Fred Anderson, *A People's Army: Massachusetts' Soldiers and Society in the Seven Years' War* (New York: W. W. Norton, 1984), 77.

84. Wraxall to Fox, September 27, 1755, in Pargellis, *Military Affairs*, 141.

85. Johnson to De Lancey, September 4, 1755, in Sullivan, *Johnson Papers*, 2: 7–8.

86. Wright, *Colonel Williams*, 120.

87. Johnson to Phineas Lyman, July 27, 1755, in Sullivan, *Johnson Papers*, 1: 783.

88. Thomas Williams to his wife, October 8, 1755, "Correspondence of Doctor Williams," 213, quoted in Milton W. Hamilton, *Sir William Johnson: Colonial American, 1715–1763* (Port Washington, N.Y.: Kennikat Press, 1976).

89. Johnson to Pownall, August 25, 1755, in Sullivan, *Johnson Papers*, 1:886.

90. Johnson to Shirley, September 1, 1755, ibid., 1:892–93.

91. Council of War Minutes, August 22, 1755, NYCD, 6:1001; Dieskau to d'Argenson, September 14, 1755, NYCD, 10: 317; Dieskau to Vaudreuil, September 15, NYCD, 10: 318; "Dialogue" with Marshal Saxe, n.d., NYCD, 10:342; Montreuil to d'Argenson, October 10, 1755, NYCD, 10: 353–54; Vaudreuil to Machault, September 25, 1755, NYCD, 10:318–23.

92. Dieskau to Vaudreuil, September 15, 1755, NYCD. 10:318.

93. Dieskau to d'Argenson, September 14, 1755, NYCD, 10:317.

94. Minutes of War Council, September 7, 1755, in Sullivan, *Johnson Papers*, 2: 16–17.

95. Claus Narrative, ibid., 3:58–65; For Johnson's account see Johnson to Shirley, September 9, 1755, in Lincoln, *Shirley Correspondance*, 2:253–59.

96. Claus Narrative, in Sullivan, *Johnson Papers*, 13:58–65.

97. Quoted in Hamilton, *Sir William Johnson*, 160.

98. Wraxwall to Fox, September 27, 1755, in Pargellis, *Military Affairs*, 139.

99. Wraxall to Fox, September 27, 1755, ibid., 140.

100. Wraxall, Return of Casualties, September 11, 1755, NYCD, 6:1006–7; Wraxall to De Lancey, September 10, 1755, NYCD, 6:1003–4; Doreil to Argenson, October 20, 1755, NYCD, 10:360–61; Gunner to his Cousin, September 10, 1755, NYCD, 6:1005; Thomas Pownall to Board of Trade, September 20, 1755, NYCD, 6:1008–9; Journal of Army Operations, July 22 to September 30, 1755, NYCD, 10: 337–40; Dialogue between Saxe and Dieskau in Elysian Fields, NYCD, 10:340–45; Sullivan, *Johnson Papers*, 9:234–38.

101. Journal of Proceedings, July 23, 1755, in Pargellis, *Military Affairs*, 107–8.

102. Wraxall to Fox, September 27, 1755, ibid., 140.

103. Ian K. Steele, *Warpaths: Invasions of North America* (New York: Oxford University Press, 1994), 193.

104. Eyre to Shirley, September 10, 1755, in Lincoln, *Shirley Correspondance*, 2: 260; Wraxall to De Lancey, September 10, 1755, NYCD, 6:1004; *New York Gazette*, October 6, 1755.

105. Shirley to Johnson, September 19, 1755, in Lincoln, *Shirley Correspondance*, 2:270–76; Shirley to Johnson, September 24, 1755, ibid, 2:280–83. Johnson to Shirley, in Sullivan, *Johnson Papers*, 2:74.

106. Johnson to Shirley, ibid., 2:74.

107. Shirley to Johnson, December 7, 1755, NYCD, 6:1024–28.

108. Dumas au ministre, 24 Juillet, 1756, in F.-J. Audet, *Jean Daniel Dumas: Le Hero de la Monongahela* (Montreal: G. Ducharme, 1920), 22–24.

109. Dieskau to d'Argenson, June 22, 1756, NYCD, 10:423.

110. Dinwiddie's commission to Washington, August 14, 1755, in Brock, *Dinwiddie Papers*, 2:184.

111. Adam Stephens to George Washington, October 4, 1755, in W. W. Abbott, ed., *The Papers of George Washington* (Charlottesville: University Press of Virginia, 1984), 2:72.

112. Pennsylvania Council Minutes, August 22, 1755, in Pa. *Council Minutes*, 6: 588–91.

113. Jennings, *Empire of Fortune*, 244–46.

114. Council Minutes, November 3, 1755, in Pa. *Council Minutes*, 6:670–72;

for a succinct overview of Pennsylvania's politics during these years, see Jennings, *Empire of Fortune*, chaps. 11, 12; Ralph L. Ketcham, "Conscience, War, and Politics in Pennsylvania, 1755–1757," *William and Mary Quarterly* 3rd ser., 20 (1963), 416–39.

115. William A. Hunter, *Forts on the Pennsylvania Frontier, 1753–1758* (Harrisburg: Pennsylvania Historical and Museum Commission, 1960).

116. Wilbur R. Jacobs, ed., *The Appalachian Indian Frontier: The Edmund Atkin Report and Plan of 1755* (1954) (reprint, Lincoln: University of Nebraska Press, 1967); Gipson, *Great War for Empire*, 6:65, 71–72; David G. Sweet and Gary B. Nash, eds., *Struggle and Survival in Colonial America* (Berkeley: University of California Press, 1981); Samuel Cole Williams, ed., *Adair's History of the American Indians* (New York: Promontory Press, 1973); David H. Corkran, *The Cherokee Frontier: Conflict and Survival, 1740–62* (Norman: University of Oklahoma Press, 1962); Jack P. Greene, *The Quest for Power: The Lower Houses of Assembly in the Southern Royal Colonies, 1689–1776* (1963) (reprint, New York: W. W. Norton, 1972); John Philip Reid, *A Law of Blood: The Primitive Law of the Cherokee Nation* (New York: New York University Press, 1970).

117. Gipson, *Great War for Empire*, 6:399.

118. Admiralty Instructions to Keppel, November 1754, in Pargellis, *Military Affairs*, 52.

119. Thomas B. Atkins, ed., *Selections from the Public Documents of the Province of Nova Scotia* (Halifax, N.S.: Charles Annand, 1869), 207.

120. Lawrence to Board of Trade, July 18, 1755, in Atkins, *Nova Scotia Documents*, 259–60.

121. Robinson to Lawrence, August 13, 1755, ibid., 279.

122. Board of Trade to Lawrence, March 4, October 29, 1754, ibid., 207–8, 235–37.

123. Gustave Lanctot, *A History of Canada, From the Treaty of Utrecht to the Treaty of Paris, 1713–1763*, 3 vols. (trans. Josephine Hambleton and Margaret M. Cameron) (Cambridge, Mass.: Harvard University Press, 1963–1965), 99.

124. Winslow's Instructions, Council Minutes, August 11, 1755, Atkins, *Nova Scotia Documents*, 271–74.

125. "Winslow's Journal," *Nova Scotia Historical Society Collection*, 3:94–95.

126. Quoted in Gipson, *Great War for Empire*, 6:262.

127. Oscar William Winzerling, *Acadian Odyssey* (Baton Rouge: Louisana State University Press, 1955; Glenn Conrad, ed., *The Cajuns: Essays on their History and Culture* (Lafayette: University of Southwestern Louisiana Press, 1978); Carl A. Brasseaux, *The Founding of New Acadia: The Beginnings of Life in Louisiana, 1765–1803* (Baton Rouge: Louisiana State University Press, 1987); Robert Sauvageau, *Acadie: La Guerre de Cent Ans des Francais d'Amerique aux Maritimes et en Louisanne, 1670–1769* (Paris: Berger-Levrault, 1987).

128. "Sketch for Next Year's Campaign in North America, September 6, 1755," in Pargellis, *Military Affairs*, 133–37.

129. Johnson to Board of Trade, September 3, 1755, NYCD, 6:993–97.

130. Hardy to Halifax, November 27, 1755, in Pargellis, *Military Affairs*, 151–52.

131. Stanley Pargellis, *Lord Loudoun in America* (New Haven, Conn.: Yale University Press, 1933), 76.

132. See also George Arthur Wood, *William Shirley, Governor of Massachusetts, 1721–1756* (New York: Columbia University Press, 1920); John A. Schutz, *William Shirley, King's Governor of Massachusetts* (Chapel Hill: University of North Carolina Press, 1961); Stanley Nider Katz, *Newcastle's New York: Anglo-American Politics, 1732–1753* (Cambridge, Mass.: Belknap Press, 1968); Patricia U. Bonomi, *A Factious People: People and Society in Colonial New York* (New York: Columbia University Press, 1971), 175–76.

133. Claus Narrative, in Sullivan, *Johnson Papers*, 13:58–65.

134. Pargellis, *Loudoun in America*, 165.

135. Jennings, *Empire of Fortune*, 284.

136. William Livingstone, *A Review of Military Operations in North America . . . To the Surrender of Oswego, on the 14th of August, 1756* (London: R. and J. Dodsley, 1757), 58.

137. Banyar to Johnson, November 11, 1755, in Sullivan, *Johnson Papers*, 2:286.

138. Steele, *Warpaths*, 195.

139. Dunbar to Napier, July 24, 1755, in Pargellis, *Military Affairs*, 112.

Bibliography

PAPERS IN INSTITUTIONS

British Museum, London: Newcastle and Hardwicke papers.

Connecticut State Library, Hartford: Henry Champion, accounts and journal, 1758; Asa Waterman, diary, 1760; Capt. Edmund Wells, 1756–1757.

Historical Society of Pennsylvania, Harrisburg: George Croghan papers; Peters papers; Penn family papers; Gratz Collection; Col. James Burd, journal, 1756–1757; Joseph Shippen, orderly book and journals, 1756–1758; Shippen family papers.

Houghton Library, Harvard University, Cambridge, Massachusetts: Joseph Williams, orderly book, 1758.

Henry E. Huntington Library, San Marino, California: Loudoun papers; Abercromby papers; Lt. Joseph Bull, orderly book, 1759; Capt. Samuel Grubb, orderly book, 1759; John Grant, orderly book, 1761; Obadiah Harris, regimental journal, 1758; Abijah Willard, orderly book and journal, 1755–1756.

Institute of Early American History and Culture, University of North Carolina, Chapel Hill, North Carolina.

Library of Congress, Washington, D.C.: General John Forbes, orderly book; Samuel Fisher, Diary of Operations Around Lake George, 1758; John Hawks, orderly books; Lt. Spaulding, diary.

Massachusetts Historical Society, Boston: Shirley, Belknap, Pepperell, and Williams papers and the Parkman Collection.

Museum of the City of New York: Livingston papers.

New York Historical Society, New York: Sterling papers; John Bremner, journal, 1756–1764.

New York Public Library: Johnson and Schuyler Manuscripts; the Indian Affairs Collection; Emmett Collection; Chalmers Collection; William Smith diary; James Henderson, diary, 1758–1759.

Newberry Library Center for the History of the American Indian, University of Indiana, Bloomington, Indiana: biographical series.
Public Archives of Canada, Ottawa: Indian Records and Claus papers.
Public Record Office, London: Sir Jeffrey Amherst papers; William Pitt, Earl of Chatham papers.
William L. Clements Library, Ann Arbor, Michigan: Gage and Clinton papers.
Wisconsin Historical Society; Madison: Draper Collection.

PUBLISHED ORIGINAL DOCUMENTS AND SOURCES

Abbott, W. W., ed. *The Papers of George Washington*. Charlottesville: University of Virginia Press, 1984.
Arouet, Francois-Marie (Voltaire). *Candide*. New York: Dover Press, 1991.
Atkins, Thomas B., ed. Selections from *Public Documents of the Province of Nova Scotia* (PDPNS). Halifax, N.S.: Charles Annand, 1869.
"Attack and Repulse at Ticonderoga, July 1758." *The Bulletin of the Fort Ticonderoga Museum* 7, no. 1 (January 1945), 15–18.
Bailey, Kenneth P., ed. *The Ohio Company Papers, 1747–1817, Being Primarily Papers of the "Suffering Traders" of Pennsylvania*. Arcata, Calif.: Arthur H. Clark, 1947.
Bass, Benjamin. "Account of the Capture of Fort Frontenac by the Detachment under the Command of Col. Bradstreet." *New York History* 16 (1935), 449–51.
"The Battle of Carillon." *The Bulletin of the Fort Ticonderoga Museum* 2, no. 8 (July 1930), 69–78.
Benson, Adolphe B., ed. *Peter Kalm's Travels in North America: The Version of 1770*. New York: Dover Publications, 1987.
Blair, Helen, ed. *The Indian Tribes of the Upper Mississippi Valley & Region of the Great Lakes (1911)*. Lincoln: University of Nebraska Press, 1996.
Bond, Beverley W., ed. "The Captivity of Charles Stuart, 1755–57." *Mississippi Valley Historical Review* 13 (1926–1927), 58–81.
Bowen, Ashley. "Journal Kept on the Quebec Expedition, 1759, by Ashley Bowen of Marblehead." *Essex Institute of Institute Historical Collections* 70 (July 1934), 227–66.
Bradstreet, Dudley. Diary, *Massachusetts Historical Society, Proceedings*, 2nd ser., 11 (1897), 432–46.
Breslaw, Elaine G. "A Dismal Tragedy: Drs. Alexander and John Hamilton Comment on Braddock's Defeat." *Maryland Historical Magazine* 75 (1980), 118–44.
Brigham, Clarence S., ed. *British Royal Proclamations Relating to America, 1603–1783*. Worcester, Mass.: Transactions and Collection of the American Antiquarian Society, vol. 12, 1911.
"British Casualty List at Carillon." *The Bulletin of the Fort Ticonderoga Museum* 2, no. 8 (July 1930), 76–78.
Brock, R. A., ed. *The Official Records of Robert Dinwiddie, Lieutenant Governor of the Colony of Virginia, 1751–1758*. 1883. Reprint, New York: AMS Press, 1971.
Brooke, John, ed. *Horace Walpole, Memoirs of King George II*, 3 vols. New Haven, Conn.: Yale University Press, 1985.

Burnaby, Andrew. *Travels through the Middle Settlements in North America in the Years 1759 and 1760*, 2nd ed. London: 1775. Reprint, Ithaca, N.Y.: Cornell University Press, 1960.

"Captain Moneypenny's Orderly Book, July 15 to August 3, 1759." *The Bulletin of the Fort Ticonderoga Museum* 2, no. 10 (July 1932), 219–53.

"Captain Moneypenny's Orderly Book, June 30 to July 7, 1758." *The Bulletin of the Fort Ticonderoga Museum* 2, no. 8 (July 1930), 54–67.

"Captain Moneypenny's Orderly Book, June 30 to August 7, 1758." *The Bulletin of the Fort Ticonderoga Museum* 2, no. 10 (July 1932), 434–61.

Carman, Harry J., and Rexford G. Tugwell, eds. *Jared Eliot: Essays Upon Field Husbandry in New England, and Other Papers, 1748–1762*. New York: Columbia University Press, 1934.

Carter, Clarence Edwin, ed. *The Correspondance of General Thomas Gage with the Secretaries of State, 1763–1775*, 2 vols. 1931–1933. Reprint, Hamden, Conn.: Archon Books, 1969.

Casgrain, H. R. *Journal du Marquis de Montcalm durant ses campagnes en Canada, de 1756 a 1759*. Quebec: Imprimerie de L. J. Demers & Freres, 1895.

Casgrain, H. R., ed. *Collection des Manuscrits des Marechal de Levis*, 12 vols. Montreal: Public Archives of Canada, 1889–1895.

Chapin, Howard M. *A List of Rhode Island Soldiers & Sailors in the Old French & Indian War, 1755–1763*. Providence: Rhode Island Historical Society, 1918.

Chauncey, Charles. *A Letter to a Friend; Giving a Concise, but Just, Account . . . of the Ohio Defeat*. Boston, 1755.

Chauncey, Charles. *A Second Letter to a Friend; Giving a More Particular Narrative of the Defeat of the French Army at Lake George, by the New England Troops, than has Yet Been Published*. Boston, 1755.

Clark, David Saunders, ed. "Journals and Orderly Books Kept by Massachusetts Soldiers During the French and Indian War." *New England Historical and Genealogical Register* 95 (April 1941), 118–21.

Claus, Daniel. *Daniel Claus' Narrative of His Relations with Sir William Johnson and Experience in the Lake George Fight*. New York, 1904.

Colden, Cadwallader. *The History of the Five Nations of Canada, Which Are Dependent Upon the Province of New York in North America*. 1747. Reprint, New York: AMS Press, 1973.

Collections of the Nova Scotia Historical Society for the Years 1878–1884. Belleville, Ont.: Mika Publishing Company, 1976.

"Colonel Charles Clinton's Journal, July to October 1758." *The Bulletin of the Fort Ticonderoga Museum* 15, no. 4 (1992), 292–315.

Comment on Braddock's Defeat. *Maryland Historical Magazine* 75 (1980), 118–44.

Connell, Brian, ed. *The Siege of Quebec and the Campaigns in North America, 1757–1760, by Captain John Knox*. Mississauga, Ont.: Pendragon, 1980.

"Conrad Weiser's Journal." *Minutes of the Provincial Council of Pennsylvania (1851)*. New York: AMS Press, 1968.

Darlington, William M., ed. *Christopher Gist's Journals*. Cleveland: Arthur H. Clark, 1893.

Dawes, E. C., ed. *Journal of Gen. Rufus Putnam Kept in Northern New York During Four Campaigns of . . . 1757–1760*. Albany, N.Y., 1886.

Dewar, Mary, ed. *A Discource of the Commonweal of this Realm of England, Attributed to Sir Thomas Smith.* Charlottesville: University of Virginia Press, 1969.

Dobson, John. *Chronological Annals of the War: From Its Beginning to the Present Time.* Oxford: Clarendon Press, 1763.

Dorr, Moses. "A Journal of an Expedition against Canady." *New York History* 16 (October 1935), 452–64.

Dunnigan, Brian Leigh, ed. *Memoirs on the Late War in North America Between France and England, by Pierre Pouchot.* Youngstown, N.Y.: Old Fort Niagara Association, 1994.

Duverger, de Saint-Blin. *Memoire Pour le Sieur Duverger de Saint-Blin, Lieutenant d'Infanterie dans les Troupes Etant Ci-Devant en Canada.* Paris: Moreau, 1763.

Ewing, William S., ed. "An Eyewitness Account by James Furniss of the Surrender of Fort William Henry, August 1757." *New York History* 42 (July 1961), 307–16.

Fitzpatrick, John C., ed. *The Diaries of George Washington, 1748–1794,* 4 vols. Boston: Houghton Mifflin, 1925.

Fitzpatrick, John C., ed. *The Writings of George Washington,* 39 vols. Washington, D.C.: U.S. Government Printing Office, 1931–1944.

Fortescue, John, ed. *The Correspondance of King George Third from 1760 to December 1783,* 6 vols. London: Macmillan, 1927–1928.

French, Capt. Christopher. "Journal of an Expedition to South Carolina." *Journal of Cherokee Studies* 2 (1977), 275–301.

"General Orders Extracts, 1759 Carillon Campaign." *The Bulletin of the Fort Ticonderoga Museum* 6, no. 33 (January 1942), 85–105.

Goodman, Nathan G., ed. *A Benjamin Franklin Reader.* New York: Thomas Y. Crowell, 1945.

Graham, Rev. John. "The Journal of the Rev. John Graham, Chaplain to Connecticut Troops in the Expedition Toward Crown Point, 1756." *Magazine of American History* 8 (1882), 206–13.

Grant, W. L., and James Monroe, eds. *Acts of the Privy Council of England, Colonial Series, 1613–1783.* Herford, England, 1908–1912.

Grenier, Fernand, ed. *Papier Contrecoeur et autres documents concernant le conflit Anglo-Francais sur l'Ohio de 1755 a 1756.* Quebec: Les Presses Universitaires Laval, 1952.

Hamilton, Charles, ed. *Braddock's Defeat: The Journal of Captain Robert Chomley's Batman, the Journal of a British Officer, Halkett's Orderly Book.* Norman: University of Oklahoma Press, 1959.

Hamilton, Edward, ed. *Adventure in the Wilderness: The American Journals of Louis Antoine de Bougainville, 1756–1760.* Norman: University of Oklahoma Press, 1964.

Hamilton, Milton W., ed. "Battle Report, General William Johnson's Letter to the Governors, Lake George, September 9–10, 1755." *American Antiquarian Society, Proceedings* 74 (1964), 21–24.

Harrison, Fairfax, ed. "With Braddock's Army: Mrs. Browne's Diary in Virginia and Maryland." *Virginia Magazine of History and Biography* 32 (1924), 305–20.

Hastings, Hugh, ed. *Orderly Book and Journal of Major John Hawkes.* New York: Society of Colonial Wars in the State of New York, 1911.

"Henry Skinner's Journal, May 1 to July 28, 1759." *The Bulletin of the Fort Ticonderoga Museum* 15, no. 5 (1993), 363–88.

Hervey, William, ed. *Journals of the Hon. William Hervey.* Bury, St. Edmunds, England: Paul & Mathew, 1906.

Hunter, William A., ed. "Thomas Barton and the Forbes Expedition." *Pennsylvania Magazine of History and Biography* 95 (1971), 431–83.

James, Alfred P., ed. *Writings of General John Forbes Relating to His Service in North America.* Menasha, Wis.: Collegiate Press, 1938.

Jackson, Donald, ed. *The Diaries of George Washington, 1748–65.* Charlottesville: University of Virginia Press, 1976.

Jacobs, Wilbur R., ed. *The Appalachian Indian Frontier: The Edmund Atkin Report and Plan of 1755.* 1954. Reprint, Lincoln: University of Nebraska Press, 1967.

Jennings, Francis, William N. Fenton, Mary A. Druke, and David R. Miller, eds. *Iroquois Indians: A Documentary History of the Six Nations and Their League.* Woodbridge, Conn.: Research Publications, 1985.

Jennings, Francis et al. *The History and Culture of Iroquois Diplomacy: An Interdisciplinary Guide to the Treaties of the Six Nations and Their League.* Syracuse, N.Y.: Syracuse University Press, 1985.

Jordan, John W., ed. "James Kenny Journals, 1758–59." *Pennsylvania Magazine of History and Biography* 32 (1913), 1–47, 152–201, 395–449.

"Josiah Goodrich Orderbook." *The Bulletin of the Fort Ticonderoga Museum* 14, no. 1 (Summer 1981), 39–61.

"Journal of Captain Samuel Cobb." *The Bulletin of the Fort Ticonderoga Museum* 14, no. 1 (Summer 1981), 12–31.

Kellogg, Louise P., ed. "La Chapelle's Remarkable Retreat through the Mississippi Valley, 1760–61." *Mississippi Valley Historical Review* 27 (June 1935), 63–81.

Kennedy, Archibald. *Serious Consideration on the Present State of the Affairs of the Northern Colonies.* New York, 1754.

Kennedy, Archibald. *Serious Advice to the Inhabitants of the Northern Colonies on the Present Situation of Affairs.* New York, 1755.

Kimball, Gertrude Selwyn, ed. *Correspondance of William Pitt when Secretary of State with Colonial Governors and Military and Naval Commissioners in America.* London: Macmillan, 1906.

King, Duane H., and E. Raymond Evans, eds. "Special Issue: Memoirs of the Grant Expedition Against the Cherokees in 1761." *Journal of Cherokee Studies* 2 (Summer 1977).

Kochan, James L., ed. "Joseph Frye's Journal and Map of the Siege of Fort William Henry, 1757." *The Bulletin of the Fort Ticonderoga Museum* 15, no. 5 (1993), 356–57.

Kopperman, Paul E., and Michael J. Freiling, eds. "A British Officer's Journal of the Braddock Expedition—Et Cetera." *Western Pennsylvania Historical Magazine* 64 (1981), 269–87.

Labaree, Leonard W., ed. *Royal Instruction to British Colonial Governors, 1670–1776,* 2 vols. New York, 1935.

Labaree, Leonard W., ed. *The Papers of Benjamin Franklin.* New Haven, Conn.: Yale University Press, 1962.

Labaree, Leonard W. et al., eds. *The Autobiography of Benjamin Franklin.* New Haven, Conn.: Yale University Press, 1964.

"Life of David Perry." *The Bulletin of the Fort Ticonderoga Museum* 14, no. 1 (Summer 1981), 4–8.

Lincoln, Charles Henry, ed. "Manuscript Records of the French and Indian War in the Library of the Society." *Transactions and Collections of the American Antiquarian Society*, vol. 11. Worster, Mass.: American Antiquarian Society, 1909.

Lincoln, Charles Henry, ed. *The Correspondence of William Shirley*, 2 vols. New York: Macmillan, 1912.

"List of French Killed and Wounded, July 8, 1758." *The Bulletin of the Fort Ticonderoga Museum* 1, no. 3 (January 1928), 12.

Livingstone, William. *A Review of Military Operations in North America . . . To the Surrender of Oswego, on the 14th of August, 1756.* London: R. and J. Dodsley, 1757.

Marlartic, Le Comte de Maures. *Journal des Campagnes au Canada de 1755 A 1760.* Paris: Libairie Plon, 1890.

McAnear, Beverly, ed. "Personal Accounts of the Albany Congress of 1754." *Mississippi Valley Historical Review* 39 (1953), 727–46.

McDowell, William L., Jr., ed. *Documents Relating to Indian Affairs, 1754–1765.* Columbia: University of South Carolina Press, 1970.

McIlwain, Charles Howard, ed. *An Abridgement of the Indian Affairs Contained in Four Folio Volumes, Transacted in the Colony of New York, from the Year 1751 to the Year 1778* (1915). New York: Benjamin Blom, 1968.

"Memoir of an Invalid." *Amherst Papers*, Packet 54, Canadian Archives Transcripts.

"Memoir on the Defense of the Fort of Carillon." *The Bulletin of the Fort Ticonderoga Museum* 8, no. 3 (1972), 196–226.

Memoires de Commissaires du Roi et de ceux de sa Majeste Britanique, sur les Possessions & les Droits Respectifs des Deux Couronnes en Amerique, avec les Actes Publics & Pieces Justificatives, 6 vols. Paris: Imprimerie Royale, 1755–57.

Minutes of the Provincial Council of Pennsylvania. Harrisburg, Pa.: Theo, Fenn, and Co., 1851. Reprint, New York: AMS Press, 1968.

Moffett, Edna V., ed. "The Diary of a Private [James Hill] on the first Expedition to Crown Point." *New England Quarterly* 5 (1932), 602–18.

Moneypenny, Alexander. "Diary of Alexander Moneypenny." *Journal of Cherokee Studies* 2 (Summer 1877), 302–31.

"Moneypenny Orderly Book, June 30 to August 7, 1758." *The Bulletin of the Fort Ticonderoga Museum* 12, no. 6 (October 1970), 434–61.

"Moneypenny Orderly Book, March 23 to June 29, 1758." *The Bulletin of the Fort Ticonderoga Museum* 12, no. 5 (December 1969), 328–57.

"Montcalm at Carillon." *The Bulletin of the Fort Ticonderoga Museum* 1, no. 3 (January 1928), 4–11.

"Montcalm's Order of Battle." *The Bulletin of the Fort Ticonderoga Museum* 2, no. 8 (July 1930), 67–69.

Montcalm-Gozon, Louis Joseph de. "Montcalm's Correspondance." *Report of the Public Archives of Canada for the Year 1929.* Ottawa: Public Archives, 1930, 31–108.

Montresor, Col. James. "Journal of Col. James Montresor, 1757–1759." *New York Historical Society Collections* 14 (1881).

Moreau, Jacob Nicolas. *Memoire Convenant le Precis des Faits avec leur Pieces Justificatives.* Paris: L'Imprimerie Royale, 1756; translated as *The Conduct of the Late Ministry, or, A Memorial Containing A Summary of the Facts with Their Vouchers, in Answer to the Observations, sent by the English Ministry to the Courts of Europe.* London: W. Bizet, 1757.

Mulligan, Robert E., ed. "Colonel Charles Clinton's Journal of His Campaign in New York July to October, 1758 During the French War." *The Bulletin of the Fort Ticonderoga Museum* 15, no. 4 (1992), 292–315.

Murray, James. *Governor Murray's Journal of the Siege of Quebec, from September 1759 to 25th May 1760.* Toronto, 1939.

Narrative of the Military Operations in America in 1755–56. New York Historical Society, Rufus King Papers 84, no. 58.

Nevins, Allan, ed. *Ponteach, or the Savages of America: A Tragedy by Robert Rogers.* New York: Lenox Hill Publishers, 1971.

O'Callaghan, Edmund, and Berthold Fernow, eds. *Documentary History of the State of New York* (DHNY), 4 vols. Albany, N.Y.: Weed, Parsons, and Co., 1850–1851.

O'Callaghan, Edmund, and Berthold Fernow, eds. *Documents Relative to the Colonial History of the State of New York* (NYCD), 15 vols. Albany, NY: Weed, Parsons, and Co., 1853–1887.

Pargellis, Stanley, ed. *Military Affairs in North America, 1748–1763: Selected Documents from the Cumberland Papers in Windsor Castle.* 1936. Reprint, Hamden, Conn.: Archon Books, 1969.

Pease, Theodore Calvin, ed. *Anglo-French Boundary Disputes in the West, 1749–1763.* Springfield: Collections of the Illinois State Historical Library 27, French Series 2, 1936.

Pease, Theodore Calvin, and Ernestine Jenison, eds. *Illinois on the Eve of the Seven Years' War, 1747–1755,* vol. 29. Springfield: Collections of the Illinois State Historical Library, 1940.

Peckham, Howard H., ed. "Thomas Gist's Indian Captivity, 1758–59." *Pennsylvania Magazine of History and Biography* 80 (1956), 258–311.

Peckham, Howard H., ed. *Journals of Major Robert Rogers.* New York: Corinth Books, 1961.

Pell, Robert. "The Strategy of Montcalm, 1758." *The Bulletin of the Fort Ticonderoga Musuem* 9, no. 3 (Summer 1953).

Peyser, Joseph L., ed. *Letters from New France: The Upper Country, 1686–1783.* Urbana: University of Illinois Press, 1992.

Pownall, Thomas. *The Administration of the Colonies* (1764). 2nd ed. Revised, corrected, and enlarged. London: J. Dodsey and J. Walter, 1765.

Pownall, Thomas. "Personal Accounts of the Albany Congress of 1754," edited by Beverly McAnear. *Mississippi Valley Historical Review* 39:4 (March 1953), 740, 742–43.

Proctor, Jonathan. "Diary Kept at Louisbourg, 1759–1760, by Jonathan Proctor of Danvers." Essex Institute, *Historical Collections* 70 (1934), 31–57.

Quaife, Milo Milton, ed. *The Siege of Detroit in 1763: The Journal of Pontiac's Con-*

spiracy and John Rutherford's Narrative of a Captivity. Chicago: R. R. Donnelly and Sons, 1958.

"Robert Webster Journal, April 5 to November 23, 1759." *The Bulletin of the Fort Ticonderoga Museum* 2, no. 10 (July 1932), 120–53.

Rogers, Robert. "Regulations for the Rangers Drawn Up by Robert Roberts." *The Bulletin of the Fort Ticonderoga Museum* 4, no. 31 (January 1941), 1–19.

Roy, Pierre-George, ed. *Inventaries des Papiers de Lery,* 3 vols. Quebec: Archives de la Province de Quebec, 1939–1940.

Sargent, Winthrope, ed. *The History of an Expedition Against Fort Duquesne in 1755; under Major-General Braddock.* Philadelphia: Memoirs of the Historical Society of Pennsylvania 5, 1855.

Schultz, John A. "A Private Report of General Braddock's Defeat [John Bolling]." *Pennsylvania Magazine of History and Biography* 79 (1955), 374–77.

Shute, Rev. Daniel. "Rev. Daniel Shute, Journal, 1758." Essex Institute, *Historical Collections* 12 (1874), 132–51.

Simmons, R. C., and P. D. G. Thomas, eds. *Proceedings and Debates of the British Parliaments Respecting North America, 1754–1783,* vol. 1. 1754–1764. Millwood, N.Y.: Kraus International Publications, 1982.

[Smith Williams]. *A Brief State of the Province of Pennsylvania.* London: R. Griffiths, 1755.

[Smith, William]. *A Brief View of the Conduct of Pennsylvania.* London: J. Scott, 1756.

Smith, William, Jr. *A History of the Province of New York* (1757, 1826). Reprint, ed. Michael Kammen, 2 vols. Cambridge, Mass.: Belknap Press, 1972.

Stevens, Sylvester K., and Donald H. Kent, eds. *Travels in New France.* Harrisburg: Pennsylvania Historical Commission, 1941.

Stevens, Sylvester K., and Donald H. Kent, eds. *Wilderness Chronicles of Northwestern Pennsylvania.* Harrisburg: Pennsylvania Historical Commission, 1941.

Stevens, Sylvester K., Donald H. Kent, Autumn L. Leonard, Louis M. Waddell, and John Totteham, eds. *The Papers of Henry Bouquet,* 6 vols. Harrisburg: Pennsylvania Historical and Museum Commission, 1972–1984.

Stock, Leo Francis, ed. *Proceedings and Debates of the British Parliaments Respecting North America,* 5 vols. Washington, D.C.: Carnegie Institute, 1924–1941.

Stone, Albert, ed. *J. Hector St. John de Crevecoeur, Letters from an American Farmer and Sketches of Eighteenth Century America.* New York: Penguin, 1986.

Stotz, Charles M., ed. "A Letter from Will's Creek: Harry Gordon's Account of Braddock's Defeat." *Western Pennsylvania Historical Magazine* 44 (1961), 129–36.

Sullivan, James, and A. C. Flick, eds. *The Papers of Sir William Johnson,* 14 vols. Albany: State University of New York, 1921–1965.

Thomas, John. "Thomas, John, Diary, 1755." *Nova Scotia Historical Society Collections* 1 (1878), 119–40.

Thomson, Charles. *An Enquiry into the Causes of the Alienation of the Delaware and Shawanese Indians from the British Interest.* London: J. Wilkie, 1759.

Thwaites, Reuben Gold, ed. *The Jesuit Relations and Allied Documents: Travels and Explorations of the Jesuit Missionaries in New France, 1610–1791,* 73 vols., 1896–1901. Reprint, New York: Pageant Book Co., 1959.

Volwiler, A. T., ed. "William Trent's Journal at Fort Pitt." *Mississippi Valley Historical Review* 11 (1924), 408–10.

Washburn, Wilcomb E., ed. *The Garland Library of Narratives of North American Indian Captivities*, 111 vols. New York: Garland Publishing Co., 1975–1979.

Webster, J. Clarence, ed. *The Journal of Jeffrey Amherst: Recording the Military Career of General Amherst in America from 1758 to 1763*. Toronto: Ryerson Press, 1931.

Webster, J. Clarence, ed. *Journals of Beausejour: Diary of John Thomas; Journal of Louis de Courville*. Sackville, N.B.: The Tribune Press, 1937.

Webster, J. Clarence, and Alice Webster, eds. *The Siege of Beausejour in 1755: A Journal of the Attack on Beausejour Written by Jacau de Fiedmont*. St. John, N.B.: New Brunswick Museum, 1936.

Welles, Lemuel Aiken. "Letters of Col. Nathan Whiting, Written from Camp During the French and Indian War." *Papers of the New Haven Colony Historical Society*, vol. 6. New Haven, Conn.: New Haven Colony Society, 1900.

Williams, Samuel Cole, ed. *Adair's History of the American Indians*. New York: Promontory Press, 1973.

Wilson, Beckles, ed. *The Life and Letters of James Wolfe*. London: Heineman, 1909.

Winslow, Col. John. "Winslow, Col. John, Journal, 1755." *Nova Scotia Historical Society Collections* 3 (1882–1883), 71–196; (1884), 113–246.

Wood, William, ed. *The Logs of the Conquest of Canada*. Toronto: Champlain Society, publications 4, 1909.

Woodhull, Col. Nathaniel. "A Journal Kept by General Nathaniel Woodhull, When Colonel of the 3rd Regiment New York Provincials, in the Expedition to Montreal, in 1760." *The Historical Magazine* 5 (1861), 257–60.

Yorke, Philip C. *The Life and Correspondance of Philip Yorke, Earl of Hardwicke, Lord High Chancellor of Great Britain*, 3 vols. Cambridge, England: Cambridge University Press, 1913.

Zaboly, Gary S., ed. "A Royal Artillery Officer with Amherst: The Journal of Captain-Lieutenant Henry Skinner, 1 May–28 July, 1759." *The Bulletin of the Fort Ticonderoga Museum* 15, no. 5 (1993), 363–87.

SECONDARY SOURCES: BOOKS AND ARTICLES

Abbott, Raymond B. "Braddock's War Supplies and Dunbar's Camp." *Western Pennsylvania Historical Magazine* 17 (March 1934), 49–52.

Abernethy, Thomas Perkins. *Western Lands and the American Revolution*. 1937. Reprint, New York: Russell and Russell, 1959.

Abler, Thomas S. "Iroquois Cannibalism: Fact Not Fiction." *Ethnohistory* 27 (1980), 309–26.

Abler, Thomas S., and Michael H. Logan. "The Florescence and Demise of Iroquoian Cannibalism: Human Sacrifice and Malinowski's Hypothesis." *Man in the Northeast*, no. 35 (Spring 1988), 1–26.

Alberts, Robert C., *The Most Extraordinary Adventures of Major Robert Strobo*. Boston: Houghton Mifflin, 1965.

Albion, Robert G. *Forests and Sea Power: The Timber Problem of the Royal Navy, 1652–1862*. Cambridge, Mass.: Harvard University Press, 1926.

Alden, John. *General Gage in America*. Baton Rouge: University of Louisiana Press, 1948.

Alden, John R. "The Albany Congress and the Creation of the Indian Superintendencies." *Mississippi Valley History Review* 27, no. 2 (September 1940), 193–210.

Alden, John Richard. *John Stuart and Southeastern Colonial Frontier*. New York: Gordian Press, 1966.

Alford, Clarence Walworth. *The Mississippi Valley in British Politics: A Study of the Trade, Land Speculation, and Experiments in Imperialism Culminating in the American Revolution*, 2 vols. (1916). Reprint, New York: Russell and Russell, 1959.

Ambler, Charles H. *George Washington and the West*. 1936. Reprint, New York: Russell and Russell, 1971.

Anderson, F. W. "Why Did Colonial New Englanders Make Bad Soldiers? Contractual Principles and Military Conduct during the Seven Years' War." *William and Mary Quarterly* 38 (1981), 395–417.

Anderson, Fred. *A People's Army: Massachusetts' Soldiers and Society in the Seven Years' War*. New York: W. W. Norton, 1984.

Anderson, Niles. "The General Choses a Road: The Forbes Campaign of 1758 to Capture Fort Duquesne." *Western Pennsylvania Historical Magazine* 42 (1959), 109–38, 241–58, 383–401.

Anderson, Niles. "Bushy Run: Decisive Battle in the Wilderness: Pennsylvania and the Indian Rebellion of 1763." *Western Pennsylvania Magazine of History and Biography*, 46 (July 1963), 211–45.

Andre, Louis, *Michel le Tellier et l'Organization de l'Armee Monarchique*. Paris: Felix Alcan, 1906.

Andrews, Charles McLean. *The Colonial Period of American History*, 4 vols. New Haven, Conn.: Yale University Press, 1934–1938.

Antoine, Michel. "L'Entourage des ministres aux XVIIe et XVIIIe siecles." In Michael Antoine et al., eds., *Origines et Histories des Cabinets des Ministres en France*. Geneva: Librarie Droz, 1975.

Antoine, Michael. *Louis XV*. Paris: Librairie Artheme Fayard, 1989.

Aquila, Richard. "Down the Warrior's Path: The Causes of the Southern Wars of the Iroquois." *American Indian Quarterly* 4 (1978), 211–21.

Aquila, Richard. *The Iroquois Restoration: Iroquois Diplomacy on the Colonial Frontier, 1701–1754*. Detroit: Wayne State University Press, 1983.

Asprey, Robert. *Frederick the Great: The Magnificent Enigma*. New York: Ticknor & Fields, 1986.

Audet, F.-J. *Jean Daniel Dumas: Le Hero de la Monongahela*. Montreal: G. Ducharme, 1920.

Auth, Stephen. *The Ten Years' War: Indian–White Relations in Pennsylvania, 1755–1765*. New York: Garland Publishers, 1989.

Axtell, James. *The European and the Indian: Essays in the Ethnohistory of Colonial North America*. New York: Oxford University Press, 1981.

Axtell, James. *The Invasion Within: The Contest of Cultures in Colonial North America*. New York: Oxford University Press, 1985.

Axtell, James, and William C. Sturtevant. "The Unkindest Cut; or, Who Invented Scalping?" *William and Mary Quarterly* 3rd ser., 37 (1980), 451–72.

Ayling, Stanley. *The Elder Pitt, Earl of Chatham*. London: Collins, 1976.

Aymard, Maurice, ed. *Dutch Capitalism, World Capitalism*. Cambridge: Cambridge University Press, 1981.

Back, Francis, and Rene Chartrand. "Canadian Militia, 1750–1760." *Military Collector and Historian* 34, no. 1 (Spring 1984), 18–21.

Back, Francis, and Rene Chartrand. "French Engineers, New France, 175–1763." *Military Collector and Historian* 38, no. 1 (Spring 1986), 26–27.

Bailey, Alfred Goldsworthy. *The Conflict of European and Eastern Algonkian Cultures, 1504–1700*. Toronto: McClelland and Stewart, 1969.

Bailey, Kenneth P. *The Ohio Company of Virginia and the Westward Movement, 1748–1792*. Glendale, Calif.: Arthur H. Clark, 1939.

Bailyn, Bernard. *The Ideological Origins of the American Revolution*. Cambridge, Mass.: Belknap Press of Harvard University Press, 1967.

Bailyn, Bernard. *Voyagers to the West: A Passage in the Peopling of America on the Eve of Revolution*. New York: Alfred A. Knopf, 1986.

Baker, Charles E. "The William Starling Powder Horn and the Niagara Campaign of 1759." *New York Historical Society Quarterly* 32, no. 2 (April 1948).

Baker-Crothers, Hayes, and Ruth A. Hudnut. "A Private Soldier's Account of Washington's First Battles in the West: A Study in Historical Criticism." *Journal of Southern History* 8 (February 1942), 23–62.

Baker-Crothers, Hayes, and Ruth A. Hudnut. *Virginia and the French and Indian War*. Chicago: n.p., 1928.

Bancroft, George. *History of the United States*, 10 vols. Boston: Little, Brown, 1879.

Barbour, Philip L., ed. *The Complete Worlds of Captain John Smith, 1580–1631*, 3 vols. Chapel Hill: University of North Carolina Press, 1986.

Basye, Arthur Herbert. *The Lords Commissioners of Trade and Plantations, Commonly Known as the Board of Trade, 1748–1782*. New Haven, Conn.: Yale University Press, 1925.

Baugh, Daniel A. *British Naval Administration in the Age of Walpole*. Princeton, N.J.: Princeton University Press, 1965.

Bauman, Richard. *For the Reputation of Truth: Politics, Religion, and Conflict Among the Pennsylvania Quakers, 1750–1800*. Baltimore, Md.: Johns Hopkins University Press, 1971.

Baxter, Douglas Clark. "Premier Commis in the War Department in the Latter Part of the Reign of Louis XIV." In *Proceedings of the Western for French History* 8 (1981), 81–89.

Bean, Walton E. "War and the British Colonial Farmer: A Reevaluation in the Light of New Statistical Records." *Pacific Historical Review* 11 (1942), 439–47.

Beatson, Sir Robert. *Naval and Military Memoirs of Great Britain, from 1727 to 1783*, 2 vols. Boston: Gregg Press, 1972.

Beattie, Daniel J. "The Adaptation of the British Army to Wilderness Warfare, 1755–1763." In Maarten Ultee, ed., *Adapting to Conditions: War and Society in the Eighteenth Century*. Tuscaloosa: University of Alabama Press, 1986, 56–83.

Beattie, Judith, and Bernard Pothier. "The Battle of the Restigouche." *Canadian Historic Sites: Occasional Papers in Archeology and History* 16 (1977), 5–34.

Beer, George Louis. *British Colonial Policy, 1754–1765*. 1922. Reprint, facsimile, Gloucester, Mass.: Peter Smith, 1958.

Beik, Paul H. *A Judgement of the Old Regime: Being a Survey by the Parlement of Provence of the French Economic and Fiscal Policies at the Close of the Seven Years War.* New York: AMS Press, 1967.

Bell, Whitfield J., and Leonard Labaree. "Franklin and the 'Wagon Affair.'" *Proceedings of the American Philosophical Society* 101 (1957), 551–58.

Bellico, Russell P. *Chronicles of Lake George: Journeys in War and Peace.* New York: Purple Mountain Press, 1995.

Berkeley, Edmund, and Dorothy Smith Berkeley. *Dr. John Mitchell: The Man Who Made the Map of North America.* Chapel Hill: University of North Carolina Press, 1974.

Berkeley, Francis L. "The War of Jenkins Ear." In Darrett R. Rutman, ed., *The Old Dominion: Essays for Thomas Perkins Abernethy.* Charlottesville: University of Virginia Press, 1964, 41–61.

Berkhofer, Robert. "The French and Indians at Carillon." *The Bulletin of Fort Ticonderoga Museum* 9, no. 6 (1956), 134–69.

Bernier, Olivier. *Louis the Beloved: The Life of Louis XV.* Garden City, N.Y.: Doubleday and Co., 1984.

Bidwell, Percy Wells, and John I. Falconer. *History of Agriculture in the Northern United States, 1620–1860.* Washington, D.C.: Carnegie Institute, 1925.

Biggar, H. P., ed. *The Works of Samuel de Champlain,* 6 vols. Toronto: Champlain Society, 1922–1936.

Billington, Ray Allen, and Martin Ridge. *Westward Expansion: A History of the American Frontier.* 5th ed. New York: Macmillan, 1982.

Bird, Harrison. *Battle for a Continent.* New York: Oxford University Press, 1965.

Black, Jeremy. *Pitt the Elder.* New York: Cambridge University Press, 1992.

Blackey, Robert Alan. "The Political Career of George Montagu Dunk, 2nd Earl of Halifax, 1748–1771: A Study of an Eighteenth Century English Minister." Ph.D. diss., New York University, 1969.

Bond, Beverly W., ed. "The Captivity of Charles Stuart, 1755–57." *Mississippi Valley Historical Review* 13 (1926–1927), 58–81.

Bonomi, Patricia U. *A Factious People: People and Society in Colonial New York.* New York: Columbia University Press, 1971.

Boorstin, Daniel. *The Americans: The Colonial Experience.* London: Sphere Books, 1959.

Bradford, William. *Of Plymouth Plantations, 1620–1647.* Edited by Samuel E. Morrison. New York: Knopf, 1952.

Bradley, Arthur Granville. *The Fight with France for North America.* Toronto: Arno Press, 1908.

Branch, Douglas E. "Henry Bouquet: Professional Soldier." *Pennsylvania Magazine of History and Biography* 62 (1938), 41–51.

Brasseaux, Carl A. *The Founding of New Acadia: The Beginnings of Life in Louisiana, 1765–1803.* Baton Rouge: Louisiana State University Press, 1987.

Bray, George A. "Leather Caps During the French and Indian War." *Military Collector and Historian* 38, no. 2 (Summer 1966), 66.

Brebner, John Barlett. *New England's Outpost: Acadia Before the Conquest of Canada.* New York: Columbia University Press, 1927.

Brewster, William. *The Pennsylvania and New York Frontier, 1700–1763.* Philadelphia: George S. McManus Co., 1954.

Bridenbaugh, Carl. *The Colonial Craftsman*. Chicago: University of Chicago Press, 1950.

Bridenbaugh, Carl. *Cities in Revolt: Urban Life in America, 1743–1776*. New York: Alfred A. Knopf, 1955.

Bridenbaugh, Carl. *Cities in the Wilderness: The First Century of Urban Life in America*. New York: Alfred A. Knopf, 1955.

Bridenbaugh, Carl. *Mitre and Sceptre: Transatlantic Faiths, Ideas, Personalities, and Politics, 1689–1775*. New York: Oxford University Press, 1962.

Brock, Leslie V. *The Currency of the American Colonies, 1700–64*. New York: Arno Press, 1975.

Brown, Douglas. *The Catawba Indians: The People of the River*. Columbia: University of South Carolina Press, 1966.

Brown, George et al., eds. *Dictionary of Canadian Biography*. Toronto: University of Toronto Press, 1966–.

Brown, M. L., *Firearms in Colonial America: The Impact of History and Technology, 1492–1792*. Washington, D.C.: Smithsonian Institute, 1980.

Brown, Peter Douglas. *William Pitt, Earl of Chatham: The Great Commoner*. London: George Allen and Unwin, 1978.

Browning, Reed. *The Duke of Newcastle*. New Haven, Conn: Yale University Press. 1975.

Brownlee, W. Elliot. *Dynamics of Ascent: A History of the American Economy*. New York: Alfred A. Knopf, 1974.

Bruchey, Stuart. *Enterprise: The Dynamic Economy of a Free People*. Cambridge, Mass.: Harvard University Press, 1990.

Bruchey, Stuart, ed. *The Colonial Merchant: Sources and Readings*. New York: Harcourt, Brace, & World, 1966.

Brunet, Michel. *Les Canadiens Apres La Conquete, 1759–1775*. Montreal: Fides, 1969.

Buell, Leslie. "In Defense of the General." *The Bulletin of the Fort Ticonderoga Museum* 12, no. 3 (October 1967), 223–32.

Burrows, Edwin, and Michael Wallace. "The American Revolution: The Ideology and Psychology of National Liberation." *Perspectives on Early American History* 6 (1972), 208–15.

Butterfield, Herbert. *George III and the Historians*. Rev. ed. New York: Macmillan, 1969.

Buxbaum, Melvin H. *Benjamin Franklin and the Zealous Presbyterians*. University Park: Pennsylvania State University Press, 1975.

Calhoun, Arthur W. *A Social History of the American Family*. New York: Barnes & Noble, 1945.

Calloway, Colin. *The Abenaki*. New York: Chelsea House, 1989.

Calloway, Colin G. *The Western Abenaki of Vermont, 1600–1800: War, Migration, and the Survival of an Indian People*. Norman: University of Oklahoma Press, 1991.

Calloway, Colin G., ed. *North Country Captives: Selected Narratives of Indian Captivity from Vermont and New Hampshire*. Hanover, N.H.: University Press of New England, 1992.

Calmes, Alan. "The Lyttelton Expedition of 1759: Military Failures and Financial Successes." *South Carolina Historical Magazine* 77 (1976), 10–33.

288 BIBLIOGRAPHY

Cardwell, John M. "Mismanagement: The 1758 Expedition Against Carillon." *The Bulletin of the Fort Ticonderoga Museum* 15, no. 4 (1992), 236–91.

Cardy, Michael. "The Memoirs of Pierre Pouchot: A Soldier's View of a Doomed Campaign." *War, Literature, and the Arts* 4 (Spring 1992), 1–23.

Cardy, Michael, ed. "The Iroquois in the Eighteenth Century: A Neglected Source." *Man in the Northeast* 38 (Fall 1989), 1–20.

Caroll, Charles F. *The Timber Economy of Puritan New England.* Providence, R.I.: Brown University Press, 1973.

Carp, E. Wayne. "Early American Military History: A Review of Recent Work." *Virginia Magazine of History and Biography* 94 (1986), 259–84.

Carville, V. Earle. "Environment, Disease, and Mortality in Early Virginia." In Thad Tate and David Ammerman, eds., *The Chesapeake in the Seventeenth Century.* Chapel Hill: University of North Carolina Press, 1979.

Casgrain, H. R. *Guerre du Canada, 1760–1760, Montcalm et Levis,* 2 vols. Quebec: Imprimeries de L. J. Demers & Freres, 1891.

Cassady, James M. *Demography in Early America.* Cambridge, Mass.: Harvard University Press, 1969.

Cave, Alfred A. "Who Killed John Stone? A Note on the Origins of the Pequot War." *William and Mary Quarterly* 49 (1992), 509–21.

Champagne, Duane. "The Delaware Revitalization Movement of the Early 1760s: A Suggested Reinterpretation." *American Indian Quarterly* 12 (1988), 107–26.

Champion, Walter T. "Christian Frederick Post and the Winning of the West." *Pennsylvania Magazine of History and Biography* 104, no 3. (July 1980), 308–25.

Chapais, Thomas. *Le Marquis de Montcalm.* Quebec: J. P. Garneau, 1911.

Charland, Thomas M. "The Lake Champlain Army and the Fall of Montreal." *Vermont History* 28 (1960), 293–301.

Chartrand, Rene. "The Troops of French Louisiana, 1699–1769." *Military Collector and Historian* 25, no. 2 (Summer 1973), 58–65.

Chartrand, Rene. *The French Soldier in North America.* Bloomfield, Ont.: Museum Restoration Service, 1984.

Chartrand, Rene. *Canadian Military Heritage 1000–1754,* vol. 1. Montreal: Art Global, 1993.

Chartrand, Rene. *Canadian Military Heritage, 1755–1871,* vol. 2. Montreal: Art Global, 1995.

Chitwood, Oliver P. *A History of Colonial America.* New York: Harper & Bros., 1961.

Church, Clive H. *Revolution and Red Tape: The French Ministerial Bureaucracy, 1770–1850.* Oxford: Clarendon Press, 1981.

Clark, Andrew Hill. *Acadia: The Geography of Early Nova Scotia to 1760.* Madison: University of Wisconsin Press, 1968.

Clark, Charles E. "The Colonial Press." In Jacob Ernest Cooke, ed., *The Encyclopedia of the North American Colonies.* New York: Charles Scribner's Sons, 1993.

Clark, Victor S. *History of Manufacturing in the United States, 1607–1860,* 3 vols. Washington, D.C.: Carnegie Institute, 1929.

Clarke, Desmond. *Arthur Dobbs, Esquire, 1689–1765, Surveyor-General of Ireland,*

Prospector and Governor of North Carolina. Chapel Hill: University of North Carolina Press, 1957.

Clay, C. G. A. *Economic Expansion and Social Change: England, 1500–1700,* 2 vols. Cambridge: Cambridge University Press, 1984.

Clayton, T. R. "The Duke of Newcastle, the Earl of Halifax, and the American Origins of the Seven Years' War." *The Historical Journal* (Cambridge, England) 24, no. 3 (September 1981), 571–603.

Cleland, Hugh. *George Washington in the Ohio Valley.* Pittsburgh: University of Pittsburgh Press, 1955.

Clowes, Sir William Laird. *The Royal Navy: A History from the Earliest Times to the Present,* 7 vols. London: S. Low Martson and Company, 1897–1903.

Cognets, Louis des. *Amherst and Canada.* Princeton, N.J.: Princeton University Press, 1962.

Conrad, Glenn, ed. *The Cajuns: Essays on their History and Culture.* Lafayette: University of Southwestern Louisiana Press, 1978.

Cook, Roy Bird. "Virginia Frontier Defenses, 1719–1795." *West Virginia History* (1940), 119–30.

Cook, Sherburne F. "Interracial Warfare and Population Decline among the New England Indians." *Ethnohistory* 20 (1973), 1–24.

Cook, Sherburne F. "The Significance of Disease in the Extinction of the New England Indians." *Human Biology* 44 (1973), 485–508.

Corbett, Sir Julian S. *England in the Seven Years' War: A Study in Combined Strategy,* 2 vols. 2nd ed. London: Longmans, Green, 1907.

Corkran, David H. *The Cherokee Frontier: Conflict and Survival, 1740–62.* Norman: University of Oklahoma Press, 1962.

Corkran, David H. *The Creek Frontier, 1540–1783.* Norman: University of Oklahoma Press, 1967.

Corvisier, Andre. "Clienteles et fidelites dans l'armee francaise aux XVIIe et XVIIIe siecles." In Yves Durand, ed., *Homage a Roland Mousnier, Clienteles et Fidelities en Europe a l'Epoque Moderne.* Paris: Presses Universitaires de France, 1981, 217–18.

Countryman, Edward. *A People in Revolution: The American Revolution and Political Society in New York, 1760–1790.* Baltimore, Md.: Johns Hopkins University Press, 1981.

Coupland, Sir Reginald. *The Quebec Act: A Study in Statesmanship.* Oxford: Clarendon Press, 1925.

Cowan, John P. "George Washington at Fort Necessity." *Western Pennsylvania Historical Magazine* 37 (1954–1955), 153–80.

Cox, Bruce A., ed. *Native People, Native Lands.* Ottawa: Carleton University Press, 1988.

Crane, Verner W. *The Southern Frontier: 1670–1732.* Ann Arbor: University of Michigan Press, 1929.

Cress, Lawrence D. *Citizens in Arms: The Army and Militia in American Society to the War of 1812.* Chapel Hill: University of North Carolina Press, 1982.

Cress, Lawrence Delbert. "Radical Wiggery on the Role of the Military: Ideological Roots of the American Revolutionary Militia." *Journal of the History of Ideas* 40 (1979), 43–60.

Cressy, David. *Coming Over: Migration and Communication Between England and*

New England in the Seventeenth Century. Cambridge: Cambridge University Press, 1987.

Cronon, William. *Changes in the Land: Indians, Colonists, and the Ecology of New England.* New York: Hill and Wang, 1983.

Cuneo, John R. *Robert Rogers of the Rangers.* Ticonderoga, N.Y.: Fort Ticonderoga Museum, 1988.

Cutcliffe, Stephen H. "Colonial Indian Policy as a Measure of Rising Imperialism: New York and Pennsylvania, 1700–1755." *Western Pennsylvania Historical Magazine* 64 (1981), 237–68.

Dahlinger, Charles W. "The Marquis Duquesne, Sieur de Mennevilles, Founder of the City of Pittsburgh." *Western Pennsylvania Historical Magazine* 15 (1932), 2–23.

Daniels, John D. "The Indian Population of North America in 1492." *William and Mary Quarterly* 49 (1992), 298–320.

Darlington, William M., ed. *Christopher Gist's Journals.* Cleveland: Arthur H. Clark, 1893.

Davies, Ralph. *The Rise of the Atlantic Economies.* Ithaca, N.Y.: Cornell University Press, 1973.

Day, Gordon M. "Rogers' Raid in Indian Tradition." *Historical New Hampshire* 17 (1962), 3–17.

Day, Gordon M. *The Identity of the St. Francis Indians.* Ottawa: National Museum of Man Mercury Series, Canadian Ethnology Service Paper 71, 1981.

Demos, John. *The Unredeemed Captive: A Family Story from Early America.* New York: Vintage Books, 1995.

Dickerson, Oliver M. *The Navigation Acts and the American Revolution.* New York: Octagon, 1978.

Dickinson, John A. "La Guerre Iroquoise et la mortalite en Nouvelle-France, 1608–1666." *Revue d'Histoire de l'Amerique Francaise* 36 (1982–1983), 31–54.

Dobyns, Henry F. *Their Numbers Became Thinned: Native American Population Dynamics in Eastern North America.* Knoxville: University of Tennessee Press, 1983.

Dolan, Jay P. *The American Catholic Experience: A History from Colonial Times to the Present.* Garden City, N.Y.: Doubleday and Co., 1985.

Donaldson, Gordon. *Battle for a Continent: Quebec 1759.* Toronto: Doubleday, 1973.

Dorn, Walter Louis. *Competition for Empire, 1740–1763.* New York: Harper and Row, 1940.

Doughty, Howard. *Francis Parkman.* New York: Macmillan, 1962.

Dowd, Gregory Evans. "The French King Wakes Up in Detroit: Pontiac's War in Rumor and History." *Ethnohistory* 37 (1990), 254–78.

Dowd, Gregory Evans. *A Spiritual Resistance: The North American Indian Struggle for Unity, 1745–1812.* Baltimore: Johns Hopkins University Press, 1992.

Dowd, Gregory Evans. "Thinking and Believing: Nativism and Unity in the Ages of Pontiac and Tecumseh." *American Indian Quarterly* 16 (1992), 309–35.

Downes, Randolph C. *Council Fires on the Upper Ohio: A Narrative of Indian Affairs in the Upper Ohio Valley until 1795.* Pittsburgh: University of Pittsburgh Press, 1969.

Downey, Fairfax. *Louisbourg: Key to a Continent.* Englewood Cliffs, N.J.: Prentice-Hall, 1965.

Doyle, J. A. *The Colonies Under the House of Hanover.* London: Longmans, Green and Co., 1907.

Drake, Samuel G. *A Particular History of the Five Years French and Indian War.* Boston: J. Munsell, 1870.

Duffy, Christopher. *The Fortress in the Age of Vauban and Frederick the Great.* London: Routledge and Kegan Paul, 1985.

Duffy, Christopher. *The Military Experience in the Age of Reason, 1715–1789.* New York: Barnes & Noble, 1987.

Dunnigan, Brian Leigh. "Portaging Niagara," *Inland Seas,* 42, no. 3 (Fall 1986), 177–83, 216–23.

Dunnigan, Brian Leigh. *Glorious Old Relic: The French Castle and Old Fort Niagara.* Youngstown, N.Y.: Old Fort Niagara Association, 1987.

Dunnigan, Brian Leigh. *Siege 1759: The Campaign Against Niagara.* Youngstown, N.Y.: Old Fort Niagara Association, 1996.

Durant, Will, and Ariel Durant. *Rousseau and Revolution: A History of Civilization in France, England and Germany from 1756, and in the Remainder of Europe from 1715 to 1789.* New York: Simon and Schuster, 1967.

Eccles, W. J. "The History of New France According to Francis Parkman." *William and Mary Quarterly* 3rd ser., 18 (1961), 163–75.

Eccles, W. J. *Canada Under Louis XIV 1663–1701.* Toronto: McClelland and Stewart, 1964.

Eccles, W. J. "Coulon de Villers de Jumonville, Joseph." *Dictionary of Canadian Biography.* Toronto: University of Toronto Press, 1966–, 3:150–51.

Eccles, W. J. "The French Forces in North America During the Seven Years' War." *Dictionary of Canadian Biography.* Toronto: University of Toronto Press, 1966–, 3, xv–xxii.

Eccles, W. J. "Montcalm, Louis-Joseph de, Marquis de Montcalm." *Dictionary of Canadian Biography.* Toronto: University of Toronto Press, 1966–, 3, 458–69.

Eccles, W. J. *The Canadian Frontier, 1535–1760.* New York: Holt, Rinehart and Winston, 1969.

Eccles, W. J. *France in America.* New York: Harper and Row, 1972.

Eccles, W. J. "A Belated Review of Harold Adams Innis, The Fur Trade in Canada." *Canadian Historical Review* 60 (1983), 341–441.

Eccles, W. J. "The Fur Trade and Eighteenth Century Imperialism." *William and Mary Quarterly* 3rd ser., 40 (1983), 341–62.

Eckert, Alan. *Wilderness Empire: A Narrative.* Boston: Little, Brown, 1969.

Edmunds, David. "Pickawillany: French Military Power Versus British Economics." *Western Pennsylvania Historical Magazine* 58 (1975), 169–84.

Edmunds, David R. *The Potawatomis: Keepers of the Fire.* Norman: University of Oklahoma Press, 1978.

Eid, Leroy V. "The Objibwa–Iroquois War: The War the Five Nations Did Not Win." *Ethnohistory* 26, no. 4 (Fall 1979), 297–324.

Eid, Leroy V. " 'National' War Among Indians of Northeastern North America." *Canadian Review of North American Studies* 16, no. 2 (Summer 1985), 125–54.

Eid, Leroy V. " 'A Kind of Running Fight': Indian Battlefield Tactics in the Late Eighteenth Century." *Western Pennsylvania Historical Magazine* 71 (1988), 147–71.

Eliot, Emory, ed. *American Literature: A Prentice-Hall Anthology*, vol. 1. Englewood Cliffs, N.J.: Prentice-Hall, 1991.

Elliott, J. H. *Imperial Spain, 1469–1716*. New York: St. Martin's Press, 1963.

Elliott, J. H. *The Old World and the New, 1492–1650*. Cambridge: Cambridge University Press, 1970.

Ellis, John Tracy. *Catholics in Colonial America*. Baltimore, Md.: Helicon Press,
1965.

Entick, John. *General History of the Late War: Containing its Rise, Progress, and
Events in Europe, Asia, Africa, and America*, 5 vols. London: Edward Dilly
and John Millan, 1763–1764.

Ernest, Joseph Albert. *Money and Politics in America, 1755–65: A Study in the Currency Act of 1764 and the Political Economy of Revolution*. Chapel Hill: University of North Carolina Press, 1973.

Evans, Gregory. "Thinking and Believing: Nativism and Unity in the Ages of Pontiac
and Tecumseh." *American Indian Quarterly* 16 (1992), 309–35.

Everett, Edward G. "Pennsylvania's Indian Diplomacy, 1747–1753." *Western Pennsylvania Historical Magazine* 44 (September 1961), 241–56.

"The Examination of Benjamin Franklin." In A. H. Smyth, ed., *Writings of Benjamin Franklin*, 10 vols. New York: n.p., 1905–1907, 4:424.

Fausz, J. Frederick. "The 'Barbarous Massacre' Reconsidered: The Powhatan Uprising of 1622 and the Historians." *Explorations in Ethnic Studies* 1 (1978), 16–
36.

Fausz, J. Frederick. "Fighting Fire with Firearms: The Anglo-Powhatan Arms Race
in Early Virginia." *American Indian Culture and Research Journal* 3 (1979),
39–47.

Fausz, J. Frederick. "An 'Abundance of Blood Shed on Both Sides': England's First
Indian War, 1609–1614." *Virginia Magazine of History and Biography* 98
(1990), 9–16.

Fautaux, Aegidius. *Les Chevaliers de Saint-Lousi en Canada*. Montreal: Les Edition
Dix, 1940.

Fautaux, Aegidius. "Officier e Montcalm." *Revue d'Historique de l'Amerique Francaise* 3, no. 3 (December 1949), 367–82.

Fautaux, Aegidius. "Quelques officiers de Montcalm." *Revue d'Historique de
l'Amerique Francaise* 5, no. 3 (December 1951), 404–15.

Fenton, William, ed. *Parker on the Iroquois*. Syracuse, N.Y.: Syracuse University Press,
1968.

Ferguson, E. James. *The Power of the Purse*. Chapel Hill: University of North Carolina
Press, 1961.

Ferguson, E. James. *The American Revolution: A General History, 1763–1790*.
Homewood, Ill.: Dorsey Press, 1979.

Ferling, John E. *A Wilderness of Miseries: War and Warriors in Early America*. Westport, Conn.: Greenwood Press, 1980.

Finn, Gerald. "Le Loutre, Jean-Louis." *Dictionary of Canadian Biography*. Toronto:
University of Toronto Press, 1966–, 4:453–58.

Firth, Sir Charles Harding. *Cromwell's Army: A History of the English Soldier during
the Civil Wars, the Commonwealth, and the Protectorate*. London: Methuen,
1962.

Fischer, David Hackett. *Paul Revere's Ride*. New York: Oxford University Press, 1994.

Fisher, John S. "Colonel Armstrong's Expedition Against Kittanning." *Pennsylvania Magazine of History and Biography* 51 (January 1927), 1–14.

Fitzhugh, William W., ed. *Cultures in Contact: The Impact of European Contacts on Native American Institutions, A.D. 1000–1800*. Washington, D.C.: Smithsonian Institution, 1985.

Flexner, James Thomas. *First Flowers of Our Wilderness: American Painting*. Boston: Houghton Mifflin, 1947.

Flexner, James Thomas. *George Washington: The Forge of Experience, 1732–1775*. Boston: Little, Brown, 1965.

Flexner, James Thomas. *Mohawk Baronet: A Biography of Sir William Johnson*. 1959. Reprint, Syracuse, N.Y.: Syracuse University Press, 1979.

Foote, William A. "The South Carolina Independents." *South Carolina Historical Magazine* 62 (1961), 195–99.

Foote, William A. "The Pennsylvania Men of the American Regiment." *Pennsylvania Magazine of History and Biography* 87 (1963), 31–38.

Fortescue, Sir John W. *A History of the British Army*, 13 vols. 1910–1935. Reprint, New York: AMS Press, 1976.

Fortier, John. *Fortress of Louisbourg*. Toronto: Oxford University Press, 1979.

Franklin, W. Neil. "Pennsylvania-Virginia Rivalry for the Indian Trade of the Ohio Valley." *Mississippi Valley Historical Review* 20 (March 1934), 463–80.

Fregault, Guy. *Francois Bigot: Administrateur Francais*, 2 vols. Montreal: Universite de Montreal Institute d'Histoire de l'Amerique Francaise, 1948.

Fregault, Guy. *Canada: The War of the Conquest, 1754–1760*. 1955. Trans. Margaret M. Cameron. Toronto: Oxford University Press, 1969.

Frey, Sylvia R. "Courts and Cats: British Military Justice in the Eighteenth Century." *Military Affairs* 43 (1979), 5–9.

Frey, Sylvia R. *The British Soldier in America: A Social History of Military Life in the Revolutionary Period*. Austin: University of Texas Press, 1981.

Fry, Bruce W. *"An Appearance of Strength": The Fortifications of Louisbourg*, 2 vols. Ottawa: Parks Commission, 1984.

Furcron, Thomas B., and Elizabeth Ann Boyle. "The Building of Fort Carillon, 1755–1758." *The Bulletin of the Fort Ticonderoga Museum* 10 (1955), 13–67.

Gaboury, Jean-Pierre. *Le Nationalism de Lionel Groulx: Aspects Ideologiques*. Ottawa: Editions de l'Universite d'Ottawa, 1970.

Gagnon, Serge. *Le Quebec et ses Historiens de 1840 a 1920*. Quebec: Presses de l'Universite Laval, 1978.

Galenson, David W. *White Servitude in Colonial America: An Economic Analysis*. Cambridge: Cambridge University Press, 1981.

Galloway, Patricia, ed. *La Salle and His Legacy: Frenchmen and Indians in the Lower Mississippi Valley*. Jackson: University of Mississippi Press, 1982.

Garneau, Francois-Xavier. *Histoire du Canada*, 4 vols. Quebec: Lacour, Gayet, Robert, 1852.

Gegenheimer, Albert Frank. *William Smith, Educator and Churchman, 1727–1803*. Philadelphia: University of Pennsylvania Press, 1943.

Gelinas, Cyrille. *The Role of Fort Chambly in the Development of New France, 1665–1760*. Ottawa: Parks Canada, 1983.

Gilbert, Arthur N. "The Changing Face of British Military Justice, 1757–1783." *Military Affairs* 49 (1979), 80–84.

Gipson, L. H. "A French Project for Victory Short of a Declaration of War, 1755." *Canadian Historical Review* 26 (1945).

Gipson, Lawrence Henry. *The Great War for Empire: The Victorious Years, 1758–1760*. New York: Alfred A. Knopf, 1949.

Gipson, Lawrence Henry. "Thomas Hutchinson and the Framing of the Albany Plan of Union, 1754." *Pennsylvania Magazine of History and Biography* 74 (January 1950), 5–35.

Gipson, Lawrence Henry. *Zones of International Friction: The Great Lakes Frontier, Canada, the West Indies, India, 1748–1754*. New York: Alfred A. Knopf, 1952.

Gipson, Lawrence Henry. *The British Empire before the American Revolution*, 12 vols. New York: Alfred A. Knopf, 1958–1970.

Gipson, Lawrence Henry. *The Great War for Empire: The Years of Defeat, 1754–1757*. New York: Alfred A. Knopf, 1959.

Gipson, Lawrence Henry. *The Triumphant Empire: Thunder Clouds Gather in the West, 1763–1766*. New York: Alfred A. Knopf, 1961.

Gipson, Lawrence Henry. *The Great War for Empire: The Culmination, 1760–1763*. New York: Alfred A. Knopf, 1964.

Gipson, Lawrence Henry. *A Biographical Guide to the History of the British Empire, 1748–1776*. New York: Alfred A. Knopf, 1968.

Godfrey, William G. "Bradstreet, John (baptised Jean-Baptiste)." *Dictionary of Canadian Biography*. Toronto: University of Toronto Press, 1966–, 4:83–87.

Godfrey, William G. *Pursuit of a Profit and Preferment in Colonial North America: John Bradstreet's Quest*. Waterloo, Ont.: Wilfred Laurier University Press, 1982.

Goldstein, Robert. *French-Iroquois Diplomatic and Military Relations 1609–1701*. The Hague: PMA Publishing Corp., 1969.

Goodwin, Gary C. *Cherokees in Transition: A Study of Changing Culture and Environment Prior to 1775*. Chicago: University of Chicago, Department of Geography, 1977.

Gradish, Stephen F. *The Manning of the British Navy during the Seven Years' War*. London: Royal Historical Society, 1980.

Graham, Dominick. "Lawrence, Charles." *Dictionary of Canadian Biography*. Toronto: University of Toronto Press, 1966–, 3:361–67.

Graham, Dominick. "The Planning of the Beausejour Operation and the Approaches to War in 1755." *New England Quarterly* 41 (1968), 551–66.

Graham, G. S. *Empire of the North Atlantic: The Maritime Struggle for North America*. Toronto: University of Toronto Press, 1950.

Graham, Gerald S. "The Naval Defense of British North America, 1739–1763." *Royal Historical Society Transactions* 4th ser., 30 (1948), 95–110.

Graham, Gerald S., ed. *The Walker Expedition to Quebec, 1711*. Toronto: Champlain Society Publications 32, 1953.

Graham, James. *History of the United State of North America, From the Plantations of the British Colonies Till Their Assumption of National Independence*, 4 vols. Boston: C. C. Little & J. Brown, 1845.

Grant, Charles S. "Pontiac's Rebellion and the British Troop Moves of 1763." *Mississippi Valley Historical Review* 40 (June 1953), 75–88.

Grant, William L. "Canada Versus Guadeloupe, an Episode of the Seven Years' War." *American Historical Review* 17, no. 4 (July 1912), 735–43.

Grant, William L. "The Capture of Oswego in 1756." *Proceedings of the New York State Historical Association* 8 (1914), 338–67.

Graves, Donald E. *French Military Terminology, 1670–1815.* St. John, N.B.: The New Brunswick Museum, 1979.

Gray, Lewis C., *History of Agriculture in the Southern United States to 1860.* Washington, D.C.: Carnegie Institute, 1933.

Greene, Jack P. "The South Carolina Quartering Dispute, 1757–1758." *South Carolina Historical Magazine* 60 (1959), 193–204.

Greene, Jack P. *The Reinterpretation of the American Revolution, 1763–1789.* New York: Harper and Row, 1968.

Greene, Jack P. *The Quest for Power: The Lower Houses of Assembly in the Southern Royal Colonies, 1689–1776.* 1963. Reprint, New York: W. W. Norton, 1972.

Greene, Jack P. "The Social Origins of the American Revolution: An Evaluation and Interpretation." *Political Science Quarterly* 88 (1973), 1–14.

Greene, Jack P. "An Uneasy Connection: An Analysis of the Preconditions of the American Revolution." In Stephen G. Kurtz and James H. Hutson, eds., *Essays on the American Revolution.* Chapel Hill: University of North Carolina Press, 1973, 35–45.

Greene, Jack P. " 'A Posture of Hostility': A Reconsideration of Some Aspects of the Origins of the American Revolution." *Proceedings of the American Antiquarian Society* 87 (April–October 1977), 27–68.

Greene, Jack P. "The Seven Years' War and the American Revolution: The Causal Relationship Reconsidered." In Peter Marshall and Glyn Williams, eds., *The British Atlantic Empire Before the American Revolution.* London: Frank Cass, 1980.

Grinnel-Milne, Duncan. *Man Is He? The Character and Achievement of James Wolfe.* London: Bodley Head, 1963.

Groulx, Lionel Adolphe. *Lendemain de Conquete.* Montreal: Universite de Montreal, 1920.

Gwyn, Julian. "British Government Spending and the North American Colonies, 1740–1775." In Peter Marshall and Glyn Williams, eds., *The British Atlantic Empire before the American Revolution.* London: Frank Cass, 1980.

Haan, Richard L. "Covenant and Consensus: Iroquois and English, 1676–1760." In Daniel K. Richter and James H. Merrell, eds., *Beyond the Covenant Chain: The Iroquois and Their Neighbors in Indian North America, 1600–1800.* Syracuse, N.Y.: Syracuse University Press, 1987, 41–57.

Hadlock, Wendell Stanwood. "War Among the Northeastern Woodland Indians." *American Anthropologist* 59 (April–June 1947), 204–21.

Hagerty, Gilbert. *Massacre at Fort Bull: The De Lery Expedition against the Oneida Carry, 1756.* Providence, R.I.: Mowbray Company Publishers, 1971.

Hamer, P. M. "Anglo-French Rivalry in the Cherokee Country, 1754–1757." *North Carolina Historical Review* 2 (July 1925), 303–22.

Hamer, P. M. "Fort Loudoun in the Cherokee War, 1758–1761." *North Carolina Historical Review* 2 (October 1925), 442–48.

Hamer, Philip M., ed. *A Guide to Archives and Manuscripts in the United States.* New Haven, Conn.: Yale University Press, 1961.

Hamilton, Edward. *The French and Indian Wars: The Story of Battles and Forts in the Wilderness.* Garden City, N.Y.: Doubleday and Co., 1962.

Hamilton, Edward. *Fort Ticonderoga: Key to a Continent.* Boston: Little, Brown, 1964.

Hamilton, Edward P. *The French Army in America.* Ottawa: Museum Restoration Service, 1967.

Hamilton, Edward Pierce. "Colonial Warfare in North America." *Massachusetts Historical Society Proceedings* 80 (1968), 3–15.

Hamilton, Milton W. "Battle Report, General William Johnson's Letter to the Governors, Lake George, September 9–10, 1755." *American Antiquarian Society Proceedings* 74 (1964), 19–36.

Hamilton, Milton W. *Sir William Johnson: Colonial America, 1715–1763.* Port Washington, N.Y.: Kennikat Press, 1976.

Hanna, Charles A. *The Wilderness Trail, or the Ventures and Adventures of Pennsylvania Traders on the Allegheny Path,* 2 vols. New York: Putnam and Sons, 1911.

Hardaway, John A. "Colonial and Revolutionary War Origins of American Military Policy." *Military Review* 56 (1976), 77–89.

Harkness, Albert. "Americanism and Jenkins' Ear." *Mississippi Valley Historical Review* 37 (June 1950), 57–91.

Harrington, J. C. *New Light on Washington's Fort Necessity: A Report on the Archeological Explorations at Fort Necessity National Battlefield Site.* Richmond, Va.: Eastern National Park and Monument Association, 1957.

Hauptman, Laurence M., and James D. Wherry, eds. *The Pequots in Southern New England: The Fall and Rise of an American Indian Nation.* Norman: University of Oklahoma Press, 1990.

Heard, J. Norman. *White Unto Red: A Study of the Assimilation of White Persons Captured by Indians.* Methuen, N.J.: Scarecrow Press, 1973.

Henretta, James A. *"Salutary Neglect": Colonial Administration Under the Duke of Newcastle.* Princeton, N.J.: Princeton University Press, 1972.

Henretta, James A. *The Evolution of American Society, 1700–1815: An Interdisciplinary Analysis.* Lexington, Mass.: D.C. Heath, 1973.

Hibbert, C. *Wolfe at Quebec.* Cleveland: World Publishing Company, 1959.

Higginbotham, Don. *The War of American Independence: Military Attitudes, Policies, and Practice, 1763–1789.* Boston: Northeastern University Press, 1983.

Higginbotham, Don. "Early American Way of War: Reconnaissance and Appraisal." *William and Mary Quarterly* 44 (1987), 226–41.

Higonnet, Patrice Louis-Rene. "The Origins of the Seven Years' War." *Journal of Military History* 40 (March 1968), 57–90.

Hitsman, J. Mackay. "Order before Landing at Louisbourg, 1758." *Military Affairs* 22 (Fall 1958), 146–48.

Hitsman, J. Mackay, and C. C. J. Bond. "The Assault Landing at Louisbourg, 1758." *Canadian Historical Review* 35 (1954), 323–24.

Hoffman, Paul E. *The Spanish Crown and the Defense of the Caribbean, 1565–1568: Precedent, Patrimonialism, and Royal Parsimony.* Baton Rouge: University of Louisiana Press, 1980.

Houlding, J. A. *Fit for Service: The Training of the British Army, 1715–1795.* Oxford: Oxford University Press, 1980.

Houlding, J. A. *French Arms Drill of the 18th Century.* Bloomfield, Ont.: Museum Restoration, 1988.

Howard, C. N. "The Military Occupation of British West Florida, 1763." *Florida Historical Quarterly* 17 (January 1939), 181–99.

Howard, James H. *Shawnee: The Ceremonialism of a Native American Tribe and Its Cultural Background.* Athens: University of Ohio Press, 1981.

Hudson, Charles. *The Southeastern Indians.* Knoxville: University of Tennessee Press, 1976.

Hunt, George T. *Wars of the Iroquois.* Madison: University of Wisconsin Press, 1960.

Hunter, William A. "Provincial Negotiations with the Western Indians, 1754–58." *Pennsylvania History* 18 (July 1951), 213–19.

Hunter, William A. *Forts on the Pennsylvania Frontier, 1753–1758.* Harrisburg: Pennsylvania Historical and Museum Commission, 1960.

Hunter, William A. "Documented Subdivisions of the Delaware Indians." *Bulletin of the Archaeological Society of New Jersey* 20 (1978).

Hutson, James. *Pennsylvania, 1949–1770: The Movement for Royal Government and Its Consequences.* Princeton, N.J.: Princeton University Press, 1972.

Hutson, James H. "Benjamin Franklin and Pennsylvanian Politics, 1751–1735: A Reappraisal." *Pennsylvania Magazine of History and Biography* 93 (1969), 303–71.

Innis, Harold. *The Cod Fisheries: The History of An International Economy.* New Haven, Conn.: Yale University Press, 1940.

Innis, Harold A. *The Fur Trade in Canada: An Introduction to Canadian Economic History.* New Haven, Conn.: Yale University Press, 1930.

Israel, Jonathan I. *Dutch Primacy in World Trade, 1585–1740.* Oxford: Clarendon Press, 1989.

Ivers, Larry E. *British Drums on the Southern Frontier: The Military Colonization of Georgia, 1733–1749.* Chapel Hill: University of North Carolina Press, 1974.

Jacobs, Wilbur R. "Presents to Indians as a Factor in the Conspiracy of Pontiac." *Michigan History* 33 (December 1949), 314–22.

Jacobs, Wilbur R. *Wilderness Politics and Indian Gifts: The Northern Colonial Frontier, 1748–1763.* Lincoln: University of Nebraska Press, 1950.

Jacobs, Wilbur R. "A Message to Fort William Henry: An Incident in the French and Indian War." *Huntington Library Quarterly* 16 (August 1953), 371–81.

Jacobs, Wilbur R., ed. *The Appalachian Indian Frontier: The Edmond Atkin Report and Plan of 1755.* 1954. Reprint, Lincoln: University of Nebraska Press, 1967.

Jacobs, Wilbur R. *Francis Parkman: The Historian as Hero: The Formative Years.* Austin: University of Texas Press, 1991.

Jaenen, Cornelius J. *The French Relationship with the Indian Peoples of New France and Acadia.* Ottawa: Research Branch, Indian and Northern Affairs, 1984.

Jaenen, Randolph C. Cornelius. "The Role of Presents in French-Amerindian Trade." In *Explorations in Canadian Economic History: Essays in Honor of Irene M. Spry.* Ottawa: University of Ottawa Press, 1985, 231–50.

James, Alfred P. *The Ohio Company: Its Inner History.* Pittsburgh: University of Pittsburgh Press, 1959.

James, Alfred P., and Charles M. Stotz. "Drums in the Forest." *Western Pennsylvania Historical Magazine* 41 (Autumn 1958), 3–27.

James, Alfred Procter. "Decision at the Forks." *Western Pennsylvania Historical Magazine* 41, nos. 3 and 4 (Autumn 1958), 39–56.

Jameson, J. Franklin. *The American Revolution Considered as a Social Movement.* Princeton, N.J.: Princeton University Press, 1967.

Jansen, Cornelius J. *The Relationship with the Native People of New France and Acadia.* Ottawa: Research Branch, Indian and Northern Affairs Canada, 1984.

Jennings, Francis. "A Vanishing Indian: Francis Parkman Versus His Sources." *Pennsylvania Magazine of History and Biography* (1963), 306–23.

Jennings, Francis. "Glory, Death, and Transfiguration: The Susquehannock Indians in the Seventeenth Century." *Proceedings of the American Philosophical Society* 112 (1968), 15–53.

Jennings, Francis. *The Invasion of America: Indians, Colonialism, and the Cant of Conquest.* Chapel Hill: University of North Carolina Press, 1975.

Jennings, Francis. *The Ambiguous Iroquois Empire: The Covenant Chain Confederation of Indian Tribes with English Colonies.* New York: W. W. Norton, 1984.

Jennings, Francis. "Francis Parkman: A Brahmin Among Untouchables." *William and Mary Quarterly*, 3rd ser., 42 (1985), 305–28.

Jennings, Francis. *Empire of Fortune: Crowns, Colonies, & Tribes in the Seven Years War in America.* New York: W. W. Norton, 1988.

Jensen, Merrill. *The Founding of a Nation: A History of the American Revolution, 1763–1776.* New York: Oxford University Press, 1968.

Johnson, Allen, and Dumas Malone, eds. *Dictionary of American Biography.* New York: Charles Scribner's Sons, 1928–1944.

Johnson, Emory R. et al. *History of Domestic and Foreign Commerce of the United States,* vol. 1. Washington, D.C.: Carnegie Institute, 1915.

Johnson, James Guyton. "The Colonial Southeast, 1732–1763; An International Contest for Territorial and Economic Control." *University of Colorado Studies* 19, no. 3 (1932), 163–225.

Johnson, James M. *Militia, Rangers, and Redcoats: The Military in Georgia, 1754–1776.* Macon, Georgia: Mercer University Press, 1994.

Johnson, Richard R. *Adjustment to Empire: The New England Colonies, 1675–1715.* New Brunswick, N.J.: Rutgers University Press, 1981.

Johnson, Richard R. "The Imperial Webb: The Thesis of Garrison Government in Early America Considered." *William and Mary Quarterly* 43 (1986), 408–30.

Johnson, Victor L. "Fair Traders and Smugglers in Philadelphia, 1754–1763." *Pennsylvania Magazine of History and Biography* 83 (1959), 125–49.

Johnston, Susan. "Epidemics: The Forgotten Factor in Seventeenth Century Native Warfare in the St. Lawrence Region." In Bruce A. Cox, ed., *Native Peoples, Native Lands.* Ottawa: Carleton University Press, 1988.

Jones, Alice Hanson. *Wealth of a Nation to Be: The American Colonies on the Eve of the Revolution.* New York: Columbia University Press, 1980.

Jordan, Winthrop D. *White Over Black.* Chapel Hill: University of North Carolina Press, 1968.

Kamen, Henry. *Spain, 1469–1714: A Society in Conflict.* London: Longman, 1983.

Kammen, Michael. *A Rope of Sand: The Colonial Agents, British Politics, and the American Revolution.* Ithaca, N.Y.: Cornell University Press, 1968.

Katz, Stanley Nider. *Newcastle's New York: Anglo-American Politics, 1732–1753.* Cambridge, Mass.: Belknap Press, 1968.

Katz, Steven T. "The Pequot War Reconsidered." *New England Quarterly* 64 (1991), 26–34.

Kawashima, Yasuhide. *Puritan Justice and the Indian: White Man's Law in Massachusetts, 1630–1763.* Middletown, Conn.: Wesleyan University Press, 1986.

Keeler, Mary Frear, ed. *Sir Francis Drake's West Indian Voyage, 1585–86.* London: Hakylut Society, 1981.

Kennett, Lee. *The French Armies in the Seven Years' War: A Study in Military Organization and Administration.* Durham, N.C.: Duke University Press, 1967.

Kent, Donald. *The French Invasion of Western Pennsylvania.* Harrisburg: Pennsylvania Historical and Museum Commission, 1954.

Kerr, Wilfred B. "Fort Niagara, 1759–1763." *New York History* 15 (July 1934), 281–301.

Kerridge, Eric. *The Agricultural Revolution.* London: Allen & Unwin, 1973.

Ketcham, Ralph L. "Conscience, War, and Politics in Pennsylvania, 1755–1757." *William and Mary Quarterly* 3rd ser., 20 (1963), 416–39.

Ketcham, Ralph L. "Benjamin Franklin William Smith: New Light on an Old Philadelphia Quarrel." *Pennsylvania Magazine of History and Geography* 88, no. 2 (April 1964), 143–44, 146.

Kingsford, William. *The History of Canada,* 10 vols. London: Roswell, Hutchinson, 1887–1898.

Kinietz, W. Vernon. *The Indians of the Western Great Lakes, 1615–1760.* 1940. Reprint, Ann Arbor: University of Michigan Press, 1996.

Klinefelter, Walter. *Lewis Evans and His Maps.* Philadelphia: American Philosophical Society, new series 61:7 (July 1971).

Knollenberg, Bernard. "General Amherst and Germ Warfare." *Mississippi Valley Historical Review* 41 (1954), 489–94.

Knollenberg, Bernard. *The Origins of the American Revolution 1759–1775.* New York: Macmillan, 1960.

Knollenberg, Bernard. *George Washington: the Virginia Period, 1732–1775.* Durham, N.C.: Duke University Press, 1964.

Koontz, Louis Knott. *Robert Dinwiddie, His Career in American Colonial Government and Westward Expansion.* Glendale, Calif.: Arthur H. Clark, 1941.

Kopperman, Paul E. *Braddock at the Monongahela.* Pittsburgh: University of Pennsylvania Press, 1977.

Kopperman, Paul E. "An Assessment of the Cholmley's Batman and British A Journals of Braddock's Campaign." *Western Pennsylvania Historical Magazine* 62 (1979), 197–218.

Krech, Shepard, ed. *Indians, Animals, and the Fur Trade: A Critique of Keepers of the Game.* Athens: University of Georgia Press, 1981.

Kupperman, Karen O. *Settling with the Indians: The Meeting of English and Indian Cultures 1580–1640.* Totowa, N.J.: Rowman & Littlefield, 1981.

Labaree, Leonard Woods. *Royal Government in America: A Study of the British Colonial System Before 1783.* New Haven, Conn.: Yale University Press, 1930.

Labaree, Leonard Woods. "Benjamin Franklin and the Defense of Pennsylvania, 1754–1757." *Pennsylvania History* 29 (1962), 7–23.

Lacour-Gayet, G. *La Marine Militaire de la France sous la Regne de Louis XV.* Paris: Librarie Ancienne, 1910.

Lanctot, Gustave. *Garneau, Historien National.* Montreal: Eides, 1946.

Lanctot, Gustave. *A History of Canada: From the Treaty of Utrecht to the Treaty of Paris, 1713–1763*, trans. Josephine Hambleton and Margaret M. Cameron, 3 vols. Cambridge, Mass.: Harvard University Press, 1963–1965.

Langdon, George D. *Pilgrim Colony: A History of New Plymouth, 1620–1691*. New Haven, Conn.: Yale University Press, 1966.

Lanning, John Tate. *The Diplomatic History of Georgia: A Study of the Epoch of Jenkins' Ear*. Chapel Hill: University of North Carolina Press, 1936.

LaPierre, Laurier. *1759: The Battle for Canada*. Toronto: McClelland and Stewart, 1990.

Lawson, Murray G. Fur: *A Study in English Mercantilism, 1700–1775*. Toronto: University of Toronto Press, 1975.

Leach, Douglas. *Roots of Conflict: British Armed Forces and Colonial Americans, 1677–1763*. Chapel Hill: University of North Carolina Press, 1986.

Leach, Douglas E. "The Military System of Plymouth Colony." *New England Quarterly* 24 (1951), 342–64.

Leach, Douglas Edward. *Flintlock and Tomahawk: New England and King Philip's War*. New York: Macmillan, 1958.

Leach, Douglas Edward. *The Northern Colonial Frontier, 1607–1763*. New York: Histories of the American Frontier Series, 1966.

Leach, Douglas Edward. *Arms for Empire: A Military History of the British Colonies in North America, 1607–1763*. New York: Macmillan, 1973.

Leach, Douglas Edward. "Brothers in Arms?—Anglo-American Friction at Louisbourg, 1745–1746." *Massachusetts Historical Society Proceedings* 89 (1977), 36–54.

Leach, Douglas Edward. "The Cartegena Expedition, 1740–42." In Maarten Ultree, ed., *Adapting to Conditions: War and Society in the Eighteenth Century*. Auburn: University of Alabama Press, 1986, 43–55.

Leliepvre, Eugene, and Rene Chartrand. "Corps of Cavalry, Canada, 1759–1760." *Military Collector and Historian* 28, no. 3 (Fall 1976), 131–32.

Leliepvre, Eugene, and Rene Chartrand. "Bearn Regiment, New France, 1755–1757." *Military Collector and Historian* 39, no. 3 (Fall 1987), 126–27.

Lemisch, Jess. "Jack Tar in the Streets: Merchant Seamen in the Politics of Revolutionary America." *William and Mary Quarterly* 3rd ser., 25, no. 3 (1968), 371–407.

Lenman, Bruce. *The Jacobite Risings in Britain, 1689–1746*. London: Eyre Methuen, 1980.

L'Epine, Anne Buot de. "Les Bureaux de la Guerre a la fin de l'Ancien Regime." *Revue d'Historique de Droit Francais et Etrangere* 54 (1976).

Lewis, Dennis M. "The Naval Campaign of 1759 on Lake Champlain." *The Bulletin of the Fort Ticonderoga Museum* 14, no. 4 (Fall 1983), 201–16.

Lincoln, Charles H., ed. *Narratives of the Indian Wars, 1675–1699*. 1913. Reprint, New York: Barnes & Noble, 1958.

Lloyd, Christopher. *The Capture of Quebec*. New York: Macmillan, 1959.

Lloyd, E. M. "William Augustus, Duke of Cumberland." *Dictionary of National Biography*. Toronto: University of Toronto Press, 1966–, 61:341.

Locke, Audrey. *The Hanbury Family*, 2 vols. London: Arthur L. Humphreys, 1916.

Lockridge, Kenneth L. "Land, Population, and the Evolution of New England Society, 1630–1790." *Past and Present* 39 (1968), 66, 68–69.

Long, J. C. *Mr. Pitt and America's Birthright: A Biography of the Earl of Chatham, 1708–1778.* New York: Frederick A. Stokes, 1940.

Long, John C. *Lord Jeffrey Amherst, A Soldier of the King.* New York: Macmillan, 1933.

Lovejoy, David S. *The Glorious Revolution in America* (1972). Middletown, Conn.: Wesleyan University Press, 1987.

Lunn, Jean Elizabeth. "Agriculture and War in Canada, 1740–1760." *Canadian Historical Review* 16 (June 1935), 123–36.

Lynch, John. *Spain, 1516–1598: From Nation State to World Empire.* Oxford: Oxford University Press, 1992.

Lyon, Eugene. *The Enterprise of Florida: Pedro Menendez de Aviles and the Spanish Conquest of 1565–1568.* Gainesville: University of Florida Press, 1976.

MacFarlane, Ronald O. "British Indian Policy in Nova Scotia to 1760." *Canadian Historical Review* 19 (June 1938), 154–67.

MacLennan, Alastair. "Highland Regiments in North America." *The Bulletin of the Fort Ticonderoga Museum* 12, no. 2 (September 1966), 118–25.

MacNutt, W. S. *The Atlantic Provinces: The Emergence of Colonial Society, 1712–1857.* Toronto: McClelland and Stewart, 1965.

Mahan, A. T. *The Influence of Sea Power Upon History, 1660–1783.* 1890. Reprint, Boston: Little, and Company, 1928.

Mahon, John K. "Anglo-American Methods of Indian Warfare, 1676–1794." *Mississippi Valley Historical Review* 45 (1970), 3–35.

Maier, Pauline. "Popular Uprisings and Civil Authority in Eighteenth-Century America." *William and Mary Quarterly* 27 (1970), 3–35.

Main, Jackson Turner. *The Social Structure of Revolutionary America.* Princeton, N.J.: Princeton University Press, 1965.

Malone, Patrick M. "Changing Military Technology Among the Indians of Southern New England, 1600–1677." *American Quarterly* 25 (1973), 49–71.

Mante, Thomas. *History of the Late War in North America, and the Islands of the West Indies, Including the Campaigns of 1763 and 1764 Against His Majesty's Enemies.* London: W. Strahan and T. Codell, 1792; New York: Research Reprints, 1970.

Marcus, G. J. *Heart of Oak: A Survey of British Sea Power in the Georgian Era.* London: Oxford University Press, 1975.

Marietta, Jack D. "Conscience, the Quaker Community, and the French and Indian War." *Pennsylvania Magazine of History and Biography* 95, no. 1 (January 1971), 3–5, 19–21.

Marshall, Peter. "Colonial Protest and Imperial Retrenchment: Indian Policy, 1764–1768." *Journal of American Studies* 5 (1971), 1–17.

Marshall, Peter, and Glyn Williams, eds. *The British Atlantic Empire before the American Revolution.* London: Frank Cass, 1980.

Marten, Catherine. "The Wampanoags, in the Seventeenth Century: An Ethnological Study." *Occasional Papers in Old Colony Studies* 2 (1970), 3–40.

Martin, Calvin. *Keepers of the Game: Indian-Animal Relationships and the Fur Trade.* Berkeley: University of California Press, 1978.

Martin, Felix. *Le Marquis de Montcalm et les Dernieres Annees de la Colonie Francaise au Canada.* Paris: P. M. Laroche, 1879.

Mauders, Eric, Brian Leigh Dunnigan, and John Elting. "80th Regiment of Foot,

1757–1764." *Military Collector and Historian* 36, no. 4 (Winter 1987), 172–73.

May, Robin, and G. A. Embleton. *Wolfe's Army*. London: Osprey Military Men at Arms Series, 1974.

McAlister, Lyle N. *Spain and Portugal in the New World, 1492–1700*. Minneapolis: University of Minnesota Press, 1971.

McCardell, Lee. *Ill-Starred General: Braddock of the Coldstream Guards*. 1958. Reprint, Pittsburgh: University of Pennsylvania Press, 1986.

McCorison, Marcus A. "Colonial Defense of the Upper Connecticut Valley." *Vermont History* 30 (January 1962), 50–62.

McCusker, John J., and Russell R. Menard. *The Economy of British America, 1607–1789*. Chapel Hill: University of North Carolina Press, 1991.

McLennan, J. S. *Louisbourg from Its Foundation to Its Fall: 1713–1758*. 1918. Reprint, Halifax, N.S.: The Book Room Limited, 1994.

McNear, Beverly, ed. "Personal Accounts of the Albany Congress of 1754." *Mississippi Valley Historical Review* 39, no. 4 (March 1953), 740–41.

McNeill, John Robert. *Atlantic Empires of France and Spain: Louisbourg and Havana, 1700–1763*. Chapel Hill: University of North Carolina Press, 1985.

Menard, Russell. "Growth and Welfare." In Jacob Ernest Cooke, ed., *Encyclopedia of the North American Colonies*. New York: Charles Scribner's Sons, 1993, 467–82.

Meriwether, Robert L. *The Expansion of South Carolina, 1729–1765*. Kingsport: University of Tennessee Press, 1940.

Merrell, James H. *The Indians' World: Catawbas and Their Neighbors from European Contact Through the Era of Removal*. Chapel Hill: University of North Carolina Press, 1989.

Merritt, Richard L. *Symbols of American Community, 1735–1775*. New Haven, Conn.: Yale University Press, 1966.

Merwick, Donna. "Becoming English: Anglo-Dutch Conflict in the 1670s in Albany, New York." *New York History* 62 (1981), 389–414.

Metzger, Charles H. *The Quebec Act: A Primary Cause of the American Revolution*. New York: United States Catholic Historical Society Monography Series 16, 1936.

Michalon, Roger. "Vaudreuil et Montcalm, les hommes, leurs relations, influence de ces relations sur la conduite de la guerre, 1756–1759." In Jean Delmas, ed., *Conflits des Societes au Canada Francais Pendant la Guerre de Sept Ans et Leurs Influence sur les Operations*. Vincennes, France: S.M.M., 1978.

Middleton, Richard. *The Bells of Victory: The Pitt-Newcastle Ministry and the Conduct of the Seven Years' War 1757–1762*. Cambridge: Cambridge University Press, 1985.

Milanich, Jerald T., and Susan Mibrath, eds. *First Encounters: Spanish Explorations in the Caribbean and the United States, 1492–1570*. Gainesville: University of Florida Press, 1989.

Miquelon, Don. *New France, 1701–1744: "A Supplement to Europe."* Toronto: McClelland and Stewart, 1987.

Mitchell, John. *The Conquest in America between Great Britain and France with Its Consequences and Importance*. New York: Johnson Reprint and Company, 1965.

Mitford, Nancy. *Madame de Pompadour*. New York: Random House, 1953.

Morgan, Edmund S. *American Slavery, American Freedom: The Ordeal of Colonial Virginia*. New York: W. W. Norton, 1975.

Morgan, Edmund S. *The Birth of the Republic, 1763–1789*. Chicago: University of Chicago Press, 1977.

Morgan, Edmund S., and Helen M. Morgan. *The Stamp Act Crisis: Prologue to Revolution*. Rev. ed. New York: Alfred A. Knopf, 1963.

Morgan Gwenda. "Virginia and the French and Indian War: A Case Study of the War's Effects on Imperial Relations." *Virginia Magazine of History and Biography* 81 (1973), 23–48.

Morison, Samuel E., ed. *William Bradford of Plymouth Plantation, 1620–1647*. New York: Knopf, 1952.

Morris, Richard B. *Government and Labor in Early America*. New York: Columbia University Press, 1946.

Morrison, Kenneth M. *The Embattled Northeast: The Elusive Ideal of Alliance in Abenaki-EuroAmerican Relations*. Berkeley: University of California Press, 1984.

Morton, Louis. "The Origins of American Military Policy." *Military Affairs* 22 (1958), 75–82.

Morton, Richard L. *Colonial Virginia*, 2 vols. Chapel Hill: University of North Carolina Press, 1960.

Mouillard, Lucien. *Les Regiments sous Louis XV*. Paris: Librarie Militaire de J. Dumaine, 1882.

Mousnier, Roland. *Institutions de la France sous la Monarchie Absolue*, 2 vols. Les Organes de l'Etat et la Societe. Paris: Universataires de France, 1974, 1980.

Mousnier, Roland. "La Fonction publique en France du debut du seizieme siecle a la fin du dix-huitieme siecle. Des officiers aux commissaires puis aux commis, puis aux fonctionnaires." *Revue Historique* 530 (April–June 1979), 321–35.

Muhlstein, Anka. *La Salle: Explorer of the North American Frontier*. New York: Arcade Publishing, 1992.

Mulkearn, Lois. "Why the Treaty of Logstown, 1752." *Virginia Magazine of History and Biography* 59 (January 1951), 3–20.

Mullet, Charles F. "James Abercromby and the French Encroachments in America." *Canadian Historical Review* 26 (1945), 48–59.

Murrin, John M. "The French and Indian War, the American Revolution, and the Counterfactual Hypothesis: Reflections on Henry Gipson and John Shy." *Reviews in American History* 1 (1973), 307–18.

Namier, Sir Lewis. *The Structure of Politics at the Accession of George III*. 2nd ed. London: Macmillan, 1957.

Namier, Sir Lewis. *England in the Age of the American Revolution*. 2nd ed. London: Macmillan, 1961.

Nammack, Georgiana C. *Fraud, Politics, and Dispossession of the Indians: The Iroquois Land Frontier in the Colonial Period*. Norman: University of Oklahoma Press, 1969.

Naroll, Raoul. "The Causes of the Fourth Iroquois War." *Ethnohistory* 16 (1969), 51–81.

Nash, Gary. *The Urban Crucible: Social Change, Political Consciousness, and the Or-*

igins of the American Revolution. Cambridge, Mass.: Harvard University Press, 1979.

Nash Gary B. *Class and Society in Early America.* Englewood Cliffs, N.J.: Prentice-Hall, 1970.

Nettels, Curtis P. *The Money Supply of the American Colonies Before 1720.* Madison: University of Wisconsin Press, 1934.

Nettels, Curtis P. *The Emergence of a National Economy, 1775–1815.* New York: M. E. Sharpe, 1962.

Nichols, Franklin Thayer. "The Organization of Braddock's Army." *William and Mary Quarterly* 4 (1947), 125–47.

Nish, C. *The French Canadians, 1759–1766: Conquered? Half Conquered? Liberated?* Toronto: Copp Clark Publishers, 1966.

Nixon, Lily Lee. "Colonel James Burd in the Campaign of 1759." *Western Pennsylvania Historical Review* 18 (1935), 109–24.

Nixon, Lily Lee. "Colonel James Burd in the Forbes Campaign." *Pennsylvania Magazine of History and Biography* 59 (1935), 106–33.

Norkus, Nellie. "Virginia's Role in the Capture of Fort Duquesne, 1758." *Western Pennsylvania Historical Magazine* 45 (1962), 291–308.

North, Douglas C., and Robert Paul Thomas. *The Rise of the Western World: A New Economic History.* Cambridge: Cambridge University Press, 1976.

Norton, Thomas Elliot. *The Fur Trade in Colonial New York, 1686–1776.* Madison: University of Wisconsin Press, 1974.

Nye, Russel Baine. *George Bancroft, Brahmin Rebel.* New York: Alfred A. Knopf, 1944.

O'Donnell, James Howlett III. *Southeastern Frontiers: Europeans, Africans, and American Indians, 1513–1840, A Critical Bibliography.* Bloomington: Indiana University Press, 1982.

Olson, Alison G. "The Board of Trade and London-American Interest Groups in the Eighteenth Century." In Peter Marshall and Glyn Williams, eds., *The British Atlantic Empire before the American Revolution.* London: Frank Cass, 1980.

Olson, Alison Gilbert. "The British Government and Colonial Union, 1754." *William and Mary Quarterly* 3rd ser., 17, no. 1 (January 1960), 22–34.

Olson, Alison Gilbert. "Relations with the Parent Country: Britain." In Jacob Ernest Cooke, ed., *Encyclopedia of the North American Colonies.* New York: Charles Scribner's Sons, 1993, 1:330–38.

O'Meara, Walter. *Guns at the Forks.* Englewood Cliffs, N.J.: Prentice-Hall, 1965.

Osgood, Herbert L. *The American Colonies in the Eighteenth Century,* 4 vols. 1924. Reprint, Gloucester, Mass.: Peter Smith, 1958.

Ostrander, Gilman M. "The Colonial Molasses Trade." *Agricultural History* 30 (1956), 77–84.

Otterbein, Keith F. "Why the Iroquois Won: An Analysis of Iroquois Military Tactics." *Ethnohistory* 11 (1964), 56–63.

Otterbein, Keith F. "Huron vs. Iroquois: A Case Study in Inter-Tribal Warfare." *Ethnohistory* 26 (1979), 141–52.

Pares, Richard. *Colonial Blockade and Neutral Rights, 1739–1763.* Oxford: Oxford University Press, 1938.

Pares, Richard. *War and Trade in the West Indes, 1739–1763.* 1936. Reprint, London: F. Cass, 1963.

Pargellis, Stanley. "Braddock's Defeat." *American Historical Review* 41 (1936), 253–69.

Pargellis, S. M. "Webb, Daniel." *Dictionary of American Biography.* Toronto: University of Toronto Press, 1966–, 19:573–74.

Pargellis, S. M. "Winslow, John." *Dictionary of American Biography.* Toronto: University of Toronto Press, 1966–, 20:396–97.

Pargellis, Stanley McCrory. *Lord Loudoun in America.* New Haven, Conn.: Yale University Press, 1933.

Parkman, Francis. *Montcalm and Wolfe: The French and Indian War.* 1886. Reprint, New York: Da Capo Press, 1995.

Parry, Peter, "Colonial Development and International Rivalries Outside Europe." In R. B. Wernham, ed., *The New Cambridge Modern History,* vol. 3. Cambridge: Cambridge University Press, 1968, 540–42.

Pease, Theodore Calvin. "The Mississippi Boundary of 1763: A Reappraisal of Responsibility." *American Historical Review* 40 (January 1935), 278–86.

Peckham, Howard. *The Colonial Wars 1689–1762.* Chicago: University of Chicago Press, 1964.

Peckham, Howard H. "Speculations on the Colonial Wars." *William and Mary Quarterly* 17 (1960), 463–72.

Peckham, Howard H. *Pontiac and the Indian Uprising.* 1947. Reprint, Chicago: University of Chicago Press, 1961.

Peckham, Howard H., ed. "Thomas Gist's Indian Captivity, 1758–1759." *Pennsylvania Magazine of History and Biography* 80, no. 3 (July 1956), 285–311.

Pencak, William. "Thomas Hutchinson's Fight Against Naval Impressment." *New England Historical and Genealogical Register* 132 (1978), 25–36.

Pencak, William. "Warfare and Political Change in Mid-Eighteenth Century Massachusetts." In Peter Marshall and Glyn Williams, eds., *The British Atlantic Empire Before the American Revolution.* London: Frank Cass, 1980.

Pencak, William. *War, Politics, & Revolution in Provincial Massachusetts.* Boston: Northeastern University Press, 1981.

Perdue, Theda. *Slavery and the Evolution of Cherokee Society, 1540–1866.* Knoxville: University of Tennessee Press, 1979.

Perkins, Edwin J. *The Economy of Colonial America.* New York: Columbia University Press, 1980.

Peters, Marie. *Pitt and Popularity: The Patriot Minister and London Opinion during the Seven Years' War.* Oxford: Clarendon Press, 1980.

Peters, Marie. "The Myth of William Pitt, Earl of Chatham, Great Imperialist, Part I: Pitt and Imperial Expansion, 1738–1763." *Journal of Imperial and Commonwealth History* 21 (1993), 31–74.

Peterson, H. L. "The Military Equipment of the Plymouth and Bay Colonies, 1620–1690." *New England Quarterly* 20 (1947), 197–208.

Peterson, Harold L. *Arms and Armour in Colonial America, 1526–1783.* New York: Bramball House, 1956.

Phelps, Dawson A. "The Vaudreuil Expedition, 1752." *William and Mary Quarterly* 3rd ser., 15 (October 1958), 483–93.

Phillips, Paul Chrisler. *The Fur Trade*, vol. 1. Norman: University of Oklahoma Press, 1961.

Powell, Philip Wayne. *Soldiers, Indians, & Silver: The Northward Advance of New Spain, 1550–1600*. Berkeley: University of Calfornia Press, 1969.

Pownall, Charles. *Thomas Pownall*. London: Henry Stevens, Son and Stiles, 1908.

Prebble, John. *Culloden*. Harmondsworth: Penguin Books, 1967.

Preston, Richard A., and Leopold LaMontagne. *Royal Fort Frontenac*. Toronto: The Champlain Society, 1958.

Price, Jacob M. "The Great Quaker Business Families of the Eighteenth Century." In Richard S. Dunn and Mary Maples Dunn, eds., *The World of William Penn*. Philadelphia: University of Pennsylvania Press, 1986, 363–99.

Pritchard, James. *Louis XV's Navy, 1748–1762: A Study of Organization and Administration*. Kingston, Ont.: McGill–Queen's University Press, 1982.

Pritchard, James S. "Some Aspects of the Thought of F. X. Garneau." *Canadian Historical Review* 1 (1970), 276–91.

Procter, James. *The Ohio Company: Its Inner History*. Pittsburgh: University of Pittsburgh Press, 1959.

Proulx, Gilles. "Le Dernier Effort de la France au Canada—secours au fraude?" *Revue de l'Amerique Francaise* 36 (1982), 413–26.

Proulx, Gilles. *The Garrison of Quebec from 1748 to 1759: A Study of Organization and Administration*. Ottawa: National Historic Sites Parks Service, 1991.

Quarles, Benjamin. "The Colonial Militia and Negro Manpower." *Mississippi Valley Historical Review* 45 (March 1959), 643–52.

Quimby, Ian, ed, *The Craftsman in Early America*. New York: W. W. Norton, 1984.

Quinn, D. B., ed. *New American World: A Documentary History of North America to 1612*, 5 vols. New York: Arno and Bye, 1979.

Quinn, David B. *England and the Discovery of America, 1481–1620*. New York: Knopf, 1974.

Rabb, Theodore K. *Enterprise and Empire: Merchant and Gentry Investment in the Expansion of England, 1575–1630*. Cambridge, Mass.: Harvard University Press, 1967.

Rahmer, Frederick A. *Dash to Frontenac: An Account of Lt. Col. John Bradstreet's Expedition to and Capture of Fort Frontenac*. Rome, N.Y.: Frederick A. Rahmer, 1973.

Ralyk, George A. *Nova Scotia's Massachusetts: A Study of Massachusetts–Nova Scotia Relations, 1630–1784*. Montreal: McGill–Queen's University Press, 1973.

Ranlet, Philip. "Another Look at the Causes of King Philip's War." *New England Quarterly* 61 (1988), 79–100.

Ray, Arthur J. *Indians in the Fur Trade: Their Role as Trappers, Hunters, and Middlemen in the Lands Southwest of Hudson Bay, 1660–1870*. Toronto: University of Toronto Press, 1974.

Ray, Arthur J., and Donald Freeman. *"Give Us Good Measure": An Economic Analysis of Relations Between the Indians and the Hudson's Bay Company Before 1763*. Toronto: University of Toronto Press, 1978.

Reddaway, W. F. "The Seven Years' War." In J. Holland et al., eds. *The Old Empire*, vol. 1 of *The Cambridge History of the British Empire*. New York: Macmillan, 1929.

Reid, John Philip. *A Law of Blood: The Primitive Law of the Cherokee Nation*. New York: New York University Press, 1970.

Reid, John Philip. *In Defiance of the Law: The Standing Army Controversy, the Two Constitutions, and the Coming of the American Revolution*. Chapel Hill: University of North Carolina Press, 1981.

Reid, Marjorie. "Pitt's Decision to Keep Canada in 1761." *Canadian Historical Association Report for 1926* (Ottawa 1927), 1–24.

Reid, Stuart. *King George's Army, 1740–93*, vols. 1–2. London: Osprey Books, 1995.

Rice, Otis. "The French and Indian War in West Virginia." *West Virginia History* 24 (1963), 134–46.

Rice, Otis K. "The Sandy Creek Expedition of 1756." *West Virginia History* 13 (October 1951), 5–19.

Richards, Frederick B. *The Black Watch at Ticonderoga and Major Duncan Campbell of Inverawase*. Ticonderoga, N.Y: Fort Ticonderoga Museum, 1926.

Richter, Daniel K. "War and Culture: The Iroquois Experience." *William and Mary Quarterly* 3rd ser., 60 (1983), 528–59.

Richter, Daniel K. Essay Review of Henry F. Dobyns, *Their Numbers Became Thinned: Native American Population Dynamics in Eastern North America*. *William and Mary Quarterly* 3rd ser., 41 (1984), 649–53.

Richter, Daniel K. "Iroquois vs. Iroquois: Jesuit Mission and Christianity in Village Politics, 1642–1686." *Ethnohistory* 32, 1985, 363–69.

Richter, Daniel K. "Up the Cultural Stream: Three Recent Works in Iroquois Studies." *Ethnohistory* 3rd ser., 32 (1985), 363–69.

Richter, Daniel K. "Cultural Brokers and Intercultural Politics: New York–Iroquois Relations, 1664–1701." *Journal of American History* 75 (1988–1989), 40–67.

Richter, Daniel K. *The Ordeal of the Longhouse: The Peoples of the Iroquois League in the Era of European Colonization*. Chapel Hill: University of North Carolina Press, 1992.

Richter, Daniel K., and James H. Merrell, eds. *Beyond the Covenant Chain: The Iroquois and their Neighbors in North America, 1600–1800*. Syracuse, N.Y.: Syracuse University Press, 1987.

Riker, Thad W. "The Politics Behind Braddock's Expedition." *American Historical Review* 13 (1908), 742–52.

Robbins, Caroline. *The Eighteenth Century Commonwealman: Studies in the Transmission, Development, and Circumstances of English Liberal Thought From the Restoration of Charles II until the War with the Thirteen Colonies*. Cambridge, Mass.: Harvard University Press, 1959.

Robinson, W. Stitt. "Virginia and the Cherokees: Indian Policy from Spotswood to Dinwiddie." In Darrett B. Rutman, ed., *The Old Dominion: Essays for Thomas Perkins Abernethy*. Charlottesville: University of Virginia Press, 1964, 21–40.

Robinson, W. Slitt. *The Southern Colonial Frontier, 1607–1763*. Albuquerque: University of New Mexico Press, 1979.

Robitaille, Georges. *Montcalm et ses Historiens: Etude Critique*. Montreal: Levis, 1936.

Robson, Eric. "British Light Infantry in the Mid-Eighteenth Century: The Effect of American Conditions." *Army Quarterly* 62 (1952), 209–22.

Rodgers, N. A. M. *The Wooden World: An Anatomy of the Georgian Navy.* Annapolis, Md.: Naval Institute Press, 1982.

Rogers, Alan. *Empire and Liberty: American Resistance to British Authority, 1755–1763.* Berkeley: University of California Press, 1974.

Rogers, H. C. B. *The British Army of the Eighteenth Century.* London: Allen & Unwin, 1977.

Rogers, J. Alan. "Impressment in Western Pennsylvania, 1755–1759." *Western Pennsylvania Historical Magazine* 52 (1969), 255–62.

Rogers, J. Alan. "Colonial Opposition to the Quartering of Troops During the French and Indian War." *Military Affairs* 34 (1970), 7–11.

Rothermund, Dietmar. "The German Problem of Colonial Pennsylvania." *Pennsylvania Magazine of History and Biography* 84, no. 1 (January 1960), 10–13.

Rothermund, Dietmar. *The Layman's Progress: Religious and Political Experience in Colonial Pennsylvania, 1740–1770.* Philadelphia: University of Pennsylvania Press, 1961.

Roundtree, Helen C. *Powhatan's People: The Powhatan Indians of Virginia through Four Centuries.* Norman: University of Oklahoma Press, 1990.

Roundtree, Helen C. *The Powhatan Indians of Virginia: Their Traditional Culture.* Norman: University of Oklahoma Press, 1992.

Roy, Pierre-George. "Les Commandants du Saint Frederic." *Le Bulletin des Recherches Historique* 51 (September 1945), 317–32.

Roy, Pierre-George. *Homme et Choses du Fort Saint Frederic.* Montreal: Les Editions Dix, 1946.

Roy, Pierre-George. "Les Commandants du Fort Niagara." *Le Bulletin des Recherches Historiques* 54, nos. 5–7 (May–July 1948), 131–40, 163–77, 195–99.

Rule, John. "The Commis of the Department of Foreign Affairs Under the Administration of Colbert de Croissey and Colbert de Torcy, 1680–1715." In *Proceedings of the Western Society for French History* 8 (1981), 69–80.

Russell, Peter E. "Redcoats in the Wilderness: British Officers and Irregular Warfare in Europe and America, 1740–1760." *William and Mary Quarterly* 35 (1978), 629–52.

Rutman, Darrett B. "The Virginia Company and Its Military Regime." In Darrett B. Rutman, ed., *The Old Dominion: Essays for Thomas Perkins Abernethy.* Charlottesville: University of Virginia Press, 1964.

Salisbury, Neal. *Manitou and Providence: Indians, Europeans, and the Making of New England, 1500–1643.* New York: Oxford University Press, 1982.

Salisbury, Neal. "Indians and Colonists in Southern New England after the Pequot War: An Uneasy Balance." In Laurence M. Hauptman and James D. Wherry, eds., *The Pequots in Southern New England: The Fall and Rise of an American Indian Nation.* Norman: University of Oklahoma Press, 1990.

Samoyault, Jean-Pierre. *Les Bureaux du Secretariat d'Etat des Affaires Etrangeres sous Louis XV.* Paris: Editions A. Pedrone, 1971.

Samuel, Sigmund. *The Seven Years' War in Canada, 1756–1763.* Toronto: Ryerson Press, 1934.

Sauer, Carl Ortwin. *Sixteenth Century North America.* Berkeley: University of California Press, 1971.

Sauer, Carl, Ortwin. *Seventeenth Century North America.* Berkeley: University of California Press, 1980.

Sautai, Maurice. *Montcalm at the Battle of Carillon*. Ticonderoga, N.Y.: Fort Ticonderoga Museum, 1941.

Sauvageau, Robert. *Acadie: La Guerre de Cent Ans des Francais d'Amerique aux Maritimes et en Louisanne, 1670–1769*. Paris: Berger-Levrault, 1987.

Savelle, Max. "Diplomatic Preliminaries of the Seven Years' War in America." *Canadian Historical Review* 20 (1939), 1–43.

Savelle, Max. *The Diplomatic History of the Canadian Boundary, 1749–1763*. New Haven, Conn: Yale University Press, 1940.

Savelle, Max. *Seeds of Liberty: The Genesis of the American Mind*. New York: Alfred A. Knopf, 1948.

Savelle, Max. *The Origins of American Diplomacy: The International History of Anglo-America, 1492–1763*. New York: Macmillan, 1967.

Savelle, Max, and Robert Middlekauff. *A History of Colonial America*. New York: Holt, Rinehart and Winston, 1964.

Schoenfeld, Max. *Fort de la Presqu'ile*. Erie, Pa.: Erie County Historical Society, 1989.

Schumacher, Max G. *The Northern Farmer and His Markest During the Late Colonial Period*. New York: Arno Press, 1975.

Schutz, John A. "The Disaster of Fort Ticonderoga: The Shortage of Muskets During the Mobilization of 1758." *Huntington Library Quarterly* 14 (May 1951), 307–15.

Schutz, John A. *Thomas Pownall: British Defender of American Liberty*. Glendale, Calif.: Arthur Clark, 1951.

Schutz, John A. "Imperialism in Massachusetts during the Governance of William Shirley, 1741–1756." *Huntington Library Quarterly* 23 (1960), 217–36.

Schutz, John A. *William Shirley: King's Governor of Massachusetts*. Chapel Hill: University of North Carolina Press, 1961.

Selesky, Harold. *War and Society in Colonial Connecticut*. New Haven, Conn.: Yale University Press, 1990.

Shammas, Carole. "How Self-Sufficient Was Early America." *Journal of Interdisciplinary History* 13 (1982), 247–72.

Shea, William L. *The Virginia Militia in the Seventeenth Century*. Baton Rouge: Louisiana State University Press, 1983.

Shepherd, James T., and Gary M. Walton. *Shipping, Maritime Trade, and the Economic Development of Colonial North America*. Cambridge: Cambridge University Press, 1972.

Sherman, Richard P. *Robert Johnson: Proprietary & Royal Governor of South Carolina*. Columbia: University of South Carolina Press, 1966.

Sherrard, D. A. *Lord Chatham: Pitt and the Seven Years' War*. London: The Bodley Head, 1955.

Shy, John. "Quartering His Majesty's Forces in New Jersey." *New Jersey Historical Society Proceedings* 78 (1960), 82–94.

Shy, John. "A New Look at Colonial Militia." *William and Mary Quarterly* 3rd ser., 20 (1963), 175–85.

Shy, John. *Toward Lexington: The Role of the British Army in the Coming of the American Revolution*. Princeton, N.J.: Princeton University Press, 1965.

Shy, John W., ed. *A People Numerous and Armed*. New York: Oxford University Press, 1976.

Siebert, Wilbur H. "How the Spaniards Evacuated Pensacola in 1763." *Florida Historical Society Quarterly* 11 (October 1932), 48–57.

Siebert, Wilbur H. "Spanish and French Privateering in Southern Waters, July 1762 to March 1756." *Georgia Historical Quarterly* 16 (September 1932), 163–78.

Sigmund, Samuel. *The Seven Years' War in Canada, 1756–1763*. Toronto: Ryerson Books, 1934.

Smith, Abbott Emerson. *Colonists in Bondage: White Servitude and Convict Labor in America, 1607–1776*. Chapel Hill: University of North Carolina Press, 1947.

Smith, James M., ed. *Seventeenth Century America*. Chapel Hill: University of North Carolina Press, 1959.

Smith, Page. *A New Age Begins: A People's History of the American Revolution*. New York: Penguin Books, 1976.

Smollet, Thomas. *History of England from the Revolution to the Death of George II*, 5 vols. London: Cooke Publisher, 1790.

Snow, Dean R., and Kim M. Lanphear. "European Contact and Indian Depopulation in the Northeast: The Timing of the First Epidemics." *Ethnohistory* 35 (1988), 15–33.

Sosin, Jack M. *Whitehall and the Wilderness: The Middle West in British Colonial Policy, 1760–1775*. Lincoln: University of Nebraska Press, 1961.

Stacey, C. P. "The Anse au Foulon, 1759: Montcalm and Vaudreuil." *Canadian Historical Review* 40 (March 1959), 27–37.

Stacey, C. P. *Quebec, 1759: The Siege and Battle*. Toronto: Macmillan, 1959.

Stacey, C. P. "Quebec, 1759: Some New Documents." *Canadian Historical Review* 47 (December 1966), 344–55.

Stagg, Jack. *Anglo-Indian Relations in North America to 1763 and an Analysis of the Royal Proclamation of 7 October 1763*. Ottawa: Research Branch, Indian and Northern Affairs, Canada, 1981.

Stanley, George F. G. *New France: The Last Phase, 1740–1760*. Toronto: McClelland and Stewart, 1968.

Stearn, Wagner E., and Allen E. Stearn. *The Effect of Small-pox on the Destiny of the American Indian*. Boston: B. Humphries, 1945.

Steele, Ian K. *The Politics of Colonial Policy: The Board of Trade in Colonial Administration, 1696–1720*. Oxford: Oxford University Press, 1968.

Steele, Ian K. *Guerrillas and Grenadiers: The Struggle for Canada, 1689–1760*. Toronto: McClelland and Stewart, 1969.

Steele, Ian K. *The English Atlantic, 1675–1740*. New York: Oxford University Press, 1986.

Steele, Ian K. *Betrayals: Fort William Henry & the "Massacre."* New York: Oxford University Press, 1990.

Steele, Ian K. *Warpaths: Invasions of North America, 1513–1765*. New York: Oxford University Press, 1994.

Stotz, Charles Morse. *Outposts of the War for Empire: The French and English in Western Pennsylvania: Their Armies, their Forts, their People, 1749–1764*. Pittsburgh, Pa.: Historical Society of Western Pennsylvania, 1985.

Stout, Neil R. *The Royal Navy in America, 1760–1775: A Study in Enforcement of*

British Colonial Policy in the Era of the American Revolution. Annapolis, Md.: Naval Institute Press, 1973.

Summers, Jack L., and Rene Chartrand. *Military Uniforms in Canada, 1665–1970.* Ottawa: Canadian War Museum, 1981.

Sweet, David G., and Gary B. Nash, eds. *Struggle and Survival in Colonial America.* Berkeley: University of California Press, 1981.

Syrett, David. "American Provincials and the Havanna Campaign of 1762." *New York History* 49 (1968), 375–90.

Tanner, Helen Hornbeck. *Atlas of Great Lakes Indian History.* Norman: University of Oklahoma Press, 1987.

Temperly, H. W. V. "The Peace of Paris." In *The Old Empire,* vol. 1 of *The Cambridge History of the British Empire.* J. Holland Rose, A. P. Newton, and E. A. Benians, eds. New York: Macmillan, 1929, pp. 485–506.

Thayer, Theodore. *Israel Pemberton: King of the Quakers.* Philadelphia: Historical Society of Pennsylvania, 1943.

Thayer, Theodore. *Pennsylvania Politics and the Growth of Democracy, 1740–1776.* Harrisburg: Pennsylvania Historical and Museum Commission, 1953.

Thayer, Theodore. "The Army Contractors for the Niagara Campaign, 1755–56." *William and Mary Quarterly,* 3rd ser., 14 (1957), 31–46.

Thomas, Daniel H. "Fort Toulouse—in Tradition and Fact." *Alabama Review* 13 (October 1960), 243–57.

Thomas, Daniel H. "Fort Toulouse: The French Outpost at the Alibamos on the Coosa." *Alabama Historical Quarterly* 22 (Fall 1960), 135–230.

Thomas, Hugh. *Conquest: Montezuma, Cortes, and the Fall of Old Mexico.* New York: Simon and Schuster, 1993.

Thomas, Peter D. G. "The Reorganization of Empires: British." In Jacob Ernest Cooke, ed., *Encyclopedia of the North American Colonies.* New York: Charles Scribner's Sons, 1993.

Thomson, Charles. *An Enquiry into the Causes of the Alienation of the Delaware and Shawanese Indians from the British Interest.* London: J. Wilkie, 1759.

Thorton, Russell. *American Indian Holocaust and Survival: A Population History Since 1492.* Norman: University of Oklahoma Press, 1987.

Thorpe, F. J. "Chaussegros de Lery, Gaspard-Joseph." *Dictionary of Canadian Biography.* Toronto: University of Toronto Press, 1966–, 4:145–47.

Titus, James. *The Old Dominion at War: Society, Politics, and Warfare in Late Colonial Virginia.* Columbia: University of South Carolina Press, 1991.

Tooker, Elisabeth. "The Iroquois Defeat of the Huron: A Review of the Causes." *Pennsylvania Archeologist* 33, nos. 1–2 (1963), 115–23.

Tooker, Elizabeth. "The Demise of the Susquehannock: A 17th Century Mystery." *Pennsylvania Archeologist* 54 (1984), 1–10.

Trealease, Allen W. "The Iroquois and the Western Fur Trade: A Problem in Interpretation." *Mississippi Valley Historical Review* 49 (June 1962), 32–51.

Trigger, Bruce G. *Natives and Newcomers: Canada's "Heroic Age" Reconsidered.* Montreal: McGill–Queens University Press, 1985.

Trigger, Bruce G. "Early Native American Responses to European Contact: Romantic versus Rationalistic Interpretations." *Journal of American History* 77 (1990–1991), 1195–1215.

Trimble, David B. "Christopher Gist and the Indian Service in Virginia, 1757–1759." *Virginia Magazine of History and Biography* 65 (January 1956), 143–65.

Trudel, Marcel. *The Beginnings of New France, 1524–1663.* Toronto: McClelland and Stewart, 1973.

Turnbull, J. R. "Jean-Armand Dieskau." *Dictionary of Canadian Biography.* Toronto: University of Toronto Press, 1966–, 3:185–86.

Tyler, John W. *Smugglers and Patriots: Boston Merchants and the Advent of the American Revolution.* Boston: Northeastern University Press, 1986.

Ultree, Maarten, ed. *Adapting to Conditions: War and Society in the Eighteenth Century.* Tuscaloosa: University of Alabama Press, 1986.

Upton, L. F. S. *Micmacs and Colonists: Indian–White Relations in the Maritimes, 1713–1867.* Vancouver: University of British Columbia Press, 1979.

Usner, Daniel H. *Indians, Settlers, & Slavers in a Frontier Exchange Economy: The Lower Mississippi Valley Before 1783.* Chapel Hill: University of North Carolina Press, 1992.

Varg, Paul A. "The Advent of Nationalism." *American Quarterly* 16 (1964), 169–81.

Vaughan, Alden T. " 'Expulsion of the Savages': English Policy and the Virginia Massacre of 1622." *William and Mary Quarterly* 35 (1978), 57–84.

Vaughan, Alden T., and Edward W. Clark, eds. *Puritans Among the Indians: Accounts of Captivity and Redemption, 1676–1724.* Cambridge, Mass.: Harvard University Press, 1981.

Verge-Franceshi, Michel. *La Marine Francaise au XVIIIe Siecle.* Paris: Sedes, 1996.

Verney, Jack. *The Good Regiment: The Carignan-Salieres Regiment in Canada, 1665–1668.* Montreal: McGill–Queens University Press, 1991.

Vitzhum, R. C. "The Historian as Editor: Francis Parkman's Reconstruction of Sources in Montcalm and Wolfe." *Journal of American History* 52 (1966–1967), 471–86.

Vitzthum, Richard C. *The American Compromise: Theme and Method in the Histories of Bancroft, Parkman, and Adams.* Norman: University of Oklahoma Press, 1974.

Volwiler, Albert T. *George Croghan and the Westward Movement, 1741–1782.* Cleveland: Arthur H. Clark, 1926.

Waddington, Richard. *La Guerre de Sept Ans: Histoire Diplomatique et Militaire,* 5 vols. Paris: Firmin-Didot et Cie, 1888–1910.

Wade, Mason. *Francis Parkman: Heroic Historian.* New York: Viking Press, 1942.

Wainwright, Nicolas B. "Governor William Denny in Pennsylvania." *Pennsylvania Magazine of History and Biography* 81 (1957), 170–98.

Wainwright, Nicholas B. *George Croghan: Wilderness Diplomat.* Chapel Hill: University of North Carolina Press, 1959.

Wallace, Anthony F. C. *King of the Delawares: Teedyuscung, 1700–1763.* 1949. Reprint, Syracuse, N.Y.: Syracuse University Press, 1990.

Wallace, Paul A. W. *Conrad Weiser, Friend of Colonists and Mohawk, 1696–1760.* Chapel Hill: University of North Carolina Press, 1959.

Wallace, Paul A. W. *Indians in Pennsylvania.* Harrisburg: Pennsylvania Historical and Museum Commission, 1961.

Wallace, Paul A. W. " 'Blunder Camp': A Note on the Braddock Road." *Pennsylvania Magazine of History and Biography* 87 (January 1963), 21–30.

Wallace, Paul A. W. *Indian Paths of Pennsylvania*. Harrisburg: Pennsylvania Historical and Museum Commission, 1965.

Warburton, George. *The Conquest of Canada*, 2 vols. London: R. Benteley, 1857.

Ward, Harry M. *The United Colonies of New England, 1643–1690*. New York: Vantage Press, 1961.

Washburn, Wilcomb E. *The Governor and the Rebel: A History of Bacon's Rebellion in Virginia*. Chapel Hill: University of North Carolina Press, 1957.

Waugh, W. T. *James Wolfe: The Man and Soldier*. Montreal: L. L. Carrier and Company, 1928.

Webb, Stephens Saunders. "Army and Empire: English Garrison Government in Britain and America, 1569–1763." *William and Mary Quarterly* 34 (1977), 1–31.

Webb, Stephen Saunders. *1676: The End of American Independence*. New York: Alfred A. Knopf, 1984.

Webster, John Clarence. *The Career of the Abbe Le Loutre in Nova Scotia with a Translation of His Autobiography*. Shedia, N.B.: Privately Printed, 1933.

Wells, Robert V. *The Population of the British Colonies in North America before 1776: A Survey of Census Data*. Princeton, N.J.: Princeton University Press, 1975.

Weslager, C. A. *The Delaware Indians: A History*. New Brunswick, N.J.: Rutgers University Press, 1991.

West, Martin, ed. *War for Empire in Western Pennsylvania*. Ligonier, Pa.: Fort Ligonier Association, 1993.

Western, J. R. "Professionalism in Armies, Navies and Diplomacy." In Alfred Cobban, ed., *The Eighteenth Century: Europe in the Age of Enlightenment*. New York: McGraw-Hill, 1969, 181–216.

White, Richard. *The Middle Ground: Indians, Empires, and Republics in the Great Lakes Regions, 1650–1815*. Cambridge: Cambridge University Press, 1991.

Williams, Basil. *The Whig Supremacy, 1714–1760*. 2nd ed. Rev. by C. H. Stuart, *Oxford History of England*. Oxford: Clarendon Press, 1962.

Williams, Basil. *The Life of William Pitt, Earl of Chatham*, 2 vols. 1913. Reprint, New York: Octagon Books, 1966.

Williams, W. R. "British-American Officers, 1720–1763." *South Carolina Historical and Genealogical Magazine* 33 (1932), 183–96, 290–96.

Willison, George F. *Saints and Strangers*. New York: Reynal and Hitchcock, 1945.

Willison, George F. *Behold Virginia: The Fifth Crown*. New York: Harcourt, Brace, and Company, 1952.

Wilson, A. M. *French Foreign Policy during the Administration of Cardinal Fleury, 1726–1743*. Cambridge: Cambridge University Press, 1936.

Winzerling, Oscar William. *Acadian Odyssey*. Baton Rouge: Louisana State University Press, 1955.

Wood, George Arthur. *William Shirley, Governor of Massachusetts, 1721–1756*. New York: Columbia University Press, 1920.

Wood, George Arthur. "Celeron de Blainville and French Expansion in the Ohio Valley." *Mississippi Valley Historical Review* 9 (March 1923), 302–19.

Wood, Peter H., Gregory A. Waselkov, and M. Thomas Hatley, eds. *Powhatan's*

Mantle: Indians in the Colonial Southeast. Lincoln: University of Nebraska Press, 1989.

Wood, William Charles Henry. *The Fight for Canada*. Boston: Little, Brown, 1906.

Wood, William Charles Henry. *The Passing of New France*. Toronto: Glasgow Brook, 1915.

Woods, Patricia D. "The French and the Natchez Indians in Louisana, 1700–1731." *Louisiana History* 19 (1978), 421–38.

Woods, Patricia D. *French-Indian Relations on the Southern Frontier, 1699–1762*. Ann Arbor: University of Michigan Press, 1980.

Worrall, Arthur J. "Persecution, Politics, and War: Roger Williams, Quakers, and King Philip's War." *Quaker History* 66 (1977), 73–86.

Worth, Lawrence C., ed. *The Voyages of Giovanni da Verrazzano, 1524–1528*. New Haven, Conn.: Yale University Press, 1970.

Wright, J. Leitch, Jr. *The Only Land They Knew: The Tragic Story of the American Indians in the Old South*. New York: The Free Press, 1981.

Wright, J. Leitch, Jr. *Anglo-Spanish Rivalry in North America*. Athens: University of Georgia Press, 1971.

Yorke, Philip C. *The Life and Correspondence of Philip Yorke, Earl of Hardwicke, Lord High Chancellor of Great Britain*, 3 vols. Cambridge: Cambridge University Press, 1913, 2:256–57.

Zimmerman, John J. "Benjamin Franklin and the Quaker Party, 1755–1756." *William and Mary Quarterly* 17 (1960), 291–313.

Zimmerman, John J. "Governor Denny and the Quartering Act of 1756." *Pennsylvania Magazine of History and Biography* 91 (1967), 266–81.

Zoltvany, Yves F. *The Government of New France: Royal, Clerical, or Class Rule*. Scarbrough, Ont.: Prentice-Hall, 1971.

Index

About the Author

WILLIAM R. NESTER is Professor in the Department of Government and Politics at St. John's University in New York. He is the author of eleven books which explore various aspects of international relations and political economy and two books on the American frontier.

ISBN 0-275-96772-7

HARDCOVER BAR CODE